The ADMINISTRATOR'S GUIDE to

MICROSOFT SQL SERVER 6.5

KEVIN COX
WILLIAM JONES

A Division of
DUKE COMMUNICATIONS INTERNATIONAL
221 E. 29th Street • Loveland, CO 80538
(800) 621-1544 • (970) 663-4700 • www.dukepress.com

Library of Congress Cataloging-in-Publication Data

Cox, Kevin.
    The administrator's guide to Microsoft SQL Server 6.5 / by Kevin Cox and
        Bill Jones. — 1st ed.
    p.   cm.
    Includes index.
    ISBN 1-882419-53-7 (pbk.)
    1. Client/server computing. 2. SQL server. I. Jones, Bill, 1968– .
      II. Title.
QA76.9.C55C69 1997
005.75'85—dc21   97-4755
                                        CIP

Published by DUKE PRESS
DUKE COMMUNICATIONS INTERNATIONAL
Loveland, Colorado

This book was printed in Canada.

ISBN 1-882419-53-7

1 2 3 4 5 6 WL 1 0 9 8 7

Acknowledgments

I would like to thank my family — Yvonne, Nicole, and Mark — for all their wonderful support. I would also like to thank Sharon Brigner for her commitment, time, and effort in doing the technical editing. Special thanks go to the team members at MCI in Colorado Springs, Colorado, and Austin, Texas, for their input into the replication chapter, especially Tim Ling, who was on the other end of the phone when we were trying to get replication to work between two domains without a trusted connection.

Bill Jones, my coauthor, deserves a lot of credit for helping get this book to market. His perseverance in finding the small details behind some of the SQL Server features has brought him a long way since his first exposure to SQL Server.

And last, but certainly not least, I would like to thank Janet Robbins and Marion Agnew at Duke Press for their lessons and guidance in writing a book, as well as Dave Bernard, Martha Nichols, John Morris-Reihl, and Rob Carson, who labored behind the scenes. If they can manage other projects as well as this one, they will have a long career of successful ventures!

Kevin Cox

I would like to express the appreciation I have for my wife Susan and our children Emily and Jacob. Without them, this effort would have had significantly less meaning. This book would not have been possible without all the hard work by the people at Duke Press. It was quite an experience, and I recommend that all of you reading this book take the opportunity to experience it for yourselves.

Bill Jones

About the Authors

 **Kevin Cox** is President of Computer Peritia, an Aurora, Colorado-based consulting company. He has 17 years of experience in the computer industry and has been using relational databases since the early 1980s. He was one of the first Microsoft certified SQL Server instructors in the country and has mentored many technical professionals in the correct use of SQL Server in a client-server environment. Kevin carries almost all Microsoft Professional and Training certifications, such as MCSE, MCSD, and MCT. Kevin is in the fortunate position to have participated in some of the best SQL Server projects in the country. He lives in Aurora, Colorado, with his family.

 **William D. Jones** (a.k.a. Bill Jones) is a displaced physicist who spends his spare time contemplating the mysteries of modern physics. He was awarded his Master's degree in physics at the University of Denver for computer modeling of atmospheric scattering of infrared light. He received his BS in Physics from the University of California at Santa Barbara. He has a diverse background in mathematics and enjoys coding very complex algorithms in C++ and SQL. He experiments continuously in database connectivity, the use of databases as organized storage for complex programs and extending database capabilities through C++.

Table of Contents at a Glance

Table of Contents

Acronyms

ACID	atomicity, consistency, isolation, durability
ACL	access control list
ADO	active data objects
API	application programming interface
ASP	active server pages
BCP	Bulk Copy Program
COM	component object model
DAC	Distributed Transaction Coordinator Administrative Console
DBA	database administrator
DBCC	Database Consistency Checker
DBO	database owner
DBOO	database object owner
DHCP	Dynamic Host Configuration Protocol
DLL	dynamic link library
DMO	Distributed Management Objects
DNS	Domain Name System
DRI	declarative referential integrity
DSN	data source name
DTC	Distributed Transaction Coordinator
FAT	file allocation table
FIPS	Federal Information Processing Standards
GID	group ID
GSNW	gateway services for netware
GUI	graphical user interface
HAL	hardware abstraction layer
HR	human resources
HTML	HyperText Markup Language
IRL	insert row-level locking
ISAPI	interactive services application programming interface; also Internet Services application programming interface
ISQL	interactive SQL
LE	lock escalation

LRU	least recently used
MIB	Management Information Base
MPNL	multiprotocol network library
MS DTC	Microsoft Distributed Transaction Coordinator
MSSQL-MIB	Microsoft SQL Server Management Information Base
MTS	Microsoft Transaction Server
NIC	Network Interface Card
NIST	National Institute of Standards and Technology
NTFS	Windows NT file system
ODBC	open database connectivity
ODS	Open Data Services
OLE	object linking and embedding
OLTP	online transaction processing
PK	primary key
RA	read ahead
RAID	redundant array of inexpensive disks
RAS	Remote Access Service
RDBM	relational database management
RPC	remote procedure call
SA	system administrator
SARG	search argument
SMP	symmetric multiprocessing
SNA	systems network architecture
SNMP	simple network management protocol
SQL-DMO	SQL distributed management objects
SUID	system user ID
TCP/IP	Transmission Control Protocol/Internet Protocol
TDS	tabular data stream
TSR	terminate and stay resident
UI	user interface
UID	user ID
UPS	uninterruptable power supply
URL	universal resource locator
VB	Visual Basic
VBA	Visual Basic for Applications
VLDB	very large databases

Chapter 1

Overview of Microsoft SQL Server

What Is SQL Server?

Microsoft SQL Server is a database management system. It is portable, reliable, flexible, fast, and easy to manage. SQL Server has been developed specifically to take advantage of the best features Microsoft Windows NT has to offer. It is optimized for the multithreaded, preemptive multiprocessing kernel of Windows NT. The many features and options in SQL Server are geared toward multiple users who need concurrent access to high volumes of data. In this chapter, we discuss the primary features that differentiate SQL Server from other database management software.

Portability

SQL Server is portable across all platforms on which Windows NT runs, including Alpha AXP, Intel x86, MIPS, and PowerPC architectures. The Windows NT hardware abstract layer (HAL) and other kernel processes create layers between the hardware and services like SQL Server.

Besides being portable across platforms, SQL Server and Windows NT support many different types of hardware devices. The recent and ever-changing improvements in hardware devices include support for symmetric multiprocessing (multiple CPUs), high-bandwidth network cards, striped backups, and RAID disk striping. RAID, an acronym for Redundant Array of Inexpensive Disks, can provide performance and/or reliability improvements. SQL Server will also support multiple tape drives for striped backups, which are useful for very large databases; striped backups write to multiple backup devices simultaneously.

More on NT Integration

This section is a preview of Chapter 4, which is devoted to a discussion of the close integration of SQL Server with Windows NT.

SQL Server runs as a service under Windows NT. Services in NT can start when the machine restarts and can broadcast their service names and types over the network. For example, SQL Server will broadcast its type of service as SQL Server as well as the name of the server. This feature allows other machines, whether clients or servers, to query a network to find out which servers are providing database services. Two other services come with SQL Server — the SQL Executive and the Distributed Transaction Coordinator. These services are separate programs that run under Windows NT and can be started and stopped from the Services applet in the Control Panel. Other processes, such as replication, run as different threads under the SQL Server process.

Errors in SQL Server appear in the Windows NT event log and can be seen in the Application section of the Event Viewer program. The errors also appear in the SQL Server error log. Programmers can set their application errors to appear in the NT event log.

The NT registry controls the basic SQL Server installation parameters. It is used to save the default login name, the standard named pipe configuration, the SQL Server startup parameters, and more. It also saves parameters for SQL Executive, as well as for tools like SQLTrace.

The Windows NT Performance Monitor has a special addition for SQL Server. It includes pre-defined counters that give an in-depth look at what is happening behind the scenes. In addition, programmers and administrators can define new counters to track application-based performance. The Performance

Monitor shows more detail than most people will use, but the detail is very beneficial when your system is showing signs of performance problems.

SQL Server can take advantage of Windows NT's security models. The three choices — integrated, mixed, and standard security — give SQL Server the flexibility to fit into any security scheme. The SQL Security Manager program makes it easier to administer large groups of users because SQL user and login information is integrated with Windows NT user information.

Batch jobs use Windows NT command-line utilities, such as ISQL (Interactive SQL) and BCP (Bulk Copy Program). Windows NT is not considered to have the most powerful scripting language for command-line batch programs, but it is usually adequate for background database jobs. Other popular scripting languages, such as PERL, are available for Windows NT if the standard language is not sufficient. Combining the scheduler (new in 6.0) with the power of the batch scripting languages makes it easier to program and manage background jobs for all Windows NT jobs, not just those related to SQL Server.

Reliability

SQL Server is reliable because of the enforced transaction logging in all versions of SQL Server, complete with roll-forward and roll-backward recovery. Recovery from application and system errors and from hardware problems has always been a solid part of the Windows NT/SQL Server cohesiveness.

Another new feature in the hardware/software combination arena is the fallback support in SQL Server. This option lets two servers share one disk tower. If one server fails, the other can be brought up very quickly.

Flexibility

Because SQL Server is a Win32 application, it is network independent and supports all major networks, including TCP/IP, NetBEUI, IPX/SPX, DECNet Sockets, Banyan Vines, and AppleTalk (or Apple Datastream Protocol). The Win32 API lets services like SQL Server take advantage of all networks that work with Windows NT. The network library (new in SQL 6.0) called MPNL, or Multiprotocol Network Library, integrates common network services and remote procedure calls (RPCs) to offer additional features. The Windows NT RPC allows two-way encryption so that SQL Server can encrypt both the queries and the results. The MPNL option is found in the SQL Server installation process.

Client/Server Orientation

SQL Server has all the right pieces to be a very good element of a client/server environment. Support for the major network protocols, standard database links with ODBC, new OLE automation, and multiple choices for client-side data management make it very versatile. DB-Library, ODBC, and Microsoft Jet Engine are choices for getting data from SQL Server to client machines and back. SQL Server is also one of the best databases for the back end of an Internet application. The new tools, such as ISAPI (Internet Services Application Programming Interface), ADO (Active Data Objects), OLE-DB, and ASP (Active Server Pages), make it relatively easy to set up and manage Web servers.

Efficiency

The heart of SQL Server's good performance lies in its ability to manage memory pages and process threads efficiently. These concepts apply to SQL Server in general and not necessarily to a specific version.

Let's look at the thread management first. Windows NT splits very large programs into smaller segments, called *threads*, to manage many tasks happening on the server at the same time. If you have only one CPU, then the tasks only appear to be happening at the same time, because each thread gets a small slice of time to do its work on the CPU. However, if your setup has more than one CPU, different threads can be executing simultaneously.

Because SQL Server manages its threads efficiently, it has very good response time. The Read-Ahead Manager for parallel data scanning runs on a separate thread, so it can operate independently from the user session it is working for. Other SQL Server processes, such as the checkpoint process and any backup processes started by the administrator, work on separate threads behind the scenes. You can configure thread usage for SQL Server from the standard SQL Server configuration screen. Refer to Chapter 16, "Performance Tuning," for more information about configuring SQL Server.

Now let's look at SQL's memory management. SQL Server does everything in 2K blocks called *pages*. There are many different page types, each with its own purpose and format. Most pages handled by SQL Server are data and index pages, so most of the optimization techniques internal to SQL Server focus on these page types.

SQL Server reads a 2K page from the physical disk into memory and leaves it there as long as it can. Optimizing the task of getting data from disk to memory includes processes such as the Read-Ahead Manager. To be technically correct, the Read-Ahead Manager is a thread within the SQL Server process. The memory manager keeps track of available memory blocks to know where to put the pages coming from disk. If no pages are available, the memory manager knows which pages haven't been used for a while and will discard them. This type of memory management is based on the least recently used (LRU) algorithm. Of course, before discarding the page, the memory manager writes it back to disk if the page has been modified. Because all the pages are the same size, the memory manager does not care about the type of page it is because the page is handed off to other threads for the actual processing.

Query Optimizer

SQL Server uses a cost-based optimizer to determine the best method of processing a query. The basis of the optimizer is the distribution page, which keeps a statistical distribution of the values in the first field of an index. Every index gets a distribution page. From this, the optimizer can determine the selectivity of the index and determine if it is the best one to use.

Developers and administrators can use tools that show what the optimizer has chosen and the steps it goes through to get to a final decision. The SET SHOWPLAN ON option is one of the most helpful techniques for programmers to learn. Several DBCC TRACEON options show the join order and index selections made by the optimizer.

Manageability

In SQL Server, Microsoft has provided some of the best administrative and operations tools for managing your SQL Server environment. For example, the Enterprise Manager program allows administration of all your servers from one central location. SQL Server uses its own services to manage a server. System databases and system stored procedures perform various administrative functions.

System Databases

SQL Server uses its own databases to manage the user databases, which means that the same tools and techniques can be used to manage SQL Server as well as all the databases on the system.

The main database is the Master database. It is used to control devices, other databases, logins, remote connections, and configurations. Another system database, Tempdb, is used for temporary workspace, such as large sorts and work tables for complex queries. The Model database is used as a template when creating application databases — any objects added to the Model database are added to any new application databases created after the object was added. The Msdb database (new in SQL 6.0) keeps track of scheduled jobs and job history. One other system database, Distribution, is created only when replication is installed.

Ability to Handle Very Large Databases (VLDB)

SQL Server's architecture, its integration with Windows NT, and its expandable hardware bring Microsoft SQL Server into the big leagues. The combination of operating system and hardware features allows for very large databases at reasonable prices. The largest production databases on Microsoft SQL Server machines have exceeded 100 gigabytes. The largest current project in development using SQL Server exceeds 1 terabyte.

What's in this Book

This book is written with the advanced administrator in mind. It assumes that the reader has received training in the SQL Server basics from another source, but it does cover some basic information about the new features, new programs, and new tools. Chapter 2 reviews all the new features, programs, and tools in SQL Server 6.5. This chapter is particularly helpful because some of the new features are mentioned only in this chapter, although others are discussed in later chapters. Chapter 3 focuses on the tools that come with version 6.5. Chapter 4 is a treatise on the close integration of SQL Server and Windows NT. Chapters 5 and 6 tell you how to install and upgrade SQL Server. The chapters in the rest of the book can help you get the most out of SQL Server. They cover performance and tuning, backups, recovery, logins, and security. Chapter 11 is an in-depth article about replication and replication troubleshooting. The last chapter covers extended stored procedures. The appendices cover three topics: internals of the transaction log, other knowledge resources, and more about SQL 7.0.

Everyone can learn something from the tips and techniques, as well as the occasional notes and cautions, in every chapter. Some tips and topics are more for beginners; some are for experts. However, regardless of your expertise, the information in this book will give you new ideas and reminders that will help make you a more effective administrator.

Summary

Microsoft SQL Server is portable, reliable, flexible, efficient, and easy to manage. It has been written to take advantage of the architecture of Windows NT. Other database management systems are written to be very portable between operating systems, which limits their opportunities for specific performance enhancements. In contrast, SQL Server is portable only to the platforms supported by Windows NT, and this tight integration lets SQL Server become more powerful with each enhancement to Windows NT and the underlying hardware.

SQL Server is reliable. SQL Server is oriented toward client/server applications. SQL Server is fast and has good performance tuning options. SQL Server has some of the best administrative tools on the market. This book will help you make the most of your database choice.

Chapter 2

What's New in SQL Server 6.5

This chapter briefly discusses the features of SQL Server that are new in version 6.5. We have grouped these new features into those that will be used primarily by administrators and those that will be used more often by programmers; however, because this book is intended primarily for administrators, the programming tools are examined from an administrator's point of view. Some of the features in this chapter get only a short explanation because they are covered more thoroughly in a later chapter. Some features get several paragraphs in this chapter because they don't need a complete chapter of their own. Although you aren't likely to use every single feature we mention, the improvements from version 6.0 to 6.5 are significant and make SQL Server even more useful.

What's New for Administrators

SQL Server 6.5 offers many new features for database administrators. As you can see from the list below, there are many changes between SQL Server 6.0 and 6.5. The look and feel of the tools is basically the same between the two most recent versions. However, if you are converting from a SQL Server 4.2 database, the changes are tremendous. In general, the new tools are easier to use and make it easier to manage all the SQL Server databases in your organization from one desk.

The top 10 new features for administrators are

- Replication enhancements
  - Replicates a SQL Server database to any database that supports open database connectivity (ODBC)
  - Supports text and image data types
  - Disables constraints during replication
- Database Maintenance Planning Wizard
- Object transfer between databases and servers (in Enterprise Manager)
- Table dump and load
- Point-in-time recovery
- Fallback support
- Performance Monitor enhancements
- Simple network management protocol (SNMP) support for monitoring SQL Server
- New setup features
- New server and client tools

New administrative features that deserve honorable mention include

- Create Schema statement
- SQLExecutiveCmdExec account
- DBCC REINDEX command
- Two new performance-tuning enhancements
  - Thread affinity
  - Remote connection timeout
- SQLMail enhancements
- User-defined error messages at the Management Screen
- More ANSI-standard extensions

Administrators' Top 10 New Features

We chose the following features as the top 10 new features because of the value they bring, the problems they help solve, the workarounds they help avoid, and their expected benefit to professional database administrators.

Replication Enhancements

You can now use SQL Server to replicate any ODBC-compliant database, such as Microsoft Access or Oracle. You can manage replication either through the SQL Enterprise Manager or with stored procedures, which is more difficult. Replication to ODBC databases is currently a one-way transaction from SQL Server to the ODBC database. However, it is rumored that two-way replication will be added to SQL 7.0.

Both text and image data types are now supported in replication. However, logging, limiting size, and replicating to other database management systems can still be difficult. For more detailed information about replication in SQL Server 6.5, see Chapter 11, "Replication."

Some of the problems with constraints in subscribing tables, such as records coming from the publisher before the primary key record has been sent, are now solved by a new feature that lets you disable constraints during replication. This feature allows the record to be added to the detail table before the record is added to the Master table. Of course, this feature means that even though you might not get a replication failure in certain situations, you must have your own application integrity checks in case the Master record never comes down.

Database Maintenance Planning Wizard

This wizard is a great addition for all SQL Server newcomers. It eases setup for many maintenance tasks, such as database consistency checks, optimization updates, and backups.

You can run the wizard in three ways:

- Click the button on the toolbar in the SQL Enterprise Manager (Figure 2.1).

Figure 2.1
Database Maintenance
Planning Wizard Button

- Click the Help menu and choose the Database Maintenance Wizard.
- From a Command Prompt (CmdExec window), run the Sqlmaint.exe program. You can find the parameters with the /? option.

We examine this wizard in more detail in Chapter 7.

Object Transfer in Enterprise Manager

Did you miss the SQL Object Manager 4.2 transfer option that disappeared in SQL Server 6.0? This option is back in SQL Server 6.5 in another form and better than ever. Database objects are now Object Linking and Embedding (OLE) objects, and the transfer object feature in SQL Enterprise Manager has been completely rewritten to handle OLE objects. This option lets you easily write a Visual Basic (VB) or Visual Basic for Applications (VBA) program to do your own custom transfer.

You can copy all objects of all types, or all objects of one type, or one object of one type. You can copy an object with or without the data it is linked to. You can even append or replace data that is linked to an object before you copy the object.

Although these object-copying features are important additions, they do not always work correctly because the sysdepends table is not always up to date. The sysdepends table stores dependencies between database objects; for example, when a stored procedure refers to a table, the stored procedure is said to depend upon that table. So if procedure A executes procedure B, the entries in sysdepends properly show that B depends upon A. However, if you drop (delete) and recreate procedure A, the system assigns a new number to A, but the record in sysdepends for B still points to the original number for A.

If you don't use the dependency options, the objects are created in alphabetical order, so the primary key and foreign key references can cause errors when the created script is run in the destination database. The errors occur when a foreign key references a primary key table that is later in the alphabetical order and hasn't been built yet.

The default setting is to have the dependency options checked. It is best to clear this checkbox because all the dependencies will be copied when you may be expecting only the one object you have chosen. For example, even though you only want a copy of one stored procedure to be transferred, all of the tables, views, and stored procedures referenced will also be copied if you have the dependencies checked.

We also recommend that you turn off the default scripting options, which will copy users, logins, and permissions when you don't want them copied.

The source database in a transfer can be older versions of SQL Server, but the destination database can only be a registered SQL 6.5 database. *Registered* in this case means that the other server has been entered as a valid server in the SQL Enterprise Manager program.

Table Dump and Load

These new features let you back up (dump) and restore (load) one table at a time. However, we don't recommend using these features, because when a prior version of a table is restored and primary keys are missing, referential integrity can be violated. For example, let's say you add a customer and some sales orders referencing this new customer to a table, then restore a prior version of the customer table. The new customer is gone, but the sales orders are still there.

Although table dump and load are described in the documentation for SQL Server 6.0, these features never actually appeared. In SQL Server 6.5, the Enterprise Manager's backup and load dialog boxes have been enhanced to support these features by giving you a choice of which table to dump or load. All backup information is kept in the Msdb system database, so that the system can track which tables and databases are contained in a backup file or tape.

Point-in-Time Recovery

This feature lets you recover a database as it existed at a certain time. When you load a log file with the Load command, you specify a time interval for recovering transactions. So if you know a corruption occurred at a certain time, you can restore up to the point of the failure.

Fallback Support

This feature lets you configure a server for different data-protection options, such as two servers sharing one disk array. If the primary server goes down, the secondary server takes over. This feature is especially useful for administrators whose servers run 24 hours a day, seven days a week.

Performance Monitor Enhancements

You can track your own statistics in SQL Server 6.5's Performance Monitor using 10 new user-defined counters. These counters let you monitor system and database performance statistics from your application. The counters are implemented through skeleton stored procedures sp_user_counter1 through sp_user_counter10 in the Master database. In these procedures, you can write code to track your application.

To use these procedures, you must return one integer value and give the probe user (a special user added by the system for use by Performance Monitor) Execute permission for the procedures. Then you run Performance Monitor, find the SQL Server section, and add User Counter 1 to the tracking display. Unfortunately, you cannot rename a user-defined counter to more accurately reflect what you are tracking. For more information about using Performance Monitor, see Chapter 15.

SNMP Support for Monitoring SQL Server

SQL Server 6.5 now supports programs that use SNMP, an industry-standard protocol for tracking the status of servers and networks. You can use a third-party SNMP program to monitor SQL Server 6.5 installations and server performance information, explore defined SQL Server databases, and view server and database configuration parameters.

Workstations running an SNMP monitor are notified by SQL Server of a particular status or that a particular condition has occurred. An SNMP trap in SQL Server sends a notification to an SNMP agent — hardware or software that reports network activity to the network management console — which forwards it to the SNMP monitor.

The SNMP enhancements are part of the SQL Server Management Information Base, or MIB (MSSQL-MIB). Microsoft developed this MIB using the proposed Internet Engineering Task Force SNMP RDBMS-MIB (RFC 1697) and enhanced it specifically for use with Microsoft SQL Server.

New Setup Features

The setup program has been enhanced with new keywords and character sets and new setup options and tools. Platform support for the PowerPC is now included, so you can now run SQL Server on PowerPC systems.

Before you upgrade to SQL Server 6.5, you should run Chkupg.exe to check your SQL Server 4.2 or SQL Server 6.0 databases for keyword conflicts. The new keywords in SQL Server 6.5 are

- Authorization
- Cascade
- Cross
- Escape
- Full

- Inner
- Join
- Left
- Outer
- Privileges

- Restrict
- Right
- Schema
- Work

SQL Server 6.5 also supports the following new characters:

- CP932, Japanese
- CP936, Chinese (simplified)
- CP949, Korean
- CP950, Chinese (traditional)

Two sort orders are included with all supported character sets: binary and Windows NT provided. A *sort order* is a dictionary that gives SQL Server a place to look up the order of the characters in a language. A *binary sort order* sorts the characters according to their ASCII value.

New Server and Client Tools

SQL Server 6.5 includes the following new server tools:

- Microsoft Query — a point-and-click tool for looking at data
- SQLTrace — a spy tool that shows commands being received by SQL Server
- Microsoft Distributed Transaction Coordinator (MS-DTC) — runs as a Windows NT service
- SQL Web Page Wizard — lets you build World Wide Web pages from query results
- SNMP MIBs and SNMP Agent — these tools are discussed above

SQL Server 6.5 includes the new client installation tools and changes listed below. You will notice that some of these tools can be run on both the client and the server.

- Microsoft Query
- SQLTrace
- MS DTC (client support installed)
- SQL Web Page Wizard
- Other ODBC client drivers for heterogeneous replication use

Administrators' Honorable-Mention Features

These items are not in the top 10 because they will probably not be used often — perhaps only once, at installation. But they are still great new features.

Create Schema Statement

This statement is an ANSI-standard extension that lets you create objects and privileges within a single batch of statements. Because all actions are considered to be created at the same time, it is not necessary to create the objects in dependent order. For example, you can create a view before creating its base table, and a Grant statement can establish permissions before the object has been created.

The Create Schema statement makes it possible to create two tables with mutually dependent foreign keys. Of course, you can still do it the old-fashioned way — creating the tables first, then adding the foreign key constraints with the Alter Table command.

SQLExecutiveCmdExec Account

SQL Server 6.5 includes a new account — SQLExecutiveCmdExec — that is installed during SQL Server setup. This account is for CmdExec tasks owned by users who aren't system administrators; the tasks run in SQLExecutiveCmdExec's security context. By default, this account is a member of the Users local group on the Windows NT server.

Do not confuse the SQLExecutiveCmdExec account with the requirement that Microsoft SQL Server run under a user account instead of the default LocalAccount to take advantage of some of the new network features (such as ODBC replication and Web page generation). These features must have SQL Executive running in an account other than the LocalAccount, whereas the SQLExecutiveCmdExec account is used by background jobs (tasks) that execute a Windows NT command in a CmdExec session.

DBCC REINDEX Command

The Data Base Consistency Checker (DBCC) extensions make administrative tasks easier. For example, the DBCC REINDEX command rebuilds all indexes for a table.

Performance-Tuning Enhancements

- Thread affinity — If your server has four or more processors, you can now assign certain processors to SQL Server. For example, you could dedicate one processor to Windows NT and network traffic and the other processors to SQL Server. This setup helps minimize the amount of memory that must be copied to another processor when a program or thread is moved to another CPU. Refer to Chapters 15 and 16 about performance tuning for a more detailed explanation of this feature.

- Remote connection timeout — You can choose the time period during which remote procedure calls (RPCs) keep open their connection to other server(s) after the RPCs are complete. In earlier versions of SQL Server, every call to a remote stored procedure required a new connection. This feature keeps the first connection active, letting any more calls during the chosen time period bypass the slow connection process.

SQLMail Enhancements

- New SQLMail icon in the Server Manager tree — You can start and stop SQLMail from SQL Enterprise Manager's Server Manager window. A SQLMail icon appears in the expanded tree under each server name. To start or stop SQLMail, open the tree for a server, right-click its SQLMail icon, and then choose Start or Stop. You can also assign a mail login name and password to SQLMail from the Server Manager window of SQL Enterprise Manager. Simply right-click the SQLMail icon, choose Configure, and complete the SQLMail Configuration dialog box that appears.

- Microsoft Exchange compatibility — SQLMail is now compatible with Microsoft Exchange. See Chapter 3, "Administrative and Programming Tools," for step-by-step instructions on how to configure Exchange for use with SQLMail.

User-Defined Error Messages at the Management Screen

Although user-defined error messages are not a new feature of SQL Server, you can now define error messages through the Management window. Using the Enterprise Manager, choose Server, Error Messages. For more information about this feature, see Chapter 7, "Scheduling and Performing Administrative Tasks."

SQL Enterprise Refresh

In SQL Server 6.0, newly added objects, such as a new table, did not automatically appear in the Server Manager window; you had to refresh the list manually. When an object is added or deleted with a Transact-SQL command, the Refresh statement still does not automatically refresh the SQL Enterprise Manager window; however, refreshing works when it's done with the Enterprise Manager screens. To be on the safe side, you should learn how to refresh the list manually. You can refresh the list manually in two ways:

- Click a folder, select the View menu, and choose Refresh.
- Right-click a folder and choose Refresh.

More ANSI-Standard Extensions

Microsoft SQL Server 6.5 has been certified as compliant with Federal Information Processing Standards (FIPS 127-2) established by the National Institute of Standards and Technology (NIST). It has also been enhanced to meet the ANSI SQL-92 standards. This compliance certification is important for interoperability between databases from different vendors and for portability of applications. SQL Server 6.5 features that comply with these standards include

- The Create Schema statement
- The Grant With Grant Option and Revoke Grant Option For statements
- The Select statement (support for ANSI-standard joins)
- ANSI-standard null and default support

The ANSI-standard joins, which are explained in more detail in the next section, include Inner Join and Outer Join extensions that make Microsoft Access queries more compatible with SQL Server queries.

What's New for Programmers

SQL Server 6.5's top 10 new features for programmers are listed below. We will consider each feature in more detail.

- The Web Page Wizard, which lets you build Web pages from query results.
- The ability to create objects within a transaction, so that you can copy the Inserted and Deleted tables to a temporary table within a trigger.

- The ability to return results and populate local tables from remote procedures with the Insert...Exec statement.

- Bound connections for multiple connections sharing the same lock space, so that one program with multiple connections can have these connections participate in one transaction. Bound connections also speed up the programs because the connections are not dropped after a statement has completed.

- The Insert Row-Level Locking (IRL) feature — until now, the lowest granularity of lock for SQL Server was one page (2K). When a page was locked, all records on that page were locked. Although this locking strategy was the fastest for most applications, it caused serious problems for high-volume transaction processing applications. Row-level locking was instituted, for Insert statements only, to allow one row at a time to be locked.

- Select statement enhancements.

  – Group By enhancements — With Cube and With Rollup.

  – ANSI-standard join options.

- Cursor enhancements.

  – The ability to update tables without unique indexes.

  – The option to close the cursor automatically when Commit or Rollback is complete.

- The Distributed Transaction Coordinator (MS DTC), which lets you update, insert, and delete records on multiple servers in different locations.

- Distributed Management Objects (SQL-DMO) enhancements, which let you use the OLE features of SQL Server for specialized programming.

- ODBC API enhancements.

  Honorable-mention features for programmers include

- DB-Library enhancements
- Open Data Services
- Embedded SQL for C enhancements
- More ANSI-standard extensions

Programmers' Top 10 New Features

These features are not just for programmers; they are also important for administrators who need to do support programming, such as importing data from external sources, writing database installation scripts, or just fixing data problems. Reading this section is imperative for database administrators, because it is important to know what the development staff will be trying to apply as they use this new version of SQL Server.

Using the Web Page Wizard

This wizard creates HyperText Markup Language (HTML) 3.0 pages. The wizard comes in a variety of flavors — one for Access, one for FoxPro, one for SQL Server, and one that can be used with both Excel and Word. Regardless of software, these wizards perform the same basic function. The SQL Server Wizard lets you use the results of a query to create an HTML page, which you can then view with any of the popular Web browsers. One of the best features of this wizard is its ability to schedule times when the data on the HTML page will be refreshed. You can set the page to be refreshed whenever the data changes or at regular intervals (for example, every hour).

With SQL Server 6.5's wizard, you can create your first Web page in just a few minutes. If you have installed the Pubs database, type the following query in the wizard screen:

```
SELECT au_fname, au_lname from authors
```

After the page is created, open the file with a Web browser. The basic screen is attractive, even without the graphics you will add later (using a pre-built template). After you have viewed the page, you can open the .htm file with an HTML editor and teach yourself the basics of HTML by looking at the code.

Creating Objects within a Transaction

You can now create any object within a transaction; one example is copying SQL Server's special Inserted and Deleted tables to a temporary table within a trigger. Now, the created objects are a part of a transaction, so you can use Rollback to remove the object. In prior versions of SQL Server, data modifications in these special tables were available only to the trigger, so the current applications have had to do creative workarounds for complex processing in triggers. Cursors, which first became available in SQL 6.0, were the first big improvement in handling the Inserted and Deleted tables. In SQL 6.5, you can save the data modifications in a temporary table and access them in a stored procedure, which gives you greater control over data manipulation.

For example, let's look at a trigger that saves the Inserted table and calls a stored procedure. The trigger below will call a stored procedure named prMyProcedure, which can retrieve records from the #tblTemp table. Note that this table is a temporary table; you can tell by the # designation as the first character of the table name. In prior versions of SQL Server, all the code accessing the Inserted table had to reside in the trigger itself.

```
CREATE TRIGGER trMyTrigger ON myTable FOR insert, update AS
BEGIN
    SELECT * INTO #tblTemp FROM INSERTED
    EXEC prMyProcedure
END
```

Here is a trick you need to know when you use a stored procedure to access a temporary table created by another object. To compile the stored procedure, all table objects need to be created before they are referenced in the code. In the above example, the procedure called by the trigger, prMyProcedure, will not compile when it tries to reference the #tblTemp, because this table is created at runtime by the trMyTrigger object. The trick is to put a Create Table statement in the same script as the stored procedure, but before the Create Procedure statement, as in the example below.

```
CREATE TABLE #tblTemp (myColumn1 int, myColumn2, etc)
GO
CREATE PROCEDURE prMyProcedure AS
    BEGIN
        SELECT * FROM #tblTemp
    END — of procedure
```

Of course, the #tblTemp table must have the same structure as myTable, referenced in the first trigger above. A safer way of creating it would be

```
SELECT * INTO #tblTemp FROM myTable WHERE 1 = 2
```

instead of using the Create Table command. This method would ensure that the temporary table always had the current structure of myTable.

Another example of creating objects within a transaction is creating tables and rolling them back if necessary. The example below starts a transaction, creates a permanent table called myTable, then cancels the transaction via the Rollback command. When the code is finished running, myTable does not exist.

```
BEGIN TRANSACTION
    CREATE TABLE myTable (myColumn1 int, etc)
ROLLBACK TRANSACTION
```

Returning Results and Populating Local Tables from Remote Procedures

This feature considerably improves on SQL Server 6.0's row-at-a-time method of returning query results from another server. You can now use the Insert...Exec statement to return data obtained from remote procedures to tables in your local server. If you want the results returned to a stored procedure, you can insert the rows into a prebuilt temporary table.

The example below selects rows from one server and saves them on another server. The first step is to create a stored procedure on Server 1.

```
CREATE PROCEDURE prCalledByRemoteServer AS
    SELECT * FROM MyTable
```

The second step is to insert the rows from Server 1 into a table on your local server.

```
INSERT MyLocalTable EXEC SERVER1.myDatabase.owner.prCalled-
ByRemoteServer
```

The first step, creating the stored procedure, returns a result set. The second step inserts those rows with the Insert statement, combined with an Execute (or Exec) statement. (This process is an easy way to do "pull" replication, which is explained more in Chapter 11, "Replication.")

Creating Bound Connections

This feature lets two or more connections share the same lock space and transaction. This capability can be useful in several situations. First, dynamic link libraries (DLLs) for an extended stored procedure that is run within a transaction can now access data locked by the transaction, which was not possible in SQL Server 6.0 and earlier versions.

Second, the SQL Server 6.0 extension to the Execute command lets you build an SQL statement in a string and run it. In SQL Server 6.5, the Execute statement runs in another connection, so calling it inside a transaction means it cannot access data already locked by the transaction.

In the following example, the first two lines declare and seed a variable. We begin a transaction to keep the pages locked until the end of the transaction. The Update statement modifies every row and locks all the pages in the table. (It modifies every row because it contains no Where clause.) The Exec statement will perform two tasks:

1. Create a new session, which under earlier versions of SQL Server would not be able to access the locked pages.
2. Select all the rows in the table, even if they are locked. This step is an example of a bound connection.

The last statement will save (commit) the changes.

```
DECLARE @sCmd varchar(255)
SELECT @sCmd = "SELECT * FROM MyTable"
BEGIN TRANSACTION tranSample
    UPDATE MyTable SET MyColumn = MyColumn
    EXEC (@sCmd)
COMMIT TRANSACTION tranSample
```

Using Insert Row-Level Locking (IRL)

Row-level locking is an option an administrator can use for each table in a database. The first part of this section explains row-level locking; the last part explains when it is useful and when to avoid it. This discussion is intended to be a short definition of the new locking feature, not an exhaustive discussion of SQL Server's locking mechanisms.

Row-Level Locking

Row-level locking in SQL Server 6.5 applies to rows being inserted. It is controlled by the stored procedure sp_tableoption and can be turned on or off for all tables in a database or for one table at a time. The first example below shows how to control all tables in a database; the second example shows control for one table.

```
sp_tableoption '%.%', 'insert row lock', 'true'
sp_tableoption 'myTable', 'insert row lock', 'false'
```

By default, SQL Server uses page-level locking, which means that when a lock is granted, the whole 2K page is locked, and all records on the page are accessible only to the session that has acquired the lock. On some applications, this restriction can result in too many sessions waiting for locks to become free. With the addition of row-level locking, it is possible for a session to lock one record at a time. The only current restriction is that row-level locking is limited only to records being added to a table.

Row-level locking helps avoid database *hot spots*, or tables in which more than one session tries to lock the same pages at the same time. A typical example of a hot spot occurs when new records are always added to the end of the table. Everyone who is inserting records tries to lock the last page. For an application with hundreds of users, this situation can become a problem very quickly.

There are several ways around this problem. In prior versions, the best way was to create a clustered index with a 50 to 75 percent fill factor on a field (or fields) that would cause the inserts to be randomly spread throughout a file. For example, you might have a hot spot on the customer number in a customer table if this number is an identity field and the table has a clustered index. This setup creates a hot spot because SQL Server is always assigning the next greater number to the identity counter, and the clustered index dictates that the records are always added at the bottom of the file. Changing the clustered index to another field — customer name, for example — spreads the inserts throughout the file instead of always adding them to the end.

Another way around the hot spot problem is to turn on row-level locking for the table with the problem. Then the rows that are inserted acquire row locks on the last page. More than one session can then insert to the same page at the same time.

Now for a word of caution: Row-level locking works only for rows being inserted; the other commands — Select, Update, and Delete — require page-level locks. An Update statement on a page with several Insert locks would have to wait until all Insert locks are released on that page, so it is possible for a session to deadlock itself. For example, in one transaction, an Insert followed by an Update to the row will cause a deadlock if another Insert lock is already held on the same page. The deadlock occurs because Insert locks only one row, while the Update waits for a page lock.

Select Statement Enhancements

Group By Enhancements — With Cube and With Rollup

The Cube operator creates an *n*-dimensional view of your data, where *n* is the number of fields in the Group By clause plus one. You get one total for every combination of fields in the Group By clause, and then one is added to give you a final grand total. The Group By…With Cube command is a powerful and useful feature, but you should note a few caveats.

First, this command transfers data-summarizing work performed on the client side to the server; therefore, using this command may not be advisable if your server is already overloaded. Most client machines have idle horse-power these days, and you may want to let the client-side report writers do some of the work.

Second, Group By…With Cube returns summary rows with null values in the key fields. Some applications and report writers may not be able to deal with these rows or handle them properly, at least not in their current versions.

The With Rollup option applies to cumulative aggregates, such as a running sum or a running average. The Rollup option differs from the Cube operator only in that the position of the aggregate columns control the subtotal breaks — for example, it never aggregates the column to the left of a column unless the left column is also an aggregate.

The difference between the With Rollup and With Cube options is illustrated in the examples below.

```
SELECT Department, Account, "Total" = Sum(Amount) FROM
       AccountHistory
GROUP BY Department, Account
WITH ROLLUP
```

The above example returns the following result:

Department	Account	Total
Accounting	1000	100.00
Accounting	1100	200.00
Accounting	(null)	300.00
Sales	1000	100.00
Sales	1100	500.00
Sales	(null)	600.00
(null)	(null)	900.00

If you use the With Cube option instead of the With Rollup option, the Select statement returns a different result, as you can see below.

Department	Account	Total
Accounting	1000	100.00
Accounting	1100	200.00
Accounting	(null)	300.00
Sales	1000	100.00

Sales	1100	500.00
Sales	(null)	600.00
(null)	(null)	900.00
(null)	1000	200.00
(null)	1100	700.00

ANSI-Standard Join Options

The new options in the Select statement's From clause comply with the ANSI SQL-92 standard. This feature is great because SQL Server will now recognize queries built with the Access query builder. Table 2.1 summarizes the new extensions for supporting Joins.

TABLE 2.1 NEW JOIN OPTIONS

Join Type	Description
Inner Join	Returns all rows that meet the specified condition and discards unmatched rows.
Cross Join	Returns the cross product of tables when no condition is specified in the Where clause.
Left Outer Join	Returns all rows that meet the specified condition. All rows from the left table that do not meet the specified condition are included in the result set; output columns corresponding to the other table are set to null.
Right Outer Join	Returns all rows that meet the specified condition. All rows from the right table that do not meet the specified condition are included in the result set; output columns corresponding to the other table are set to null.
Full Outer Join	Returns all rows from both tables that meet the condition specified. If a row from other table does not match the selection criteria, that row is included in the result set and its output columns that correspond to the other table are set to null.

Old-style SQL Server outer Joins using =* or *= syntax are still supported, but you cannot use them in the same statement as ANSI-style joins.

Cursor Enhancements

- Updates for tables without unique indexes. In SQL Server 6.0, an updatable cursor's underlying table required a unique index. With SQL Server 6.5, the Update Where Current Of cursor name statement updates the row regardless of the index condition.

- Automatic Close Cursor when Commit or Rollback is complete. When declaring a cursor, you can choose to close the cursor automatically when a Commit or Rollback occurs. This feature solves a problem that previously occurred when a stored procedure aborted with a cursor open — when the front-end application called the stored procedure again, the application returned an error message that the cursor already existed.

Distributed Transaction Coordinator (MS DTC)

SQL Server 6.5 supports MS DTC, which lets programmers and administrators control transactions across a distributed set of software components. Transactions can be on the same server or across multiple servers. Remote stored procedures can now participate in transactions, with a transaction spanning all servers treated as a single unit of work. The transactions can also participate with other XA-compliant transaction managers — data can reside on other database management systems on other operating systems. For example, one transaction can insert records in a Microsoft SQL Server database on a Windows NT machine, insert records in an Oracle database on a Unix machine, then issue one Commit statement to save the work on both machines. If one machine fails, the entire transaction fails and is rolled back.

MS DTC is compatible with distributed transaction controllers from other vendors, such as Tuxedo, Top-End, and Encina; it passes data and SQL commands to the other controllers. These other controllers can be other Windows NT machines, Unix machines, IBM Mainframe machines, and others.

SQL Enterprise Manager also has a new screen that lets you view the status of and control the completion of distributed transactions. You can manually resolve a transaction or force its completion.

SQL Distributed Management Objects (SQL-DMO)

SQL Server is becoming more object oriented. SQL Server is defined as a collection of objects that can contain other objects. For example, a device object can contain other objects and collections, such as a database collection, which in turn can contain other objects, such as tables and stored procedures. Each collection or object has its own properties.

Some of the more popular data manipulation features are becoming OLE objects. SQL Server's OLE features are implemented using SQL-DMO.

The following SQL-DMO objects and functions are new:

- Transfer
- BulkCopy
- ServerGroup
- RegisteredServer

You can use these objects to write your own data-handling routines with Visual Basic or other languages. Some of the SQL-DMO objects support ConnectionPoint events; this support lets you create COM (Common Object Model) objects that are notified by SQL-DMO when certain events occur.

In addition to the new SQL-DMO objects, you can now write extended stored procedures with Visual Basic using the ODSConnection SQL-DMO object. ODS (Open Data Services) is an API that lets you write a server program that appears to clients to be SQL Server. It accepts SQL Connections and can process any command that comes from the clients. For example, you can use an ODS server as a traffic cop to pass commands to the appropriate server, or you can use ODS to intercept SQL Server commands, write them to a log file, and pass them on to SQL Server.

ODBC API Enhancements

The ODBC API is used by programmers to access any database that has the appropriate drivers. One of the advantages of using ODBC is that the same program can be used to access different databases. We don't spend much time on this subject; we include the following list of enhancements only to help database administrators who also do database programming or support a programming staff and are expected to know everything there is to know about SQL Server.

The ODBC API enhancements include

- MS DTC support that treats multiple updates to different servers as one transaction.
- Static server-side cursors on ODBC catalog functions.
- The ability to call ODBC catalog functions inside a transaction.
- Better support for retrieving column attributes (SQLColAttributes) similar to the DB-Library functions.
- The ability to log performance data and long-running queries.

- Other SQL 6.5 enhancements and language changes. An example is the syntax changes for Right Outer Join and Left Outer Join in the From clause of an SQL statement. The ODBC API supports these syntax changes.

Programmers' Honorable-Mention Features

These options are not in the Top 10 list because they are not widely used. However, to the small percentage of the people who use them, the changes are potentially significant. Some of the new features make life easier by giving options and workarounds to difficult problems. Some of the features are not improvements; they are merely syntax changes to support the ANSI-standard SQL language.

DB-Library Enhancements

DB-Library for VB (Visual Basic)

- VB OLE custom control is a 32-bit OLE DB-Library for Visual Basic
- SQLCursorOpen& function no longer supports a pstatus&() row status indicator
- SQLCursorRowStatus& function lets you obtain the row status indicator
- Support for the other new SQL Server 6.5 enhancements is also provided, so that the new features can be used in a VB program

DB-Library for C

- MS DTC support
- Ability to open a cursor on a stored procedure using dynamic parameters
- Support for the other new SQL Server 6.5 enhancements, so that the new features can be used in a C or C++ program

Open Data Services (ODS)

- Bound session support using the new srv_getbindtoken function
- Support for the other new SQL Server 6.5 enhancements in the ODS API

Embedded SQL for C Enhancements

- ANSI compatibility
- Although Embedded SQL for C is not widely used, it can allow greater portability for your application programs among platforms, especially when combined with the ANSI-standard enhancements

More ANSI-Standard Extensions

- Transact-SQL language extensions such as Right Outer Join, Left Outer Join, etc.
- Changes to the Grant and Revoke syntax to be more ANSI-standard

Did We Lose Any Features?

Not yet. However, it appears that SQL 6.5 is preparing us to change the way we use some features, because they may not be supported in the future. SQL Server *Books Online* (available on the Microsoft SQL Server CD-ROM) advises that the following features may be phased out of future versions.

- As mentioned above, outer join syntax is changing from *= or =* to the ANSI-standard Left Outer Join, Right Outer Join, and Full Outer Join. Most programmers agree that using *= and =* in the Where clause are easier to read and to code, but they are not ANSI-standard. The Left Outer Join and Right Outer Join options are used in the From clause and seem to be harder to read. The new Full Outer Join does not have an equivalent in prior versions, because *=* is invalid.
- You are encouraged to use Windows NT's mirroring or hardware mirroring instead of the SQL Server device mirroring.
- You should consider using cursors instead of the Select...For Browse option to step through a result set one record at a time. DB-Library's For Browse option is a method that gives multiple users concurrent access to the same data.

Summary

Exploring the new features in SQL Server 6.5 requires some time. Fortunately, the learning curve is not very steep because the new tools and wizards are easy to learn. Our jobs as developers and administrators are made easier because of the solid support by SQL Server tools and add-on products such as the SQLTrace program.

The language extensions will be important to some people and not to others. For example, the ability to create tables and other objects in a transaction will be important to the applications that are using triggers to enforce complex business rules. Other applications will benefit more from the low-level ODBC extensions, while others will rely more on the new reporting features of With Rollup and With Cube.

In general, the number of improvements and changes from SQL 6.0 and 6.5 is very significant. New tools, new commands, and new features combine to make SQL Server 6.5 a very solid and robust database system. The next chapter gives an overview of the new tools, as well as the new features in the existing tools.

Chapter 3

Administrative and Programming Tools

In this chapter, we look at the programs new in SQL 6.5 and the new features of existing programs. Plenty of documentation is available that explains the basic uses of these tools. Some of the tools are only briefly mentioned here because they are covered in greater detail in later chapters.

We begin by carefully examining the new features in the Enterprise Manager. We then note changes in SQL Task Manager, Service Manager, Security Manager, and Transfer Manager, as well as the Client Configuration Utility. The SQL Trace Manager and the new Web Page Wizard will be explained in some detail. We also discuss several utilities, such as DAC.exe and Textcopy.exe, found in the MSSQL\Binn folder, that have very little documentation.

Enterprise Manager

The Enterprise Manager program administers all the SQL Server installations within the company. Before most of the options in the Enterprise Manager are available, you must have chosen or clicked a server or database. The last server and database you clicked are tagged the current values.

The features of the Enterprise Manager listed below are new in SQL Server 6.5. We consider each of these features briefly in this chapter; several are also covered in more depth in subsequent chapters.

- Startup Tips
- Toolbar buttons
- Menu changes
- Graph controls and print support
- Server Manager Window changes
- Links to external programs (customizable tool bar)
- SQLMail Manager
- Distributed Transaction Coordinator (DTC) Manager
- DTC Administrator Console (DAC)
- Extended Stored Procedures manager
- Alerter changes
- Transfer Manager
- User-defined error messages
- Database Maintenance Wizard

Startup Tips

The Enterprise Manager now provides 25–30 startup tips. These tips appear whenever you start the program, unless you check the box to turn off this feature. You can read all the tips in one sitting by pressing the Next Tip button — the entire process takes only a few minutes. When you are done, you can choose to turn off the tips by clicking the box at the bottom of the screen. You can reactivate this feature at any time by choosing the Tip of the Day item from the Help menu. The tips are excellent and cover a wide range of topics for both the beginner and advanced user.

Toolbar Buttons

Figure 3.1 gives you a quick glance at the new toolbar layout. Notice the last icon on the right for the new Maintenance Plan Wizard. (This great new wizard is covered in detail in Chapter 7, "Scheduling and Performing Administrative Tasks.") The new toolbar also includes three new buttons, which you use to configure SQL Server, SQLMail, and SQL Executive.

Figure 3.1
SQL Enterprise Manager Toolbar

Menu Changes

Several items in the menus have changed. We only mention them here without going into depth because you can get to the changed options more quickly using the toolbar. The two major changes are

- Tools, Task Scheduling is now available in Server, Scheduled Tasks
- Tools, Query Analyzer is now available in Tools, SQL Query Tool

   Six of the menus have changed (the Window and Options menus remain the same). The new additions to the menu are

- File: Server, Toggle Legend, and Print Setup choices
- View: Tools Bar (links to external programs) and Refresh
- Server: Task Scheduler (moved from Tools), Remote Servers, SQL Server (replaces configuration), SQLMail, and SQL Executive
- Tools: DB/Object Transfer, Set up Links to External Tools
- Manage: Extended Stored Procedures
- Help: Tip of the Day and Maintenance Wizard

Where Did It Go?

To configure SQL Server 6.0, you chose the Configurations option from the Server menu. In SQL 6.5, this option is one level deeper. From the Server menu, choose the SQL Server option, and then choose Configure. Or, right-click the server name in the Server Manager window and choose Configure.

Graph Controls and Print Support

Some of the dialog boxes that you use to manage databases and devices also let you control the graph display. For instance, you can turn the graph labels on and off and you can set the bars for horizontal or vertical view. The best feature, however, is the ability to print the reports.

Server Manager Window Changes

The new SQLMail Manager (see page 37) and Distributed Transaction Coordinator (DTC) Manager (see page 39) programs are the two most significant changes in the Server Manager. Each of these Managers is covered in more detail later in this chapter.

Another significant change is the improved menu that is available by clicking the right mouse button. You can reach almost any feature by right-clicking and choosing the appropriate topic. Between the right mouse button and the toolbar, you may hardly ever use the menu options.

Links to External Programs

This feature lets you customize your toolbar by adding your own favorite programs, such as Performance Monitor or other third-party database tools. To add links to external programs, click the Tools menu and choose External Tools to display the dialog box in Figure 3.2. Let's add the performance monitor as an example.

Figure 3.2
Linking External Tools

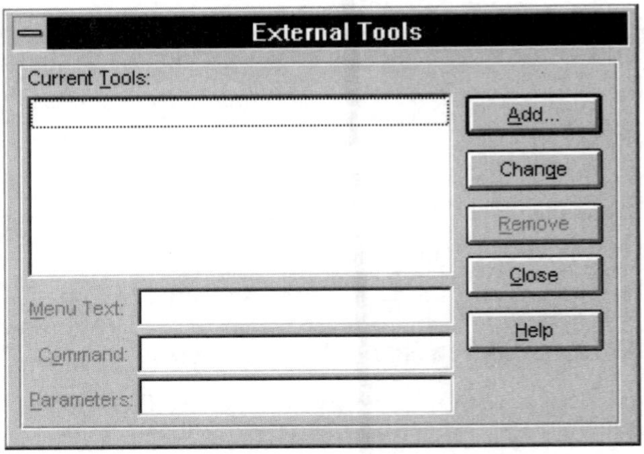

1. Click the Add button. A dialog box appears with program files displayed.
2. Click the Browse button.
3. Change to the directory where you have installed Windows NT.
4. Find the program called Perfmon.exe.
5. Click this file to highlight it, then click OK.
6. The Perfmon.exe program will appear in the box shown in Figure 3.2.
7. Type the following file name in the Parameters box:
   C:\MSSQL\Binn\Sqlctrs.pmc, using the drive and directory that contains the Sqlctrs.pmc — it is not necessarily in the C:\MSSQL\Binn directory. Because Perfmon.exe is the regular Windows NT Performance Monitor, you must specify the Sqlctrs file to get to the special counters for SQL Server.

   You can define standard parameters to be used with the program you're linking to with the [SRV] and [DBN] options in the parameter box. The current server name and database name will be sent to the program each time it is started. Be aware that if you have not chosen a server and database name, the current values are null.

After you complete this procedure, a floating, dockable tool window showing Performance Monitor will appear. It is best to put it with the main toolbar to keep it out of the way because it is always kept on top of all the other windows. To put it with the main tool bar, click the colored title bar of the floating tool window and drag it to the end of the gray area of the main tool bar. Experiment by dragging it to all four corners of the main SQL Enterprise Manager window. If you have added too many icons to the main toolbar, you may need to dock this tool window someplace else.

Our hats are off to the developers of this feature. It even has a menu that provides tips for the added programs. It also adds the program to the bottom of the Tools menu. This tool window can be displayed or hidden using the View, Tools Bar option — not to be confused with the standard toolbar option under Views, Toolbar.

SQLMail Manager

The SQLMail Manager starts, stops, and configures the mail login. To get to the configuration dialog box, right-click the SQLMail icon in the Server Manager window or choose the SQLMail option from the Server menu and click the Configure option. The dialog box shown in Figure 3.3 will appear. Enter the mail login account and password.

Figure 3.3
SQLMail Configuration
Dialog Box

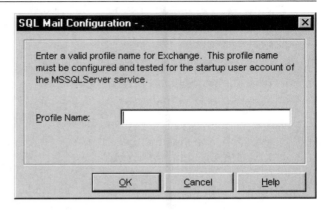

If you are using Microsoft Exchange (instead of Microsoft Mail), the setup requires more steps. SQLMail is compatible with Microsoft Exchange, but you cannot use the Microsoft Exchange client to communicate with Microsoft Mail. To configure SQLMail to work with Microsoft Exchange, follow these steps.

1. On the SQL Server machine, go into Control Panel, choose Services, then choose MSSQLServer service and click Startup. Make sure it is logging on to a user account; e.g., SQLAccount, and not the System Account.

2. At the Exchange server, type the name of a user account in the current domain, one name for each SQL Server user who needs a mail account. For example, in the Account field, type **MyDomain\SQLAccount**; in the Mailbox field, type **MySQLServer**. You must use the same account that MSSQLServer is logging into; e.g., SQLAccount.

3. At the SQL Server machine, log on to Windows NT using the same account that MSSQLServer is logging on to: MyDomain\SQLAccount.

4. Install the Exchange client on the SQL Server machine.

5. Start the Exchange client, and start the Exchange Setup Wizard. When the setup is complete, verify that you can send and receive mail.

6. Go into Control Panel and start the Mail and Fax program, which starts the Microsoft Exchange Services application. Click the Show Profiles button and choose the profile you set up using the wizard in the previous step.

7. Stop and start or restart MSSQLServer.

8. Start SQL Enterprise Manager, choose a server, right-click the SQLMail icon, and choose the Configure option.

9. When the account and password dialog boxes come up, supply the same profile name used in the setup wizard above. Do not enter a password here, because it will communicate with Exchange using the account and password you gave to the MSSQLServer service. If you have forgotten the user account, you can look it up in the Services Program of the Control Panel.

10. From the Server Manager window, right-click the SQLMail icon and choose Start. The icon will change from red to green when it is successfully started. If it doesn't start, look in the Windows NT Event Viewer for an error message.

Distributed Transaction Coordinator (DTC) Manager

SQL Server 6.5 can participate in industry-standard transaction controllers from other vendors, such as Tuxedo®, Top-End®, or Encina®. These products are transaction coordinators that run on Unix and other platforms. They let you start a transaction, do inserts and updates on local and remote servers, then commit or roll back the entire transaction. The Microsoft DTC manages transactions across a network of Windows NT and Windows 95 systems and communicates with the other transaction controllers on other types of servers.

Replication (see Chapter 11) and the DTC are two different distributed computing concepts. Replication allows data to be distributed to other databases and servers after the transactions are committed on the primary server. DTC ensures that the data is committed on all servers in one transaction. Therefore, DTC is the solution when you need synchronized databases in real time, and replication is better when real-enough-time is OK.

You may remember the two-phase commit portion of the DB-LIB API, which has been in part of SQL Server from the very beginning. The SQL DTC is a grown-up version of the same concept. Anyone who attempted a two-phase commit program knows that although it worked well, it was difficult to manage. It was hard to control when a network or other problem occurred. Sometimes it was necessary to stop and restart all the SQL Servers involved to kill a two-phase commit session.

Now, the DTC manager allows many different ways to view and control these distributed transactions. You can select Distributed Transaction Coordinator from the Server menu or click a server in the Server Manager window and right-click Distributed Transaction Coordinator. In either case, the dialog box in Figure 3.4 appears. Your choices are Start, Stop, Transactions, Trace, Statistics, and Configure.

Figure 3.4
DTC Menu

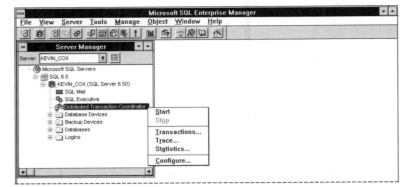

Choosing Start or Stop from the menu, obviously, either stops or starts the DTC. When you choose Transactions from the menu, the window shown in Figure 3.5 will appear. This window lets you see the transactions in progress. It shows the Status of the transaction, the Parent Node controlling the transaction, and the Unit of Work ID that is assigned to the transaction.

Figure 3.5
DTC Transactions

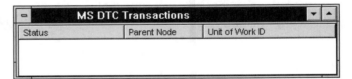

The Trace option on the DTC menu lets you see all the errors and warnings associated with the transactions and the transaction controller (see Figure 3.6). (All the errors and messages generated by distributed transactions will appear in the Windows NT event log, regardless of the slider bar setting.) This trace information is the same dialog box you see when you run the DTC-trace.exe program in the MSSQL\Binn folder.

Figure 3.6
DTC Trace

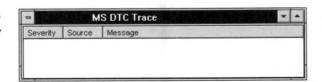

Choosing Statistics from the DTC menu will bring up the window in Figure 3.7, which lets you see the performance of the transactions. Each time the DTC Coordinator starts, the statistics are also reset.

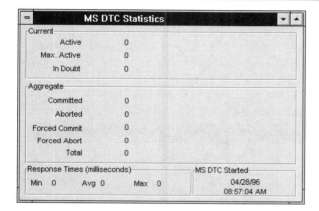

Figure 3.7
DTC Statistics

You can save the trace and statistics in the log file from the Configuration dialog box shown in Figure 3.8, which appears when you choose Configure from the DTC menu. From this dialog box, you can set the controlling parameters for the DTC Manager.

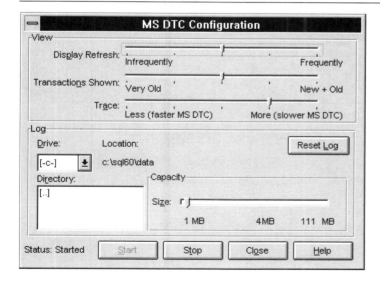

Figure 3.8
DTC Configuration

Microsoft DTC Administrator Console (DAC.exe)

DAC.exe can be run either from the server or from a client machine. You can use it and the DTC Manager to perform the same functions. You can see from the tabs in Figure 3.9 that you can view transactions, trace the transactions, look at the statistics collected, and configure the transactions coordinator (using the Advanced tab). DAC.exe combines all the DTC windows in the SQL Enterprise Manager into one program. DAC.exe is a good tool to add to your customizable toolbar if you are running distributed transactions; having this one program running makes it easy to view the status and tracing of transactions.

Figure 3.9

DTC Administrator Console

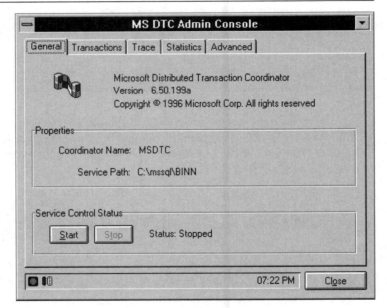

Extended Stored Procedures Manager

The simple dialog box shown in Figure 3.10 is the only dialog box you need to add and edit extended stored procedures. It is a much easier process than trying to remember the syntax of adding an extended procedure with the sp_addextendedproc command.

To get to this dialog box, highlight the Master database and choose Manage, Extended Stored Procedures. For more information about extended stored procedures, see Chapter 20, "Extended Stored Procedures," which covers them in more detail.

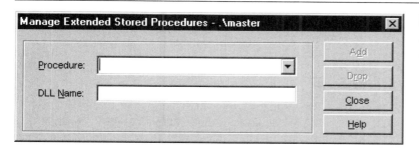

Figure 3.10
Extended Stored Procedures Dialog Box

Alerter Changes

SNMP traps can be sent when an alert occurs. SNMP stands for Simple Network Management Protocol, and it is an industry-standard method for managing and monitoring networks, messages, errors, and processes. Of course, you must be running an SNMP agent first. To set up an SNMP trap, use the Manage Alerts and Operators toolbar button (or the Alerts/Operators option under the Server menu). Click the Alerts tab and either find the alert you want to edit or add a new one. Then choose the Raise an SNMP Trap When Alert Occurs option. If you are not running an SNMP agent when the trap is set, an error message appears in the Windows NT system event log and in the SQL Server error log.

An alert can be forwarded to other servers if they are properly registered as remote servers. To find out if each server has a proper name, open a query window on the server and execute the following command: **SELECT @@servername**. If the result is NULL, then use the sp_addserver stored procedure to give the server a proper name.

Alerts raised from batch scripts can take advantage of the Sqlalrtr.exe program. This program runs as a command line executable to send alerts to SQL Server and Windows NT. It has a new parameter, -M, that lets you send parameters to error messages. With this -M parameter, you can take advantage of the fact that SQL Server error messages can be set up as generic messages that will substitute your parameters into the error message. For example,

```
SQLALRTR.EXE -E 50001 -M, 'text parm 1',9,'text parm2'
```

where 50,001 is the error number and 9 is a numeric parameter, will find error message number 50,001 in the Master..sysmessages table, retrieve the text, substitute the parameters, send it to the Windows NT event log and the SQL Server error log, and look in the SQL Server alert setup to see what actions to take. Some of the possible actions are to page or e-mail someone or to run a task that runs a program. To use the customizable error message feature of SQL Server, you need to separate the parameters with commas and no extra spaces.

The other change in the Alerts/Operator dialog box is the ability to send a mail message to an operator. The Send Mail button is available only when the local mail client is running. Clicking the Send Mail button opens the Send Note window.

Transfer Manager

The Transfer Manager in the SQL Enterprise Manager has made the old SQL Transfer program obsolete. All the transfer objects are now OLE objects and are now published as part of the Data Management Objects (DMO), which lets you easily write your own specialized transfer programs. Writing your own transfer program is beyond the scope of this book, but the documentation on SQL-DMO in the SQL Server box and SQL Server *Books Online* will get you started.

To get to the Transfer Manager, choose the Database/Object Transfer option from the Tools menu. The dialog box shown in Figure 3.11 will appear. The new items in the Transfer Manager include the Foreign Source and the Scripting Options buttons.

Figure 3.11
Database/Object Transfer

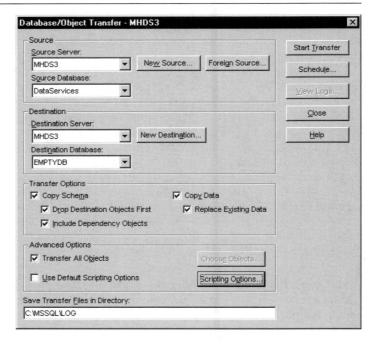

The Foreign Source button lets you enter a user name and password for another SQL Server that you don't want to register in your Enterprise Manager — for example, you may not want to register a data source that will be used only one time. If you do want to register a data source, choose the New Source button, which will switch you to the familiar dialog box for registering servers.

The Scripting Options button includes several options from the old transfer program along with some new choices. The new dialog box is shown in Figure 3.12. This dialog box and others are covered in greater detail in Chapter 14, "Importing and Exporting Data."

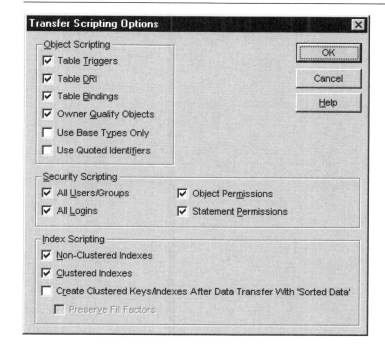

Figure 3.12
Scripting Options

User-Defined Error Messages

To get to the dialog box to add new error messages, use the Messages option on the Server menu. The dialog box shown in Figure 3.13 will appear. To add a new message, click the New button to bring up a dialog box that lets you add a new user-defined error message. Because the first 50,000 numbers for error messages, as well as all negative numbers, are reserved by Microsoft, your custom error messages should start at number 50,001.

The two notes about ad hoc error messages in the SQL Server *Books Online* give conflicting information. One states that ad hoc error messages receive the number 14,000, while another statement says that they receive the number 50,000. The 50,000 number seems to be the correct one.

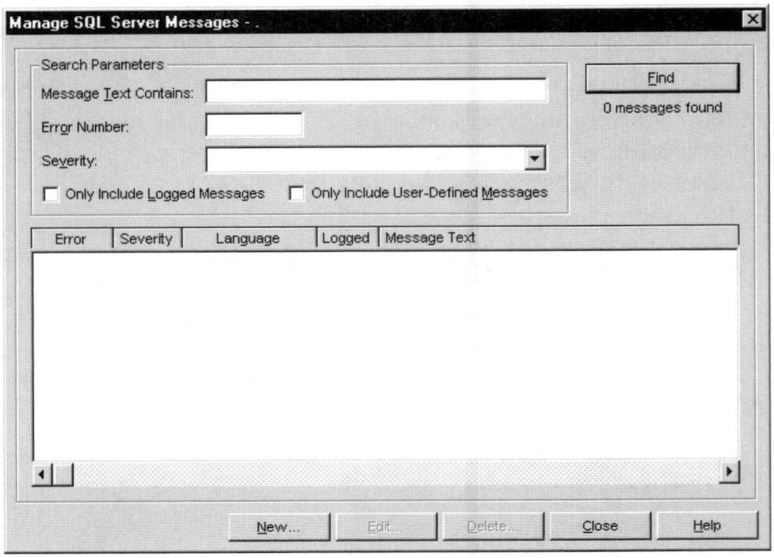

Figure 3.13
Messages

Error messages can now take parameters, much like the C printf function, and can contain up to 255 characters before expansion with substitutions. An example is listed below and shown in Figure 3.14.

```
RAISERROR (50001, "Error occurred while writing to table %s in
procedure %s", 16, -1, 'myTable', @myProcedure) WITH LOG
```

In this message, 16 is the severity, -1 is the state, and %s is a string substitution; the first string is 'myTable', and the second string is a variable you have populated with the current procedure. The With Log parameter will record this error in the SQL Server error log and the Windows NT event log.

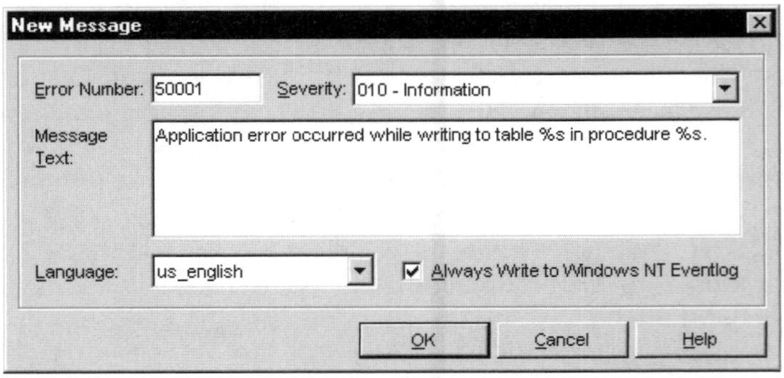

Figure 3.14
*New User-Defined Message
With Parameters*

The error number of 50,001 in the above example will be available in a global SQL variable @@error, and the error message will be sent back to the calling program. If the calling program is a Windows program, the error message will be handled by the call-back message-handling function, and a popup message box will be displayed. Sometimes the actual error message will be wrapped inside another error message, such as an ODBC error message.

Errors with a severity level of 16 to 25 will cause the front-end program to abort after receiving the error message. The error will then be logged in the SQL error log and the Windows NT event log.

You have many options for formatting your error messages, as shown in the following example and Tables 3.1 and 3.2.

```
% [[flag] [width] [precision] [{h | l}]] type
```

where the flag parameter defines the spacing and justification according to Table 3.1, below. The width parameter defines the minimum width — you can use an asterisk (*) to allow the width to be determined from the parameters. The precision parameter defines the maximum characters, or the minimum number of digits needed in an integer field, and the [{h | l}] type parameter defines the data type according to Table 3.2. Note that floating-point and single-character numbers are not supported.

TABLE 3.1 FLAG FIELD CODES FOR FORMATTING ERROR MESSAGES		
Code	**Prefix or justification**	**Description**
− (minus)	Left justified	Starts the field on the left of output area.
+ (plus)	Signed number	Adds a sign (+ or −) depending upon the value of the number.
0 (zero)	Zero padding	If width is prefaced with 0, zeros are added until the minimum width is reached. If 0 and − appear, 0 is ignored. If 0 is specified with an integer format (i, u, x, X, o, d), 0 is ignored.
		continued

TABLE 3.1 FLAG FIELD CODES FOR FORMATTING ERROR MESSAGES, CONTINUED

Code	Prefix or justification	Description
# (number)	0x prefix for hexadecimal number	When used with the o, x, or X format, the # flag prefaces any nonzero value with 0, 0x, or 0X, respectively. When d, i, or u are prefaced by the # flag, the flag is ignored.
' ' (blank)	Space padding	Preface the output value with blank spaces if the value is signed and positive. This will be ignored if included with the + flag.

TABLE 3.2 DATA TYPES FOR FORMATTING ERROR MESSAGES

Type	Description
d or I	Signed integer
o	Unsigned octal
p	Pointer
s	String
u	Unsigned integer
x or X	Unsigned hexadecimal

Database Maintenance Wizard

This wizard is one of the better features added to the Enterprise Manager. It will start putting those high-priced consultants out of business, or at least allow them to concentrate on areas of concern besides the routine operations of SQL Server. We recommend that you schedule as many tasks as this wizard allows you to run. In Chapter 7, "Scheduling and Performing Administrative Tasks," we document this utility in detail.

What Didn't Change (but Should Have)

Two items come under the category of things in the Enterprise Manager that didn't change but should have. The first is getting triggers to show in the objects list; the second is having a standard operations login.

Triggers still do not show up under the objects in the Server Manager window. Go to Manage, Triggers to find the trigger you want to work with. Choose the table, then pick the type (add, change, or delete) of trigger you want to work with.

SQL Server should come with a standard login and group for operations, because at remote sites, the servers should be registered using an operator's login, with special security rights. SQL Server does not come with a standard operator group or login, as Windows NT does, so you will have to create your own. This standard login will prevent the operators at the remote sites having SA privileges.

Task Manager

The most significant change in the Task Manager is that you can now run more than one Transact-SQL command without creating a batch file. For example, in the command line of the task window, the following command is now possible because the text window has been enlarged:

```
sp_spaceused
go
sp_help
go
```

Another change is that non-administrative users can now see only the tasks they own. With this feature, you can set up operator accounts on remote servers and allow operators to see only certain tasks.

In another new feature, the system procedure sp_runtask allows you to spawn a task from a Transact-SQL query window, batch file, or front-end application.

Although it is generally true that certain Windows NT commands run only if formatted properly, it is critical to format carefully when you're using the Task Manager. For example, the Rename command works with the following syntax:

```
RENAME c:\myfile c:\newfile
```

When you're scheduling tasks, you should also remember that commands that ask for user input do not run. Tasks created to respond to alerts can use the following parameters: [SVR], [DBN], [ERR], [SEV], and [MSG]; they refer to the server name, database name, error number, error severity, and message text. You can use these parameters to format special commands to respond to the alerts.

SQL Service Manager

Also known as the SQL traffic light program, this feature lets you start and stop all SQL-related services. The only new option in this program is the ability to start and stop the SQL DTC service.

Incidentally, you can start these services in at least four other ways. The first way is through the Control Panel by choosing the Services option; the second is to go to the Program Manager, Administrative Tools group, Server Manager program, Computer menu, Services option. The third method is to use the SQL Enterprise Manager (which itself provides several ways to start each service); the fourth is the MS-DOS-style command prompt (Net Start servicename, Net Stop servicename) for special purposes, such as scheduling the shutdown in a batch command file.

SQL Security Manager

This feature makes an administrator's job much easier by setting up SQL Server access for the Windows NT user groups and accounts. For more information about the Security Manager, see Chapter 10, "Administering Users and Security."

Client Configuration Utility

The SQL Client Configuration Utility is installed as one of the SQL Tools programs. It is used by Windows NT server clients, Windows NT workstation clients, Windows 95 clients, and Windows 3.x clients to view and modify the following components:

- DBLIB versions (for example, Ntwdblib.dll)
- Net library .dlls (for example, Dbnmpntw.dll)
- Server Connection Information (if necessary)

DOS clients do not use this program to establish connection parameters. Instead, a terminate-and-stay-resident (TSR) program is run once to provide the same information. It is best to add a line to the Autoexec.bat file to run this TSR or add it to a .bat file before starting your application. The TSR to run is located in the MSSQL\Bin folder and depends upon your network protocol, as listed in Table 3.3.

TABLE 3.3 NETWORK LIBRARIES			
Network	**Windows NT or Windows 95**	**Windows 3.x**	**MS-DOS**
Named Pipes	Dbnmpntw.dll	Dbnmp3.dll	Dbnmpipe.exe
NWLink, IPX/SPX	Dbmsspxn.dll	Dbmsspx3.dll	Dbmsspx.exe
Banyan VINES	Ddbmsvinn.dll	Dbmsvin3.dll	Dbmsvine.exe
TCP/IP Sockets	Dbmssocn.dll	Dbmssoc3.dll	N/A
Multiprotocol	Dbmsrpcn.dll	Dbmsrpc3.dll	N/A

The multiprotocol option is necessary if you want to use encrypted packets or if you have Macintosh clients. The installation and setup processes will add the MSSQL\Binn or MSSQL\Bin folder to your path for Windows 3.x or MS-DOS.

Table 3.4 shows the number of connections possible for each network protocol under the different operating systems.

TABLE 3.4 NUMBER OF CONNECTIONS SUPPORTED

Network	Windows NT or Windows 95	Windows 3.x	MS-DOS
Named Pipes	Limited by memory	34	15[1]
NWLink, IPX/SPX	Limited by memory	25[2]	15[3]
Banyan VINES	Limited by memory	15	15
TCP/IP Sockets	Limited by memory	6	N/A
Multi-Protocol	Limited by memory	Limited by underlying protocol.	N/A

[1] Can be further limited by the number of available DOS file handles. Look in Config.sys to see the current handle limit.

[2] Uses one IPX socket per connection and one to three SPX sessions per connection. To get the maximum connections, open the Shell.cfg file and change the IPX Sockets parameter to 32 and the SPX Connections to 96. You may also need to change the Net.cfg file in either the root directory or the Novell configuration directory.

[3] Uses one IPX socket per connection and one to three SPX sessions per connection. To get the maximum connections, open the Shell.cfg file and change the IPX Sockets parameter to 22 and the SPX Connections to 66. You do not need to change the Net.cfg file.

To run the SQL Client Configuration Utility for Windows NT or Windows 95, go to your program manager icon or Start button, or use Windows Explorer to locate and run Windbver.exe (on Windows 3.x systems, use W3dbver.exe). On Windows NT or Windows 95 systems, the dialog box shown in Figure 3.15 will appear (Windows 3.x uses only one dialog box instead of three).

The DBLibrary tab is the default; you can use it to view the versions and files already in place. If nothing appears in the fields, you need to install the client software on the SQL Server CD (or in the installation directory). You should not change anything on this dialog box, unless you really know what you are doing or unless Microsoft support tells you to do so.

The Automatic ANSI to OEM option translates characters coming from the client from OEM to ASCII. When a packet is returned from the server, the translation is from ASCII to OEM. This option is set on by default for Windows NT and Windows 95 clients and set off by default for Windows 3.x clients.

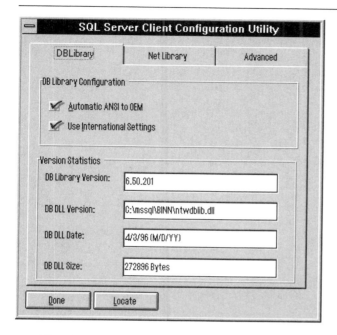

Figure 3.15
*SQL Server Client Configuration —
DBLibrary Tab*

The Use International Settings option informs SQL Server to get date, time, and currency settings from the system. This option is available only for Windows NT and Windows 95 clients and is turned on by default. If the option is set off here, the parameters can also be set in the Sqlcommn.loc file; you can also manipulate the parameters in the application programs by API calls and formatting options. We recommend that you leave this option turned on.

You can set the appropriate network library using the Net Library tab, shown in Figure 3.16. For any client application to run, you need both a database library and an appropriate network library. If nothing appears in the fields, you need to install the client software on the SQL Server CD (or in the installation directory). Install whatever network library each client will need.

Using the Advanced tab, you can connect to SQL Server using a network protocol not among the normal choices in the install/setup program, connect to a SQL Server that is listening on another named pipe, or connect to an ODS (Open Data Services) source that may need a special connection string. For most applications, you do not need to use this tab.

For ODBC to use the information on this tab, all three of the following conditions must be met.

- The name in the Server field in Figure 3.17 must match a valid Data Source Name (DSN) in the ODBC configuration dialog box in the Control Panel.

Figure 3.16
*SQL Server Client
Configuration —
Net Library Tab*

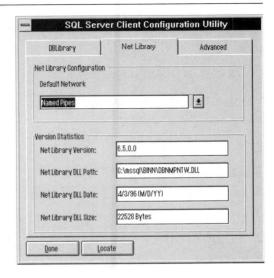

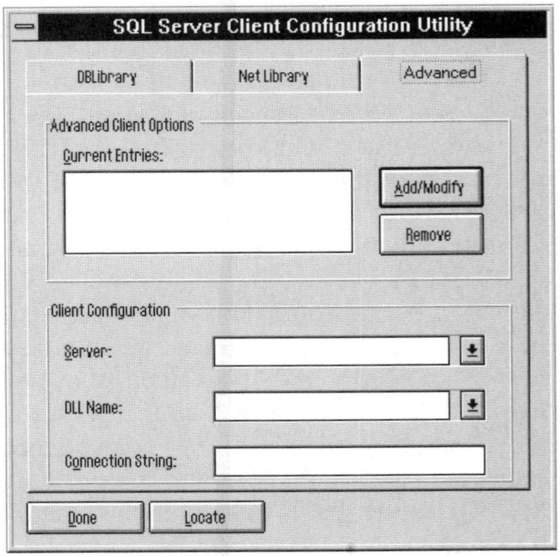

Figure 3.17
*SQL Server Client
Configuration —
Advanced Tab*

- The network address in the Control Panel's ODBC dialog box must remain the default.
- The network library in the Control Panel's ODBC dialog box must remain the default.

In Figure 3.17, the Server name can be either a valid server name on the network or an ODBC data source name, depending upon your intended use. If you are not sure, make two entries, one with the ODBC data source name, and one with a valid server name.

In the DLL Name field, you can enter either a DLL name (for example, Dbmssocn) without the .dll extension or the library type (for example, TCP/IP). In the Connection String field, enter either the server name or a special connection string. The connection string must be a valid value as determined by the application (usually ODS) you are connecting to.

Transfer Manager

The old transfer manager program has been replaced by the Database/Object Transfer option under the Tools menu in the Enterprise Manager. Refer to the Transfer part of the above Enterprise Manager section. This extra note is included here in case you are scanning the chapter for information on the Transfer Manager.

Interactive SQL (ISQL/w)

Not much has changed in ISQL/w since version 6.0. The best new feature is the improved Help information. In fact, the first Help dialog box has a very good list of what is new and what is modified in Transact-SQL. If you are upgrading from MS SQL 4.2, you probably don't know that ISQL/w has most of the good features of a good programming tool — cut and paste from the keyboard, undo, find and replace, and much more. It is the same SQL Query tool that you access from within Enterprise Manager.

Bulk Copy Program (BCP)

BCP is one of the oldest tools available for importing and exporting with SQL Server. It is a command-prompt program, so you can schedule the imports and exports in batch mode. No new options were added to SQL Server 6.0's BCP function for SQL Server 6.5. If you are migrating from SQL Server 4.2, the /E option is newly available to help you manage identity (counter) values. This tool is covered in more detail in Chapter 14, "Importing and Exporting Data."

ISQL

ISQL is another command-prompt program useful for creating and scheduling batches of Transact-SQL commands. It is also one of the oldest tools available with SQL Server. The following options are new for SQL 6.5:

- /b: returns a DOS ERRORLEVEL
- /O: runs the old version of ISQL
- /I timeout: declares a login timeout
- ISQLPASSWORD environment variable

The /b parameter will return a DOS ERRORLEVEL code of 1 if an error of severity level 10 or greater occurs. This feature will give you more control of the batch files by responding to severe errors.

The ISQLPASSWORD environment variable can be set for a session to avoid hard-coding a password in a batch file. For example,

```
SET ISQLPASSWORD=MYPASSWORD
```

will set this variable. If the /P parameter is not supplied to ISQL, it will check this environment variable. If it does not find one, it will prompt for one. To get ISQL to accept a NULL password, try the following statement:

```
SET ISQLPASSWORD=    (an equal sign followed by nothing)
```

Registry Font Writer [REGFONT.EXE]

This utility, virtually undocumented in the SQL books (that come with SQL Server) and SQL Server *Books Online*, lets you set the font used by the dialog boxes in the SQL Enterprise Manager and ISQL/w. It also lets you set the general query font for both the query and results dialog boxes. The Registry Font Writer is shown in Figure 3.18. Be aware that the results dialog boxes look better if they use fixed-width fonts.

Those of you who are doing presentations will find this a good program to run and test while setting up for your presentation. Most small to medium-sized rooms work well with a 14-point font. If you are going to use this utility, it is a good program to add to your customizable, dockable tool bar because it does not have its own icon on the main tool list. You will need to find it in File Manager or Windows Explorer, depending upon which version of Windows NT or Windows you are running.

You can also change the font in the Query System field by going to Tools, Preferences and choosing the Fonts button from the Query System tab.

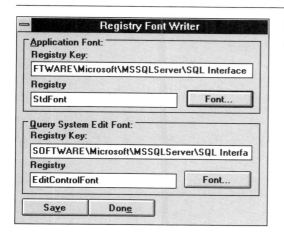

Figure 3.18
Registry Font Writer

SQL Trace Manager

This new tool lets you view all the buffers passed between one client and the server or all clients and the server. It fills a gap in the tool set because it gives you another level of detail to use to debug the problems occurring on your server. The program is run on the server, not the client. It is a good program to add to your customizable, dockable tool bar in the SQL Enterprise Manager.

The first time you run this program, it will bring up a dialog box that lets you add filters (Figure 3.19). These filters are used to define how SQL Trace monitors the server activity, which activity to monitor, and how the results are displayed and/or saved.

Let's go through all the fields and options to learn how to manage the traces.

- Filter Name: type the name you want to use to refer to this trace definition.

- Login Name: if you want to watch one particular login name, type the name here. The list of names (available by clicking the ... button at the end of the field) comes from the logins on the server you are monitoring.

- Application: the application names are built from running programs that currently have a SQL connection. An easy way to see the application names for all current SQL connections is to run Enterprise Manager, open the current activity dialog box, and pick the Detail Activity tab. Then maximize the dialog box, or scroll over to the right until you can see the application column.

- Host Name: type the computer name of the client machines.

Figure 3.19
SQL Trace Filter

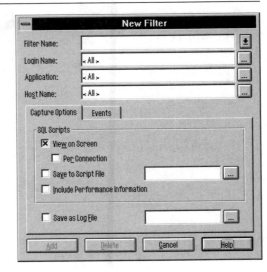

Capture Options Tab

Now let's go through the Capture Options tab at the bottom of Figure 3.19, which lets you control the output generated from the trace.

- View on Screen: results from all filtered connections will be displayed in one window.
- Per Connection: each connection will get a separate window.
- Save to Script File: you must specify a fully qualified path name and file name, including the drive letter; for example, C:\Trace file for Tuesday.sql. SQL commands from all filtered connections are saved to this trace file. You do not have an option to save each connection to a separate log file. You may need to edit this script file before running the commands, because some case-sensitive function names are saved as lower case in this script file.
- Include Performance Information: several statistics are gathered for each connection, including the duration of the event, CPU usage for the event, disk reads for the event, and synchronous writes for the event. Synchronous writes indicate that the event is waiting for writes to complete instead of continuing with the task while the server is processing the writes in another thread.
- Save as Log File: saves all information from all filtered connections generated from the trace in this log file. Specify a drive, path, and file name or click the browse button to find an existing file to overwrite.

The lists for the Login Name, Application, and Host Name fields are built from current and past connections. Multiple entries are separated with a semi-colon (;). Wild card entries are allowed with a percent sign (%).

Events Tab

The other tab on the dialog box in Figure 3.19 lets you select which commands are shown during the trace. As you can see from Figure 3.20, you have a wide range of options.

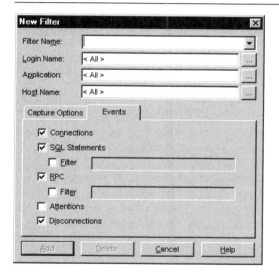

Figure 3.20
SQL Trace Filter Events Tab

- Connections: declare connection events to be filtered; for example, "Kevin just connected from host" would be shown only if you set a filter to show commands from certain workstations.

- SQL Statements: all SQL commands will be trapped and displayed.

- SQL Statements Filter: specific SQL commands, commands using a certain table or column, and commands with an Order By or Group By parameter are examples of filtering certain statements. Multiple entries are separated with a semicolon (;). Wild card entries are allowed with a percent sign (%). You cannot use these signs inside your SQL statements.

- RPC: all Remote Procedure Calls for the filtered connections will be tracked.

- RPC Filter: RPC calls containing certain key words can be filtered. Multiple entries are separated with a semicolon (;). Wild card entries are allowed with a percent sign (%).

- Attentions: an attention event is one in which a client has canceled or interrupted a running statement. Checking this box lets you monitor the attention events.

- Disconnections: all disconnects will be tracked.

SQL Web Page Wizard

One of the most significant new tools in SQL 6.5 is the SQL Web Page Wizard. It reduces the learning curve for HTML and lets you develop an Internet or intranet application around a database, which makes for fast coding and low maintenance. You can use the Web wizard to publish the results of a query or stored procedure as an HTML page. Whether the end user is on your corporate intranet or on the Web in a remote corner of the world, all a user needs is a Web browser to see the results of your query. We will guide you through building Web pages and give you a few tips and recommendations.

The SQL Web Page Wizard publishes Web pages. To collect data from Web screens, you should use the new technology of active server pages (ASP) to link the HTML screens with a database. Of course, you can use the old-fashioned CGI if you want a slower application that takes longer to code, but that is your decision.

The first dialog box of the wizard, shown in Figure 3.21, is a simple dialog box where you log on. Be sure to use a login that will get you to all the objects you need to use on your Web page — you can use tables, views, and stored procedures that return result sets. Enter a server name; then either enter a login name and password or check the "Use Windows NT security" box at the bottom. You can check this box only if you have integrated or mixed security and your current Windows NT login is mapped to a valid SQL Server login. (Use the SQL Security Manager program to map your Windows NT users to SQL logins. For more information about the SQL Security Manager, see Chapter 10, "Administering Users and Security.")

After you have entered the information, click the Next button. The query window will appear; it gives you three choices for building a query.

- Build a query from a database hierarchy
- Enter a query as free-form text
- Use a query in a stored procedure

The first choice, "Build a query from a database hierarchy," is shown in Figure 3.22. To see all the tables and views in a database, click the plus (+) sign next to the databases. Next, click a table name or view name.

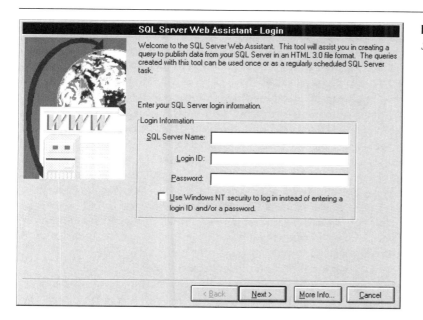

Figure 3.21
SQL Web Login

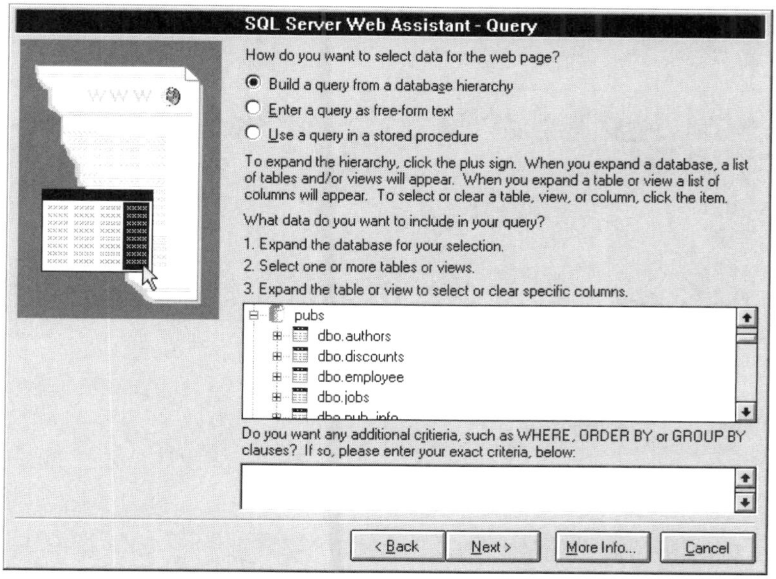

Figure 3.22
Building a Query from a Database Hierarchy

At this point, you can continue to select information as if you were creating a Select * From table. To join multiple tables, click all the tables you want to see in your From clause. To show certain fields, click the plus sign next to the table or view name. By default, all the fields are highlighted. Click the ones you do not want to see in the results, and they will no longer be highlighted. At the bottom of the dialog box, you can enter Where, Order By, Group By, Having, Compute, or any other extension to the normal Select clause. Of course, you must use appropriate Join clauses (Inner Join, or Where Pkey = Fkey) if you have selected multiple tables; otherwise you will get a Cartesian product or unrestricted Join as a result set.

The final result of this dialog box must be a valid SQL Select statement. One problem with this wizard is that at this point in building the query, you cannot view your Select statement or copy it to a query window in ISQL/w to test it. So, for more complex queries, use the free-form query window to create your query. For example, although you can enter a Union statement and the second Select part of the union in this last box, it is much easier to use the free-form query window to use a Union statement.

The second option on the query dialog box in Figure 3.22 is "Enter a query as free-form text." When you choose this option, the dialog box in Figure 3.23 will appear. Pick the database you want to query, then type your query in the box or copy and paste it from another query tool. You should test the query in ISQL/w (or your favorite query tool) before committing it to this dialog box. It would be nice if you could open a file and paste a saved query in here, but perhaps the next version will have that feature.

Figure 3.23

Free-Form Query Builder

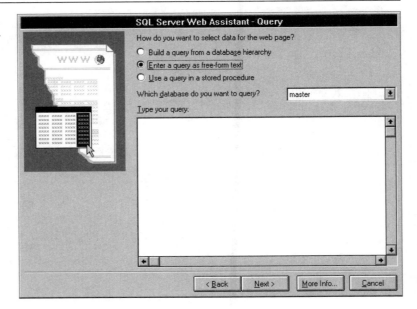

The third option on the query dialog box in Figure 3.22 is "Use a query in a stored procedure" (see Figure 3.24). With this option, you can base your Web page on the results of a stored procedure. The only requirement is that the last statement in the stored procedure must be a Select statement that returns results. Stored procedures let you use many steps to manipulate data and use temporary tables, local variables, and other Transact-SQL features to build the final result set. When you choose a database, the names of all the procedures in that database will show in the field below.

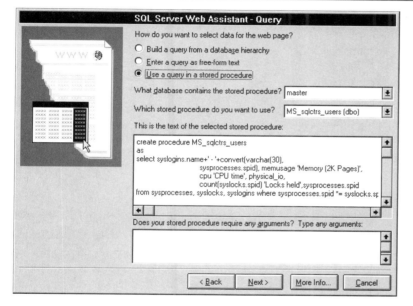

Figure 3.24

Web Query Builder Using Stored Procedures

Choose the stored procedure you want to run. (The procedure must already exist — you cannot build stored procedures here.) The source code for the procedure will appear for you to view. Although you can change this code, you cannot save the changes. Enter any parameters here so that the procedure will run. It is a good idea to write the procedure so that it creates defaults for all parameters not supplied so that the procedure can be run in batch and scheduled at different times.

We have now created a query. The next step is to schedule when the query is run and create your Web page (see Figure 3.25). This scheduling ability is the most powerful feature of this tool. Your options are Now, Later, When Data Changes, On Certain Days of the Week, and On a Regular Basis. If you choose Now or Later, the Web page will be created only once. However, if you choose one of the other options, you set a schedule for your page to be refreshed. For static lookup tables, it is best to choose When Data Changes, which should be seldom. For dynamic transaction tables you can choose either On Certain Days of the Week or On a Regular Basis. Either of these options will bring up the task scheduler so you can create a schedule.

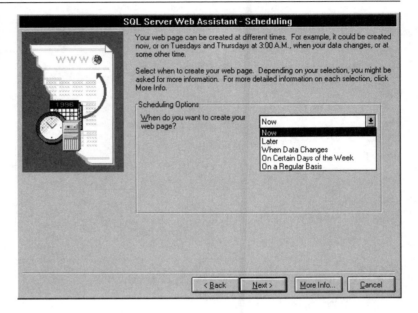

Figure 3.25
Web Assistant —
Scheduling

Guess what happens when you choose When Data Changes? That's right, three triggers are created — one for Insert, one for Update, and one for Delete. The wizard uses its own naming convention for creating the triggers. For example, the name Web_16003088_1 is derived from "Web" to designate it as a Web trigger and a system-assigned number. If triggers already exist on this table, they are extended and the sp_makewebtask stored procedure is added at the bottom of the existing triggers. If multiple tables exist in the query and you want to make sure that the page gets rebuilt whenever data in any of the tables changes, then click each relevant table to highlight it. The wizard will create triggers in each table highlighted.

After you have chosen your scheduling option, click the Next button. Now you are ready to add more information to the page (see Figure 3.26). First, type the file name where the Web page will be saved. This information is critical because the file must be saved to a location where the user can see it and where SQL Server can write to it if it is refreshed regularly.

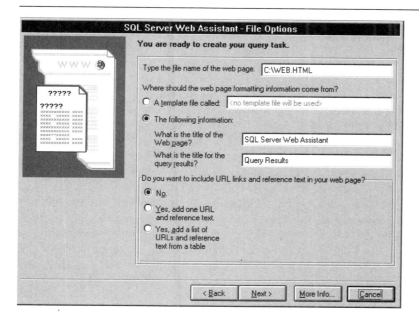

Figure 3.26

*Web Assistant —
File Options*

The best place to save the file is on the Internet server box, under the C:\Inetserv\WWWRoot directory (or wherever your Internet server is installed). If you are running multiple Internet services on one box, you should have a root directory for each service. For example, if you have one service for Bill and one for Kevin, then you should have a Bill\WWWRoot and a Kevin\WWWRoot. Be sure to save the file in the appropriate directory. Unfortunately, you can only save it to one directory from this dialog box. If you need the file to be in multiple locations, you need to devise a strategy for copying or replicating it to the necessary directories.

After determining your file name, you will next determine where the formatting information for the Web page should come from. You can either use a template file or type in the title for the Web page and for your query results. We recommended that you use a template, so that you can have your company's logo and other attractive-looking bitmaps. This dialog box doesn't let you add graphics, so you must use a template to add other elements. Add <%insert_data_here%> to your template to indicate where the query results are inserted into the page. Remember the Internet etiquette that says to limit the large bitmaps on your dialog box, because the files take too long to download.

If you are using a template, skip this paragraph and the next one, because the options in these paragraphs are unavailable when you use a template.

Otherwise, type the title you want to appear in the colored bar at the top of the main Web page window in the first field under the "The following information" option. Then tab to the next field and type the heading to appear at the top of the query results. Try to be more creative and pick something other than the default Query Results.

If you choose not to use a template, you can enter URL (Universal Resource Locator) links in your document using the next section of the dialog box. Otherwise, the wizard assumes that your template already contains the necessary URL links. You can enter one link, along with the text to display on the dialog box, or enter a list of URLs stored in a table by entering the Select statement in the box provided. We recommend that you store the link in a table, even if you only need one link, because it's easier to modify.

The Web Assistant dialog box in Figure 3.27 lets you perform minimal formatting. If you have used a template, the first field is unavailable because the template will control how the title looks. You can experiment with the font options; it doesn't take long to view the different resulting combinations. At the bottom, you have the option of adding a date and time stamp, adding the column names, and limiting the query results.

Figure 3.27

*Web Assistant —
Formatting Options*

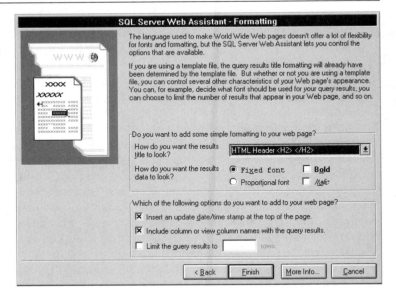

We recommend that you include a date and time stamp to indicate the last time the page was built. You should also include column names in the query results as a general practice — but make them meaningful names. The column names from the table become the default heading names. If they are not easy to read, format your query so that each column has an alias.

Last, we suggest that you limit the number of results rows. It would be nice if you could set up this dialog box to supply your own default, of 100 rows, for example. It is not difficult to put a Previous, Next, First, and Last button on the HTML screens as a standard toolbar and only bring down a small portion of the data at a time. The latest HTML samples show good examples of how to create this kind of toolbar, including the sample .asp or .idc and .htx files to do Previous, Next, First, and Last records.

The last step is to click Finish. A message telling you that a task was scheduled will appear. Any of the scheduling options except the Later option will create the page when you click Finish; triggers will also be created at this time. Unless your query is very large, the execution is very fast.

One last note on using this Web wizard: it currently supports the HTML 3.0 specification. We have had no problems viewing pages published with this wizard using all the major browsers. Wizards and tools for Microsoft Word, Excel, Access, FoxPro and other Microsoft products are also available. If you are a Visual Basic user, you will probably want to get VBScripts to go along with this wizard. You don't need these wizards and tools to create HTML pages from SQL Server 6.5, but if you are using a Microsoft development front end, you can use the same programs you are already familiar with to create HTML screens.

Textcopy.exe

This new program, virtually undocumented, copies a single text or image value into or out of SQL Server. The value is a text or image column of a single row (specified by the Where clause) of the specified table. The options following the forward slash (/) are case-sensitive.

It is easy to tell that this is just the 1.0 version of Textcopy, because it is temperamental. It will only update records, not insert them, and the text and image fields must already have a value. The documentation says that you must have a timestamp field in the record for this program to work, but it seems to work if you put any initial non-null value in these fields. Therefore, you must find a way to insert all the records you will need in the table and seed the text and image values with any non-null value. Remember that seeding these records with one character in the text and image fields will fill a 2K page for each non-null text and image field in each row. So, in our example below, we insert two rows with seed values, and one row with null values. In addition to the normal space reserved for the table, the non-null values will have an extra three pages (at 2K each).

If the direction is In (/I), the data from the specified file is copied into SQL Server, replacing the existing text or image value. If the direction is Out (/O), the text or image value is copied from SQL Server into the specified file, replacing any existing file.

The command and its parameters are explained below.

```
TEXTCOPY [/S [sqlserver]] [/U [login]] [/P [password]]
[/D [database]] [/T table] [/C column] [/W "where clause"]
[/F file] [{/I | /O}] [/K chunksize] [/Z] [/?]
```

- /S sqlserver: the SQL server to connect to. If this parameter is not specified, the local SQL server is used.
- /U login: the user name to connect with. If a login is not specified, a trusted connection will be used.
- /P password: the password for login. If a password is not specified, a null password will be used. The new environment variable SET ISQLPASS-WORD= is not available for this program.
- /D database: the database that contains the table with the text or image data. If a database is not specified, the default database specified with login (/U) is used.
- /T table: The table that contains the text or image value.
- /C column: The text or image column in the table specified.
- /W "where clause": A complete Where clause (including the Where keyword) that specifies a single row of the table specified with /T. If multiple rows of a table are in the result set, this clause will not work. This entry is required unless the table has only one row.
- /F file: The file name containing the text to copy from with the /I option, or to copy into with the /O option.
- /I: Copy text or image value into SQL Server from the file specified in /F.
- /O: Copy text or image value out of SQL Server into the file specified in /F.
- /K chunksize: Size of the data transfer buffer in bytes. The minimum value is 1024 bytes; the default value is 4096 bytes. It would be nice if the default were the same as the network buffer size configured with SQL Server.
- /Z: Display debug information while running.
- /?: Display this usage information and exit without copying anything.

You will be prompted for any required options you did not specify. For example, if you leave out /S (when you are on the server) and /P, you will be prompted for them. If you are running commands in a batch file, you should include the required options followed by a blank space, without putting a parameter. Figure 3.28 shows a sample script you can use to test Textcopy.exe.

```
/* TEST SCRIPT FOR TEXTCOPY.EXE */
USE PUBS
GO
CREATE TABLE TextCopy
    (
    iKey INT NOT NULL IDENTITY,
    txtDocument TEXT NULL,
    imgPicture IMAGE NULL,

    CONSTRAINT pkTextCopy PRIMARY KEY (iKey)
    )
GO

/* Add 3 blank records to the table. Notice that we are not
including the iKey field in the column list because it is
an identity column and this is the best way to get values
into the table without error messages.
    Even though we are entering the word 'Test' into an
image column below, it will print as a hex value, as shown
in the results from the select.

*/
INSERT TextCopy (txtDocument, imgPicture) VALUES ('Test',
'Test')
INSERT TextCopy (txtDocument, imgPicture) VALUES ('Test',
null)
INSERT TextCopy (txtDocument, imgPicture) VALUES (NULL,
NULL) - - to demonstrate errors
GO

/* Check the results */
SELECT * FROM TextCopy
GO
RESULTS
iKey    txtDocument    imgPicture
1    test        0x74657374
2    test        (null)
3    (null)      (null)

(3 row(s) affected)
```

Figure 3.28

Sample Script for Testing Textcopy.exe

Textcopy.exe Example

Now we will look at a real example, which we will run from a DOS-style console window. First, we will see what is in the files we are importing (Figure 3.29).

Figure 3.29

*Example Files for
Textcopy.exe*

```
TYPE myfile1.txt
Now is the time for all good programmers to go to bed.

TYPE myfile2.txt
Except me, who will continue to stay up and work on this book.

TYPE myfile3.txt
End of story
```

Test 1

We are ready to import these three files. Go to a console window and type the following text. Don't hit a carriage return at the end of the line; the text will wrap by itself.

```
TEXTCOPY /SmyServer /Usa /Psapass /Dpubs /TTextCopy
 /CtxtDocument /I /Fmyfile1.txt /W"WHERE iKey = 1"
```

Go back to SQL Enterprise Manager, a query window, or ISQL/w and do a Select * From Textcopy. You should get the following results.

iKey	txtDocument	imgPicture
1	Now is the time for all good programmers to go to bed.	0x74657374
2	test	(null)
3	(null)	(null)
(3 row(s) affected)		

If you use the /Z option, you get all the messages and steps the program goes through, including how many bytes were in the file, and how many were written to the table.

Test 2

In this test, we will put a picture in the imgPicture field of the first record. Type the text below.

```
TEXTCOPY /SmyServer /Usa /Psapass /Dpubs /TTextCopy
 /CimgPicture /I /Fc:\winnt\marble.bmp /W"WHERE iKey = 1"
Data copied into SQL Server image column from
c:\winnt\marble.bmp
```

Now when you do a Select * From TextCopy, it will show the first 255 characters of a hex stream.

Test 3

The next step is to copy the text from myFile2.txt into the second record.

```
TEXTCOPY /SmyServer /Usa /Psapass /Dpubs /TTextCopy
 /CtxtDocument /I /Fmyfile2.txt /W"WHERE iKey = 2"
```

The results, after selecting the records again, are shown below.

iKey	txtDocument	imgPicture
1	Now is the time for all good programmers to go to bed.	0x424dfe6b0000000000000...
2	Except me, who will continue to stay up and work on this book.	(null)
3	(null)	(null)

(3 row(s) affected)

Test 4

Now, let's add a picture to the second row. Type the following text.

```
TEXTCOPY /SmyServer /Usa /Psapass /Dpubs /TTextCopy
 /CimgPicture /I /Fc:\winnt\marble.bmp /W"WHERE iKey = 2"
```

From this TEXTCOPY command, you should get the result shown below.

```
ERROR: Text and image pointer and timestamp retrieval failed.
```

As you can see, the error is caused by a null value in the imgPicture field in the second record before the attempted update. It has nothing to do with a timestamp field, because it will still not add the picture when the record has a timestamp. This same error will occur when you try to insert the third record, with either the text or the picture.

If all the text and image fields must contain a value before the Textcopy program will work, your initial database will be huge. Even if you initialize each column with one space, it will assign one 2K page for each text column and one for each image column for each row. In the example above, we had three rows, each with one text field and one image field, so it would assign six 2K pages, or 12K. This size may not sound like much with only three rows, but what if you had 1,000 rows or a million rows? Adding 1,000 rows to the above example and initializing the text and image fields to one space each would take an additional 4 MB of data space. Adding a million rows would require 4 GB of space!

Summary

SQL Server 6.5 includes some great new tools and new features in the old tools. Don't be afraid to experiment. Take advantage of the online help that is available for most options. In light of the paradigm shift to the Internet/intranet focus, the Web Wizard gets our vote as the best and most usable tool, followed closely by SQLTrace and SQLMAINT.

Chapter 4

Windows NT Integration

One of the most significant differences between SQL Server 6.5 and other relational database management systems is the tight integration of the database server with the network server. SQL Server 6.5 is a platform-specific product. It does not run on any operating system other than Windows NT. Server and Workstation versions are available.

The level of integration between Windows NT and SQL Server 6.5 has advantages and disadvantages, with the disadvantages centering on the portability of the database. However, because Windows NT Server can exist in a heterogeneous network environment, SQL Server 6.5's platform-specific nature is seldom a complete roadblock to its implementation.

In this chapter, we examine the advantages of the integration between SQL Server and Windows NT, including the Service Management System, the User Security System, the Event Viewer, and Performance Monitor, as well as SQL Server's multithreaded execution. We will also briefly consider the drawbacks of the tight integration.

The Advantages

Services on Windows NT

The Windows NT operating system comes with a built-in service management system that registers and controls services through a single interface. These services range from network communication services and uninterruptable power supply (UPS) monitoring to third-party systems that track performance or perform backups.

To work with these services, use the Services applet in the Control Panel. When you select this applet, you will see a scrolling list of all the services currently installed on the system (Figure 4.1). This list displays the current status of the service and its current startup configuration.

Figure 4.1
Services Dialog Box

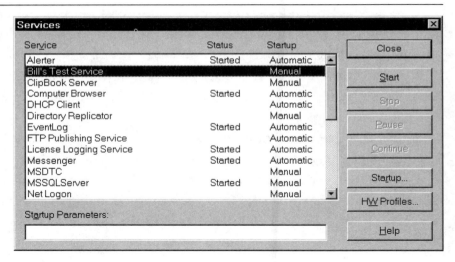

To bring up the configuration settings for the currently selected service, click the Startup button on the Services dialog box. The dialog box in Figure 4.2 appears. Here, you can specify whether the service will start up automatically when the system starts up or whether it will require a user to start it manually. For example, you can set SQL Server and the SQL Executive to be started when the system boots and, barring any errors in initialization, these two applications will be running whenever the Windows NT Server is active. You can also disable a service without removing it from the list of services, allowing the service to be reestablished in the future.

Figure 4.2
Service Configuration Profile

In the dialog box shown in Figure 4.2, you can also specify the security rights that the service will use under Windows NT. A service can access the resources in the system either as a local system account or through an account defined under Windows NT. By letting a service log on to the local system account, the service can be granted the right to access the graphical interface of the desktop and perform user interface (UI) tasks, such as creating message boxes. If you specify a user account for the service to use to log on, you preclude the service from interacting with the desktop, but you can assign network rights to the account you specify. For services such as the Directory Replicator, this feature lets you grant permissions on remote machines so that the service has access to perform its tasks.

In most production environments, you set up SQL Server to start automatically when the system boots and to log on to the local system account. In situations where no replication or remote procedures are used, neither of these services needs network permissions. However, if the database is to be a publishing server in a replication topology, the SQL Executive service will need a network-enabled account.

Likewise, if you will use SQL Server as a remote alert system, the SQL Executive should be provided with an account that is created with the User Manager administrator's tool. In this case, the account that is assigned to SQL Executive should be granted the right to log on as a service. The account should be in the administrator's group and allowed to log on 24 hours a day. This account can be assigned to SQL Executive from the Enterprise Manager through the Configure SQL Executive option (Figure 4.3).

Figure 4.3
*Configure SQL Executive
Dialog Box*

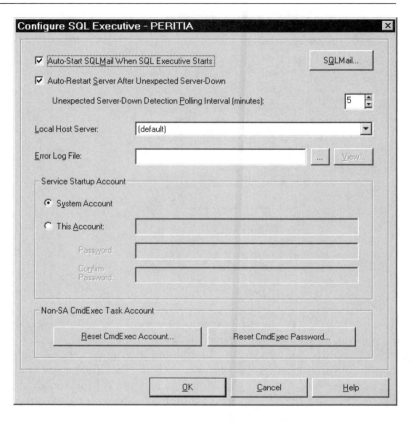

You access this dialog box by right-clicking the SQL Executive icon under the server name in the Server Manager window and then choosing the Configuration menu entry. It is also available by selecting Manage, SQL Executive, Configuration from the Enterprise Manager's main menu. The SQL Server logon account can also be set through the Control Panel Services applet. We cover the requirements for setting a replication topology in Chapter 11, "Replication," and examine the interaction between the SQL Executive and the database in more detail.

Special Note

The exact security setup for any given situation will depend on the overall security setup of the Windows NT network. The domain trust relationships have a significant impact on the required security for performing various tasks.

Windows NT and User Security

SQL Server 6.5 can be set up to allow Windows NT-integrated security access. This setup lets SQL Server accept user login requests using the Windows NT Security System to validate login and password information. Using Windows NT security in this fashion makes it possible for a user to access multiple protected services with a single login, which creates a relatively seamless work environment.

This security model also ensures that the database remains very secure because the Windows NT security system is much better than SQL Server's. Connecting to SQL Server using false credentials through Windows NT's security system is nearly impossible — it would require a falsified login through Windows NT's C2-compliant security. See Chapter 10, "Administering Users and Security," for a more detailed examination of user access to SQL Server.

The Registry

The Windows NT operating system has a secure configuration management system called the registry. The registry stores hardware and software configurations in a hierarchical database that allows intuitive grouping and organization. SQL Server creates a hive under the HKEY_LOCAL_MACHINE\ Software\Microsoft key called MSSQLServer. The hive's subkeys and values hold configuration information for all the interface programs as well as the setup values for SQL Executive and SQL Server. The registry entries for SQL Server are shown in Figure 4.4.

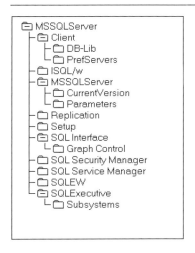

Figure 4.4
The Registry for SQL Server

Whenever you make changes to SQL Server's configuration or, for example, to SQL Executive or SQLMail, the changes are recorded in the registry. The registry acts as a central repository for all of the configuration information needed for both the operating system and programs. It contains device driver information; startup parameters for programs (replacing the config.sys and autoexec.bat files); information that was in DOS, such as path and environment information; and information that was in the .ini files for Windows programs.

The safest way to make changes in the registry is to use the Registry Editor or the Control Panel. Although it might sometimes seem necessary to make the changes directly to the registry, be careful.

Caution

Changing the registry can make a system fail to boot. You should not directly edit the registry entries unless you are absolutely sure of the impact of those changes. It is highly recommended that you save a key before altering it and make sure that the Emergency Repair Disk for the machine is up to date and usable.

Event Viewer

Windows NT also has a common interface for posting and reading application, system, and security events. The Event Viewer in the Administrative Tools program group displays recorded events for all three logs. These events represent both failures and successes as well as simple information. You can set up SQL Server to log events to the Windows NT event log, which logs status during startup and provides runtime errors and warnings. Also, applications running with SQL Server can log application-specific error messages into the event log from within stored procedures and triggers; these messages give you information you can use to completely customize SQL Server database applications.

The SQL Executive uses the Windows NT event log to trap errors for alerts and notifications; this integrated notification gives you exceptional monitoring ability for both the local system and remote systems. You can use the SQL Executive to create alerts and notifications based on errors logged to the Windows NT event log. Using this process, SQL Server and SQL Executive can significantly enhance Windows NT's notification process and provide remote notification for almost any system or application event.

You can also examine the event log on remote machines through the Event Viewer. SQL Executive can respond to events posted in those locations using locally stored alert configurations, thereby centralizing alert handling and notifications. These alerts need not relate only to administrative tasks; they can easily be extended to program-specific notifications, such as stocking requirements or large transactions on a sales system. For more information about alerts, see Chapter 7, "Scheduling and Performing Administrative Tasks."

Performance Monitor

The Windows NT Performance Monitor can also display SQL Server-specific counters, which let you view all the server activities as charts and graphs. You can use the performance log files for long-term performance monitoring. Both system-level and SQL Server-specific information is useful for optimizing performance. Performance Monitor displays disk access and CPU usage at the system level, which is an excellent overall usage metric. Performance Monitor can display a tremendous amount of useful information about SQL Server, such as the number of pages locked in the database, the number of transactions per second executed, and data about read-ahead performance.

Performance Monitor is an excellent tool for system troubleshooting and can be useful in determining the activity that specific database processes generate. Constantly monitoring performance metrics can help you identify potential problems early in their development, and these counters provide excellent information on which to base initial analysis. We recommend that you take time to examine the available counters within Performance Monitor and understand their significance to system operation. A more detailed examination of the counters specific to SQL Server is in Chapter 15, "Performance Monitoring Guidelines."

Windows NT, the Database, and Threads

One advantage of the tight integration of SQL Server 6.5 with the Windows NT operating system is the way the two programs handle process threading. Under SQL Server, each user connection, up to 1024 connections, can generate and be serviced by its own thread. Each thread is created under the operating context of SQL Server, sharing memory resources and inheriting the security of the account that SQL Server is running under. The Windows NT operating system processes every thread waiting for CPU time based on the thread's priority, regardless of the process under which it exists. The more threads that exist under SQL Server, the more time the processor spends executing SQL Server requests relative to other processes.

You can configure SQL Server to specify the number of threads that will be used to perform striped backups. Although up to 32 threads can be specified for parallel backups, setting this value to a number larger than the number of backup devices participating in the striped set will not improve performance. You can also set the maximum number of threads created for read-ahead operations within SQL Server. The limiting factor for creating threads in these cases is the availability of overhead memory.

Windows NT threads have many advantages over many operating systems' multiprocess-based architectures, including smaller overhead requirements, shared memory, and shared security access. However, this Windows NT-specific component of SQL Server contributes substantially to the lack of cross-system portability of SQL Server.

The Shortcomings

The strong integration of SQL Server 6.5 with Windows NT has its drawbacks, particularly in the area of portability. If you want a uniform computing platform and Microsoft SQL Server is part of your information services system, the whole system must ride on the Windows NT operating system. For some businesses, this restriction is unacceptable, usually because they have legacy systems that are bound to a different specific operating system. Often the choice is between creating a heterogeneous network on one hand and, on the other, using a single operating system and not using SQL Server.

Luckily, Microsoft has worked long and hard to create an operating system capable of communicating and working with many other network systems. Services such as Systems Network Architecture (SNA) Server and Gateway Services for NetWare (GSNW) allow Windows NT Server to be integrated immediately into NetWare and IBM mainframe and minicomputer environments. When combined with the variety of network protocols, Domain Name System (DNS) and Dynamic Host Configuration Protocol (DHCP), the Windows NT operating system can interact with nearly any existing network.

However, another shortcoming of a Microsoft-based solution is Microsoft's failure to use any open standards in developing its products. Many IS shops prefer to work with open, nonproprietary operating systems and communications protocols to ensure the long-term viability of their investments. Without a commitment from Microsoft to help generate and follow an open standard, some degree of cross-platform incompatibility is inevitable. The current implementation of TCP/IP on Microsoft operating systems is a reasonable start and the ODBC standards help in continuing compatibility, but future plans are not well publicized.

Summary

All the support structures that Windows NT provides as an application server also enhance SQL Server's database services. SQL Server's multithreaded execution, its tight integration with the operating system's security subsystem and error logging capability, and its compatibility with Windows NT's services control system all make for a broad-spectrum information service provider.

If you are not averse to maintaining a Windows NT server in your network, SQL Server's tight integration with the operating system provides a highly tuned enterprise solution for almost all database requirements. Microsoft's continued development of the database product and the development tools for user access will certainly continue to produce some of the most advanced information service applications available. The cost of integrating SQL Server with the operating system is outweighed by the benefits, and future versions will likely only continue to exploit this advantage.

Many good references on the internal operations of Windows NT are available, such as *Inside Windows NT*, by Helen Custer (Microsoft Press). A thorough understanding of Windows NT's system components will certainly help you understand how SQL Server functions at a basic level.

Chapter 5

Getting Ready to Install SQL Server 6.5

You have the SQL Server 6.5 CD-ROM in hand and wonder whether it will be a late-night installation. It doesn't have to be if you understand the options and have prepared a list of the basic requirements. This chapter covers information for a new installation of SQL Server. Once you're familiar with the preinstallation information in this chapter, proceed to Chapter 6, which contains detailed instructions for installing and upgrading SQL Server 6.5. If you are upgrading from an earlier version of SQL Server, you may want to review this chapter briefly, then proceed to Chapter 6.

The checklist in Table 5.1 shows the minimum requirements for running SQL Server 6.5. Fill in the third column with the appropriate choices for your environment. The rest of this chapter explains each checklist option.

TABLE 5.1 PREINSTALLATION CHECKLIST		
Option	**Minimum**	**Your Environment**
Server	Windows NT 3.51 build 1057	
Platform	Intel, Alpha, MIPS, PowerPC	
Number of CPUs	1	
Memory	16 MB	
Disk space	100 MB. Remember that this is just the minimum space required to install. Don't forget to plan for the sizes of your databases.	
Network software	AppleTalk (ADSP), Banyan Vines, DECNet, DEC Pathworks, NETBEUI, Multiprotocol, Novell NetWare, TCP/IP	
Network adapter	Any adapter on the Windows NT Hardware Compatibility List (HCL)	
File system	FAT or NTFS	
Server name	Your choice	
Licensing	Per Server or Per Seat	
Add user account for SQL Executive	Pick a user name and security options to use	
Remove Read-Only flag from databases you're upgrading	N/A	

Two Versions of SQL Server

SQL Server comes in two forms: the Server version for enterprise use and the Workstation version for development and small systems use. Most features and options are the same in the two versions except that the Workstation version allows only 15 simultaneous connections. The server version allows up to 32,767 user connections (although this many connections would require 1.2 GB of RAM, assuming 37K per user connection). The Workstation version also contains all of the Programmer's Tool Kit, including DBLIB. It is designed for developers, not your enterprise installation. One major difference in the preparation and installation of the Workstation version is that in the Workstation version, you don't need to install any network options.

Hardware

Hardware Platforms

SQL Server 6.5 supports the hardware platforms listed below. For more specific information about each platform, refer to the Windows NT Hardware Compatibility List. Be aware, however, that a device on the compatibility list for the current version of Windows NT won't necessarily be supported for future Windows NT versions.

- Alpha AXP
- Intel 32-bit-based (80486 or later)
- MIPS
- PowerPC

Hardware Requirements

Table 5.2 shows the minimum hardware requirements for SQL Server 6.5.

TABLE 5.2 HARDWARE REQUIREMENTS		
Resource	**Amount**	**Notes**
Memory	16 MB	Minimum for a base SQL Server installation (i.e., a small development staff or a small department).
	32 MB	Minimum if you intend to use this server as the distribution server for replication.
Disk space	85 MB	Total disk space for programs and SQL databases if you take the default Master database size.
	15 MB	Additional disk space for installing SQL Server *Books Online* (recommended). Add only 1 MB if you run the online books from the CD-ROM (which is very slow).
	65 MB	If upgrading from a SQL 4.2 or 6.0 database.

You need at least 85 MB of free disk on your server for the files SQL Server 6.5 installs. In addition, you must allow enough disk space for the Windows NT virtual memory file (Pagefile.sys) to grow. During heavy loads on SQL Server, Pagefile.sys can grow to a maximum size of the system memory plus 12 MB. For example, if you have 32 MB of memory, Pagefile.sys can grow to 44 MB.

Installation Tips

As you prepare your hardware to install SQL Server 6.5, keep these tips in mind:

- Make sure your server has at least 32 MB of memory. SQL Server 6.5 runs well with 64 MB or more memory. Also, use at least two processors in the server for better speed. SQL Server will now run with four or more processors. Some hardware vendors, such as TriCord and Sequent, have recently demonstrated Windows NT running with 8 and 16 processors. SQL Server will eventually run with as many CPUs as Windows NT will support, up to the maximum configurable value of 64 processors.

- Install the SQL Server *Books Online* CD-ROM on your server's hard drive. You can also install it on a Windows client with the setup program in the installation CD-ROM's Client directory. Also, it's wise to install SQL Server *Books Online* on every PC in your software development group.

Software Requirements

SQL Server 6.5 requires Windows NT Server 3.51 build 1057 or later. SQL Server will not run on Windows NT Server 3.5. SQL Workstation will run on Windows NT Workstation 3.51 or later (any nonbeta version should work well).

To use some of the advanced networking features, such as data encryption, you must also install Service Pack 4 for Windows NT 3.51.

Network Software

SQL Server 6.5 runs with most popular network packages. Table 5.3 shows the network protocols that SQL Server 6.5 supports.

TABLE 5.3 SUPPORTED NETWORK SOFTWARE	
Network	**Notes**
Multiprotocol	Uses Windows NT's Remote Procedure Call (RPC) feature. RPC enables communications over most popular protocols, but TCP/IP, NetBEUI named pipes, and IPX/SPX are the most stable (supported and tested) for multiprotocol networking.
TCP/IP	Microsoft TCP/IP is recommended. If you use another vendor's TCP/IP, you may need new drivers.
NetBEUI	Uses named pipes, the default.
Novell NetWare	Requires NWLINK IPX/SPX software for full support.
Banyan Vines	Requires additional network software from Banyan.
DEC Pathworks	Requires additional network software from Digital Equipment Corporation.
AppleTalk ADSP	Enables native AppleTalk connections to SQL Server.
DECnet	Lets VMS clients connect to SQL Server via DECnet sockets.

Network Adapter

SQL Server 6.5 supports all network adapters that Windows NT supports. You even need a network adapter if you're running a standalone server (for example, for development purposes). You must install the Microsoft loop-back adapter if you don't have a network card; otherwise, SQL Server will not complete the installation.

File System

SQL Server 6.5 supports two file systems: NT File System (NTFS) and File Allocation Table (FAT). NTFS is the recommended file system, because it's written specifically for Windows NT and offers security and recovery advantages over a FAT file system. You should use FAT only if you need a dual-boot system. Although you can install SQL Server 6.5 on a compressed NTFS volume, this installation isn't advisable because it causes additional overhead and poorer performance.

Server Name

Before you install SQL Server 6.5, make sure your server has a name conforming to the SQL Server naming conventions:

- The name must begin with a letter or an underscore (_).
- The name must have 30 or fewer characters.
- Characters after the first character can include letters; numbers; the #, $, or _ symbols; or any combination of these.
- The name cannot contain spaces.

If you must rename your server, do it *before* you install SQL Server. Remember to contact your system administrator to add the new server name to the domain and remove the old name. Plan ahead for the name change because the old server name in any .ini files or other configuration files can cause problems during installation.

Licensing Terms

Microsoft's licensing requirements for SQL Server 6.5 are confusing, so read this section carefully to ensure you understand the legal implications.

Microsoft SQL Server 6.5 requires a Server License plus a Client Access License for each client computer that accesses the server. You must acquire these licenses before using SQL Server 6.5. You obtain the base Server License when you buy the SQL Server 6.5 CD-ROM containing the software you'll install. You buy Client Access licenses separately. The setup program won't proceed until you make your selection and accept the terms of the license agreement.

You have two choices of Client Access licenses:

- Per Seat — Each computer or workstation that will use SQL Server via either Microsoft-provided client software or third-party software requires a Client Access License.
- Per Server — You specify a maximum number of simultaneous user connections for the server and purchase an equal number of Client Access licenses for that server.

Note that multiple connections from one client machine to the same SQL Server system count as only one licensed connection (i.e., node-based Client Access). However, only newer versions (SQL Server 6.0 and later) of ODBC and DBLIB can take advantage of this feature. Older versions count each connection as a separate license.

Which License Do I Choose?

The Per Seat licensing option is cheaper when your clients need to connect to more than one server running SQL Server 6.5 (the connections need not be simultaneous).

The Per Server option is better for department or regional offices where most users connect to only one server. You specify how many simultaneous connections to a SQL Server system you want. When this limit is reached, the next user trying to log on receives an error message and is asked to wait.

In other words, if you have 20 client licenses and one server, then go with the Per Server option, and any 20 computers can connect simultaneously. If you have 20 client licenses and 10 servers, then the Per Seat option lets 20 clients connect to any or all servers simultaneously.

What if you have a mixture of the two scenarios? For example, your company's regional staff must access one SQL Server system, while the corporate staff must access all the regional servers. According to Microsoft, you can mix and match SQL Server 6.5 licenses. The regional server could have the Per Server license, and the corporate staff could have the Per Seat option. Be aware that mixing and matching might not be the most cost-effective option: The user with a Per Seat license in effect pays twice to log on to a server with Per Server licensing by using a connection paid for by both the client and the server. Instead of mixing and matching, you might be better off choosing one corporate strategy and sticking with it.

If you aren't sure which license to choose, select Per Server so you can proceed with installing SQL Server 6.5; later, if you want to convert to Per Seat mode, you can do so at no additional cost (you don't have to notify Microsoft of this change). Note that once you change from Per Server to Per Seat licensing, you must keep that licensing — you aren't legally allowed to change back to Per Server.

To change licensing to Per Seat after you've installed SQL Server 6.5, use the Licensing application from the Control Panel. For more information about changing licensing, see SQL Server 6.5's online Help for the Licensing application. To review the licensing agreement, see the Client License Access Agreement or the Licensing application's online Help.

User Accounts

The Windows NT User Account for SQL Executive

Before you install SQL Server 6.5, you should add a new Windows NT user account for SQL Executive. This account is different from another new Windows NT account, SQLExecutiveCmdExec, which is explained in the next section. The default setup lets SQL Executive log on to LocalSystem; however, a LocalSystem account can't replicate the system's database to other servers or run scheduled tasks involving other servers.

The new user account should be a domain user account instead of an account on the local server, which can't be shared with other servers. For example, a publication server and all its subscription servers should share the same account. And the local accounts run in the security context of that account and cannot complete connectivity-related tasks — so, for example, using the local account for a Windows NT service would restrict it from communicating with other servers, and features such as replication and remote stored procedures would not run.

When creating a new user account, select the following user attributes (these attributes are found on different screens in the Windows NT User Manager application):

- Add the user to the Administrators domain administrators group on the SQL Server system.
- Select the Password Never Expires option.
- Grant the Log On as a Service right.

- Allow all logon hours (required for domain accounts only).

If you plan to replicate data between SQL Server databases in different domains, it's advisable to assign all SQL Executive services the same user name and password (replication seems to perform more reliably this way).

If you're pressed for time when installing SQL Server 6.5, you don't have to specify a new user account. If you don't specify this account, SQL Executive will be installed with the default account, LocalSystem. If you want to change the account later, you can add the user by clicking the Services icon in the Control Panel to assign the user to the SQL Executive service. You must also add the new user account with the Services command in the Server Manager or SQL Enterprise Manager's facility for managing the SQL Executive login.

The SQLExecutiveCmdExec User Account

As part of the setup process, the setup program will create a new user account for SQL Executive, SQLExecutiveCmdExec. CmdExec tasks owned by users who are not system administrators (SAs) run in the security context of this account. By default, this account is a member of the Users local group on the server.

Windows NT administrators can control the operating system privileges of tasks owned by users who aren't SAs by controlling the rights, permissions, and group memberships of the SQLExecutiveCmdExec account. To configure these attributes, use Windows NT's User Manager application, but don't change the SQLExecutiveCmdExec password from User Manager. If you do, CmdExec tasks owned by users who aren't SAs won't run successfully. When you need to change the password, use the Configure option in SQL Enterprise Manager. It is a good idea to use User Manager to configure the SQLExecutiveCmdExec account in such a way that the password never expires and jobs do not quit running unexpectedly.

Read-Only Flags

Before you install SQL Server 6.5, remove the Read-Only flag from any databases you intend to upgrade to version 6.5 from earlier SQL Server versions. SQL Server 6.5 includes additions and enhancements to the system tables, so it must have both read and write access to those tables.

Summary

Our discussion of SQL Server's hardware and software prerequisites in this chapter should help your installation or upgrade process run smoothly. Using our Preinstallation Checklist in Table 5.1, plan which networking software, adapter, file system, and server name you'll use with SQL Server 6.5. You should also understand SQL Server 6.5's licensing options and know which option you want to select during your installation or upgrade. In addition, you should take care of other details before installation, including adding a new user account for SQL Executive instead of using the default LocalSystem account and removing Read-Only flags. At this point, you're ready to install or upgrade to SQL Server 6.5.

Chapter 6

Installing and Upgrading SQL Server 6.5

This chapter gives detailed instructions for installing and upgrading to SQL Server 6.5. If you're installing SQL Server for the first time, or if you're running a SQL Server version that can't be upgraded to version 6.5, read the section called "Installing SQL Server 6.5" (versions of SQL server that can be upgraded are named later in this chapter). If you're running an earlier SQL Server version that is upgradable to version 6.5, read the section called "Upgrading to SQL Server 6.5." Suggestions for troubleshooting both installation and upgrade problems are at the end of the chapter.

Installing SQL Server 6.5 can be as simple as choosing all the default options and can take 20 to 30 minutes. If you have complex networking and connectivity requirements, you can save yourself many hours of troubleshooting time later by spending a few minutes learning the SQL networking options. These options are best reviewed in the SQL Server *Books Online* or the Windows NT *Books Online*. Also, be sure you've performed the necessary preinstallation tasks; for more information about preinstallation, see Chapter 5.

Installing SQL Server 6.5

Running the Setup Program

The SQL setup program (Setup.exe) installs SQL Server 6.5; you can also use this program or the SQL Enterprise Manager to change SQL Server configuration options after SQL Server is up and running.

To install SQL Server 6.5, you must first log on to your Windows NT Server system as a system administrator (SA). Using File Manager or Windows Explorer, find the directory on the installation CD-ROM that has your server computer's processor architecture (e.g., for systems with Intel processors, use the I386 directory). Then double-click Setup.exe.

At the first dialog box, fill in your name, organization, and product ID. The product ID is a recommended, but optional, entry used for Microsoft support purposes.

Next, choose the licensing mode, either Per Seat or Per Server, and enter the number of licenses you have purchased. The licensing options are explained in more detail in Chapter 5. The next two dialog boxes ask which drive to install SQL Server on, then where and what size to make the Master device. The Master device is OK at its default size of 25 MB, although if you have enough disk space it may be better to create it at 35 MB to protect yourself against mistakenly filling it up.

At the next dialog box, choose the Install SQL Server and Utilities option. You then see the dialog box in Figure 6.1, SQL Server Installation Options dialog box, which includes three buttons and two options. The first button sets the character set. (For detailed information about character sets and sort orders, see the setup manual that comes with the SQL Server 6.5 installation software. You can't read SQL Server *Books Online* until after the install.) Usually you can select the default ISO character set. Consider your choice of character set carefully, because you cannot perform replication or tape restores when the originating and target databases have different character sets.

Figure 6.1
Installation Options Dialog Box

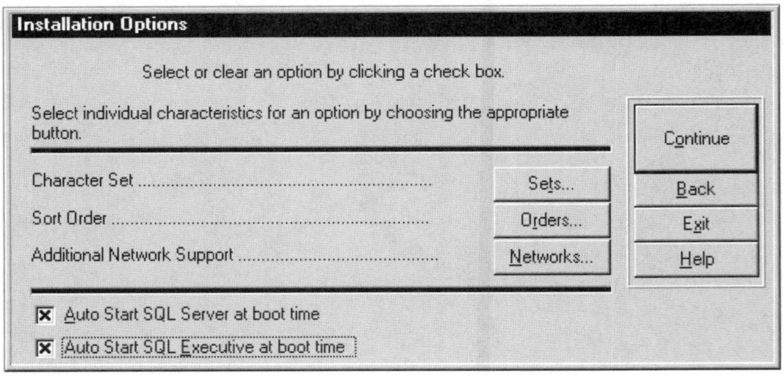

The second button lets you choose the sort order. The sort order is the method SQL Server uses to perform sorts, create indexes, and compare values. The sort order comes into play when Order By, Group By, or Distinct clauses are used in SQL statements. Again, in most cases, you use the default — Dictionary Order, Case-Insensitive. The Binary sort order option can be up to 20 percent faster than most other options. As long as you can guarantee that all your data will be saved as uppercase, you can use the Binary option, because it sorts all the lowercase letters after the last uppercase letter. If you have mixed-case data, do not use the Binary option. Your reports will not be sorted and printed in the order you expect: uppercase letters A through Z are sorted (and thus printed) before lowercase a through z (e.g., Ziegler is printed before adams). Also, any performance gains from the binary option will be negated by the extra work the server does when you constantly must use the Upper( ) function to compare data.

The defaults have changed from SQL Server 4.2 to 6.x. Installing SQL 6.5 with the default sort order and character set does not allow for restoring a version 4.2 database with a different sort order and character set. You will need to use the Transfer Manager utility if your character sets and sort orders are different.

Clicking the third button, Networks, lets you choose the network protocol you'll use for your SQL Server system. At the Select Network Protocols dialog box (Figure 6.2), choose your protocol (Named Pipes is the default).

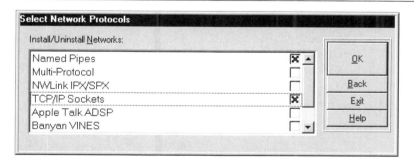

Figure 6.2
Select Network Protocols Dialog Box

The last items to set are the two options at the bottom of the main setup dialog box in Figure 6.1. Click the boxes to add SQL Server and SQL Executive as automatic services that will start whenever the server is restarted. (You can also set this option later with the Services applet in the Control Panel.)

Next, click Continue, which displays the Master Device Creation dialog box in Figure 6.3. Increase the Master device's default size from 25 MB to 35 MB. Click Continue and choose to install SQL Server *Books Online*. From this point, as you go through the dialog boxes you can keep the options at their defaults. After you click the last Continue button, you will wait 10 to 15 minutes for the installation to finish. When it is done, choose to reboot the computer.

Figure 6.3

MASTER Device Creation
Dialog Box

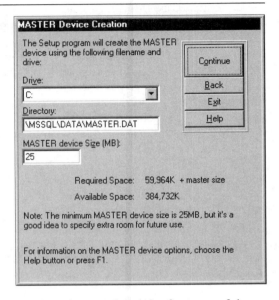

Once you've rebooted the system, you've completed the first part of the installation. If you want to perform an unattended setup of SQL Server 6.5 (for example, to install the product at a remote site), read the "Unattended Setup" section later in this chapter. After you finish installing SQL Server, you must perform the postinstallation tasks described below.

Postinstallation Tasks

After you install your production databases, you should run the Setup.exe program again to set up other server options, such as tape backup support, mail support, license monitoring, and security.

When you run Setup.exe again, the setup dialog box in Figure 6.4 is displayed. Although the Upgrade option is the default after SQL Server 6.5 is installed, instead choose Set Server Options and click Continue to display the dialog box in Figure 6.5. The Select Server Options dialog box is also available through the Enterprise Manager. In SQL Server 6.0, you found Set Server Options in the Enterprise Manager by choosing the Configuration option from the Server menu and selecting the Security Options tab. In the 6.5 Enterprise

Manager, you select SQL Server from the Server menu and then choose Configure; you can also right-click the name of the server.

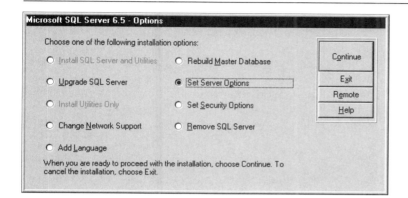

Figure 6.4
Main Dialog Box with Set Server Options Checked

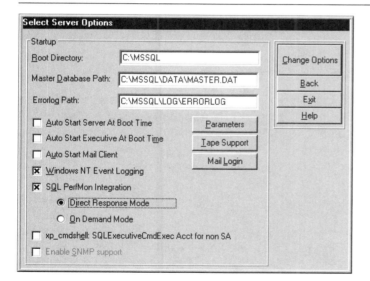

Figure 6.5
Select Server Options Dialog Box

Tape and Mail Support

If you plan to back up SQL Server databases to tape, click the Tape Support button and fill in the dialog box options. If you use SQL Server to send and receive mail, click the Mail Login button and fill in the dialog box. When the Select Server Options dialog box returns, click Auto Start Mail Client, which starts Microsoft Mail or Microsoft Exchange to send and receive mail messages.

Setting Security Options

You can set up SQL Server security from the SQL Setup dialog box
(Figure 6.4) by choosing Set Security Options and clicking Continue. Doing so
displays the dialog box in Figure 6.6. Choose the appropriate login security
mode of Integrated, Standard, or Mixed. These options are explained fully in
Chapter 10, "Administering Users and Security." You have the option to Set
Hostname to User Name, which you should choose when the client machines
are not individually named. The host name is the workstation name. The user
names can be viewed via the Enterprise Manager in the Current Activity dialog
box, to see who is logged on, which workstation they are using, and what
application and command they are executing.

Audit Level

To enable auditing, select Failed Logins from the Set Security Options dialog
box in Figure 6.6, which traces failed attempts to log on. (Most failed log on
attempts are from users entering their password incorrectly.) Remember that it
doesn't do much good to turn on auditing unless you review error logs regularly. You should be monitoring both the SQL Server error log and the
Windows NT event log. The Successful Logins option puts too many entries in
the log file, so don't use it unless your company's security policy dictates
doing so.

Figure 6.6

*Set Security Options
Dialog Box*

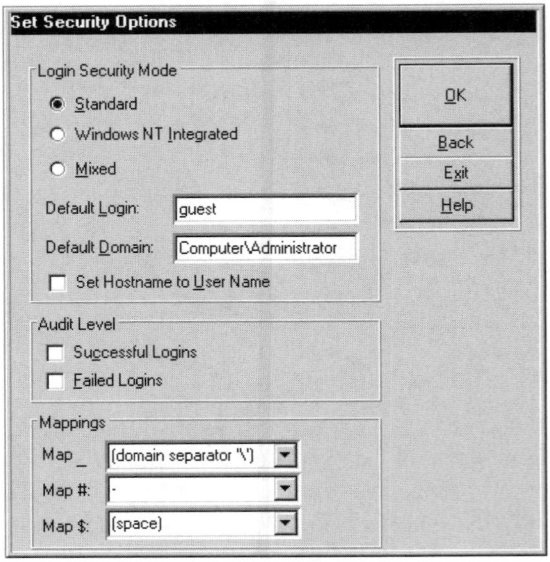

Mappings

The mappings option translates Windows NT user names into valid SQL Server user names. Leave the mappings option alone for now, unless you know of a user name that will cause a problem. You can always set mappings later via the Server, Configurations menu option from the SQL Enterprise Manager.

Other Uses for SQL Setup

Once you've installed SQL Server 6.5, you can use the SQL Setup program to perform the following tasks in addition to those discussed earlier:

* Add a language
* Add or drop MSSQL-MIB and the SQL Server SNMP extension agent, which lets SNMP monitors on your network receive alerts and performance data from SQL Server 6.5
* Rebuild the Master database
* Remove SQL Server

Changing Configuration with the SQL Enterprise Manager

You can use the SQL Enterprise Manager instead of SQL Setup to change your SQL Server configuration after you've installed SQL Server 6.5. For a newly installed server, you'd typically use the SQL Enterprise Manager to

* Register the server and add it to a server group
* Add a password for the SA and then change the registration to use this password
* Set security options
* Set server options
* Set configuration options

SQL Setup and the SQL Enterprise Manager keep the Windows NT registry up-to-date. It's important that you use SQL Setup to change the registry options instead of using Regedt32.exe, because the SQL Setup dialog boxes record other information and do other tasks.

Server Tools Installed

During SQL Server installation, several components are installed *in addition to those provided with SQL Server 6.5*. These tools, listed below, are discussed in Chapter 3 and are installed automatically when SQL Server is installed.

- Microsoft Query
- SQLTrace
- Microsoft Distributed Transaction Coordinator (MS DTC runs as a Windows NT service)
- SQL Web Page Wizard
- SNMP MIBs and SNMP Agent

Client Tools Installed

When you install the SQL Workstation version on a client, the components listed below are automatically installed *in addition to those provided with SQL Server 6.5* when SQL Workstation is installed. These tools are discussed in detail in Chapter 3.

- Microsoft Query
- SQLTrace
- MS DTC (client support installed)
- SQL Web Page Wizard
- Other ODBC client drivers for heterogeneous replication use

Unattended Setup

SQL Server 6.5's unattended setup feature is useful for installing the product at remote sites. It's also useful if you want to schedule an installation for a specific time using the At command from Windows NT or by setting up a SQL Executive task from a SQL Server 6.0 or 6.5 installation. For unattended setup, you run Setup.exe from a command prompt using a Setup.ini file instead of prompting for user input, as in the following example.

```
setup.exe /t IniFilePath = c:\myapps\mysetup.ini
```

Figure 6.7 shows a sample .ini file for unattended setup, and Table 6.1 shows the file documentation for unattended setup (entries are indented for readability).

```
[License]
FullName=Kevin Cox
    OrgName=Computer Peritia
    ProductID=XX98765
    PerServerUsers=50
    Mode=0
[SQLPath]
SQLPath=\SQL65
LogicalSQLDrive=C:
[MasterPath]
MasterSize=50
LogicalDBDrive=C:
MasterDBPath=\SQL65\DATA
MasterDBFileName=MASTER.DAT
[NewOptions]
AutoServerService=CHECKED
AutoExecutiveService=CHECKED
BooksOnline=1
[CharSet]
CharSet=CPISO
[SortOrder]
SortFileName=NOCASE.ISO
    SortConfigValue=52
[Network]
NetLibList={"SSNMPN65","SSMSRP65","SSMSSP65","SSMSSO65"}
ServerNMPipe=\\.\pipe\sql\query
MultiProtEncrypt=NOTCHECKED
SPXServiceName=MY_SQL_SERVER
TCPIPSocketNumber=1433
[LogonAccount]
LocalSystem=NOTCHECKED
Username= SQLExecutiveCmdExec
    Password=THISISAPASSWORD
[Scripts]
CustomScPath=C:\TEMP
CustScriptList={"MyScript.sql","MyScript2.sql","MyScript3.sql"}
```

Figure 6.7
Sample .ini File for Unattended Setup

TABLE 6.1 UNATTENDED SETUP FILE DOCUMENTATION

[Section]	Entry	Description	Valid Values	Notes
[License]	FullName			
	OrgName			
	ProductId			
	PerServerUsers			
	Mode			
[SQLPath]	SQLPath			
	LogicalSQLDrive			
[MasterPath]	MasterSize			
	LogicalDBDrive			
	MasterDBPath			
	MasterDBFileName			
[NewOptions]	AutoServerService			
	AutoExecutiveService			
	BooksOnline			
[CharSet]	CharSet			
[SortOrder]	SortFileName			
	SortConfigValue			
[Network]	NetLibList			
	ServerNMPipe			
	MultiProtEncrypt			
	SPXServiceName			
	TCPIPSocketNumber			
[LogonAccount]	LocalSystem			
	UserName			
	Password			
[Scripts]	CustomScPath			
	CustScriptList			

When you use unattended setup, keep in mind the following hints:

- You must be in the appropriate directory for your hardware architecture: Alpha, Mips, PPC, or I386.
- The /t switch tells the setup program to perform an unattended installation.
- You must add the keyword IniFilePath after the /t option and before the equal (=) sign. This keyword is case sensitive: You must type it exactly as shown.
- You must include a space before and after the equal sign.

- After the installation is completed, delete the .ini file, because it contains the password to the account used by the SQL Executive service. (You can also simply remove the password from the file.)
- If you rely on "Set quoted_identifier on" being set in any of your databases, you must run the unattended setup program from a command prompt with the following option added:

```
setup /t SetQuoteID = ON
```

Upgrading to SQL Server 6.5

This section explains how to upgrade to SQL Server 6.5 from any the versions of SQL Server listed below.

- SQL Server 6.0
- SQL Server 4.2
- SQL Server for OS/2 4.2
- Earlier SQL Server 6.5 versions
- Any Sybase SQL Server version

You can no longer upgrade from SQL Server 1.*x*.

The first four supported upgrades above, plus any Sybase SQL Server 4.*x* or System 10 versions, can be transferred to SQL Server 6.5 using SQL Server's transfer features. You can upgrade from the above versions, except the Sybase databases. The Sybase database must be transferred to a newly installed Microsoft SQL Server 6.5 database. The OS/2 database can be upgraded directly only after OS/2 has been replaced by Windows NT.

Upgrade Plan

Before you upgrade SQL Server, it is wise to have an upgrade plan, which includes an extra backup and an estimate of how long the upgrade will take. Table 6.2 is a basic pre-upgrade checklist with suggestions and recommendations; you can amend this list with your own action items. The items in this list are explained in this chapter.

TABLE 6.2 PRE-UPGRADE CHECKLIST		
Task	**Notes**	**Your Notes**
Run Chkupg.exe	Resolve keyword conflicts before upgrading	
Create a recovery plan	In case anything goes wrong	
Check required disk space	Need 50 MB for upgrade, plus 15 MB for SQL Server *Books Online*	
Check free space in Master database	Need 8 MB; however, the setup program expands Master.dat if it needs more space	
Estimate downtime	The bigger the database, the longer the downtime	
Inform users of scheduled downtime		
SQL Server backup of Master database		
SQL Server backup of application databases		
Log everyone off		
Make sure all transactions have been replicated, then stop replication		
Stop SQL Server and SQL Executive		

continued

TABLE 6.2 PRE-UPGRADE CHECKLIST, CONTINUED

Task	Notes	Your Notes
Using your favorite Windows NT backup utility, back up all database files, including Master.dat and the Windows NT registry	Yes, this is a second backup. You can't be too careful	
Run Rdisk.exe to create a new Emergency Repair Disk	In case your old one does not have the latest changes	
Insert the SQL Server 6.5 CD-ROM		
Use File Manager or Explorer to find the correct directory on CD-ROM (I386 for Intel x86 based machines, etc.)		
Turn off the Read-Only flag on databases		
Run Setup.exe		
Choose the Upgrade SQL Server option		

Before You Upgrade

Before you start your upgrade, you should perform the five following tasks, as applicable:

1. If you are installing SQL Server 6.5 over an existing database, back up everything on your server first. An upgrade to SQL Server 6.5 is one-way only. You cannot use the database again with SQL Server 4.2*x* or SQL Server 6.0 if something goes wrong with the upgrade, unless you restore the old database, programs, tools, and registry entries that you backed up.

   Back up once to tape and once to a database dump device, if you have extra disk space. One backup should be a SQL Server dump, the other a Windows NT backup. (Note that you can load SQL Server 6.0 dumps into version 6.5, but not vice versa.)

   Make a backup copy of your Windows NT registry. Also make a new Windows NT Emergency Repair Disk by using the Windows NT Rdisk.exe utility.

2. Shut down earlier versions of Microsoft SQL Server before you install or upgrade to SQL Server 6.5. Also, before an upgrade, stop replication and make sure the log is empty.

3. Resolve keyword conflicts between your older database and SQL Server 6.5. To check the old database for new keyword violations, first run Chkupg65.exe. For example, if a SQL Server 4.2 database includes a column named Action, you must modify your database before doing the upgrade, because that column name is now a new keyword in SQL Server 6.5. Chkupg65.exe runs very quickly. Because it searches only the structure of database objects, it does not affect the data itself, so you can run Chkupg65.exe while users are on the system.

   If you have a development database that uses the same structure as the production database, you should run Chkupg65.exe on the development server only, because deleting the text of your stored procedures from the syscomments table makes it impossible for the program to check for keywords. It is best if you drop and re-create them before running the program. You can now encrypt the text so you no longer have to delete source code that you don't want visible to customers.

   Keyword conflicts don't prevent SQL Server 6.5 upgrades from being completed. However, your applications won't run until the conflicts are resolved. Thus, you should not continue with the upgrade until you've identified and resolved keyword conflicts. You can find the list of SQL Server 6.5 keywords in SQL Server *Books Online*.

You also should run Chkupg65.exe to see whether you use reserved words in your database and, if so, you should change applications that use keywords or reserved words in their code. To run Chkupg65.exe, use a statement like the following from a prompt:

```
chkupg65/Usa/Pyourpassword/Sservername
/ooutputfile
```

Note that ChkupgG65.exe doesn't check your front-end applications for keyword conflicts. However, checking the database is sufficient; it just doesn't show the extent of the usage of the keywords in the front-end application.

4. If possible, install SQL Server 6.5 on a nonproduction server first to test the system. If you plan to run SQL Server 6.5 on more than one system, it's advisable to first install the product on a server running Windows NT 3.51 or later, create devices and databases, and then use the Transfer Manager program (found in Enterprise Manager or in the SQL Server 6.5 program group in Program Manager/Windows Explorer) or SQL Server restore (load), provided your sort orders and character sets match. Installing SQL Server 6.5 first on a nonproduction system lets you run application and system tests before you officially move over from production.

5. Use Transfer Manager if you are changing processor platforms. If you're upgrading your SQL Server installation to a different processor platform (e.g., an Intel server to a Digital Alpha server), you must use the Transfer Manager utility to transfer the data between servers.

   You cannot upgrade databases between processor architectures or restore across architectures. The SQL Restore facility won't let you restore a SQL Server 6.0 database to a different platform. If you try to restore a 4.2x database, SQL Restore doesn't record the processor type during backup and continues the reload. Of course, after the reload, the database doesn't start and is marked suspect by SQL Server. If it is marked suspect, all you can do is drop the database, rebuild it, and then restore an earlier version.

   You must also use Transfer Manager if you change the character set or sort order in the new database if you're upgrading across platforms. (If you're using the same processor for the upgrade, you can use either Transfer Manager or SQL Restore.) Do not perform a Windows NT restore because this restore replaces the .dat files and overlays the new system table structure that SQL Server 6.5 installs with the old 6.0 or 4.2 formats.

Disk Space Requirements

Upgrading from 6.0 takes about 20 MB of disk space and 2 MB of free space in the Master database (Master.dat). Upgrading from 4.2*x* takes about 65 MB of disk space and 9 MB of free space in the Master database. These figures are for the extra disk space required for an upgrade. The requirements for disk space discussed in the preinstallation section of Chapter 5 are for new installations only. The setup program automatically expands the Master database if necessary.

Doing the Upgrade

For the OS/2 upgrade, install Windows NT 3.51 (or later) over OS/2. For all five upgrades, go to the appropriate platform directory on your SQL Server 6.5 CD-ROM and run Setup.exe. Choose the Upgrade SQL Server option. The dialog box in Figure 6.8 is displayed. Click the Continue button. The next few dialog boxes go through the typical setup questions, such as who the program is registered to, what the SA password is, what directory you want this installed in, and where Master.dat is. Watch carefully, because the big default button on the dialog box changes from Continue to Exit on certain dialog boxes. (Note that Setup.exe always uses Named Pipes for the upgrade process regardless of what network[s] SQL Server is configured for.)

Figure 6.8

Upgrade SQL Server Dialog Box

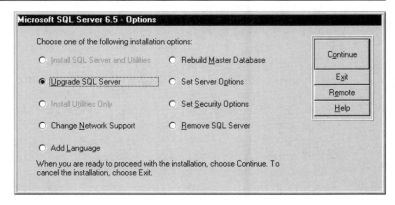

Check the open databases option using the stored procedure sp_configure. SQL Server attempts to open all your databases simultaneously, including the system databases — Master, Model, Tempdb, Msdb, Distribution, and Pubs (if it's installed). To verify the databases on your system, get the actual count of how many databases are installed on your server by typing **Select COUNT(*) From master..sysdatabases** in a query window. Then run EXEC sp_configure and check to see whether the number of open databases is set to a value greater than or equal to the actual count.

Once you've performed the above sequence of tasks, the setup program starts copying files to disk, updating the Master database, and installing new stored procedures in both the Master and Msdb databases and also in the Distribution database if replication is installed. This process takes 15–30 minutes, depending on your system's speed.

Troubleshooting Installations and Upgrades

After you install SQL Server 6.5, you should check in three main places for errors: the .out files in the MSSQL65\Install directory, the Windows NT event logs (using Windows NT Event Viewer), and the MSSQL65\Log\Errorlog file. To open the last file, use SQL Enterprise Manager and click the Server menu option, then choose Error_Log.

Most installation and upgrade errors are caused by lack of disk space. Refer to Chapter 5 for information about estimating the amount of disk space you need for SQL Server 6.5. Installation errors require that the database backup be used to restore the database. In cases of extreme problems, you may need to install the prior version of SQL Server.

Summary

The key to a successful SQL Server 6.5 installation or upgrade is making the necessary preinstallation preparations ahead of time. Review the checklists in this and the previous chapter, make several backups of your databases *before* you install or upgrade, and make sure you have a solid recovery plan. Also run Chkupg.exe before upgrading to check for keyword conflicts in table names, column names, stored procedure code, view statements, rules, defaults, and user-defined data types.

Chapter 7

Scheduling and Performing Administrative Tasks

To ensure that your databases are stable and run efficiently, you should perform certain administrative tasks regularly. Checking file consistency, updating index statistics, re-packing indexes, and archiving data all help maintain system performance and proactively address problems that can arise when your database is used heavily. In addition, scheduling backup routines reduces the amount of hands-on attention you need to devote to the database to protect the integrity of the data.

The interaction of SQL Server and the SQL Executive gives you a variety of methods for setting up regularly executed procedures. Combined with the Database Maintenance Plan Wizard, these tools provide all the functions that any database administrator (DBA) needs to maintain a database in optimal form. We will consider the SQL Executive, the Database Maintenance Plan Wizard, and the SQL Executive Task Manager in detail in this chapter. In addition, we will detail the procedures you can use to define operators and assign alert notifications to them so that appropriate people can be contacted automatically to handle specific problems.

SQL Executive

The principal component of SQL Server's administrative control mechanism is the SQL Executive, a Windows NT service that monitors the activity of SQL Server, executes maintenance chores, and sends notifications to specified operators. It is supported by the Msdb system tables. For SQL Executive to function correctly, SQL Server must be running.

The SQL Executive keeps in constant contact with SQL Server and uses the database to store task, alert, notification, and operator information. The SQL Executive service also monitors the Windows NT event log. If you set up SQL Server at installation to write its error events to the Windows NT application log, SQL Executive can send messages and alerts in response to events in the log filtered by error number, severity, or message content. For example, if a database's transaction log fills up, SQL Executive can respond by dumping the log.

The Executive can also send mail through the SQL Mail agent. To take full advantage of the hands-off administration tasks, you must enable SQL Mail. Without SQL Mail, most operator notifications cannot take place.

The configuration options for the SQL Executive are stored in the registry under the HKEY_LOCAL_MACHINE\Software\Microsoft\MSSQLServer\SQLExecutive key and can be set through the Enterprise Manager. These configuration values govern such things as SQL Executive's ability to restart SQL Server and the number of history records to keep after a scheduled task is executed.

Many administrative tasks are necessary to maintain a database. SQL Executive and the graphical interface of the Enterprise Manager make the job easier. SQL Executive lets you create and execute a neat and orderly process definition with very little operator intervention, notifying operators of the success or failure of these tasks and even responding to the completion of scheduled tasks with additional tasks.

The Database Maintenance Plan Wizard

The primary purpose of the Database Maintenance Plan Wizard is to create a scheduled maintenance plan for a database that is easy to use and covers the common tasks. We will go through the wizard step by step and then consider in greater detail the options that you can choose through the wizard.

The Wizard

The Maintenance Plan Wizard consists of eight dialog boxes that lead you through a set of questions that cover the basics of database maintenance. Although you can choose any option on each dialog box, the options with "Recommended" in parentheses after the option label are the wizard's recommended choice, based on your previous choices.

You can start the Maintenance Plan Wizard from the Enterprise Manager's Help Menu by selecting the menu item or by using the wizard button at the far right of the toolbar.

On the first dialog box (Figure 7.1), you choose the database for which you want to create the maintenance plan.

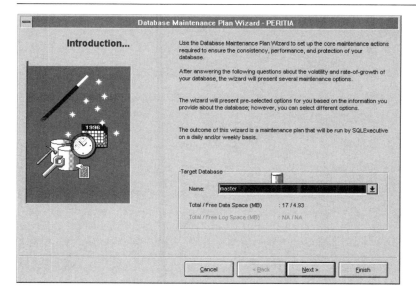

Figure 7.1
Introduction to the Maintenance Wizard

The second dialog box (Figure 7.2) lets you specify the volatility of the data, encompassing both the percent of data that is changed and the rate of growth of the database given as a percentage of the size of the database.

The Data Verification dialog box (Figure 7.3) is used to specify which consistency checks should be run and how often they are to be run. The wizard recommends that all of the checks be run at least once a week, more often on more volatile data systems.

At the next dialog box (Figure 7.4), you determine the data optimization schedule. You can set the statistics pages to be updated and the indexes reor-

Figure 7.2

About the Data Dialog Box of the Maintenance Wizard

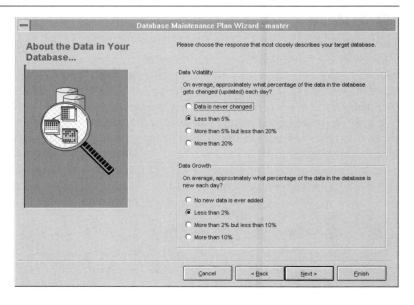

Figure 7.3

Data Verification Dialog Box of the Maintenance Wizard

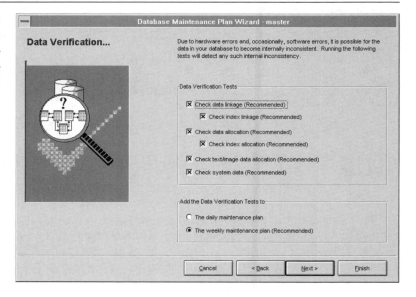

ganized daily or weekly. You can set the data pages to a specific free space value if the indexes are to be reorganized.

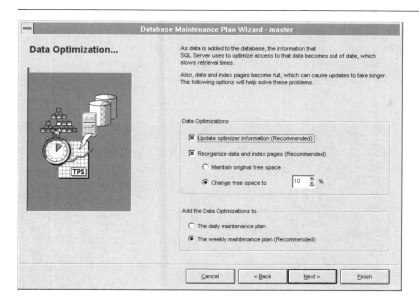

Figure 7.4

Data Optimization Dialog Box of the Maintenance Wizard

The Data Protection screen (Figure 7.5) sets the backup schedule. It lets you choose not to back up your data or to back up daily or weekly. You can also make the backup conditional upon the success of the consistency checks.

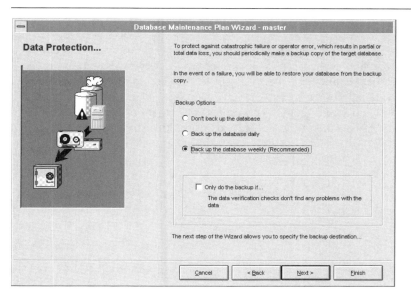

Figure 7.5

Data Protection Dialog Box of the Maintenance Wizard

At the next dialog box (Figure 7.6), you specify the destination path for the backup. SQL Server makes these scheduled dumps to temporary backup devices as either tape or disk dumps, so you only specify a path or tape drive, not a dump device. This procedure lets the wizard-generated maintenance plans dump to unique names and not overwrite previous dumps.

Figure 7.6
Backup Destination Dialog Box of the Maintenance Wizard

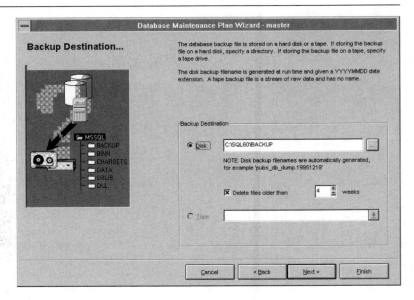

The next dialog box (Figure 7.7) sets the time of day at which the daily and weekly routines will be run. You can have SQL Server generate a log file for the maintenance tasks and the results of the execution of the procedures; this file can be mailed to an operator.

The last dialog box (Figure 7.8) presents a summary of the maintenance procedures that you scheduled. You can also print this summary.

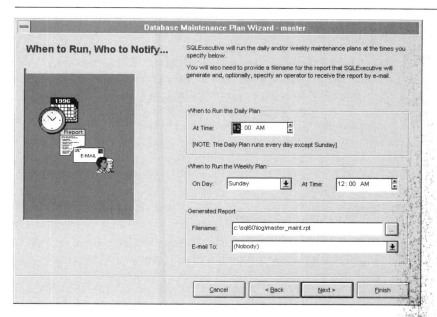

Figure 7.7
When to Run, Who to Notify Dialog Box of the Maintenance Wizard

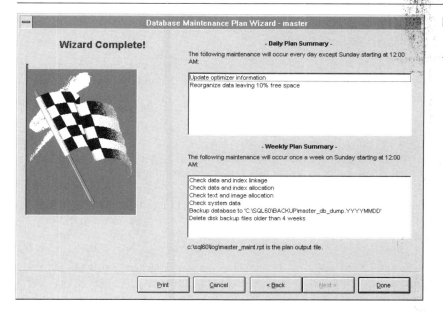

Figure 7.8
Wizard Complete Dialog Box

Understanding the Variables

The Database Maintenance Plan Wizard gives you a road map to the analysis that determines when maintenance needs to be performed. It is important to understand why the wizard queries you for the information it does and why it recommends the settings it does. By examining the relationship between the queries and the recommendations, you can understand what a maintenance plan should do. With this understanding, you can create maintenance plans more tailored to a specific situation than the wizard can create.

The relationships among the kinds of information the wizard requests can be best illustrated by considering data volatility. Data volatility affects database maintenance in three ways.

Volatility and Backup Frequency

First, data volatility affects backup frequency. The more volatile the data, the faster the transaction log grows. If this growth in the transaction log is accompanied by a steady increase in size of the database, the transaction log dumps become larger, more prone to error, and more time-consuming to complete. Therefore, database dumps for volatile databases should be performed more often. (For more detail about data dumps, see Chapter 12, "Database Backup," in which we discuss backing up the server.)

Volatility and Index Structures

The second way in which volatility affects maintenance scheduling is related to maintenance of index structures. The Transact-SQL statement (given as the SQLMAINT option -UpdSts)

```
UPDATE STATISTICS [[database.]owner.]table_name [index_name]
```

refreshes the distribution page for the index, which helps the query optimizer perform better. The higher the volatility of your data, the more frequently your indexes' distribution pages should be refreshed. In addition, index pages themselves can become fragmented on the disk when data is inserted and deleted frequently. You can rebuild an index by dropping and recreating the clustered index, if one exists. If you create this index with a fill factor other than zero, the leaf pages of the index will contain free space for new inserts, which minimizes page splitting as new data is added. Because this fill factor is not maintained, it is a good idea to re-create the indexes periodically by simply rebuilding them, particularly if you have an on-line transaction processing (OLTP) system. For more information about index structures, see Chapter 17, "Indexing."

As a matter of performance tuning, most tables can benefit from having a clustered index. In cases where a clustered index is not desired, you can reorganize the data pages using the order of one of the non-clustered indexes by dropping the non-clustered index, re-adding it as a clustered index, dropping it again, and re-adding it as a non-clustered index. With this procedure, it is usually best not to define a fill factor, thereby packing the data pages as much as possible until the last index is built.

You can generate an SQL script (see the text associated with the sp_helpindex system stored procedure) that combines a little tricky SQL with the system tables to perform the steps described above. You can run this script as a stored procedure or you can execute it directly. Another option for performing the same task is to execute the SQLMAINT utility specifying the -RebldIdx option (for more information about the SQLMAINT utility, see the next section, "A Better Way to Perform Maintenance"). We recommend using the SQLMAINT option because it is easier and adapts itself to the current structure of the database.

Volatility and Physical Storage

The third way in which high volatility and growth affect a database relates to the physical storage of the data. The more allocation and de-allocation of storage space, the higher the likelihood of internal consistency problems. Missed allocation pages, cross-linked allocations, and pages that are allocated but not used can all cause serious problems. The DBCC utility commands help detect and fix these errors. The more frequently you use the DBCC utility commands, the more likely it is that they can repair the problem.

You can check your data with Transact-SQL or the SQLMAINT utility before you back up your database. You should create backups that do not contain allocation errors, because these errors can make reloading the database impossible. SQLMAINT checks for allocation errors before the database is backed up and can stop the backup if the checks fail. We recommend SQLMAINT for performing this type of maintenance.

A Better Way to Perform Maintenance

When the Maintenance Plan Wizard runs, it generates two tasks that are registered with the SQL Executive as database tasks. Both of these tasks use the same CmdExec utility, SQLMAINT. The utility's parameters are listed below and their corresponding Transact-SQL commands are listed in Table 7.1.

```
SQLMAINT
    [-?] | [-S server_name]
```

```
[-U login_ID [-P password]]
-D database_name
-Rpt output_file
[-To operator_name]
[-CkDB | -CkDBNoIdx]
[-CkAl | -CkAlNoIdx]
[-CkTxtAl]
[-CkCat]
[-UpdSts]
[-RebldIdx free_space]
[-BkUpDB backup_path | -BkUpLog backup_path]
[-BkUpOnlyIfClean]
[-BkUpMedia {DISK [-DelBkUps number_of_weeks] | TAPE}]
```

TABLE 7.1 COMPARING SQLMAINT TO TRANSACT-SQL

Utility Option	Equivalent Transact-SQL Commands
[-CkDB	-CkDBNoIdx]	DBCC CheckDB (,NOINDEX)
[-CkAl	-CkAlNoIdx]	DBCC CheckAlloc (,NOINDEX)
[-CkTxtAl]	DBCC Textall
[-CkCat]	DBCC CheckCat
[-UpdSts]	UPDATE STATISTICS
[-RebldIdx *free_space*]	dropping and rebuilding all the indexes with a FILLFACTOR parameter
[-BkUpDB *backup_path*	BkUpLog *backup_path*], [-BkUpMedia {DISK [-DelBkUps *number_of_weeks*]	TAPE}]	allow dumps of databases and transaction logs to the specified media location
[-BkUpOnlyIfClean]	create the dump only if the consistency checks report no errors

Once you understand what information needs to be gathered and what impact this information has, the SQLMAINT utility will prove to be one of your most useful tools. You can use it to perform all the regular maintenance.

Because it can create a log and, in combination with the SQL Executive and SQLMail, send notification of a problem, your routine maintenance needs little human intervention. If you have ever set up camp in the server room waiting for checks to run and backups to start, you will quickly understand the improvement that this represents.

The Task Manager

You can enter tasks that you want the SQL Executive to perform through the Enterprise Manager's Manage Scheduled Tasks window (Figure 7.9). This window has two tabs, one displaying the Task List and one for Running Tasks.

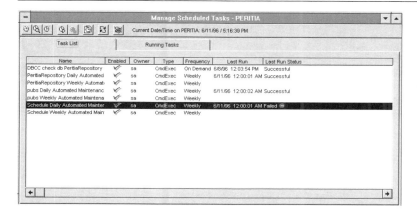

Figure 7.9

The Manage Scheduled Tasks Window, Task List Tab

The Task List tab in the Scheduled Tasks window displays the currently defined tasks. To edit a task, right-click a task in the task list and choose Edit from the menu, and the Edit Task dialog box will be displayed (Figure 7.10). You can also bring up the Edit Task window by double-clicking a task or by highlighting a task and clicking the Edit Task button on the toolbar (shown in Figure 7.11). When you right-click a task, the menu that appears lets you edit, delete, get the history of, or run a task.

In the Edit Task dialog box, you can name tasks (all task names must be unique), enable or disable tasks, and assign task types. A scheduled task falls into one of five types. The two types of tasks you will use most often are CmdExec tasks, which are operating system tasks executed outside of SQL Server, and TSQL tasks, which are Transact-SQL commands that will be executed in a database session. The Distribution, LogRead, and Sync tasks are all used in replication and you do not usually set them manually. From this dialog box, you also specify the database in which the task will run and which

Figure 7.10
Edit Task
Dialog Box

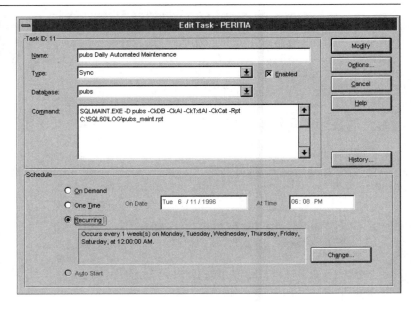

Figure 7.11
Manage
Scheduled
Tasks
Toolbar

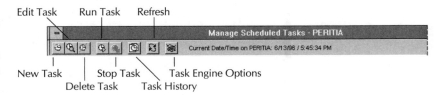

command to execute. You set the schedule for the task at the bottom of this screen.

When you click the Change button, the Task Schedule dialog box appears (Figure 7.12), which lets you set up schedules in different configurations. Events with irregular schedules — for example, twice a month — can be created as separate tasks. You can schedule a task by the day, week, or month and for a specific time of day. You can also give a task start and end dates, creating an effective date range for a task.

The Options button on the Edit Task dialog box in Figure 7.10 brings up the Task Option dialog box in Figure 7.13, which you use to set up notification of an operator by e-mail and to change the parameters of Windows NT event logging. You can also specify the number of retries and the retry delay for executing the task. For LogReader and Sync tasks, you can also set the replication server and database; however, the replication server must be added as a remote server before a task can be scheduled to access it.

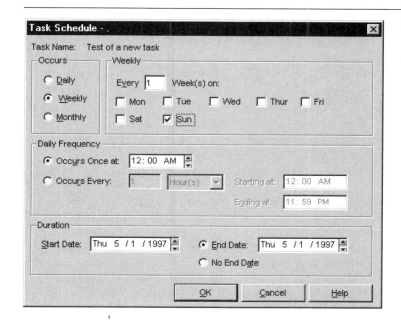

Figure 7.12
*Task Schedule
Dialog Box*

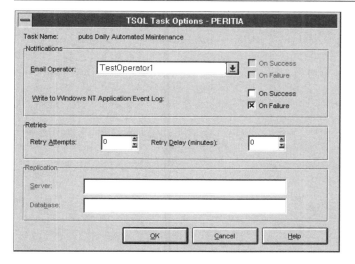

Figure 7.13
*TSQL Task Options
Dialog Box*

Three screens — the Manage Scheduled Tasks window, the Edit Task dialog box, and the Task Schedule dialog box — are equivalent to the following system stored procedure:

```
sp_addtask name [, subsystem] [, server] [, username]
[, databasename][, enabled] [, freqtype] [, freqinterval]
[, freqsubtype] [, freqsubinterval][, freqrelativeinterval]
[, freqrecurrencefactor] [, activestartdate][, activeenddate]
[, activestarttimeofday] [, activeendtimeofday][, nextrundate]
[, nextruntime] [, runpriority] [, emailoperatorname]
[, retryattempts] [, retrydelay] [, command]
[, loghistcompletionlevel][, emailcompletionlevel]
[, description] [, tagadditionalinfo] [, tagobjectid]
[, tagobjecttype] [, @newid OUTPUT], [parameters],
[cmdexecsuccesscode]
```

The last two parameters of the stored procedure are not listed in the SQL *Books Online*. The Parameters option is a text field that is passed as an argument to the command. The Cmdexecsuccesscode parameter, which applies to Cmdexec tasks, specifies the return code of the command when it succeeds. SQL Executive uses this value to determine whether the command was executed successfully.

Both the stored procedure and the task scheduling dialog boxes create a record in Systasks in the Msdb database, which the SQL Executive uses to determine when and what to execute.

You can see the task's execution history by clicking the Task History button on the toolbar (see Figure 7.11) or by clicking the History button in the Edit Task dialog box (see Figure 7.10). The task's execution history is stored in the Syshistory table in Msdb. The history record contains the date the task was executed, the last result, the operator e-mailed and the duration of the task. If the task generated an error message, the message is displayed in the text box at the bottom of the screen.

A task's most recent return status is displayed in the Manage Scheduled Tasks window (Figure 7.9), which indicates when the task was last run and whether it was successful. To limit the size of the task history list, use the Task Engine Options dialog box (Figure 7.14), which you display by clicking the Task Engine Options button on the toolbar.

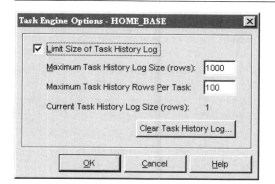

Figure 7.14
*Tasks Engine Options
Dialog Box*

Running Tasks, the second tab in the Manage Scheduled Tasks window, lists the current activity for scheduled tasks (see Figure 7.15). This list includes the task's name, owner, type, start date, and status. To stop a running task, click the Stop Task button on the toolbar or right-click the task and choose Stop. You can also display the task's history through the menu that appears when you right-click over the task in the list.

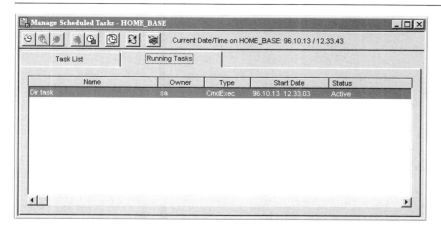

Figure 7.15
*Manage Scheduled
Tasks, Running
Tasks Tab*

To remove tasks from the Task List, select the task and click the Delete Task button on the toolbar or right-click the task and choose delete. You can also use the following system stored procedure to remove the task:

```
sp_droptask {name | loginname | id}
```

If system table updates are allowed by setting the Allow Updates flag in the server configuration values, you can remove the records from systasks directly. If you are going to update the system table directly, you should remove the history records for a task before removing the task. The sp_drop-task system procedure automatically deletes these records before dropping the task.

You can refresh the Task List by clicking the Refresh button on the toolbar (see Figure 7.11), which updates the current status, the last date run, and the execution duration. The entries in the Running Task list change quickly and are especially prone to being out of date; be sure to refresh your screen periodically.

Alerts, Operators, and Error Messages

When automated systems detect problems, some sort of human intervention is often necessary to solve the problems. SQL Server lets you define operators, specify when they are scheduled to be available, and provide information concerning how to contact them. You can assign system notifications to one or more operators, and the database can attempt to contact them through e-mail or an e-mail pager. You can also define and manipulate the error messages that users receive.

You use the Manage Alerts and Operators dialog box both to define alerts and to assign operators to handle them. To open this dialog box, you have three options: select Alerts and Operators from the Server Menu in the Enterprise Manager, right-click the SQL Executive icon in the Server manager, or click the Manage Alerts and Operators button in the Enterprise Manager's toolbar.

Alerts

Alerts are events that trigger a response from the SQL Executive. The SQL Executive constantly monitors the Windows NT event log. If SQL Server is set up to register failures in the Windows NT event log, the SQL Executive can monitor and report on specified events. It can then use e-mail facilities to contact the operator assigned to that alert.

The first tab on the Manage Alerts and Operators dialog box displays the alerts that have been defined (Figure 7.16). This list is an overview of the alerts and the last time each occurred. You can edit an alert by double-clicking it or by selecting it and clicking the Edit Alert toolbar button (Figure 7.17). The toolbar lets you access the same options as the Enterprise Manager's File Menu.

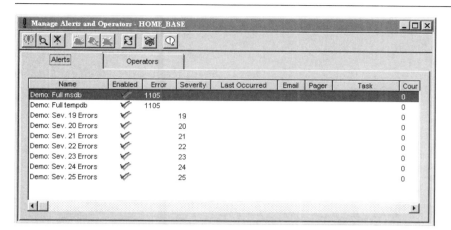

Figure 7.16
Manage Alerts and Operators, Alerts Tab

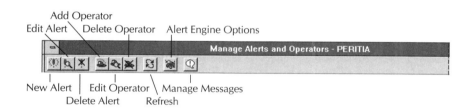

Figure 7.17
Manage Alerts and Operators Toolbar

The Edit Alert dialog box (Figure 7.18) displays the alert's ID number and name at the top. You define the event that causes the alert in the Alert Definition box. An alert can be triggered by a specific error number or by a message of a particular severity. You can also tie an alert to a specific database. If you do not specify a database in the Database Name field, the alert criteria will be applied to all databases.

You can further filter the alert so that it is triggered by messages containing certain text. The text filter can be used in conjunction with the Severity level or the Error Number filters, but it is most useful when a severity of error is specified rather than a specific error message. By setting the alert to be triggered by certain text within an error message, the alert can be directed to a specific operator depending on the databases that the error occurs in or the name of the object that is being accessed.

In the Response Definition box, you specify a task to be performed in response to the error and enable an SNMP trap to signal the SNMP agent of the alert. This agent then communicates with SNMP applications that monitor

Figure 7.18

*Edit Alert
Dialog Box*

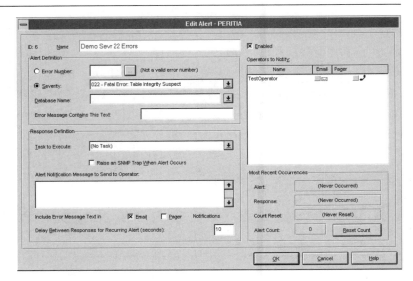

and report on the status of SQL Server databases. These monitoring applications can be resident on any platform. The agent within SQL Server recognizes the trap and relays the notification to the applications through SNMP. You can define a text message of up to 255 characters that will be sent to an operator either by pager or e-mail or both. The Delay Between Responses for Recurring Alert value sets a time that must elapse between events before the notification is sent again. This feature stops SQL Server from sending mail messages for an alert that recurs in a short period, such as a full transaction log.

You assign operators to receive the notification in the Operators to Notify section of the Edit Alert dialog box. We recommend that you build in some redundancy in notification to guarantee that at least one of the assigned operators receives and can respond to the message.

The last time the alert occurred and the last time the system responded are displayed in the lower right section of the dialog box. Every time the alert occurs, the Alert Count box is incremented. Pushing the Reset Count button sets the Alert Count to zero and sets the Count Reset date. Both the last time the count was reset and the number of times the alert has occurred since the last reset are displayed in the Count Reset field.

To add a new alert, click the New Alert button on the Manage Alerts and Operators toolbar (see Figure 7.16). The New Alert dialog box in Figure 7.19 has the same features as the Edit Alert dialog box, except that no task information appears.

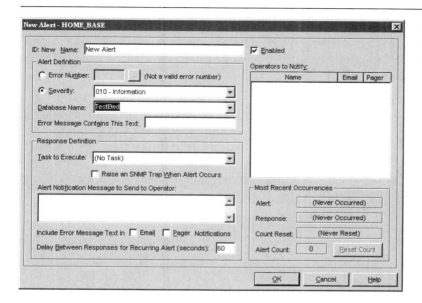

Figure 7.19
*New Alert
Dialog Box*

You can also add an alert with the Transact-SQL command below:

```
sp_addalert name, message_id, severity [, enabled]
[, delay_between_responses] [, notification_message]
[, include_event_description_in] [,database_name]
[, event_description_keyword] [, task_name]
```

To add operators for notification, the Transact-SQL command is

```
sp_addnotification alert_name, operator_name,
notification_method
```

where notification_method can be EMAIL, PAGER, or BOTH.
You modify alerts using the following two stored procedures:

```
sp_updatealert name [, new_name] [, enabled] [, message_id]
[, severity] [, delay_between_responses]
[, notification_message] [, include_event_description_in]
[, database_name] [, event_description_keyword] [, task_name]
[, occurrence_count] [, count_reset_date] [, count_reset_time]
[, last_occurrence_date] [, last_occurrence_time]
[, last_response_date] [, last_response _time]

sp_updatenotification alert_name, operator_name,
notification_method
```

To drop alerts and notifications, use the following two stored procedures:

```
sp_dropalert name
sp_dropnotification alert_name, operator_name
```

The alerts and notifications are kept as records in the Sysalerts and Sysnotifications tables in Msdb. The operator must be defined in Sysoperators and the alert must exist in Sysalerts to add a notification record using the stored procedures.

Alert Engine Options

The Alert Engine Options dialog box can be called up from the Manage Alerts and Operators toolbar and has two tabs, one to define fail-safe operators and one to set up the pager e-mail system if you need to integrate special prefixes or addresses with e-mail.

The Pager-Fail-Safe Operator (Figure 7.20) is notified if the alert is unable to notify the assigned operator because of e-mail or pager failure. The fail-safe operator is also notified if the alert notification was to be sent by a pager and the alert occurs during a gap in the pager notification schedule.

Figure 7.20

*Alert Engine Options,
Fail-Safe Tab*

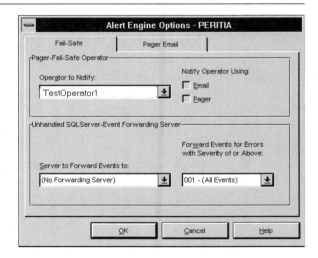

In the Unhandled SQL Server-Event Forwarding Server section, you specify a server to which alerts can be sent if they are not handled by the local alert notification setup. These events are written to the forwarding server's Windows NT event log, and if SQL Executive is running at the for-warding server, these alerts will be handled as local alerts. This feature lets you administer alert notification for several servers from one centralized location.

You should be careful when you set up tasks to handle alerts on the for-warding server. It is possible that the server may attempt to handle an alert as a local event when the alert in fact occurred on a remote server, which can lead to confusion and wasted time. It is best to put text filters on messages to determine where the message came from. If the defined error messages hold the originating server's name in the text of the message, the errors can be fil-tered more easily. Confusion can be minimized by adding the text of the error messages to the e-mail or pager notification.

With the Pager Email tab (Figure 7.21), you set up e-mail names with a prefix or suffix of a pager-specific string. Some e-mail pager systems require prefixes or suffixes to direct user mail to the pager. You can also address the CC Line prefix and suffix and, in the Subject fields, specify a subject for pages that are generated through e-mail. If your paging system will support it, you can include the body of the e-mail message in the page.

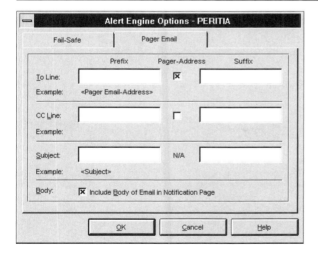

Figure 7.21
Alert Engine Options, Pager Email Tab

Operators

The second tab on the Manage Alerts window lists the defined operators (see Figure 7.22). This tab displays the operator's e-mail and pager names and the last time the operator was notified by each of these means.

Figure 7.22
Manage Alerts and Operators, Operators Tab

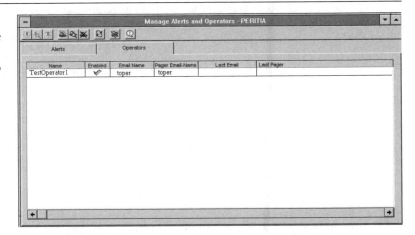

To edit an operator, double-click an operator, right-click over the operator in the list and choose Edit, or click the Edit Operator button on the toolbar. The Edit Operator dialog box appears (Figure 7.23). This dialog box presents the operator ID and the operator's e-mail and pager e-mail names. You can also define a pager schedule, setting which workdays and times to use the pager to locate the operator. You can set up different times for pager notifications on weekends. A list of defined alerts and the last time the operator received notification of each alert is on the right side of the dialog box. You assign notifications for specific alerts to the operator by checking the Pager and/or Email check boxes in the list of alerts.

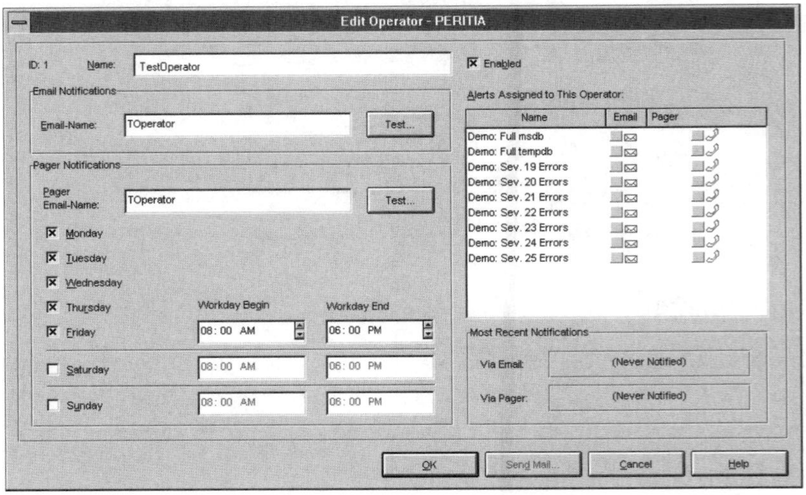

Figure 7.23
Edit Operator Dialog Box

To add new operators, click the Add Operator button on the Manage Alerts and Operators toolbar (whoever decided the icon should be a fireman's hat should be complimented). The New Operator dialog box (Figure 7.24) has the same layout and functionality as the Edit Operator dialog box.

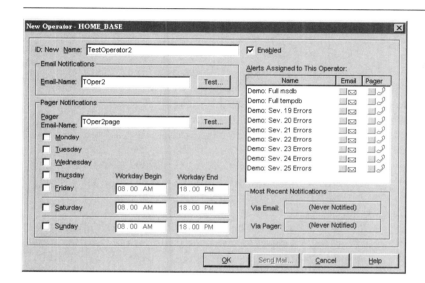

Figure 7.24
New Operator Dialog Box

The following Transact-SQL commands perform the same tasks as the Edit Operator and New Operator dialog boxes. The operator information is kept as a record in the Sysoperators table in Msdb.

```
sp_addoperator name [, enabled] [, email_address]
[, pager_number] [, weekday_pager_start_time]
[, weekday_pager_end_time] [, saturday_pager_start_time]
[, saturday_pager_end_time] [, sunday_pager_start_time]
[, sunday_pager_end_time] [, pager_days]

sp_updateoperator name [, new_name] [, enabled]
[, email_address] [, pager_number] [, weekday_pager_start_time]
[, weekday_pager_end_time] [, saturday_pager_start_time]
[, saturday_pager_end_time] [, sunday_pager_start_time]
[, sunday_pager_end_time] [, pager_days]
```

Defining Error Messages

Error message management can significantly ease the administration of a database and can also make troubleshooting in development much more straightforward. A well-laid-out procedure for creating and adding error messages to a database can make finding problems and isolating their causes relatively easy. Using error severity consistently and applying strict ranges to error numbers for various types of error messages reduces the response time in troubleshooting.

To manage your messages, select Server, Messages from the Enterprise Manager's main menu or use the Manage Messages toolbar button in the Manage Alerts and Operators dialog box. At this dialog box, you can view and edit all the error messages defined on the server and add new ones. It also is a great way to search for error messages containing specific text. This feature is particularly handy when your users call and know they received an error but can't remember the number or the exact words. Although the system messages cannot be deleted or changed, you can control whether they show up in the Windows NT event log with the "Always write to the NT Event log" check box.

You can edit, delete, or add user-defined messages by selecting a message and clicking the Edit button to display the Edit Message dialog box (Figure 7.25). Here, you can change the severity, error message, and Windows NT logging status of user-defined messages.

Figure 7.25

Manage SQL Server Messages Dialog Box

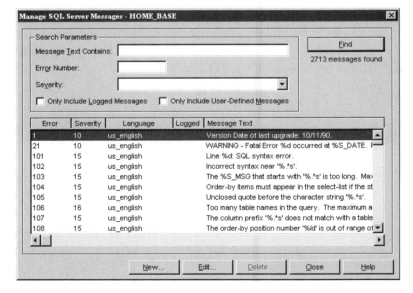

You add user messages by clicking New on the Manage Messages toolbar. User-defined messages must be assigned an error number larger than 50,000. The default method for assigning a number to a message is to assign the smallest available error number. Every new version of SQL server suggests that you use a higher starting number for user-defined error messages, because they keep adding system messages. Because these numbers keep changing, you must change your old ones when you upgrade. We recommend that you do yourself a favor and start with a bigger number than they suggest, such as 100,000 instead of 50,000. And while we're on the subject, it's helpful if you have a numbering scheme in place so that you can easily identify the module, screen, and database activity that generates a certain range of numbers. Your support desk will thank you for it.

You use the Severity field to set the severity of an error. Any message text up to 255 characters can be assigned to the error. The error message can have formatting parameters that may be used with RAISERROR, allowing the message to be customized at the time of the error.

User-defined messages can signal many events on the database. Typically, these messages are customized error messages for an application. You can also use them in more inventive ways, such as sending a page to signal certain database values. For example, you could create a message that pages a sales manager when sales go above a certain level or notifies a stock clerk when an inventory value falls below a preset limit. You can also send a message to the Windows NT event log when a procedure has completed successfully, setting up this message to initiate a new task. The messages don't have to indicate errors only, so use your imagination.

Summary

SQL Server 6.5 contains many significant improvements to the administrative tools. The SQL Executive allows for hands-off maintenance and system-controlled notification. Using SQLMAINT lets you start multiple maintenance tasks with one command and execute backups that depend on the successful completion of consistency checks. The ability to signal certain operators when specific events occur dramatically reduces the need for monitoring the database. E-mail and pager notification is the first step on the way to databases that are fully integrated with e-mail systems, so that users can be notified when database information becomes significant instead of being forced to check important values constantly. As the RDBMs evolve, user notification through email and pager will most likely become part of the programming language, thereby allowing these sorts of notifications to be added directly to the database code.

Chapter 8

Database Devices

The lowest-level system construct for data storage in SQL Server is the device. A device is a disk file within which data is stored. The two types of devices are database devices and backup devices. Backup devices will be covered in Chapter 12, "Database Backup." In this chapter, we discuss database devices, how they are created, and how to manage them, including such issues as device mirroring and segmenting.

What Are Devices?

Database devices are storage locations for both data structures and transaction logs. One database device can store many databases, and a database can be stored across more than one device. Installing SQL Server creates three devices. The Master database device is used by the Master, Model, Tempdb, and Pubs databases. The Msdbdata and Msdblog database devices are used by the Msdb (scheduling) database and its transaction log, respectively.

At its most basic level, a database device is a file created by SQL Server. The device file has a fixed length when it is created and is given a .dat suffix by default. When a device is created, SQL Server initializes the file storage to create the structure needed to write and retrieve records. If you install SQL Server on a freshly formatted drive, the initialization process will create the file structure using contiguous disk space, thereby enhancing serial reads when they occur. Optimally, you should create devices as one of the first steps in configuring the network server. It is also a good practice to devote volumes (preferably physical volumes) exclusively to SQL Server to reduce fragmentation of the free space and allow future allocation to be created with minimal discontinuity.

The device initialization process relies on the operating system to provide a clean file for the device. In a FAT file system, the file bytes are set to zero on file creation. In NTFS file systems, the file image is presented to SQL Server with zeroed values. Rather than initializing every bit, the file is marked as new; when a program reads from noninitialized sectors, the operating system presents zeroed values. The initialization process also creates the logical division of the devices into allocation units, extents, and pages. An allocation unit is 512K, or 0.5 MB, and an extent is eight 2K pages, or 16K. Therefore, each allocation unit contains 32 extents or 256 pages. SQL Server ensures that each allocation unit is contiguous; that is, an allocation unit is one "chunk" of space. However, SQL Server doesn't guarantee that the device consists of contiguous allocation units; allocation units may be separated from other allocation units.

During initialization, SQL Server maps the device file storage. This process stores the page allocation information in the allocation page, which is the first page of the allocation unit (the 0 page of each block). The pages of a device are numbered consecutively starting at zero, and every 256th page holds the allocation page for the allocation unit. The allocation page holds the disk address of the header for each page within the allocation unit.

Creating Database Devices

You can create database devices through the Enterprise Manager or by using the Disk Init statement. From the Enterprise Manager, choose Database Devices from the Manage menu to display the Manage Database Devices window (Figure 8.1). The Manage Database Devices window can also be accessed by right-clicking over a Database Devices entry in the Server Manager window and choosing Edit from the menu that appears.

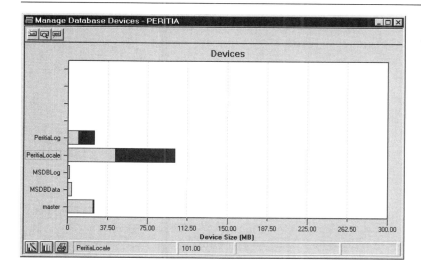

Figure 8.1

Manage Database Devices Window

This window displays all the defined database devices for the current server. The three toolbar buttons in the upper left corner create a new device, edit the currently selected device, and delete the currently selected device. The buttons in the lower left provide access to the graph display and print options. The status bar at the bottom displays the currently selected drive and the number of megabytes that have already been allocated as storage within the device.

To create a new database device, click the New Device button or choose New Device from the Enterprise Manager's File menu. (This menu option is available when the Manage Database Device dialog box is open.) The New Database Device dialog box will appear (Figure 8.2).

In this dialog box, you specify the name of the device to be created and its physical storage location. The default file name is the name of the device with a .dat extension. Although you can change this name, we recommend

Figure 8.2

New Database
Device Dialog Box

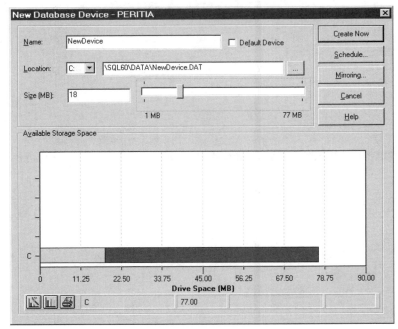

that you use the default name, because it retains the connection between the logical device name and the device's physical storage. All the storage devices to which you can write files are displayed in the drop-down box next to the Location field, and the path and name for the physical location is displayed next to the drive letter.

The Available Storage Space graph displays the amount of free space on the disk specified in the Location field and displays the relationship between the new allocation and the available space. Although SQL Server allows devices to be created in 2K increments, this user interface will allow creation of devices only in megabyte increments. You can type numbers in the Size field or use the sliding control to set the size of the device. We explain how to create smaller devices, or to specify a size that is not a whole megabyte (for example, 1.5 MB) later in this chapter.

You can mark the device you're creating as a default device by checking the Default Device box. A default device is a device on which new databases and logs are created unless a different device is specified in the Create statement or unless the Log On option is used. Any number of devices can be specified as default devices; SQL Server will use the default devices in alphabetical order, one at a time. When SQL Server is installed, the Master device is the only default device that is defined. However, you should not leave the Master device as a default device, because this device should only be used by the Master database. If no devices are set as defaults, the Create Database statement must specify which device is to be used. In most cases, you will want to control where your databases are created so you may not want to define default devices. For ease, you may want to use defaults on your development server.

The Create Now button on the New Database Device dialog box creates the device immediately. Creating database devices causes a large volume of disk I/O as the pages are initialized and allocation maps generated. Because this high volume can adversely affect users, you should consider scheduling device creation for off hours. To schedule device creation, click the Schedule button to display the Schedule Database Device Creation dialog box (Figure 8.3).

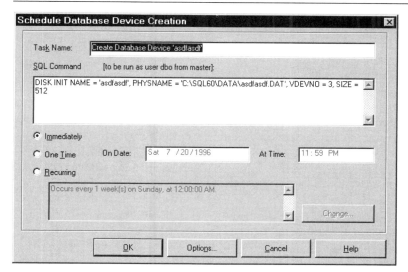

Figure 8.3
Schedule Database Device Creation Dialog Box

This dialog box is fundamentally the same as the rest of the task scheduling dialog boxes. You can launch the creation of your device at any time, on any day, or on many days. We strongly recommend that you do not schedule a device creation as a recurring event, because re-creating the device will cause errors and will be unsuccessful. By default, the task will execute in the Master database under the SA login account. Even if you want to create the device now, you can use this feature to "schedule" it and then do other things, instead of waiting for the device creation to finish before you can close this window.

You can also create database devices using the Transact-SQL statement

```
DISK INIT
NAME = 'logical_name',
PHYSNAME = 'physical_name',
VDEVNO = virtual_device_number,
SIZE = number_of_2K_blocks
[, VSTART = virtual_address]
```

The Disk Init command is also displayed in the window of the Schedule Database Device Creation dialog box in Figure 8.3. The virtual device number in the Disk Init command is a unique value that identifies the device in SQL Server. Up to 255 database devices can be defined; the device numbered 0 is reserved for the Master device.

The Disk Init statement can be executed from any command interface to the database. The virtual device number will be generated by the system if the Manage Database Device screen is used; otherwise, it must be provided by the user. An error will occur and the device will not be created if the device number is not unique.

If you wish to create a device with a size other than some whole number of megabytes, you can edit the SQL command on the scheduling screen in Figure 8.3, specifying the exact number of 2K pages that you want the device to have. It is important to remember that the size in this command is given in 2K pages. Keep in mind that when you use the Manage Database Devices window, you pick a size of the database in megabytes. Therefore, we recommend that you choose a size for your device that is a multiple of 512 (512 × 2K = 1 MB). (In cases where you want to create a database in half-megabyte increments, the device size should be given as a multiple of 256.) In reality, you can specify any number you want to here and SQL Server will build the file. However, because SQL Server divides this space into half-megabyte increments to be given to databases, any space that isn't in at least a half-megabyte chunk will be wasted. Windows NT will not give it to any other process and SQL Server cannot use it.

The stored procedure sp_helpdevice [*logical_name*] reports the critical information about the device specified or, if no database device is specified, it will display information about all of the devices. The procedure gives you the virtual device numbers, the current status of the devices, and a system description of the device. After your SQL Server implementation is complete, you should record the device numbers along with their physical file names to help you recover from failures. SQL Server doesn't really care about the device numbers when you are trying to restore, as long as you don't pick one that is in use. As you will see when we discuss recovering from a failure (Chapter 13), you should save the Disk Init commands to a file in case you need to re-execute them. Having the file will save you a lot of time and headache when you're looking for the information.

The device information is stored in the Master database's sysdevices table. The device record in the table contains the current status and type of the device, the device name, the physical file name, the name of the mirror device (mirroring is explained later in this chapter), the first and last virtual page numbers the device contains, and the size of the device. You shouldn't need to adjust these records manually, and you should not perform manual updates on the sysdevices table unless you can find no other way to resolve whatever problem exists.

Editing Devices

After you have created a database device, you may need to edit its configuration for two reasons. Occasionally, you may need to change the default device. If the current default device fills up, you can create a new device and specify it as the default instead of extending the size of the current default device. Increasing the size of a device is the other reason to edit a device configuration. You cannot reduce the size of a device, but it is often necessary to increase the size of the device as the database grows. The ability to increase the size of a device was a much-needed enhancement included first in version 6.0.

You display the Edit Database Device dialog box (Figure 8.4) by right-clicking the device name in the Server Manager and choosing Edit or by clicking the Edit button in the Manage Database Devices window.

This dialog box displays the name and location of the device and the current database usage of the device. At this dialog box, you can increase the size of the device and set it as the default device. The usage information shows which databases have allocations on the current device and the size of those allocations.

Just as you can schedule a database device to be created at a later time, you can also schedule the expansion of a device. The Schedule button on the Edit Database Device dialog box gives you the same options as the Schedule button on the New Database Device dialog box.

The Transact-SQL statement

```
DISK RESIZE
NAME = 'logical_device_name',
SIZE = final_size {Note: This is the final size, not the
amount you are adding on}
```

Figure 8.4
Edit Database Device
Dialog Box

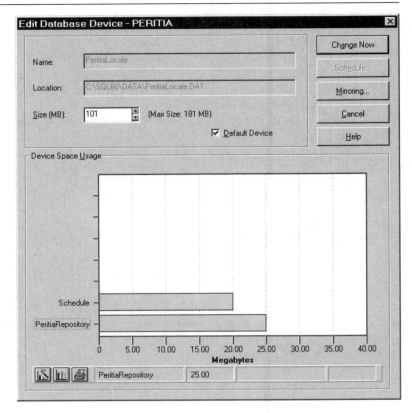

expands the device to the specified size, given in 2K pages. It will not decrease the size of the device or change any of the already-existing database allocations.

To specify a default device or remove a device from the pool of defaults, use the following stored procedure.

```
sp_diskdefault logical_device name, {defaulton | defaultoff}
```

Removing Devices

In the life cycle of a database server, it is occasionally necessary to remove database devices. You can remove a database device by right-clicking the name of the device in the Server Manager and choosing Delete. Your other two options are selecting the device and clicking the Delete button in the Manage Database Devices window or selecting Delete from the Edit menu in the Enterprise Manager.

You cannot delete a device that contains allocations for a database without first dropping those databases. If you wish to consolidate the device structure so that SQL Server will reduce the number of devices being used, first back up the databases that have allocations on the devices you wish to remove. After they are backed up, drop the databases and delete the devices that you are removing, and create the new device(s) and re-create the databases on the new device(s). Then restore the databases from the dumps.

The restoration will produce error warnings about the segment mappings of the restored databases, but the DBCC NEWALLOC command occasionally removes these errors when it is run. Allocation pages mapped to segments that do not exist because the segment mapping has changed are most easily fixed by dropping and rebuilding the clustered index on the table that has the error. If no clustered index exists, one of the nonclustered indexes can be created as a clustered index and then re-created as a nonclustered index. If DBCC reports that a system table has allocation pages on segments that no longer exist, the best course of action is to drop and re-create the user-defined objects on the database. For example, if the sysprocedures table has allocation pages that are not contained on a valid segment, the triggers, procedures, and views can be dropped and re-created.

When a device is deleted through the Enterprise Manager, the physical file is not removed. After deleting the device, you can delete the file directly using normal file deletion processes. The stored procedure

```
sp_dropdevice logical_name [, DELFILE]
```

has the optional parameter Delfile, which will remove the physical file and delete the device from SQL Server. This parameter was new in version 6.0. If you are using the Manage Database Devices window, you must manually delete the file to free up the space and reuse the file name. If you are using a version earlier than 6.0, you must stop SQL Server to close the file before you can delete it.

Device Mirroring and Segments

In a holdover from earlier versions, SQL Server still supports its own device mirroring and segment mapping. These capabilities are usually provided through hardware controllers or the operating system. Microsoft makes no promises to include support for these capabilities in future releases of SQL Server, so we generally recommend that you not use SQL Server to manage mirroring and segment mapping. Instead, we suggest that you rely on hardware-level data protection such as RAID and hardware mirroring. More modern methods of mirroring and disk striping can significantly reduce the relative complexity of administrative tasks. However, because SQL Server supports these features and they can have application in specific environments, we will consider mirroring, segments and striping, and RAID technologies.

Special Note

Note that if you are using the disk striping capabilities of Windows NT, you will need to set up disk striping before you create your SQL Server devices.

Device Mirroring

SQL Server mirrors a database device by creating a secondary device that is a copy of the primary device and duplicating all the changes written to the primary device onto the secondary device. This mirroring process is especially useful if the secondary device is on a separate disk controller and the mirroring can be done without competing for disk I/O on the primary device.

Although the secondary device is not required to be on a separate physical drive, it should be to provide reliable backup. When a device is mirrored, the secondary device will automatically be used to replace the primary device if it fails.

Remember that mirroring is done at the device level. If a database is not contained in a single device, you need to mirror *every* device that the database is using and make sure that you are not including fragments of other databases in these device files.

You display the Mirror Database Device dialog box (Figure 8.5) by clicking the Mirroring button on the New Database Device dialog box or on the Edit Database Device dialog box. You can also access this dialog box by right-clicking the device name in the Server Manager and choosing Mirror from the menu.

Figure 8.5

Mirror Database Device Dialog Box

Through this dialog box, you can specify a secondary device to act as a mirror. If you're creating a new device, the secondary device will also be created. If you want to mirror an existing device, the Mirror Database Device dialog box displays a Mirror Now button. If you are in the process of creating a new database device, the Create Mirror button is displayed on the Mirror Database Device dialog box. Clicking this button creates the secondary device immediately and prepares it to act as the mirror. If data is in the primary device, SQL Server makes a complete copy to the mirror. This process is nearly the same as creating a new database device and it creates a large amount of disk activity. We recommend creating mirrors during periods of low database usage.

Unfortunately, the Enterprise Manager does not provide a direct way to schedule when the mirroring will take place. You can use the Transact-SQL statement below and the Task Manager to schedule mirroring for off-hours.

By default, the mirror file is created with the same name as the primary device and a .mir extension. The file name specified for the mirror device cannot already exist. The Mirror Database Device dialog box truncates the mirror name to eight characters by default. As we mentioned earlier, you should create the mirror device on a separate physical storage device.

The Transact-SQL statement to create a mirror device is

```
DISK MIRROR
NAME = 'logical_name',
MIRROR = 'physical_name'
[, WRITES = {SERIAL | NOSERIAL}]
```

The Writes option is left in for compatibility with SQL Server on other platforms that could specify this option in script files. All mirroring performed by SQL Server uses the equivalent of the Serial option, which forces the write to the primary device to be completed before the secondary write begins. When mirroring is done through a single disk controller, this process can adversely affect performance, so we highly recommend using a second disk controller if SQL Server is going to provide its own mirroring. Normally, system-level mirroring uses two disk controllers to maintain throughput at reasonable levels.

Ordinarily, you create mirrors so that they are available to be used when the disk containing the primary device fails. You use the Unmirror Device dialog box (Figure 8.6) to begin using the secondary device when the primary fails. Unfortunately, it can be difficult to determine whether a device is mirrored. The Manage Database Devices window displays mirrored and unmirrored devices in the same way, so you must examine sysdevices, use the sp_helpdevice procedure, or click the Mirroring button from the Edit Database

Figure 8.6
Unmirror Device
Dialog Box

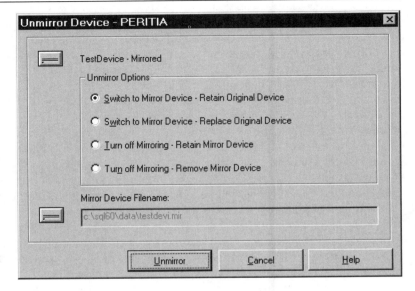

Device dialog box to see whether a particular device is mirrored. If a device has a mirror defined, the Mirroring button on the Edit Database Device dialog box displays the Unmirror Device dialog box in Figure 8.6. To use the mirrored device, select one of the first two options and click Unmirror.

If you choose Switch to Mirror Device - Retain Original Device, the secondary device is used as the primary device, any changes to data or structure are stored on it, and mirroring is turned off. The secondary device is left in the sysdevices record and the primary device name stays the same. The value of 482 in the sysdevices status field record indicates that a mirror exists but the device is currently not being mirrored.

Special Note

Typically, the status field for a physical device is 2. The status of a mirrored device that is working correctly is 738. Look under "System Tables (System Catalog)" in the Transact-SQL manual for all the status values.

You can reactivate the mirror by clicking the Mirroring button in the Edit Database Device dialog box; the secondary device name will default to the name originally defined for the mirror. Until the mirror is reactivated, the Mirror Database Device dialog box will indicate that the device is currently using the mirrored device by displaying "Running On Mirror" next to the device name.

If you choose Switch to Mirror Device - Replace Original Device, the secondary device name replaces the primary device name in the sysdevices record and the mirror name is set to null. The sysdevices record then indicates that no mirroring exists and the Mirror Database Device dialog box does not indicate the device is running from the mirror. You can re-mirror the device to another device name, which defaults to the current running device name with a .mir extension.

You can break mirroring without switching to the mirrored database by choosing one of the Turn off Mirroring options in the Unmirror Device dialog box. For example, you may wish to break a mirror if a large volume of transactions are to be processed and the database is going to be backed up afterwards; breaking the mirror will reduce the processing time. Once the backup is completed, you can reactivate the mirror.

Choosing the Turn off Mirroring - Retain Mirror Device option leaves the mirror name in the sysdevices tables and sets the status to indicate that a mirror exists and is not being used. When you click the Mirroring button in the Edit Database dialog box, the original mirror device name is displayed as the name of mirror device. Choosing Turn off Mirroring - Remove Mirror Device sets the device status to indicate that no mirroring is defined and sets the mirror device name to null.

To activate the mirror in the event of failure and then return the mirroring setup to its original configuration, follow the steps below.

1. If the physical file that originally contained the primary device still exists, switch to the mirror device using the Unmirror Device - Retain Original Device option. If the primary device file does not exist, use the Unmirror Device - Replace Original Device option.

2. If the primary device file exists, reactivate the mirror using the original mirror device name. The device is now configured as it was before the primary device failure. If the primary device file does not exist and the file was replaced in the previous step, the secondary mirror device is now the primary device. In this case, mirror the new primary device to a secondary device with the same name as the original primary device.

3. After the mirror is established using the original primary device name as the mirror, break the mirror with the Unmirror Device - Replace Original Device option. This process sets the new secondary device as the primary device and drops the mirroring. At this point the original device name has been restored and is ready to be remirrored to the original secondary device name.

4. You must delete the physical file for the original secondary device before you can mirror the primary device to a device with the same

name. After the primary device is mirrored to a secondary device with the same name as the original secondary device, the mirroring configuration will be identical to the configuration before the failure.

The process described above is much more complicated than using Windows NT's mirroring capability or a mirroring disk controller. Both methods will perform automatic mirror switching and rebuilding at startup.

Segments and Striping

SQL Server can also define segments and, through these segments, distribute I/O load across devices. A segment is a logical collection of disk storage that can consist of one or more devices. A database device can contain multiple segments, but we don't recommend this configuration because the objects using different segments will compete for the device space. You can't use the Enterprise Manager to define segments, and RAID controllers are a better method for distributing I/O.

Special Note

Disk striping is the process of writing bytes of data in parallel to two or more disks. Disk striping increases I/O capabilities and, with parity striping, can allow for on-the-fly replacement of disks in the set (hot-swap). RAID technology has greatly increased the reliability of disk storage systems and is generally more reliable and easier to administer than software-implemented data safeguarding.

The stored procedure sp_addsegment *segname, logical_name* maps the segment named to the database device given in *logical_name*. When you create a table or a nonclustered index on a table, you can specify a segment name; all data storage for that table or index then occurs on the named segment.

You can change the defined segment for a table or index using the stored procedure sp_placeobject *segname, objname*. This procedure forces future storage for the object to be written to the new segment. It does not affect the current storage, and thus splits table and index storage across the segments.

If you want to create a table or index on a specific segment, you must make sure that the database in which the table or index is created has access to the segment's database device(s) before you can build it on the segment. Therefore, either the segment must reside only on the database device that the database was created on or the device(s) that the segment is defined on must have allocations from the database that the table or index is being created in. You can create this setup by specifying the segment to be expanded onto in the Alter Database command.

This sort of segmenting is typically used to balance I/O loads across read/write heads in one of the following ways:

- Placing a table on one physical device and its nonclustered indexes on a different physical device
- Splitting a large, heavily-used table across database devices on two separate disk controllers
- Storing data for text and image columns on separate physical devices
- Placing a transaction log on a separate device so it can be dumped (usually by declaring a separate database device as the log device when creating the database)

Creating segments is quite complex, and you need a thorough understanding of devices to use segments successfully. Recovering from catastrophic failure is much more complicated when you use segments, because the segments must be completely defined before a database that uses them can be restored.

RAID Technology

If you are familiar with RAID (Redundant Array of Inexpensive Disks) technology, you will notice that SQL Server's mirroring and segmenting features are a much more complex way of accomplishing what RAID systems are designed to do. You could choose to mirror through the Windows NT operating system, but a RAID controller provides all the recoverability that a mirror provides. A notable exception is the system volume; the system volume cannot be part of a striped set, so mirroring is the only method of fault tolerance for it.

RAID controllers optimize disk access by distributing the disk I/O in parallel across multiple disks. Striped sets with parity let you recover data on one physical drive from the information stored on the other members of the striped set. Using hardware-controlled striping or mirroring is the optimal solution to data safeguarding. In general, a RAID system that allows hot-swapping of drives provides a system with the highest level of fault tolerance. We recommend this sort of setup for all production environments that require fast recovery from failure.

Typically, hardware devices that perform striping and mirroring are faster and more reliable than software implementations. More and more servers come with built-in RAID controllers and drives that can be hot-swapped. These advances in technology have made mirroring and segment mapping in SQL Server obsolete. At some point in the future, SQL Server will discontinue support for these features, so if you are responsible for a new implementation of SQL Server, don't use them unless you have no other solutions to the problems.

Summary

Database devices are the basis of SQL Server access to disk storage. Devices are organized files that are pre-allocated and mapped with extents and data pages. Database devices are used for data storage and transaction logs. SQL Server provides its own mirroring capabilities and can use segments to distribute I/O across physical volumes. This capability is a remnant of older version and should not be introduced in new implementations unless no other solution exists.

Chapter 9

Managing Databases

Database management encompasses creating, altering, and deleting databases. A database is a collection of logical pages on one or more database devices. You can think of a database as a container for related database objects. Database structure is defined by

- data tables that are defined by a set of relations,
- a group of procedures that manipulate the data in the tables, and
- a set of users and their permissions to access objects within the database.

The database is a logical construct that allows data to be stored and retrieved based on relationships within the data.

The number of databases that exist in any given SQL Server setup will vary, depending on how you implement your system. When you install SQL Server, the Master, Tempdb, Model, and Msdb databases are created; the sample database, Pubs, is optional. The Master database contains the system catalog, which describes the fundamental organization and configuration of SQL Server, including other databases, login information, and server information. Temporary objects created during the execution of queries and procedures are created in Tempdb. Other temporary workspace for sorting and joining tables also comes from Tembdb. When a database is created, its initial structure is copied from the Model database. The Msdb database contains information for system tasks such as replication, alerts, and maintenance tasks.

In this chapter, we examine

- the relationship between devices and databases
- the Master and Model databases
- creating databases
- modifying databases
- using removable media

Special Note

In the context of a database, a *relation* is an entity. A relation is a group of data that can be represented by a key and its corresponding information.

For example :

Employee ID

Employee First Name
Employee Last Name
Employee Birth Date

The relation defined above could be given a name, such as Employee Information, and be defined as a table within a database.

Devices and Databases

As discussed in Chapter 8, a database device is a collection of 2K pages grouped into 256-page allocation units. A database is a logical collection of pages from database devices. The pages are allocated to the database in 0.5 MB blocks (1 allocation unit) and need not reside on a single segment or device. The size of a device is specified in 2K pages, while the size of a database is specified in megabytes. Although it is unusual, it is possible when creating a database to ask for more space than is present in the device. As long as the device specified contains the minimum amount of space required to create the database, your database will be created, but it will have less space than you asked for — for example, it might be a 0.5 MB database instead of a 1 MB database. Fortunately, the new GUI tools make this coordination easier to manage, but be aware of it if you are creating a database from SQL commands.

Generally, it is best if the logical pages within a database device are physically contiguous and database allocations on those devices are composed of large groups of contiguous pages. It is not always possible to achieve this setup, but accurately estimating the size of the final database before you create it helps maintain the continuity of the physical storage. If the database isn't created large enough and must be enlarged later, data pages may not be contiguous and performance may be affected. If database objects are created so that they keep the data pages contiguous, the physical continuity can improve performance during scans of large tables and during mass alterations of data.

Sometimes physical continuity is undesirable. When a large number of users access the same database and database objects, it can be beneficial to split a database across multiple physical devices. Splitting the database in this way increases the likelihood that any given disk access will not be queued behind another request. You can set up devices and segments to

> **Special Note**
>
> Data pages for objects are allocated in extents of eight pages as the storage is needed. To increase the continuity of data pages, you can re-create the object on a segment that is not fragmented and then load the data immediately. As long as the logical pages of the devices are contiguous, this process will create relatively continuous allocation for the object that will be preserved when the data is relatively static. An alternative, if you have the space, is to create a clustered index for the table on the unfragmented segment. Even if you drop the index after you create it, creating the clustered index will move the data to the new segment. For more information about indexing, see Chapter 17, "Indexing."

help distribute a database across physical devices; however, data striping is more commonly performed by hardware devices.

In special cases, such as large reference tables, it may become advantageous to relocate heavily used objects on separate physical drives. As a rule of thumb, it is highly unlikely that you will derive any performance gain from allocating the table in discontinuous blocks on a single physical device; in fact, it is more likely that this sort of fragmentation will reduce disk performance.

Master and Model Databases

When you install SQL Server, it creates two databases that are instrumental: the Master database and the Model database.

Master Database

The Master database contains the system catalogs that describe other databases managed by SQL Server, the logins of database users, and information about remote servers and extended procedures. Generally, you should not add objects to the Master database and you should severely restrict access to it. You should not update the system tables directly unless no other solution to the problem exists, and then alterations should only be made by experts or under expert direction. Every time information in the Master database changes, you should make a complete backup to ensure that recovery from a severe failure is possible. If databases or devices are added and the system fails before the Master database is backed up, the added objects can be lost and recovery becomes a much more complicated process. (For more information about recovery, see Chapter 13, "Database Recovery.")

Many system stored procedures that can be used to edit data in the system tables are stored in the Master database. Some of these procedures are designed to give more "user friendly" information than just selecting raw data from the tables. Many can be called from within any database. For example, sp_remoteoption describes remote servers and logins stored in the sysservers and sysremotelogins tables.

Model Database

The Model database is the template for all databases created on SQL Server. The objects, users, and database settings in the Model database are the starting point for every new database. If any tables, procedures, rules, defaults, triggers, or other objects need to be in every database created on SQL Server, adding them to the Model database will ensure their existence in new databases.

This feature can be very useful, but it can also become problematic if users are allowed access to the Model database and add extraneous objects to it. Remember that users added to the Model database will be added to every other database created from that point forward, so exercise caution when you add users or groups to the Model database.

Tempdb, the database for temporary objects, is re-created from the Model database each time SQL Server is started, so adding objects such as user-defined datatypes to the Model database adds them not only to your new databases but to Tempdb as well. This feature is very helpful in maintaining consistency when creating temporary tables.

Creating Databases

The system administrator can create databases and can grant the Create DB permission in the Master database to other users either by using the Enterprise Manager or by using a Transact-SQL command. To use the Enterprise Manager, first access the Manage Databases window in Figure 9.1 by right-clicking the Databases collection in the Server Manager and choosing Edit or by choosing Manage, Databases from the Enterprise Manager.

The Manage Databases window displays the currently defined databases, their allocation, and their current usage. The bar graph displays the total size of the database; the used space is indicated by the secondary color fill in the bar. The graph also displays the allocation that is being defined. You can display a legend for the graph by clicking the graph wizard button in the lower left corner; the Graph Properties window will appear.

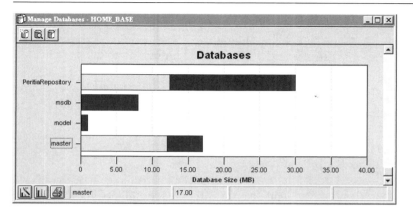

Figure 9.1
*Manage Databases
Window*

The next step in creating a database is bringing up the New Database dialog box. Click the New Database icon on the toolbar of the Manage Databases window; select Edit, New Database from the Enterprise Manager while the Manage Databases window is selected; or right-click the Databases collection in the Server Manager and select the New menu item. The New Database dialog box is shown in Figure 9.2.

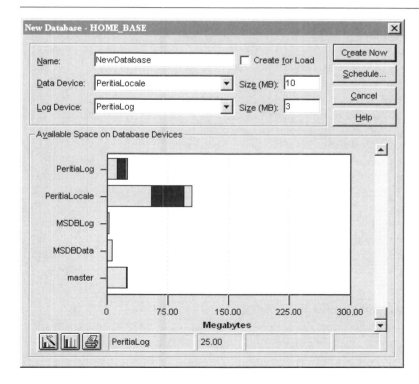

Figure 9.2
New Database Dialog Box

Enter the name for your new database in the top field. You set the names and sizes for your database device and log pages below the name. With the system administrator account, you can create a new database device from this screen by choosing New from the drop-down list for the Data Device field. The data pages and the log pages should be on separate devices if you want to dump the log independently of the database. In most circumstances, log pages should be created on separate devices from the data devices. For more details, see Chapter 12, "Database Backup."

If you are going to be restoring your database from a backup, you can create the database with the Create for Load box marked. Marking this box creates the database but doesn't initialize the pages and can be a good option to pick — the pages will be overwritten when you load the backup, so why waste time and effort? This feature can be especially useful for large databases, because initializing the pages can be a lengthy process.

The Create for Load option also sets the configuration value DBO Use Only. (Database configuration values are discussed in detail later in this chapter.) If no users have been added to the Model database, the administrator is the only user that is DBO in a new database. Setting the DBO Use Only flag effectively locks out all other users until the flag is reset, which lets the administrator completely set up new databases without interference from users. If users have been added to the Model database, they will automatically be added to newly created databases. If these users have an alias of DBO in the Model database, specifying Create for Load when you create the database won't lock these users out. (In development environments, it may be useful to map users into the Model database as DBO; however, generally mapping users into Model as DBO is NOT recommended.)

After completely setting up your database, you need to reset the For DBO Use Only configuration value with the sp_dboption stored procedure or by setting the database option through the Enterprise Manager (see "Modifying Databases," below).

You can schedule the creation of your database for a later time by clicking the Schedule button in Figure 9.2. Because the allocation process is very disk I/O intensive, it is often a good idea to schedule the creation of your database for a later time, particularly if you are creating a large database in a production environment. The scheduling process for database creation is fundamentally the same as the scheduling process for device creation and mirrors the scheduling of administrative tasks. By default, the scheduled task uses the Master database and executes the Transact-SQL statement below.

```
CREATE DATABASE database_name
[ON {DEFAULT | database_device} [= size]
```

```
  [, database_device [= size]]...]
[LOG ON database_device [= size]
  [, database_device [= size]]...]
[FOR LOAD]
```

This statement performs the same action as the New Database dialog box, with a few variations. The On Default option is not available through the user interface; it causes the new database to be created in the first available space on the default device(s). When you create a database with the Transact-SQL statement, you can specify multiple devices, whereas the window interface limits you to one device for data and one for the log. On the other hand, you cannot create the database with Transact-SQL if you haven't already created the devices. If you do not specify a size in the Transact-SQL statement, SQL Server uses the larger of two values: the size of the Model database or the server configuration value for Database Size. These values default to 1 MB and 2 MB, respectively, and are too small for most implementations. (In version 6.0, the default for the Model database changed to from 2 MB to 1 MB to accommodate users who want to create databases on a floppy disk.)

The creation of a database adds a record to the sysdatabases system table in the Master database. This record holds the database ID, the system user ID of the creator, the current status of the database, the creation date, and other detail information. (See the system table definitions in the SQL Server *Books Online*.) SQL Server can manage up to 32,767 databases, each of which can be up to 1 TB in size. Each database can have a maximum of 32 device fragments. Each of the devices specified in a Create Database statement represents a device fragment and is entered as a row in the sysusages system table. The total number of physical devices that can be used or the total size of each logical device is not limited. However, the physical device size is limited to 32 GB; and 32 device segments at 32 GB each is 1 TB.

Each device fragment can actually exist on one or more physical devices if some form of hardware or software striping is used. Striping is the process of storing information on disk in a way that allows I/O to be performed in parallel. Parity striping safeguards data by recording parity information, which allows the data to be reconstructed from the remaining drives if a disk fails.

Modifying Databases

After you create a database, you can alter its size and options. Most frequently, you will modify a database to increase its storage size. Occasionally, you will need to change the other database options, especially during recovery. To view and modify the database size and other options, right-click the database name in the Server Manager and choose Edit; double-click the database name in the Manage Databases window; or click the Edit button on the toolbar in the Manage Databases window. The Edit Database dialog box will appear. This dialog box has three tabs: Database, Options, and Permissions.

Database Size

The Database tab (Figure 9.3) displays usage information for the database, including the creation date, the database owner, the data size and data space used, the log size and log space used, and the version of SQL Server that created it. The tab also has buttons for expanding, shrinking, and recalculating the size of the database, as well as truncating the log.

Figure 9.3

Edit Database Dialog Box, Database Tab

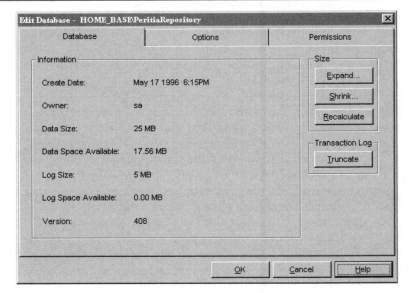

Expanding a Database

Clicking the Expand button displays the Expand Database dialog box in Figure 9.4. This dialog box is fundamentally the same as the New Database dialog box, except that you cannot specify the name and you cannot specify the Create for Load option.

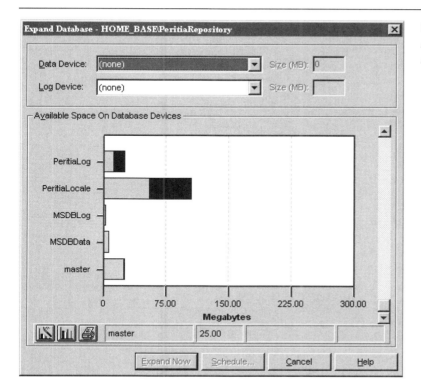

Figure 9.4
Expand Database Dialog Box

You can schedule the expansion of the database, just as you can schedule the creation of a new database. The scheduled expansion executes the Transact-SQL statement

```
ALTER DATABASE database_name
[ON {DEFAULT | database_device} [= size]
[, database_device [= size]]...]
[FOR LOAD]
```

Note that the Transact-SQL statement lets you alter the database with the For Load option. This option can be specified only if the database was originally created with the For Load option and the database option DBO Use Only has not been reset. You can specify multiple devices for the expansion; each device counts towards the limit of 32 segments per database.

If the database was originally created without the Log On option and you have not set the log device, or if you are designating an additional device for the log, you need to execute the stored procedure sp_logdevice to set the log on a separate device from the data. When the Expand Database dialog box creates the Alter Database statement for scheduling, it does not take this need into consideration. If a log expansion is specified for a database that has not had its log device separated from the data device, the scheduled task is formulated incorrectly — the scheduled task should execute the sp_logdevice stored procedure to move the log device. However, if you do not schedule your database expansion, the interface creates the correct usage information, including putting the log on a separate device.

Shrinking a Database

The Shrink button in the Edit Database dialog box in Figure 9.3 lets you reclaim unused space within a database. The database must be in single-user mode before it can be shrunk. If no one is currently connected to the database, the flag is set and the Shrink Database dialog box is displayed (Figure 9.5).

Figure 9.5
Shrink Database
Dialog Box

This dialog box shows the minimum size the database can have. The current size is displayed in the Database Size field. Although you cannot schedule shrinking a database from this screen, you can use the following DBCC command to set up a scheduled task:

```
DBCC SHRINKDB (database_name [, new_size [, 'MASTEROVERRIDE']])
```

If you do not specify a value for the size parameter, the database will be shrunk to its minimum size. Note that the new_size parameter is the final size, not the amount of space you are reclaiming. After it runs, the DBCC command displays the objects that exist in the database; the ones that are responsible for restricting the minimum size are listed as well. The minimum size is governed by both the amount of data in the database and the distribution of the pages that are in use. The less fragmented the used pages are, the smaller the minimum size, because database size can only be reduced by removing allocation units (each 512K). Knowing which objects are using a lot of space lets you drop and re-create these objects on allocations that are more contiguous and more proximal to the rest of the used pages. This process may reduce the minimum allowable size.

Shrinking a database is a fully logged event, which allows for normal recoveries, except in the case of the Master database. To shrink the Master database, you must start SQL Server in single-user mode, using the /m command-line option. If you use the DBCC SHRINKDB command, you must specify the Masteroverride option. After shrinking any database, especially the Master database, you should make a complete backup of the Master database and any user databases that were changed.

Truncating a Database Log

The Database tab of the Edit Database dialog box (Figure 9.3) also lets you truncate a log. When you click the Truncate button, the current database's log is dumped with the no_log option. (For more information about dumping logs, see Chapter 12, "Database Backup.") This option is helpful when you need to dump a completely full log.

Normally, dump operations are logged. When a transaction log becomes full, the dump operation cannot be logged, and the server will roll back the request. A full transaction log makes a database useless. The only way to get the database running again is to truncate the log — so remember where the Truncate button is.

Do not stop and start SQL Server when you get a message about a full log, because when SQL Server goes through automatic recovery, it tries to do a checkpoint in every database. It will mark a database as suspect if it can't find room in the log, and then recovery will be much harder. You may have to drop and re-create the database and restore from a backup.

Caution

You should not truncate the log using this button on production systems unless you plan to run a full database backup immediately following the truncation. (For a full discussion of backup and recovery, see Chapters 12 and 13.)

Database Options

You use the Options tab on the Edit Database dialog box (Figure 9.6) to set database options. You can set seven configurable options for each database from this dialog box.

Figure 9.6
*Edit Database Dialog
Box, Options Tab*

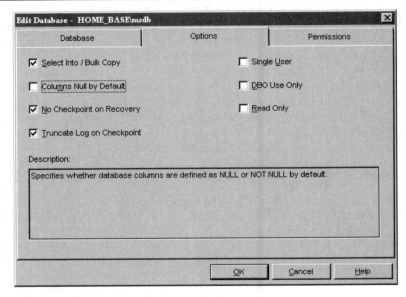

Select Into/Bulk Copy

The Select Into/Bulk Copy option allows non-logged operations to take place within the database. This option should only be used in production environments under controlled conditions — if you want to recover the database, you must dump the database in full after non-logged operations. For more information about the effect of non-logged operations on backup and recovery, see Chapters 12 and 13.

When you're troubleshooting or loading large amounts of data, it is often convenient to be able to replicate table structure, data, or both with the Select Into statement. If the database contains text fields, you must set this option to write the text pages. You must also check the box for this option if you want to perform a fast bulk copy (BCP).

Columns Null by Default

When this box is checked, newly created tables will allow nulls in columns unless the column is explicitly defined as not allowing nulls. You use this option to force SQL Server into ANSI compliance and to make your setup compatible with schemas that assume a column is null unless defined otherwise.

> **Tip**
>
> In programming, it is better not to rely on this setting, but to indicate the Null/Not Null parameter explicitly each time you create a table so that you have no question about the Null setting if you ever need to rebuild. You should specify Null/Not Null explicitly for temporary tables as well, especially when they are created inside stored procedures. If your application is using ODBC to get to SQL Server, be aware that ODBC sets this parameter on. If you have not explicitly declared Nulls, you might get a result that is exactly the opposite of what you expect.

No Checkpoint on Recovery; Read Only

These options are used primarily with standby servers. Sometimes you may want to maintain a hot backup by loading log dumps from the primary server to the secondary server. In this case, activating these two options will keep the checkpoints that are issued on shutdown and startup from recording the action in the transaction log. Future dumps from the production server can then be loaded even if the secondary server has been shut down. If you don't set these options, the checkpoint commands issued at shutdown and startup record the action in the transaction log, which causes different transaction counts on the production server and on the secondary server. Attempts to load more transactions into the database will fail.

The Read Only option is also used in static databases, such as remote reporting facilities.

Truncate Log on Checkpoint

This option forces SQL Server to perform a logged truncation of the transaction log whenever a checkpoint is issued. If the recovery interval (explained in Chapter 13, "Database Recovery") is set to a reasonable value, checking the box by this option will stop the transaction log from filling up. This feature can be useful when you're modifying very large databases or in development environments where data recoverability is not important. If you temporarily activate this option in a production environment, you should perform a complete database dump immediately after turning off this option. You cannot dump the transaction log until you reset the flag and do a full database dump. (See Chapter 12, "Database Backup.")

Single User, DBO Use Only

Checking these boxes restricts database access to a single user and to the users entering the database as DBO, respectively. If a database is created For Load, the Single User option is set automatically. It can be useful to restrict access to a single user if you're performing maintenance and you want the environment to remain stable. If many people are required to perform some maintenance chore, such as upgrades or a yearly cleaning, and you haven't given all users DBO rights within a database, the DBO Use Only option gives the proper permissions to those needing it while restricting other users.

Setting Options with Transact-SQL

You can also use the following Transact-SQL statement to set the options presented on the Options tab of the Edit Database dialog box.

```
sp_dboption [dbname, optname, {true | false}]
```

The options for this statement, listed below, are similar to those presented in the Edit Database dialog box, though the Transact-SQL statement lets you configure more options.

- ANSI Null Default
- DBO Use Only
- No Chkpt on Recovery
- Read Only
- Select Into / Bulk Copy
- Truncate Log on Checkpoint
- Offline
- Published

The ANSI Null Default option corresponds to the Columns Null by Default option in Figure 9.6. This option forces SQL Server into ANSI compliance. The rest of the options, except the Offline and Published options, all correspond directly to the options on the screen.

The Offline option is used primarily for databases on removable media and cannot be configured from the Edit Database dialog box. Setting the Offline option to True sets the status of the devices that contain the database to Deferred if the device has only allocations for the database on it. Databases placed offline are not recovered automatically at server startup. For more information about removable media, see page 168.

The Published option does not publish a database. Instead, it permits the tables of a database to be published. When set to True, the Published option lets the database publish data through replication and adds the user repl_subscriber to the database. It also marks all the tables as publishable.

By setting this option to False, you can also disable publishing, drop all publications, and unmark all transactions that were marked for replication in the transaction log. Although SQL Server *Books Online* indicates that setting this option to False also removes the database user repl_subscriber, it really doesn't under the first release version of 6.5.

In general, you usually set these options when you set up replication parameters, not from the Edit Database interface. (For more explanation of publishing and replication, see Chapter 11, "Replication.")

Database Permissions

The Permissions tab of the Edit Database dialog box (Figure 9.7) displays the statement permissions on the database. The database's users and groups are listed in the large window of this dialog box, along with the permissions they have been assigned for certain tasks. The tasks for which you can see permissions include creating and dropping database objects and dumping and recovering databases and their transaction logs. When you view this dialog box for the Master database, you can also modify users' permission to create a database. You need to be the SA or DBO to grant these permissions.

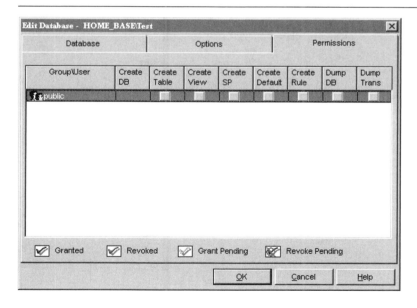

Figure 9.7
*Edit Database Dialog Box,
Permissions Tab*

Remember, if no permission is specified, it is assumed that permission does not exist. If a group is granted permission, all members of the group have permission unless their permission is explicitly revoked. For more information about permissions, see Chapter 10, "Administering Users and Security."

Tip

Generally, it is easier and safer for a single account to have permission to create and drop databases. However, if more than one administrator uses the SA account, you can't associate specific SA activities to a specific user. You may want to assign permissions to individual users so that they are forced to log on through separate accounts — in this way, their activities are logged and associated with their names.

Removable Media

It is possible to create a database on a device that uses media that can be distributed — moved around physically — such as CD-ROMs, tapes, and floppy disks. With larger removable media available, it is often more viable to distribute databases as complete entities instead of creating an installation script, creating the database, and then loading it with the necessary data at the installation site. Removable databases can also be used to secure information by keeping read-only data on removable media; for example, with some planning, you can move critical reference tables to removable media. Using removable media to create databases is particularly useful when, for example, a weekly update on reference material in a database is necessary; a CD could be distributed and used remotely without transferring the data to the server.

A database that will be used on a removable medium must be created on at least three devices: one for the system catalogs, one for the transaction log, and at least one for the data. The log device is used during development.

The following stored procedure can be used to create a database with the required device structure:

```
sp_create_removable dbname, syslogical, 'sysphysical', syssize,
loglogical, 'logphysical', logsize,
datalogical1, 'dataphysical1', datasize1
[... , datalogical16, 'dataphysical16', datasize16]
```

The syslogical, sysphysical, and syssize parameters give the logical name, physical location, and size of the device for the system catalogs. The transaction log device is defined with the Loglogical, Logphysical, and Logsize parameters. Up to 16 data devices are defined with the remaining parameters. The devices should not exceed the size of the medium being used. If necessary, you can use a third-party tool to split one file over multiple disks; however, size is usually only a problem when you're using diskettes as your removable medium.

You can also create a database for use on removable media without using the sp_create_removable procedure, as long as the following requirements are met:

- The devices the database uses must contain only the one database that is being created as removable; the allocation for the database must start at the beginning of the device.
- The administrator must be the owner of the database.
- The database must exist on at least three devices as described above.

After the database has been created, you can create tables and stored procedures, add data, and perform all the other normal development tasks. When development is complete, the following stored procedure can be used to prepare the database to be written onto the removable medium:

```
sp_certify_removable dbname[, AUTO]
```

This procedure sets the database offline and returns information that will be required when the database is later installed. This stored procedure creates a file named CertifyR_[dbname].txt, which is written to the Log subdirectory of the SQL Server installation directory. The information is delimited by commas. Records preceded by two hyphens (--) are considered comments. The permissions on xp_cmdshell must permit this file write. The Auto parameter sets the owner of the database and the database objects to SA, because the SA is the only user ID that can be guaranteed to exist on the server the database will be loaded on. The Auto parameter drops any other users (not groups) that have been created.

The certification process truncates the transaction log, moves it to the system device, and drops the log device. The physical and logical names and the size, in megabytes, of the system device and the data device(s) are returned. This information is used in the following install stored procedure:

```
sp_dbinstall database, logical_dev_name, 'physical_dev_name',
size, 'devtype' [,'location']
```

You must run this procedure wherever you are installing the database, for each device that the database is composed from. For the Devtype parameter, you can choose either Data or System, indicating a data device or the system device, respectively. The Location parameter must be provided for the system device, because the system device must be copied to the server. The data device can remain on the removable medium if it is read-only; in this case, no location needs to be specified. If the data device has been moved to a read/write medium, it can be made read/write by running sp_addsegment against the device and using sp_devoption to set the Read Only setting to False for that device.

Back at the development site, after you have copied a removable media database onto the removable medium, the stored procedure

```
sp_dbremove database[, dropdev]
```

can be run to remove the database from the system catalogs. If the Dropdev option is specified, the devices are removed from sysdevices also. The physical files are not deleted by this procedure — you can remove them using the standard file deletion process. If you prefer, you can just remove the database (without the dropdev option), then use

```
sp_dropdevice devicename, DELFILE
```

on each of the devices, and the physical files will be dropped. Neither option is better; it just depends on your preference and how many devices are involved.

Summary

The fundamental logical structure within SQL Server is the database. A database is a logical collection of logical device pages allocated on physical drives. SQL Server recognizes up to 32,768 databases of up to 1 TB apiece. Four databases are created when SQL Server is installed; these databases are used to control the server and the databases within it. The two most important of these databases are the Model database, which holds the template for the creation of new databases, and the Master database, which contains the system catalogs describing the current devices, databases, users, and other information contained in SQL Server. Databases can be expanded and shrunk and several options can be changed at any point after the database is created. Databases can be created to reside on removable media, which allows for easy installation and security for reference information.

Chapter 10

Administering Users and Security

One fundamental responsibility of a database administrator (DBA) is securing databases. In SQL Server 6.5, you manage database security by creating user accounts and groups and assigning access rights to database objects. SQL Server lets you map Windows NT users and groups into the SQL Server database, thus integrating SQL Server access with Windows NT's security. Although creating user accounts and groups and assigning rights is a straightforward process, the potential exists for DBAs to create a security system that rapidly becomes an administrative nightmare, or, even worse, fails to provide adequate protection.

This chapter shows you how to avoid such pitfalls. We cover the three models of database security — standard, integrated, and mixed — and give you issues to consider when setting up security systems for your database. Along the way, we show you the relationship among users, aliases, logins, and groups and explain the two kinds of access rights — statement permissions and object permissions.

Logins, Users, Aliases, and Groups

One of the basic challenges in any security system is keeping track of the collection of individuals that use the database. Under SQL Server's security layout, a user's rights are divided into two broad categories: the right to use the SQL server itself, which entails logging on to the SQL server (also known as login rights), and the right to use an object within a database (user access rights). Before we begin considering the various security setups available through SQL Server 6.5, let's consider some basic relationships.

Figure 10.1 shows a representation of the system tables and the relationships among logins, users, aliases, and groups (groups are stored in the user list). At the most basic level, all object rights are assigned to user IDs. These IDs can map either to group IDs or to a specific user. A login is mapped to a user in a database either directly, to a user account, or indirectly, through an alias to a current user. For example, in Figure 10.1, PeteM has the same rights in Database 1 as SueJ, because his login is mapped to Sue's userID, as shown in the alias list for Database 1.

Figure 10.1
System Tables and Relationships

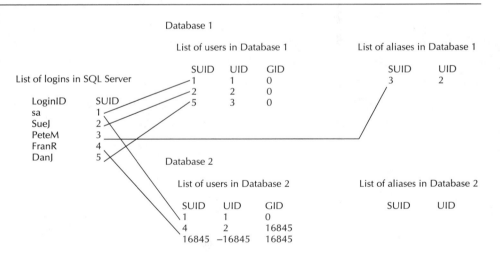

To further understand the relationships among logins, users, aliases, and groups, it's helpful to examine three system tables: syslogins, sysusers, and sysalternates.

Login information is stored in syslogins in the Master database. Here, a unique system user ID (SUID) is associated with the login name and password.

Every database the login has rights to has a record either in sysusers, with a matching SUID, or in sysalternates, also with a matching SUID.

In sysusers, the SUID is matched to a user ID (UID) unique within that database. The UID is also associated with a group ID (GID); to indicate that no GID is associated with the UID, the GID is assigned a value of zero. Although a UID is unique within a database, the UID is not unique across databases: The same UID value can exist in many databases, but it may be associated with different logins in those different databases. For example, in Figure 10.1 FranR has UID 2 in Database 2, while SueJ has UID 2 in Database 1. Group names are added to the sysusers table with a UID equal to the GID and an SUID equal to the negative of the GID.

The sysalternates table has two columns. The first column contains a valid SUID, and the second column contains a valid UID. This table provides a way to match any number of logins to a user in a database.

Standard Security

SQL Server 6.5's standard security relies on two basic concepts of user identification. The first, the user login, is the identity SQL Server associates with the right to request information from the server. The second concept is that of a user in a database, which is the identity SQL Server associates with specific access rights for objects in a database.

User Logins

To access database data, a user must first log on to SQL Server by providing a password and a login ID. This ID is associated with a user in one or more databases on the SQL Server system.

Remember that a SQL Server system can be the repository for many databases, so it's important to understand the distinction between the server and a database. A login gives access to the entire server.

Special Note

In SQL Server 6.5's standard security setup, you can create user logins either with the Manage Logins dialog box, which you can get to through several GUIs, or with stored procedures. First, we will go through your GUI options. From the Enterprise Manager, you can get to the Manage Logins dialog box by choosing Manage, Logins. From the Server Manager, go to Server Group, Server, Logins; then select Manage Logins and choose New

Login. The Enterprise Manager's toolbar also has a button that is a shortcut to this dialog box. Figure 10.2 shows the Manage Logins dialog box.

Figure 10.2

Adding User Logins with the Manage Logins Dialog Box

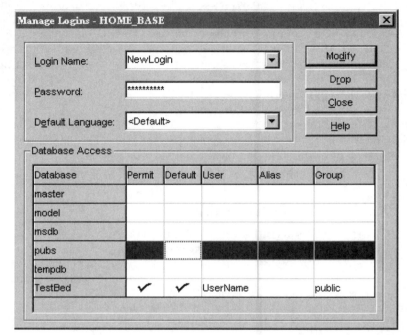

To create a new login ID with the Manage Logins dialog box, you must provide a name and password. You also have the option of specifying the login with a default database and language. If no default database is specified, SQL Server uses the Master database for the login, which means that the user will log on to the Master database. It's best to change the default from Master to another database, because the Master database contains critical system information and you should restrict access to it.

If you don't specify a default language, SQL Server uses us_english as the default. Changing the language affects database data, including the representation of dates, money, and numeric data formatting and error messages.

In addition to using the Manage Logins menu, you can add a user login with the following stored procedures:

```
sp_addlogin login_id [, passwd [, defdb [, deflanguage]]]
sp_adduser login_id [, username [, grpname]]
sp_addalias login_id, username
```

The sp_addlogin stored procedure adds a row to the syslogins table in the Master database, sp_adduser adds a record to the database's sysuser table, and sp_addalias adds a record to the database's sysalternates table. You could also add the appropriate login information directly to the Master database's syslogins table; however, we don't recommend this procedure because the user password won't be encrypted.

Adding Access Rights

The Manage Logins dialog box also lets you specify which databases a user with a particular login ID can access. To do this, you check the Permit box for the appropriate databases. Checking this box lets a user with that login ID switch context from one database to another and lets a DBA add the user's access rights for the selected databases.

The *operating context* of a user is the substrate on which the SQL server determines the validity of a request from a user. *Changing context* is the same as providing a new set of objects and permissions for queries and requests to be executed against.

Special Note

You add access rights in one of three ways:

- adding a user to a database independently (i.e., not within a group)
- giving a user an alias to a preexisting user
- adding a user to an existing group in a database

To add access rights, you modify an existing user account through the Manage Users dialog box in Figure 10.3. This dialog box is available either by choosing Users from the Manage menu or from the Server Manager window under the appropriate database's Groups/Users entry. This dialog box lets you set or change a user's group or give other users in the database the right to use the current user ID as an alias.

Figure 10.3
*Manage Users
Dialog Box*

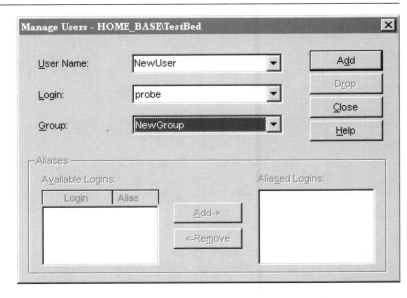

Special Note

Adding an alias for a login or assigning the user to a group assigns all the rights of that alias ID or group to the newly added login. You should carefully consider when to add aliases or insert users into existing database groups.

You can add an existing login as a user in the database by clicking the button next to the User Name field, selecting New User from the list, and then choosing the login ID from the list next to the Login field. The bottom half of the box shows the current available logins and lists those with this user ID as an alias.

User information is recorded in each database's sysusers and sysalternates tables. You should be careful about the order in which you add users and aliases. The sysusers table contains a list of the database's login IDs; only when the user's login ID cannot be found in this table will the sysalternates table be checked for an alias. Therefore, adding an alias for a user after adding the user to the database does not have the effect that might be expected — the system will first use the user ID it finds in sysusers, which directly maps to the login, instead of using the alias ID that is in sysalternates, even though the alias was added more recently than the user ID.

The only way to get into this situation is to directly alter the system tables in a database. The system stored procedures won't let you add an alias for a currently defined user, so if you want to add an alias for a current user, you must directly insert changes into the sysalternates table, which requires setting the server configuration parameter Allow Updates to True. Similarly, it is possible to unintentionally strand an alias by removing from the sysusers table the underlying user account that the alias refers to, thus making the alias meaningless. So be careful if you directly alter a database's system tables.

Once you've created a new user, SQL Server 6.5 adds that user to the public group by default. When you add a user, the user name in the database defaults to the login ID, but you may substitute any name not currently used in the database. To minimize confusion in administration, it's generally a good idea to add users to databases with the same user and login names and to keep a user name consistent across all the databases that a particular user can access.

Special Users

When you create a database, two special kinds of users are also created. The first special user is the database owner (DBO). Initially, the SA login has an alias to the DBO, although this information is not recorded in the sysalternates table. The only way to eliminate the connection between the SA and the DBO on any database is to eliminate the SA account, which we don't recommend — it can have a grave impact on the health of the SQL server.

This access by the SA login can be regarded as a security hole in highly secure databases, but many of the tools, such as ISQLw, seem to depend on its existence, and internal system procedures such as DBCC checks can only be executed under the SA account. The easiest way to overcome this security problem is to limit the number of users who know the SA password and assign the rights that are necessary to perform basic system administration tasks to another account.

The second special user is the Guest user. If the Guest user is part of the Model database, creating a database also automatically creates a Guest user. Normally, all valid logins are members of the Guest group in all the databases. Removing the Guest user makes the database invisible to those without specific permissions in the database.

Special Note

When you install SQL Server 6.5, a Probe login is added and the Probe user account is also added to the Master database. The Probe user lets Performance Monitor access the performance information, such as block counts, Tempdb space, and customized user-defined counters, as well as replication information, such as jobs replicated. (The SQL Performance Monitor is covered in more detail in Chapter 15, "Performance Monitoring Guidelines.") This account presents a small security risk, because someone using the probe account can access user-defined counters that could provide information that otherwise would not be available to that user.

Caution

When the Enterprise Manager is connected to a SQL server, it stores the password and user account information unencrypted in the registry. This entry is visible to the Windows NT account under which the connection was created and is stored as part of the user configuration under the HKEY_CURRENT_ USER\Software\Microsoft\MSSQLServer\SQLEW\RegisteredServers\<*Your ServerGroups*>\<*Your ServerNames*> key. An unattended and unlocked machine presents a significant hole in security. Generally, it is a good idea to control the profiles of users on secure systems, to eliminate registry access from all accounts except administrative accounts, and to use administrative accounts only when necessary.

Adding Groups

Grouping your users can greatly reduce the time and effort you spend in keeping a security system up-to-date, because groups can provide general access rights to many users at once. Users can belong to only one group at a time besides the public group, and the group IDs apply only within the database in which they are created. You must make a login ID a user of a database before you can add that user to a group in that database.

When you create a database, a Public group is also created and the DBO is added as a member. By default, new users are members of the Public group. The Public group is a good group to use to grant broad access rights to all new users — if that is your desired security setup.

You can add groups through the Manage Groups dialog box (Figure 10.4) by going to Manage, Groups or through the Server Manager window under the database's Groups/Users collection. Be aware of which database is highlighted in the Users in Group window, or you may add a group to the wrong database.

Figure 10.4

Manage Groups Dialog Box

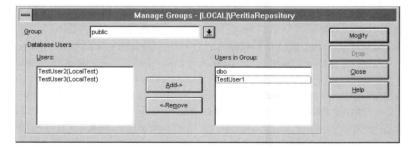

To add groups, you can also use the stored procedure

```
sp_addgroup grpname
```

Removing Users and Groups

All the stored procedures to add groups or users have "drop" counterparts. For example, you can use the stored procedure "sp_dropgroup grpname" to delete a particular group. You can also drop users, logins, and groups from their respective Manage dialog boxes by selecting the name and clicking the Remove button. To remove aliases, go to the Manage Users dialog box in Figure 10.3, highlight the alias under Aliased logins, and click Remove.

It is always possible to directly remove any of these access descriptions from the relevant system table as long as the Allow Updates flag is set to True. At some point, you may need to adjust these system tables yourself because you have removed a login before removing a user or you have made some other error. It is possible to update system tables directly if you are logged on as SA and set the Allow Updates configuration option to True. However, be very sure that you understand the structure of the tables and the relationships between the Master database, the syslogins table, your database, and the sysusers table before you make any changes. And save a copy of the data as it was before you started, just in case you get it wrong and have to go back to the beginning. At the very least, you should back up the Master database and your database.

Integrated Security

SQL Server lets you create logins, users, and groups on the server that directly relate to the users and groups defined under Windows NT. With this setup, when a user logs on to Windows NT and then requests access to SQL server, the Windows NT security tokens are passed directly to SQL Server and no local verification is performed. Users can thus access SQL Server without logging on twice, first to Windows NT and then to SQL Server. This integrated setup is particularly convenient if the access rights of users on the network (or local machine) closely match those rights assigned within the database.

For example, take two Windows NT groups, Finance and Human Resources (HR). These groups exist to control access to certain privileged files and network resources in Windows NT. If SQL Server has two databases, Finance and Employees, and the users of Finance need access only to the

Finance database, while HR users need access only to the Employees database, it makes good sense to create two groups under SQL Server that parallel the Windows NT groups, grant them the necessary rights, and add the users to the respective groups.

This setup would be simple to administer and maintain with only a few users and groups, but keeping track of hundreds or thousands of users and making sure everyone has only the appropriate rights would be a very time-consuming task. For this reason, SQL Server automates the migration of Windows NT users into SQL Server users.

Before implementing the integrated security model, the security mode for SQL Server must be set through the Enterprise Manager, Server, Configurations menus, or by setting security options with the setup program. You manage your integrated security setup through SQL Security Manager. This interface lets the SA map Windows NT Groups into SQL Server as users or administrators. When you implement your integrated security setup, members of the local Windows NT Administrator group are automatically allowed to log on to the SQL Server as SA.

The Security Manager has two components: User Mappings and Administrative Mappings. The two components are shown in Figure 10.5. The first component lets you add and remove local and domain global groups as groups on SQL Server. The second allows the SA privilege (there is only one SA account) to be granted to and revoked from the specified members of the NT groups. You can toggle between the two screens using the buttons on the left of the tool bar or by choosing the appropriate menu item under the View menu.

Figure 10.5
Security Manager—
User Mappings and
Administrative
Mappings

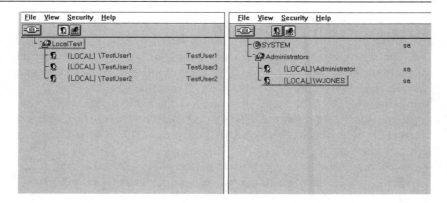

By choosing Grant New from the Security Manager's Security menu, you can display the Grant User Privilege dialog box shown in Figure 10.6. This dialog box lets you insert Windows NT groups into SQL Server. Choosing the

"Add login IDs for group members" option lets you generate logins for the members of that group either as individuals, if you are granting user rights, or as SA, if you are adding administrative groups. If the group is being added as a user group, the members of the group can be granted a login and inserted as users in a database by specifying the database name in the field at the bottom of the dialog box.

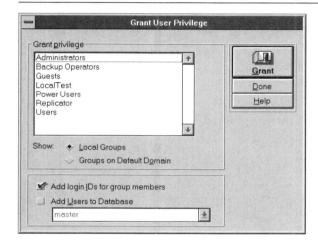

Figure 10.6
Security Manager—
Grant User Privilege
Dialog Box

These two options have interesting effects on the way users are added to SQL Server through the Security Manager. When you choose an NT group to map into SQL Server, you can elect not to add login IDs for group members. Choosing this option makes the group visible in the Grant Privilege window of the Security Manager and allows you to manipulate the users one at a time; however, no specific logins will be created for the users in that group within SQL Server. Under the covers, the users will log on to SQL Server as Guest. If the Windows NT group users are added to a database in this dialog box, the NT group will be mirrored in the database, and all the NT user IDs will be added as users under this group in the database.

To change the access rights of a specific user, select the user from the Security Manager window in Figure 10.5 and choose Account Details from the Security menu or double-click the user in the list. Either of these actions will bring up the Account Detail dialog box shown in Figure 10.7.

This dialog box lets you create or drop a login for a user and add the user to or remove the user from any database. If a group of users will be connecting on both trusted and non-trusted connections (which are discussed in more detail later in the chapter), you should make sure the "Generate random unique passwords" box is not checked and assign a password to the group. This password will be used for connections made to the database that do not first log on to Windows NT.

Figure 10.7
Security Manager —
Account Detail
Dialog Box

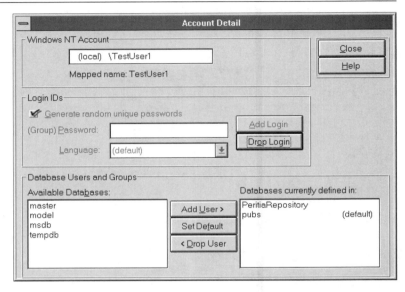

The SA Privilege component of the Security Manager lets you grant administrative rights to logins for users in the groups you choose. You can't add logins for the administrators or insert them as users in databases, because the SA is mapped to the DBO in each database. Likewise, you can't assign group passwords to these Windows NT logins; users attempting to connect to SQL Server through a non-trusted connection must use the SA password in order to use the account as SA.

The Security Manager lets you revoke access rights from a group by selecting the group and choosing Security, Revoke. To remove a user from a database, first select the user and access the Account Detail dialog box in Figure 10.7. Then remove the appropriate database from the "Databases currently defined in" box. You can also drop a specific login from this dialog box, which lets you customize the security between Windows NT groups and SQL Server groups.

Adding a user to a group under Windows NT does not add the user's login to SQL Server automatically. You must invoke the Security Manager; the new user's name should be available under the appropriate group so that you can assign a login to it. The new user is given a default login as Guest and is not inserted into any databases until you do it manually.

Adding the member of one of the Windows NT groups as a user of a database adds the NT group from which the user is being inserted to the database as well.

Special Note

It is important to note that removing a user from a group under Windows NT removes the user's ID from the Security Manager; however, it does not remove the user's SQL Server login, nor does it remove the user from any databases. To properly manage user accounts under the integrated security setup, the user should first be dropped from SQL Server through the Security Manager and then removed from the Windows NT security system. If the user is left in the database and a group password was assigned, that user still has access to the database on non-trusted connections. This oversight may never become obvious if you use only the Security Manager to manage users. However, a routine comparison of the user accounts listed under the databases in the Enterprise Manager to those listed in the Security Manager will catch these stranded accounts, and then you can remove them from the database and drop the login.

If you do not create a group password for non-trusted accounts, the act of dropping the user from the Windows NT security will effectively remove the user's access to the database, although the user login account and any access that the user has in any databases will still exist in SQL Server. Therefore, if a user can crack the random password that the Security Manager uses to map Windows NT accounts into SQL Server, that user, with a valid Windows NT login, can probably still log on to SQL Server. If you do not want a user to have this access, be sure to delete the appropriate entries from SQL Server, both in user databases (with the sp_dropuser stored procedure) and then in the Master database (using sp_droplogin). You will probably want to drop your Guest login as well.

Mixed Security

As the name implies, you can also use a combination of integrated and standard security. The mixed model lets users on trusted connections access SQL Server using their Windows NT validation and lets you restrict users on non-trusted connections to using SQL Server's security validation. This security setup lets you implement a network configuration that lets local users log on locally on trusted connections while allowing remote access through connections that are not subject to the Windows NT security validation process. The need for this setup is becoming less and less common as more integrated remote access packages are implemented. Generally speaking, using mixed security doubles both the number of administrative tasks required to maintain security and the number of places to check for leaks.

User Access Rights

After you create a group or user in a database, you need to associate access rights with that group. The two categories of access rights are statement permissions and object permissions.

The most fundamental activities in a database are creating and dropping objects. Permissions for these activities — statement permissions — are assigned by default to the DBO and are not generally assigned to other users in a database. To assign Drop and Create rights to other users, you alter the database permissions through the Edit Database dialog box, which you can get to either by right-clicking the database name in the Server Manager and choosing Edit or through the Enterprise Manager menu.

The second category of permissions, object permissions, includes both the right to use Select, Insert, Update, and Delete statements and the declarative referential integrity (DRI) creation privilege on tables and views. Users of a database are usually granted these types of access. Object permission also includes Execute permission for stored procedures. Every object in the database is owned by a user (called the Database Object Owner, or DBOO) and that owner has complete right to the object, including the right to manipulate the rights of other users to that object.

Permissions can be granted and revoked in two ways: through the user interface and through Grant and Revoke statements. To grant or revoke permissions with the user interface, choose Permissions from the Enterprise Manager's Object menu. You can also go to the Server Manager window and right-click either an object in the database or a User/Group entry under the database. The Object Permissions dialog box in Figure 10.8 will appear.

This dialog box can be used to assign or revoke permissions on any database object. It has two tabs. The By Object tab gives a view of permissions by object, listing all the users and groups within the database and the permissions that are assigned for that object. The By User tab displays permissions by user, listing all the objects in the database and the permissions that the given user has for it. The user rights are set by checking the appropriate boxes next to the user or the object and clicking Set.

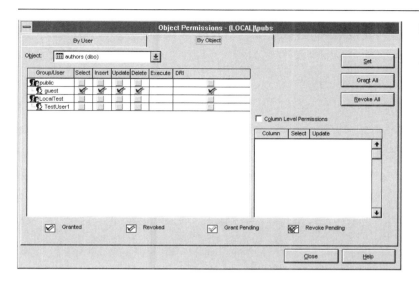

Figure 10.8
Object Permissions Dialog Box

Database object permissions are managed from the Permissions tab of the Edit Database dialog box shown in Figure 10.9. To get to the Edit Database dialog box, double-click the database name in the Server Manager window, right-click the database name and choose Edit Database from the pop-up menu, or choose the Database item from the Manage menu of the Enterprise Manager.

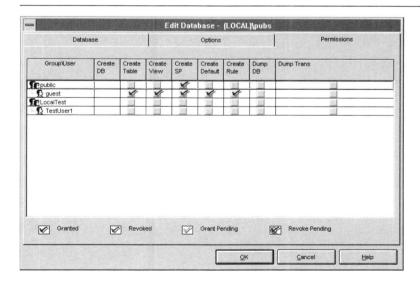

Figure 10.9
Edit Database, Permissions Tab

The second method of managing permissions is to use the Grant and Revoke statements. For statement permissions, use the following statement:

```
GRANT/REVOKE {ALL | statement_list}
TO {PUBLIC | name_list}
```

For object permissions, use this statement:

```
GRANT/REVOKE {ALL | permission_list}
ON {table_name [(column_list)] | view_name [(column_list)] |
   stored_procedure_name | extended_stored_procedure_name}
TO {PUBLIC | name_list}
```

If you list more than one permission in the above statements, separate the permissions with commas.

The statement permissions list can include Create Database (which can be granted only by the system administrator), Create Default, Create Procedure, Create Rule, Create Table, Create View, Dump Database, and Dump Transaction. The object permissions list can include Select, Insert, Delete, Update, and/or References.

When you grant or revoke object permissions on columns, you can include Select and Update in the permission list. When you revoke permissions on stored procedures, you can include only Execute in the permission list. Granting a user Create permission also lets the user Drop the specified type of object. For tables, Create permission also includes the ability to create an index on the table, alter the table, update statistics, and use DBCC CHECK-TABLE.

You can restrict the object permissions for tables and views at the column level for Select and Update permissions. By restricting permissions, an object's owner can restrict users' access to specific columns within a table. This setup is typically used in cases such as employee rosters, where you might want everyone to be able to see the list of all employees but have the related salaries visible only to the managers.

Be aware that granting and revoking permissions is order dependent, except when you explicitly grant a user rights to an object and revoke the permission from the group to which the user belongs.

Special Note

This aspect of granting and revoking permissions changed from SQL Server 6.0 to SQL Server 6.5.

In the example below, User1 belongs to Group1. Executing the revoke and grant statements in the following sequence will result in User1, along with the rest of Group1, having Select access to Table1, which is probably not what you intended.

Wrong way:

```
REVOKE SELECT ON TABLE1 TO USER1
GRANT SELECT ON TABLE1 TO GROUP1
```

If you want all of Group1 except User1 to have Select access to Table1, the correct order in which to execute the grant and revoke statements is

Right way:

```
GRANT SELECT ON TABLE1 TO GROUP1
REVOKE SELECT ON TABLE1 TO USER1
```

Database objects inherit the access permissions of their owner. For example, let's say that User1 does not have Select permission on Table1 but creates a stored procedure that includes a Select on Table1. The stored procedure will not execute properly, because the owner of the object does not have Select permission on Table1.

However, if the owner of Table1 creates a procedure that performs a Select on Table1, granting Execute permission on the stored procedure to User1 indirectly gives User1 a Select permission for Table1. Because User1 can Execute the stored procedure, User1 can perform a Select indirectly on Table1 by executing the procedure, even though User1 doesn't have Select permission on Table1. However, User1 still cannot perform a Select on the table directly.

The same permission inheritance applies to triggers and views as well as statement permissions. Creating a table within a stored procedure will be successful only if the owner of the procedure has permission to create a table in the database.

This security inheritance ensures that no unauthorized access is granted simply by wrapping the access up in another object. It can, however, cause problems if users aren't aware that the objects they create have their permissions and that they can't rely on the database to restrict access to other objects granted in this fashion.

Strategies for Managing User Security

Security Models

A discussion of trusted and non-trusted connections may help explain the various security models. When a connection is made to a Windows NT server, the operating system validates the user account and password and attaches an access control list (ACL) to the session process that is created. This ACL specifies the user's rights and privileges. This connection is called a trusted connection and the ACL is recognized by SQL Server under integrated security. In a non-trusted connection, the connection is made to SQL Server without having the operating system validate the login. In this case, the connection is passed to SQL Server and SQL Server's security mechanism validates the account and password. Because the login does not create its own Windows NT process, no ACL is attached to it. The connection operates in the security context of SQL Server and has no operating system privileges of its own.

Under SQL Server's standard security, all the connections made to the database are treated as non-trusted, which requires each connection to provide a valid ID and password that is then validated by the database's security system. In the integrated security model, all database connections are made through a valid Windows NT connection. The mixed model allows for both types of connections. Each model has its own benefits and detriments.

The standard security model allows connections to be made without requiring changes to the security on Windows NT. This model makes the database available to any user, regardless of his or her rights on the Windows NT network. It also puts all the security management in the hands of the DBA and does not require any Windows NT security rights. This model is convenient and works well in low-security environments.

However, more frequently, the users of the database are almost always the same individuals as the users of the network. The rights and privileges of the users on the network are most often reflected in their rights as database users. In these cases, it is often more convenient to map network users and groups directly into database users and groups. The integrated security model simplifies the management of this security scheme.

The mixed model provides the best and worst of the other two models. By letting you map network users into database users, it facilitates rigid organization of accounts on both Windows NT and SQL Server. To use this setup advantageously, you must manage the database users also as Windows NT users, which increases the administrative chores for both the network administrator and the database administrator. On the other hand, the mixed model also lets users who are not privileged to the other resources on the network use the database. These users can be managed from within the database, which reduces the need for intervention from the network administrator. In general, using this model increases the number of tools that you must use to manage the database and requires maintaining two separate security models.

The appropriate model for your implementation will depend on many variables, and a dialog between the DBA and the network administrator is absolutely necessary. The decision should be carefully considered from the outset, because changing from one model to another can become a very difficult procedure once a model is firmly established.

Object Permissions Options

Object permissions can be assigned in several configurations, and every project usually has several security designs that make sense. If all the database access is to be done through one front-end program — a client/server software package — you can create a single user account and login. You could control all the user access through the front end, using a user database and restricting the screens and programs that are available.

This model works well if the user population has very limited requirements or the software has a very specific and limited scope. In these cases, users do not need direct access to the database. This model is particularly attractive when you're designing a software product, because the front end will satisfy all the user requirements. However, it often becomes apparent after the software is deployed that some other product (such as Access using attached tables) is needed to perform some unanticipated requirement within the software. In situations like these you may need to change the security model, which can result either in rewriting front-end code or performing a major shift in object control security on the database.

You should carefully consider the definiteness of the specification before choosing this model. If the software is simple and the number of users few, then this model may be a viable alternative. Generally speaking, it is much more realistic to design a program around the idea that the original specifications will fall short.

Using groups, aliases, or both in a database can provide a manageable alternative to front-end-controlled methods, because you can assign security for many users at once. Using groups and aliases works well when you can divide database users into large categories. You can also assign specific privileges to users one at a time if necessary, thus customizing their access all the way down to the column level. This customization can be useful in very large, heterogeneous databases that contain a wide variety of information, such as an inventory management system that ties into a sales system with accounting facilities. This setup also lets users access the database through third-party tools, which in the long term makes the database more user friendly.

Using groups to restrict access on a rough scale and assigning specific object rights to differentiate among users works well when you have only a few users; however, this level of security can become nearly unmanageable when many users with different privileges are involved. An alternative is to create groups with general rights and a fixed set of users, each of whom has more specific rights; you can then create aliases for the users to one of these fixed users. Although this setup isn't as specifically customized as assigning rights to specific users, it does give relatively detailed rights and remains maintainable for large numbers of users. A design such as this fits well with the integrated security model.

When a database has many users, it is often well worth the investment to create and build a user management system designed around the product's requirements. A custom management system lets customers manage security on the database without needing a high level of knowledge of the database. You could also use the custom management system to make sophisticated security systems more manageable, for example, by automating some of the bookkeeping and administration. The level of detail in your security system is generally determined by the amount of time you put into designing it and creating tools to maintain it.

Summary

User security can easily become one of the most challenging aspects of creating a database-driven application. The more complicated the design of the database, the more time is needed to properly design and implement the security system. You should know from the outset that security is an integral part of designing a database and you should allocate resources to address it early in the design process.

Security can be implemented in many different ways, and usually, more than one of these ways is the "right" way. Sometimes the decision will come down to personal preference, and the DBA needs to be a primary force in making these decisions because he or she will ultimately be responsible for maintaining it.

Chapter 11

Replication

Replication — duplicating data on different servers — keeps databases in different locations synchronized and up-to-date. Replication can solve many problems, including performance problems, and can enable data sharing. SQL Server 6.5 can replicate to any ODBC-compliant database, such as Oracle, Microsoft Access, or DB2. Replication also works between SQL Server 6.0 and 6.5 databases. Table owners can now replicate their own tables. You can replicate text and image data types, up to a limited size. Replication is a very flexible process — you can set up many systems to get data from one site to another.

In this chapter, we discuss what replication is (and what it is not), replication strategies, how to set up replication, how to troubleshoot your replication setup, and how to replicate text and image data types.

What It Is, What It Is Not

Replication is the process of storing the same data in different databases, sometimes on different servers. Servers or databases can play three different roles in the replication process: publisher, distributor, and subscriber. The publisher is the source of the data, the subscriber is the destination of the data, and the distributor is the "traffic cop" between the publisher and subscriber.

Although one server can play all three roles, it is rare. Each role can also be fulfilled by more than one server. For example, one publisher can send to several subscribers. This setup works well for a corporate office sending data to regional offices. Multiple publishers can also send to one subscriber, as in the case of regional offices replicating data to the corporate office.

Replication uses a store-and-forward strategy to guarantee that a transaction committed on the original server eventually makes it to the subscriber. Transactions at the publisher are stored in the distributor before being sent to the subscriber. The transactions are applied, or recorded, at the subscriber in the same order that they were originally applied at the publisher.

The basis of replication is an *article*, which contains data from a table that has been enabled for replication. You can think of an article as a Select statement that controls which columns and rows from the table are replicated. A named collection of articles is a *publication*.

The distribution server, the "traffic cop," can control when and in what order each of the subscribers is sent an article. This process is called *push replication. Pull replication* occurs when the subscribers control replication by asking for an article. SQL Server only supports push replication, even though the replication is set up from the subscriber, or pull side.

Because it is not a real-time process, replication is not suitable for every application. For example, applications that need very tight consistency between databases should use the two-phase commit process, which commits transactions from one database to another database at the same time. Other products, such as the Microsoft Distributed Transaction Coordinator (DTC), Microsoft Transaction Server (MTS), or even the two-phase commit portion of the DBLIB API, are more suitable to a synchronous data-sharing application.

In contrast, replication provides loose consistency because time elapses between the time a transaction is committed on the publishing server and when it appears on the subscription server. You can set delivery to occur immediately or at timed intervals, such as nightly or weekly. Of course, even "immediate" replication is not the same as a two-phase commit, because it is still written to the publisher first and then sent to the subscriber, with a brief stop in the distribution database. In two-phase commit, the transaction is not finalized until the records are committed in both the source and destination databases.

The Replication Process

Getting data from one server to another takes several steps. First, the tables must be *synchronized*, which means ensuring that both the publisher and the subscriber tables contain the same data. The distribution database is not involved in the synchronization process. You must ensure that no one updates the publisher table during synchronization. The synchronization process runs in a separate thread under the SQL Executive Service and replication does not start on the table until the synchronization is complete.

After synchronization, completed transactions in the publishing database are copied to the distribution database. The log reader, which runs in a separate thread under the SQL Executive Service, manages this step. The log reader reads the completed transactions from the transaction log on the publication database; finds the corresponding article; creates an Insert, Update, Delete, or Execute command; and writes that command to the distribution database. When the log successfully writes the command to the distribution database, it marks the transaction in the log as sent.

The distribution database stores the replicated data until the subscriber is ready to receive it. The distribution database sends (pushes) the data. The command is executed at the subscriber database. As each subscriber commits the data, a record is added to the mssubscriber_status table in the distribution database and the mslast_job_info table is updated on the subscription server. Mslast_job_info is a significant table in the control and management of replication, as we see later in this chapter. Like the log reader, the distribution process is a separate thread under the SQL Executive Service. You can see the task or job in the Manage Scheduled Tasks in the Enterprise Manager.

ODBC Replication

New in SQL 6.5 is the ability to use any compatible ODBC database as a subscriber. The documentation for SQL Server says that you can only do push replication to an ODBC database. However, using Microsoft Access with attached SQL Server tables, you can use the replication feature from Access to replicate almost any ODBC database to SQL Server, too. Several of the standard replication options may not work when your subscriber is an ODBC database. Beware of different data types supported by the different databases. Some databases do not support the BIT datatype, and some do not support Identity fields (sometimes called counter or auto-number fields). Most ODBC databases cannot do clustered indexes, and Declarative Referential Integrity (DRI), the process of checking primary and foreign key references, may work differently. For example, if you attempt add an invoice record for a customer who is not in the customer table, and if you have a foreign key on the customer field in the invoice table that is linked to a primary key on the customer field in the customer table, the insert will fail.

Replication Strategies

You should keep in mind a number of issues when you set up replication. For example, it is critical to determine whether you have adequate resources for replication before you get involved in setting up the databases. We look closely at resources and other considerations in this section.

General Issues

Replication works well when you want data to be shared but the timing of that data sharing is not absolutely critical. For example, replication works well when a corporate office keeps master lists, such as a price list, and sends updates to outlying offices. It is also a good strategy when you want to have separate Online Transaction Processing (OLTP) server(s) and reporting server(s) for data warehousing and decision support.

Replication does not create a hot backup that you can use when your primary server fails. You have several other good options for fault-tolerant servers. Replication is also not the right choice when the application would better be served by a two-phase commit program, such as the new DTC or the two-phase commit API in DBLIB.

You can replicate text and image columns. You can even limit very large text and image data with the max text repl size configuration option. The default size you can replicate at any one time is 65,536 bytes, or 64K. We discuss text and image replication in detail later in this chapter.

To improve replication performance, use stored procedures to replicate as many articles as possible. (We describe how to use stored procedures in replication later in this chapter.) Because the stored procedures are already in memory when the transaction is handled, SQL Server does not have to run syntax checking or optimization processes to finalize the transaction. Stored procedures work best with transaction-based replication, in which the distribution database sends articles to the subscriber database each time a transaction occurs. Using stored procedures for scheduled replication may or may not significantly improve performance, so experiment with each individual article. In general, the smaller the data set being replicated, the more you benefit from using stored procedures.

Resource Considerations

You must plan ahead for replication, because it requires a lot of resources — at least 32 MB of memory on the distribution server. You must configure SQL

Server to have at least 16 MB of memory. The log reader and distribution manager also take process and memory space.

The extra resource required in replication that catches most installations by surprise is the log space. Normally, when a Dump Transaction command is performed to back up the transaction log, all completed transactions are cleared. However, when replication is enabled, any transactions still marked for replication remain in the log; the transactions are cleared out of the log only after they are sent to the distribution server.

Determining the size of the distribution database is the most difficult part of setting up replication. You also need to allow extra log space for the distribution database. To calculate the size of distribution database you need to

- calculate the average transaction size
- determine the maximum number of transactions
- estimate the retention time

Then use the following formula:

```
Average Transaction Size × Number of transactions per day ×
Retention Period In Days × 2
```

The minimum recommended database size is 40 MB, with 20 MB of log space. The best log file size is 50–60 percent of the size of the database.

Prerequisites to Replication

Although the documentation states that a trusted connection is required for replication, replication can work without it. However, replication does work more reliably when all the servers in different domains have two-way trusts established through Windows NT.

To set up replication without two-way trusts, you must establish a common user and password and use it for the SQL Executive on all servers. Every server must use the same user name and password for replication control. After you establish a user name and password, reboot the system.

The 32-bit ODBC drivers must be installed and set up on all the servers involved. ODBC sends individual transactions between servers. ODBC is not the only transport mechanism, because the BCP, explained in detail in Chapter 14, "Importing and Exporting Data," is used in the automatic synchronization process.

The distribution server must have a named-pipes or multiprotocol network configuration. Each server must also have the same character set installed, but the servers are not required to have the same sort order. If the servers do not have the same character set, you will get error messages.

Before a table can be replicated, you must define a primary key constraint for it. Although defining a primary key constraint also creates a unique index on the table, having only a unique index without a primary key constraint is not enough. The replication manager does not look for a unique index; it looks for a primary key.

Important Prerequisites

Install ODBC 3.0 or later and SQL Server Service Pack 2 or later before running replication in a production environment. ODBC 2.5 has documented bugs. Although workarounds to the bugs have been developed, it is advisable to upgrade to ODBC 3.0 and Service Pack 2.

Server Considerations

When you set up replication, you should consider the subscriber database to be a read-only database. At all costs, you should avoid directly updating a subscribing table that has its source on another server. It is very difficult for SQL Server to keep two tables in two databases synchronized when they are both being updated and published to each other. (You need to wait for SQL Server 7.0 and its multiple master feature to support this.) However, don't turn on the Read-Only database option, because the replication tasks won't be able to write to the subscriber tables; simply use the subscriber database for reporting purposes only.

If the publishing table has an identity field, that field must be removed on the subscribing tables, though you can leave the identity fields on the publishing table. The primary reason to remove the identify field is that the replication process tries to write the original value to the table and gets an error saying that an attempt was made to insert a value into an identity field. Another reason is that an identity field could possibly assign a different value than the original source, which would violate any foreign key constraints to other tables.

To handle identity fields on a subscribing table, create an extra column whose name does not appear in the publishing tables. This scenario works well when a table subscribes from multiple publishers. Each publisher can have the same values, so you need another primary key to give unique key values.

Also, the subscribing tables cannot have a time stamp. The synchronization process changes a time stamp on a publication table to a binary (8) column on the subscribing table when it creates the table. The synchronization process also lets you choose either to keep your user-defined data types on the column definitions or to change them to the base SQL Server data types. We recommend doing whatever is easiest for creating and maintaining your databases. Usually, the subscribers use the same creation script as the publishers, even for user-defined data types.

Remove referential integrity constraints from the subscriber database when you use automatic synchronization to keep replication errors and problems to a minimum. Referential integrity isn't necessary on the subscriber because it has already been performed on the publishing database. You are assured that the data relationships have already been verified before they are sent to the subscriber.

WAN Considerations

- Use manual synchronization for large tables or for slow connections such as a WAN to avoid tying up the WAN line with a one-time large data synchronization.

- Send the synchronize files via tape. Once the tables are synchronized, replication can begin.

- Try to minimize the volume of data transmitted over the WAN line.

- Use pull replication so that the subscribing server can ask for the replicated data when it dials in periodically.

- Expand the log space on the publisher.

- Use a larger-than-normal distributor database and log space because the transaction log does not clear until all replicated transactions have been posted to the distribution database. The transaction log could take a while to clear if the distribution database is connected over a slow WAN line.

Designing a Replication Configuration

The three most common ways to set up your replication process are in a simple topology, a star topology, or a network topology.

Simple Topology

Star Topology

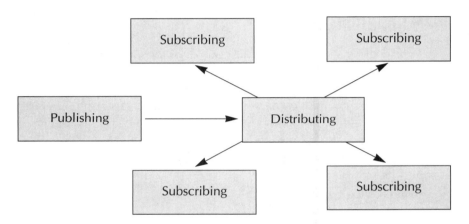

Network Topology

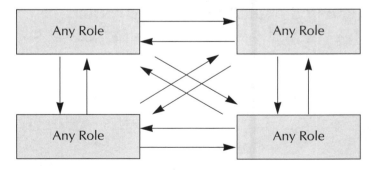

Step-By-Step Setup

Setting up replication requires choosing options for the publication, distribution, and subscription servers; setting up articles for publication; and setting other options.

Setting Up Servers

To begin setting up replication, go to Server, Replication Configuration, Install Publishing (Figure 11.1). The dialog box shown in Figure 11.2, Install Replication Publishing, will appear. Here, you can install either a local or a remote distribution database.

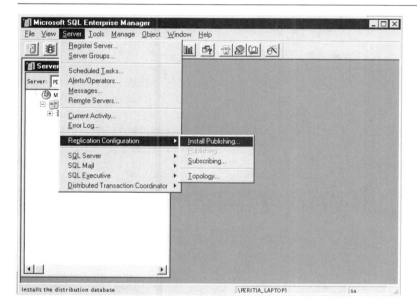

Figure 11.1
Install Publishing

If you choose to create a local distribution server, both the publisher and distributor will be on the same server, as shown in the upper right part of Figure 11.2. You are asked to install the distribution database on an existing device and log file. Your system will perform better if the log file is on a different physical disk drive (or drive array).

If you choose to use a remote distribution server, the devices and databases must already exist on the other server. You can configure a server to act as a distribution server by installing replication and no published articles. You

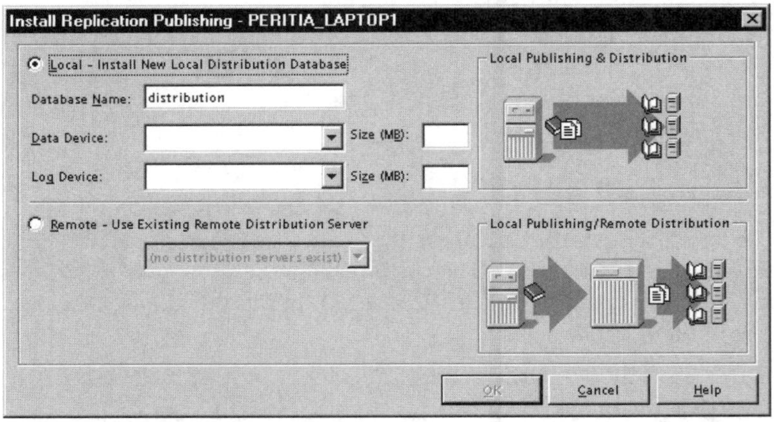

Figure 11.2
Install Replication Publishing

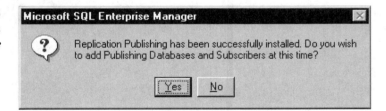

can see in the picture in the lower right of Figure 11.2 a configuration in which the publication and distribution roles are fulfilled by different servers.

When you have chosen the setup you want, click OK and the dialog box in Figure 11.3 will appear. Because you want to add publishing databases and subscribers, click Yes, and the dialog box in Figure 11.4, the Replication Publishing dialog box, will appear. You can also get to this dialog box by going to Manage, Replication.

Figure 11.3
Replication Installation Complete

At the Replication Publishing dialog box, you designate the subscribing servers and publishing databases. Select the Enable check box next to the server name in the left window. In the right window, click the databases you want to publish from. The Working Directory box shows the default directory that stores the script and data files used in replication. You can change this directory to any existing directory that SQL Executive has full rights to. You need to go into the Windows NT directory permissions section and give the appropriate rights to the account being used by SQL Executive.

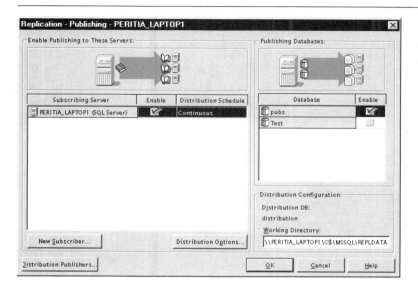

Figure 11.4
Replication Publishing Dialog Box

The Replication Publishing dialog box is very important. When your replication setup is not working correctly, and your attempts to fix it don't work, come to this dialog box, undo the necessary links, and restart SQL Server. Then return to this dialog box to redefine the replication links. Redoing the definitions doesn't take long because all the publication articles still exist.

After designating the publishing servers, you can schedule when distribution occurs. By default, distribution is continuous. To change it, click Distribution Options to bring up the dialog box in Figure 11.5. By default, transactions are sent to the subscriber every time 100 transactions accumulate. Reduce this number if you are replicating an infrequently updated table.

Do not set the set the commit batch size to 1 or 2, because these values bring out documented bugs in SQL Executive. Use a number between 20 and 50 for best results.

Special Note

For small tables, you may want to schedule when articles are fully distributed. The choices are to send each transaction to the subscriber when it occurs or always send the whole table. You can send the whole table easily when the table is small. Scheduling distribution is a good option when you have a WAN. Under Distribution Schedule, click Scheduled, then click Change to schedule when and how often the changes are transmitted. The

Figure 11.5
Distribution Options
Dialog Box

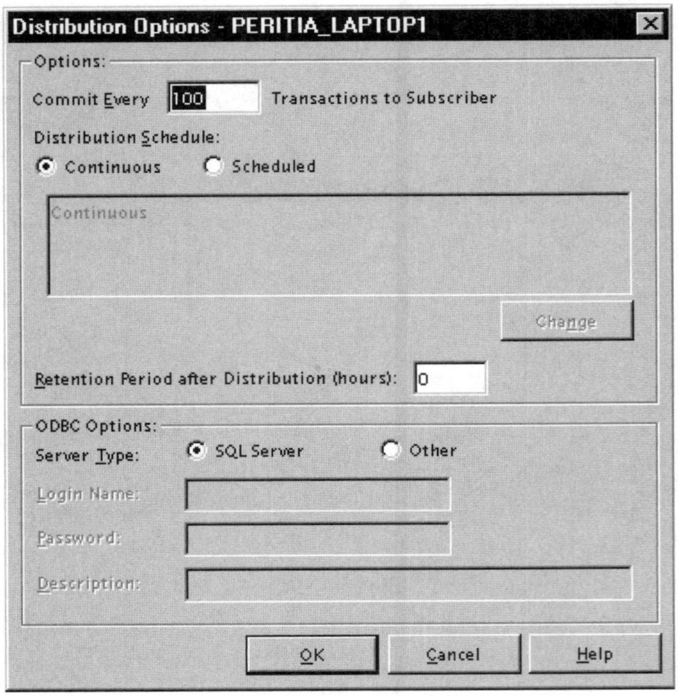

dialog box in Figure 11.6 will appear. Scheduling distribution is like scheduling any other task.

When the subscriber successfully receives the transactions, you can determine the retention period — how long, in hours, after replication the transactions stay on the distribution server. By default, the transactions are deleted immediately. To change the default, at the dialog box in Figure 11.5, type the number of hours to retain the transactions in the Retention Period field.

The dialog box in Figure 11.5 also lets you add a login name and password to be used when distributing articles to ODBC subscribers. This information is the login to an ODBC data source, if one is required. For example, if you are replicating to a Microsoft Access database that has security turned on, you supply a user name and password so the distribution task can write to the Access database. SQL Server subscribers do not need these parameters, because the SQL Executive login must have a valid login for the other server. Some ODBC management systems do not need a user name and password. In that case, click Other in Figure 11.5, but leave the Login name and Password fields blank.

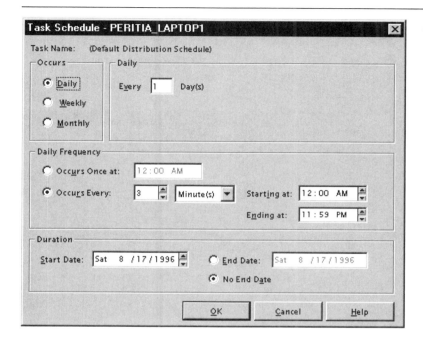

Figure 11.6
Task Schedule

The next step is to add subscribing databases, which you do at the Replication Publishing dialog box (Figure 11.4). To return, click OK on each screen until you get back. At the Replication Publishing dialog box, click New Subscriber to bring up the dialog box shown in Figure 11.7. You have three choices for adding a subscribing database. You can pick an already-registered server by using the drop-down list box, you can register a new server by clicking New Server, or you can choose an ODBC subscriber. After you make your selection, click OK.

Figure 11.7
New Subscriber Database

Back in the Replication Publishing dialog box (Figure 11.4), clicking the Distribution Publishers button brings up the dialog box in Figure 11.8. All the registered servers that have been properly set up to be distribution servers are listed in the window. Choose the one you want to use for this publication by checking the Enable box next to the server name.

Figure 11.8

Replication Distribution Dialog Box

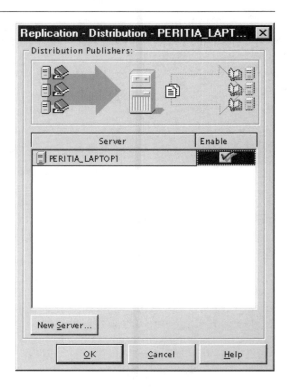

Creating Articles for Publication

Now that we have configured the publisher and distributor, it is time to create the articles for publication. From the Manage menu, go to Replication, Publications (Figure 11.9).

The Manage Publications dialog box (Figure 11.10) will appear. Here, you define a publication and its articles. The databases in the list have been enabled for publication. Remember that a publication is a collection of one or more articles, and you can transmit either the entire publication or just one article. To create a publication and its articles, click New, and the dialog box in Figure 11.11 will appear.

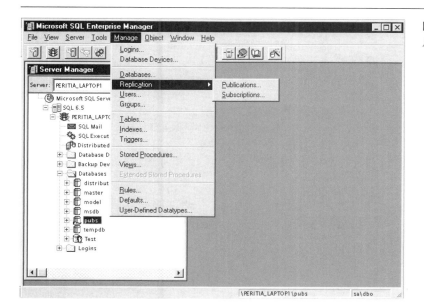

Figure 11.9
Managing Replication

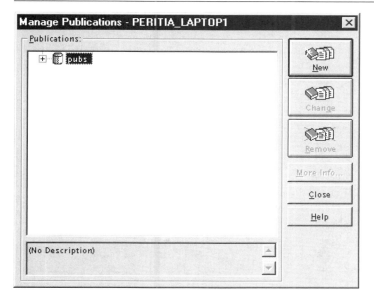

Figure 11.10
*Manage Publications
Dialog Box*

Figure 11.11
Edit Publications
Dialog Box

The Edit Publications dialog box has many purposes. First, you must give a publication a name (you can only add a new publication to the list after it has a name). You can also set a publication to be transaction- or schedule-based.

After you give the publication a name, you need to create some articles. The articles are based on tables. All the tables in the database are listed in the lower left of Figure 11.11. Click the articles you want to add to this publication, then click Add. The table names move to the right window, with a default name of the table followed by _Table. For example, choosing the authors table, as shown in Figure 11.11, creates an article with the default name authors_Table.

Clicking Edit brings up the Manage Article dialog box (Figure 11.12). The articles must have a name; the default name is the name from the previous dialog box. You can change the name here if you wish. The destination table is the name of the table that receives the data on the subscription server. You can choose to qualify the table names by the owner of the table, which is useful only if you are replicating to Microsoft SQL Server or Sybase SQL Server. For example, you could name the table dbo.authors, showing that the database owner (dbo) created the table to differentiate it from another table of the same name, created by a different owner; i.e., kevin.authors.

Figure 11.12
*Manage Article
Dialog Box*

You can also choose to use column names in the Select, Insert, Update, Updatetext, or Delete statements. In some SQL statements, the column names are optional, and choosing this option forces the field names to be used. For example, the Insert statement has these optional column names:

```
INSERT myTable (column1, column2) VALUES ('Test', 1)
```

The (column1, column2) names are optional, but if you do not specify column names, all the fields in the table must be specified in the Values clause in the order they were specified in the Create Table command.

At this dialog box, you can also specify horizontal and vertical replication. Horizontal replication copies only certain rows of a table to a subscriber. To specify horizontal replication, add a restriction, such as a Where clause, at the bottom of the dialog box. The example shows that only the authors from California are replicated. Vertical replication copies only some of the columns. You can set up vertical replication by clearing the check box to the right of the field name in the Replicated Columns list.

Before we move on, let's explore two other options available to replicated data. Click the Advanced button shown in Figure 11.12 to bring up the dialog box shown in Figure 11.13. Here, you can specify the name of an existing stored procedure to use to filter which records get replicated to a certain subscriber.

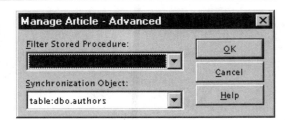

Figure 11.13
*Filter Stored Procedure
and Source Data*

The filter stored procedure must return a 1 (true) or 0 (false), indicating whether the record will be sent to the subscriber. Every modified record in a table marked for replication is sent to the filter stored procedure. If the record passes the filter criteria, the stored procedure returns a 1 and the record is marked in the transaction log for replication. If it doesn't pass the filter criteria, a 0 is returned and the record is recorded in the transaction log but is not marked for replication.

For example, consider the following filter stored procedure:

```
CREATE PROCEDURE prAuthorsFilter AS
BEGIN
    IF EXISTS (SELECT * FROM authors WHERE state = 'CA')
        RETURN 1
    ELSE
        RETURN 0
END — of stored procedure
```

This procedure publishes records only for authors who live in California. Any record with a state whose value is "CA" will be marked for publication in the transaction log. Two notes on these filter stored procedures: First, they must already exist before you get to this dialog box (Figure 11.13). If not, you must create them and come back to this dialog box later. Second, the stored procedures are restricted to one Select statement.

The synchronization object points to the data source that SQL Server uses when a synchronization is needed. By default, the table being replicated is the data source for synchronization. If you are doing horizontal or vertical replication, you can use a view or stored procedure to copy the correct rows and columns.

Other Options

We also need to examine the options in the Scripts tab of the Manage Article dialog box (Figure 11.14). For each of the basic data modification statements (Insert, Update, Delete), you can choose the default and let SQL Server create the statement for you, or you can customize the statement yourself.

Figure 11.14
*Manage Article —
Scripts Tab*

You can specify using stored procedures for articles. Whatever you typed as a command is written to the MSJob_Commands table in the distribution database, which is then transmitted to the subscriber. The field values in the record being replicated are sent as unnamed parameters to the stored procedure. Therefore, the commands you type here must result in a valid command to the subscriber. If the subscriber is another SQL Server, the commands must result in valid Transact-SQL commands.

You can look in the MSJob_Commands table in the distribution database to see the commands as they are being replicated by opening a query window and typing the following query:

```
SELECT * FROM distribution.dbo.MSJob_Commands
```

Your Select statement may different from the one shown above if you have given a new name to the distribution database. The only place the database name is stored is in the Windows NT registry. You can find it under HKEY_LOCAL_MACHINE\SOFTWARE\Microsoft\MSSQLServer\Replication. Then look at the value for the DistributionDB key, which holds the name of the distribution database.

Very advanced users can use the dialog box in Figure 11.14 to call an ODS (Open Data Services) program to replicate to a non-ODBC database. Instead of a stored procedure name here, you type a Call command that forces an RPC (remote procedure call) to your ODS program. For example, typing **call sendauthor** formats an RPC call using the fields in the record as parameters to the function. The results of a formatted call command can be viewed in the MSJob_Commands table in the distribution database, as above.

Figure 11.14 also lets you specify the script that creates the tables on the subscription database. During the initial synchronization process, SQL Server drops and re-creates the table on the subscription database. The default script is a good option only when both databases have some of the same base features. The user-defined data types and defaults must be the same to avoid problems.

To help you create a custom script, click Generate on the Manage Article dialog box shown in Figure 11.14, which brings up the dialog box in Figure 11.15. Each option in this dialog box has ramifications, so let's go through them. This dialog box is a big improvement in 6.5 that avoids the problems using replication in 6.0. The options help you support different replication architectures.

Figure 11.15

Auto-Generate Sync Scripts Dialog Box

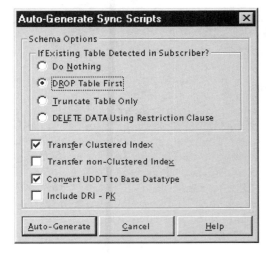

Of the responses to the question, "If existing table detected in sub-scriber?" the Do Nothing option is rarely used. It is beneficial only if you use a manual process on the subscriber to prepare the table to receive the syn-chronized data. The Drop Table First option, which attempts to drop the table on the subscriber before rebuilding and sending the data, is useful when one publisher is the source of the data and there are no foreign key references in the subscriber table. You can choose Truncate Table Only, which removes the data, but not the table. You can neither drop nor truncate a table if any other tables with foreign keys refer to this table. However, if you follow our recommendation to not use foreign keys on the subscribing server, either method is safe.

The Truncate option is good if you have different indexes on the sub-scriber than on the publisher, because the Drop Table option creates the same indexes as the publisher. This setup often occurs when the publisher is an OLTP system and the subscriber is a data warehouse or decision-support server.

The Delete Data Using Restriction Clause, which deletes only the data that matches the restriction clause, is the option to use when you have many pub-lishers going to one subscriber. The restriction clause is the same as the filter on the Filters tab of the Manage Articles dialog box (Figure 11.12).

You can also choose one of the four options at the bottom of the dialog box. The index transfer options perform as indicated; use the first option for transferring the clustered index and use the second option for transferring all the nonclustered indexes.

The third option translates all the user-defined data types into their base storage types. It is best to have the subscription server use the base SQL Server data types, because if you ever have any user-defined data type changes or additions on the publication server, you must also make those changes on the subscription servers in the same order. If you choose to use user-defined data types on all the servers, make sure that each server creates them in the same order, because a "feature" in SQL Server uses the number assigned to the data type instead of the name. If the same user-defined data types have different numbers, the system gets confused.

The last option on this dialog box includes the DRI and primary key (PK) from the table. These options should be separated, because it is best to leave off the DRI and include the PK. The main reason for keeping the PK on the table is that many of the external tools and report writers rely on the PK defin-ition to help them find the definition of unique records in the tables.

Click Auto Generate to create the base script. Once the script is generated, you can then modify the script to your satisfaction. Enter the script name in the Creation Script field shown in Figure 11.14. When you click OK, you return to the Edit Publications dialog box.

Now, let's look at the Synchronization tab, shown in Figure 11.16. Synchronization is the process that initially provides two identical copies of the tables, one on the publisher and one on the subscriber.

Figure 11.16
Edit Publications —
Synchronization Tab

You can choose one of four types of synchronization: automatic, manual, no synchronization, and snapshot only. Automatic is the default synchronization mode, which means that SQL Server checks at a specified interval to see if any new tables need synchronizing. The default interval is five minutes and is easily changed. In fact, we strongly recommend that you increase the interval, because a short interval can quickly fill up your task log in Msdb.

Manual synchronization occurs when you copy or load (restore) a table from the publication database to the subscribing database. At that point, you must manually set the synchronized status on both servers. Use this option for very large tables, for remote subscribers that have only a slow link to the main server, or for data that comes to a central location from various sources.

Choosing no synchronization puts all the burden on you to make sure that the tables on the publisher and subscriber are already synchronized. SQL Server does not check to determine whether they are the same before replication starts. This option is a good choice when the publishing table is empty.

The remaining option is snapshot only, which copies the entire table to the subscription servers at a configurable interval. Any articles on this table are ignored because all the data is copied. This option works well to schedule nightly or weekly batch copies when no one else is on the system. Do not use this option for very large tables or when multiple publishers are consolidating into one subscriber.

Whatever option you choose, SQL Server replication uses BCP to create a data file on disk, then imports it to the subscription server. The two BCP options on the Synchronization tab are for native and character mode copies. The native option keeps the data in the same internal format SQL Server uses. It is faster, but it can only be used when copying between two Microsoft SQL Server databases. The character BCP option exports the data from the publication server, converts it to character data, then saves it in an ASCII file. This method is slightly slower than the native option, but it is more flexible. You must use character mode when you are copying data to ODBC databases.

As you can see from Figure 11.16, you can also schedule the synchronization. To set up synchronization, SQL Server creates a schema file and a BCP data file in the replication working directory, and then executes these files on the subscription server. The schema is the Transact-SQL statement that creates the table, indexes, and constraints. The BCP data file is a native-mode export of the data that BCP uses to import data into the subscribing database. The data file is created with a .tmp extension and is deleted as soon as synchronization has completed. The schema file is created with a .sch extension and remains in the replication working directory.

After synchronization is set up, a task is added to the publisher database. This task is run at the interval you defined in the synchronization schedule. When the task is completed, the distribution server is notified of the successful completion, and the publication server is notified that it can begin replication. See Chapter 3, "Administrative and Programming Tools," for more information about task management.

The last part of the replication process uses the Security tab on the Edit Publications dialog box, as shown in Figure 11.17. You can see that Unrestricted is the default option. If you want to allow only certain servers to see the publication, choose "Restricted to." All the registered servers are shown in the list, so select the Allow Access box next to the servers you want to access to this publication.

When you have set all your options, you see a dialog box similar to Figure 11.18. You see that the Pubs database contains one publication, called Authors_Publication, and that publication contains the authors_table article. You can use the buttons on the right to change or remove the publication.

At the Server Manager window, you can expand the Publications folder and see the list of publications (Figure 11.19). You can see that the

Figure 11.17

Edit Publications —
Security Tab

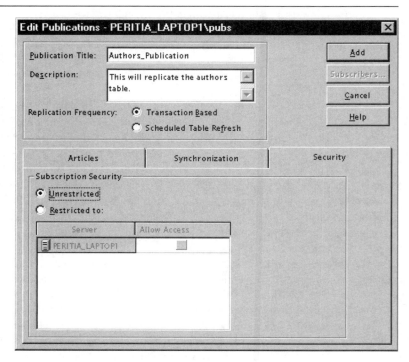

Figure 11.18

Manage Publications —
Completed Publication

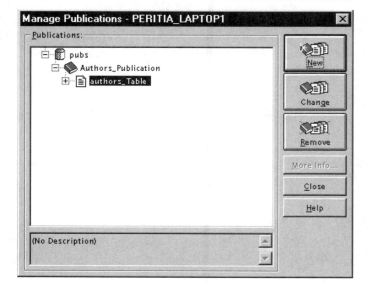

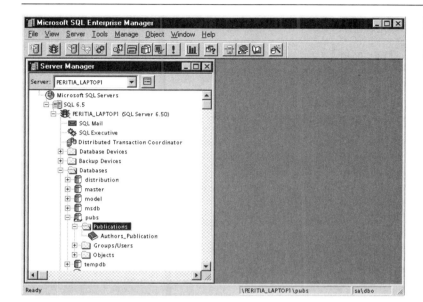

Figure 11.19
Viewing Publications in SQL Enterprise Manager

Authors_Publication appears under the pubs database, but the articles do not show here. Double-clicking on a publication brings up the Edit Publications dialog box in Figure 11.11.

Setting Up and Managing Subscription

After you have set up the publishing process and defined the articles, you must set up the subscription server to attach to the publications or articles you want to use. Choose Replication Configuration from the Server menu and click Subscribing. The Replication Subscribing dialog box shown in Figure 11.20 will appear, and you can enable the appropriate server(s) and database(s) for replication.

For our example, we use the same server for subscription that we used for publication and distribution. The Test database will subscribe to the authors table. Simply select the check boxes next to the appropriate server and database, and your subscriber is enabled.

The next step in managing subscribers is to choose the specific publications or articles defined earlier. From the Manage menu, choose Replication, Subscription. The dialog box shown in Figure 11.21 will appear. The main window displays the server, database, publications, and articles in a tree. If you want to subscribe to all the articles in a publication, highlight the publication and click Subscribe. You can also subscribe to individual articles by

Figure 11.20
Replication Subscribing

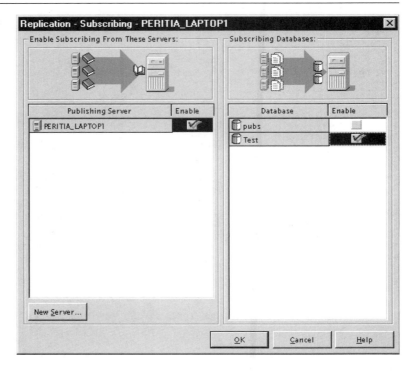

Figure 11.21
Manage Subscriptions —
Choosing Publications
or Articles

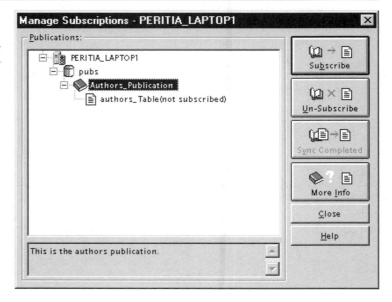

highlighting them and clicking Subscribe. Note that the Sync Completed button is available only if you are using manual synchronization.

When you click Subscribe, the Subscription Options dialog box (Figure 11.22) appears. Choose the Destination Database (subscriber) and the Sync Method, then click OK. The dialog box shown in Figure 11.21 will appear. There, the authors_Table article says Not Subscribed next to it. Highlighting it and clicking Subscribe changes the message to read "subscribed, not synchronized." If you have chosen automatic synchronization, wait until the job has completed, then come back to this dialog box. The message will read "subscribed and synchronized." If you have chosen manual synchronization, you must come back to this dialog box and click Sync Completed.

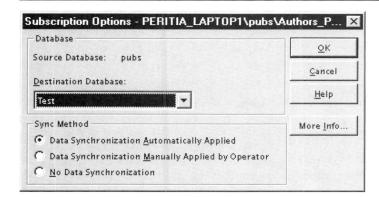

Figure 11.22
Subscription Options

As you are setting up publication and subscription, you can use the topology map shown in Figure 11.23 to give you an overall picture of the architecture. For our example, the same server is used as the publication, distribution, and subscription server. If each service is on its own server, you see three servers in the picture, with lines connecting them. Right-click on one of the servers in the picture, and a menu appears that makes it easy to manage the publications and subscriptions. Be careful, though, because if one of the servers is highlighted and you use the menus to change configuration, you change the remote server in the map, not the one you may be sitting at.

The Security tab in the Manage Publications dialog box (Figure 11.17) lets you set up your security model such that subscription servers only see certain publications. This feature lets you keep a tight reign on secure publications.

Trusted connections are not needed, as is indicated in the SQL Server *Books Online* and other publications. You can have SQL Server set up for standard security, but the SQL Executive login account and password must be the same on each server. In this scenario, each administrator of each server

Figure 11.23
Replication Topology

involved in replication must know all other administrators' login and password for the SQL Executive service. If you do not want administrators to know all the passwords, you must have a trusted connection, and then each server can have a separate login name and password.

Scheduling Replication Backups

Successfully recovering replicated databases depends heavily upon a well-coordinated backup plan. Knowing the reasons for the dependencies between the databases involved in replication can make the difference between an easy recovery and an almost impossible one.

Dependency Between the Publisher and Distributor

The dependency in this relationship is really between the publisher's transaction log and the ms_jobs table in the distribution database. The ms_jobs table contains a pointer to the last successfully replicated transaction in the publisher's transaction log. Whenever you back up this transaction log, it truncates all records that have successfully made it into the distribution database. Therefore, you must always back up the distribution database immediately after dumping the transaction log so that the ms_jobs table pointer always corresponds to the transaction log.

Dependency Between the Distributor and the Subscriber

The mslast_job_info table on the subscriber database always contains one record that is kept up-to-date after every replicated transaction. The value in this record is the job number of the last replicated transaction. Coordinating the backups of the subscriber database is not as critical as coordinating the backups between the distributor and the publisher. The most important relationship for the subscriber database is its dependence on the distribution cleanup task. The next section discusses this dependence in detail.

Troubleshooting Replication

Replication works better when it is set up correctly from the start. Most of the problems come when you try to change something after it is already running. In this section, we mention a few of the most common problems and their solutions. We start with problems commonly experienced at the beginning of replication and work our way through the process.

Synchronization may fail because the subscription database has foreign key constraints. The synchronization process attempts to drop or truncate the table first, to make sure that the subscribing table has a layout identical to the publishing table's. However, because you cannot drop a table that is being referenced by a foreign key in another table, synchronization fails at this point.

If the Msdb database or transaction log keeps filling up, increase the default synchronization time from 5 minutes to the shortest Snapshot Only time, or increase the size of the Msdb database and transaction log.

Connections are a difficult part of replication to set up. You may not be able to create the distribution database if you are connected as a local user on the current server. The synchronization jobs may not be able to log on if you haven't set up a trusted connection or if the SQL Executive logins are not the same. You may need to increase your number of user connections so that the replication processes can always get in.

If transactions are failing because the resources on the subscriber database are locked or otherwise busy, increase the task retry count to 5 and the query timeout to 2 minutes or more. By default, the retry count is 0 and the timeout is 1 minute. Use -q on the task command line to set the query timeout. No parameter in sp_update changes the retry count, so you must manually update the retryattempts column in Msdb's systasks table.

Deadlocks sometimes occur on the distribution databases. You can avoid deadlocks by decreasing the number of transactions between commits from the default value of 100. The number could be as low as 5 if it is an infrequently updated table. As mentioned earlier, don't set it at 1 or 2 because of documented bugs. If you schedule replication instead of using transaction-based replication, increase the time between refreshes. You may be in the process of doing one refresh when the next refresh command launches.

If replication is failing on the subscribing database, check to see if the database is set to read-only or is in single-user mode. To check the options for the subscribing database, go to the configuration options or open a query window and execute the system stored procedure sp_dboption to see the current settings for that database.

For replication to ODBC data sources, you may need to turn off the option to use quoted identifiers if your ODBC database does not support them.

If Sqlexec.exe is failing with Dr. Watson errors, stagger the start times of the distribution tasks. By default, they go off every 5 minutes starting at midnight. If Sqlexec.exe continues to fail, change the distribution tasks to autostart instead of letting them run every 5 minutes. However, autostart tasks must be monitored more closely, because if they fail, they must be manually restarted.

If all else fails, drop the links to the publication servers, distribution servers, and subscription servers, and start over. Sometimes this method of last resort is the only "fix" that works.

What If ...?

In this section, we consider some of the common problems and solutions in replication. For each problem after the first, we tell you how to troubleshoot the problem and provide suggested fixes. In some instances, we give you background information that explains why we suggest certain solutions.

Because the first problem, restoring data from database failure, is more complex, we focus on solutions.

What if a Database Fails and Must Be Restored?

What if any of the databases involved in replication have a catastrophic failure and must be restored? The databases are no longer synchronized. How do you recover from this problem? You may not have to recover data, because in some cases SQL Server automatically recovers the missing transactions.

Restoring a Subscriber Database (Automatic Recovery)

If the subscribing database is restored to an earlier version, the mslast_job_info table in the subscribing database is the basis for the logic behind the automatic recovery. After the database is recovered and the replication process restarts, it looks at mslast_job_info to find the job number of the last successful transaction. Then it looks in the mssubscriber_jobs table in the distribution database to see if any jobs with a higher job number are marked to go to that subscriber. If any jobs meet that criterion, the distribution task sends them to the subscriber.

For example, 100 transactions are entered in a table in the publisher database. Assume that each transaction gets a separate job number, starting at 1 and ending at 100, and enough time has passed that all these transactions have been replicated to the subscribing database successfully. As each transaction is sent to the subscriber, the mslast_job_info table is updated with the job number. When the last transaction is written, the mslast_job_info table has a value of 100. (The mslast_job_info table only contains 1 record per article/subscriber.)

Now, restore the subscriber database to a point where the mslast_job_info table has the value of 80. When the database finishes restoring and replication starts again, jobs 81–100 are replicated automatically, assuming that none of the cleanup jobs in the distribution database have cleared transactions that were successfully replicated.

As soon as the subscriber database fails, go into the Manage Tasks window and disable the cleanup tasks for this subscriber. This one action helps ensure that jobs are not cleaned up during the recovery process, which means a better chance for the automatic recovery to work.

Restoring a Publisher Database

Restoring a publisher database to an earlier date and time is a big problem because the controlling source of the data is earlier than the subscribing database and the distribution database. If you insert the missing records in the publishing database again, the replication fails because the rows it attempts to insert in the subscriber are duplicates.

The easiest recovery is to restore the subscribing database(s) and the distribution database to the same point as the publishing database, assuming that the databases were backed up at the same time. If you set up a backup schedule that backs up all databases at the same time every night, this option is your best choice.

An alternative is to re-synchronize the tables from the publisher to the subscriber, essentially restoring them to the point where the publisher is. This option works well, but you still lose the most recent transactions.

The best alternative for minimizing loss of data is to use the up-to-date subscriber database and copy all the missing transactions back to the publisher. Of course, you must turn off replication during this recovery period so that the same transactions being inserted in the publisher are not sent again to the subscriber. It is advisable to take the time to develop recovery scripts (using Transact-SQL or your other favorite language), unless you already have another mechanism to recover missing transactions after a restore.

Be on the alert for possible problems. The publisher's log reader reads the last distributed transaction from the distribution database and starts from that point. The restoration of the publisher database breaks that link and the log reader no longer has a valid pointer to the next transaction. At this point, the log reader records an error and goes into retry mode. In retry mode, the log reader tries to establish the link once every minute for 24 hours. If you are in this situation, keep reading, because the next step is recovering the distribution database.

Restoring the Distribution Database

As mentioned above, the distribution database keeps the job number of the last transaction that came from the publisher. The log reader uses this number to know where to start if the server is restarted. In the event this link is lost — usually because the publisher database has been restored to an earlier version — the log reader goes into retry mode and replication stops. If you are in this situation, follow the steps below to get replication working again.

1. From the publisher machine, unsubscribe and resubscribe all subscribers.
2. From the distribution machine, go into the Manage Tasks window and run all the cleanup jobs for subscribers associated with the publisher.
3. Stop and restart SQL Executive.

Step 1 causes a complete synchronization of all the tables. Step 2 removes all the old transactions from the distribution database. Step 3 forces the log reader to start again, which makes it reconnect to the distribution database and starts replication going again.

What if the Publication Transaction Log Is Full?

Troubleshooting

A full publication transaction log may indicate a problem with the transaction log reader. It usually means that the log reader either is not running or cannot successfully write to the distribution database.

First, go to the Manage Tasks window and switch to the Running Tasks tab. Check to see whether the log reader task is running. If it is, go to the SQL Error Log file and see if any errors are being recorded. Next, check the Windows NT event log and look for errors related to this problem. The log reader may not be able to connect to the distribution database. One common reason for this problem is that the network is down (if the distribution database is on a different server). Another reason is that no more records can be written to the distribution database, either because its transaction log is full or the database is full.

Background Information

When replication is installed, the transaction log on the publisher has a different role than it does without replication. With replication, it must keep all the transactions until they have been successfully replicated to the distribution database. Without replication, a Dump Transaction command removes all the completed transactions from the log file. When replication is installed, a Dump Transaction command removes the completed transactions only if they have been marked as successfully transferred to the distribution database.

To see if any transactions are waiting to be transferred, run the sp_repltrans stored procedure in a query window. It lists the row number and the timestamp of records waiting to go to the distribution database. If this stored procedure returns results, you can also run the sp_replcmds to see the actual commands (Select, Insert, Update, or Execute).

Fixing the Problem

First, fix any problem you found in the exploration we suggested above. Next, make more room in the transaction log. You can either expand the transaction log or clear it. We recommend expanding the transaction log so you don't lose any transactions marked to send to the subscriber. See Chapter 8, "Database Devices," for instructions on expanding a device and log file.

If you choose to clear the transaction log, you need to re-synchronize the publisher and subscriber. Because the log is full, you cannot do a normal backup of the log file, which normally clears some space, so you must truncate the entire log. First, mark all the non-replicated transactions as having been replicated with

```
sp_repldone 0, 0, NULL, 0, 0, 1
```

Next, clear the transaction log of all records using the command below.

```
DUMP TRANSACTION YourDatabase WITH NO_LOG
```

It is the No_log option that truncates the log. Then, back up your publication database:

```
DUMP DATABASE YourDatabase TO YourBackupDevice
```

Last, unsubscribe and resubscribe all the subscribers. The synchronization process restarts.

What if the Distribution or Subscription Transaction Log Is Full?

Troubleshooting

The transaction log of the distribution database and the transaction log of the subscriber database do not contain any transactions that are vital to the flow of data between the publisher and the subscriber.

Fixing the Problem

First, type the following command:

```
DUMP TRANSACTION YourDatabase WITH NO_LOG
```

Then, do a full backup of the database:

```
DUMP DATABASE YourDatabase TO YourBackupDevice
```

What if the Msdb Transaction Log Is Full?

Background Information

Msdb contains articles, publications, and the history of the tasks that have run. The data in the database is vital to replication, but the data in the transaction log is not. It is safe to truncate the transaction log and back up the Msdb database.

Fixing the Problem

First, type the following command:

```
DUMP TRANSACTION msdb WITH NO_LOG
```

Then, do a full backup of the database:

```
DUMP DATABASE msdb TO YourBackupDevice
```

What if Subscribers Do Not Receive Data?

Troubleshooting

If no subscribers are receiving data, first check to see whether the data is being inserted in the distribution database. Open a query window on the distribution server and choose the distribution database. The default is "distribution," but it can have any valid database name. Then enter the following query:

```
SELECT * FROM msjob_commands
```

If the data you expect to see does not appear in the command column, the problem is in the transaction log reader. Go to the Manage Tasks window and see whether the log reader task is running. If it is, check the task history for error messages.

   If data is in the msjob_commands table, then the problem is in the distribution task. Usually, the distribution task is not running. Sometimes, the command in the msjob_commands table cannot be written to the table. The task history gives you the specific error message.

   To find the specific command causing the problem, go to the subscriber database and type the following command in a query window:

```
SELECT * FROM mslast_job_info
```

The result gives you the last successfully replicated job number. From this job, go back to the list of msjob_commands in the distribution database and find the next greatest job number. Now you have the list of commands in the failing transaction. You can always copy this command to a separate query window, modify it so it is a valid SQL command (usually by removing extra quotes), and run the command to get the error message. The errors can range from having a different table format on the subscriber to referential integrity problems on the subscriber. Whatever the problem, you need to find the specific error message to fix it.

Background Information

The tables in the distribution database are available only to the SA, so you must be logged on with the SA account to be able to select from the tables. The main table to check is the msjob_commands table. It shows you the commands to be posted to the subscriber tables. Another table to check is mssubscriber_status, in which a record is inserted after every transaction is posted to the subscriber table.

Special Note

Most of the configuration entries you use to manage replication are kept in the Msdb, Master, and Distribution SQL Server databases. One important item is kept in the NT registry — the name of the distribution database.

Fixing the Problem

If the problem is with the log reader task, you need to see the task history for this task. If the task is not running, you can restart SQL Executive.

If the problem is in the distribution task, check to see that it is enabled. If not, double-click the task, select the enable check box, then click Modify. If it is enabled, check the task history to see whether any error messages appear. Use the Select commands in the section above to find the job number causing the problem. Then you have three choices:

- If the problem is on the subscriber table, you can fix it.
- If the problem is with the command and you are very good at Transact-SQL, you can update the msjob_commands table and fix the command.
- You can use the stored procedure sp_msKill_Job jobid to remove the transaction from msjob_commands and msjobs in the distribution database. If you do, you must manually apply the transaction in all the subscribers.

What if One Subscriber (of Many) Does Not Receive Data?

Troubleshooting

Check the subscribing server to see whether SQL Server is running, the subscribing database exists, and the subscribing table exists. If all these conditions are met, look at the repl_subscriber login. If it exists, then it is probably not the problem, unless you see login errors in the SQL error log or the Windows NT event log.

Next, run the following command in the subscriber database:

```
SELECT * FROM mslast_job_info
```

If the publication, article, and description columns are not Null (i.e., if they contain data), the distribution task is waiting until manual synchronization is completed. We'll explain finishing manual synchronization in a moment.

If the task is not waiting on manual synchronization, see instructions in the previous section about finding the command causing the problem and how to fix it.

Background Information

When setting up an article, you can choose automatic, manual, or no synchronization. If you have chosen manual synchronization, you must ensure that the data is copied to the subscriber table yourself. Then you must come back to the SQL Enterprise Manager and tell SQL Server that the synchronization is complete. Once SQL Server knows it is complete, replication of transactions can begin.

Fixing the Problem

To update the manual synchronization status, go to the Server Manager window in SQL Enterprise Manager. Click the subscription server to highlight the name, then click Manage Subscriptions on the right side of the toolbar. Expand the tree for the database you are working with by clicking the plus sign next to the database. Then select the publication you are working with and expand the tree. If you need to get to a specific article, click the name of the article. If you want to mark the entire publication and all the articles as being synchronized, click the publication name. If the publication or article is awaiting manual synchronization, the Sync Completed button will be enabled. Finally, click Sync Completed.

What if the Synchronization Task Does Not Work?

Troubleshooting

Go to the Manage Tasks window on the publication server. If the sync task for your subscriber is not there, you need to add a subscriber, as described in the first part of this chapter. If the sync task is there, check the history of the job to see whether any errors have been recorded. If no history is available, the sync task has not run yet. Click the Run Now button (the green arrow on the screen toolbar).

Commonly, either the directory for the synchronization scripts is not valid or SQL Executive does not have the appropriate permissions to read and write the synchronization scripts to the directory. To review which directory is being used, go to SQL Enterprise Manager and the Replication Publishing dialog box. The replication directory is in the lower right corner.

Another common problem is that the synchronization task cannot log on to the subscription server. This problem usually shows up in the task history. One way to determine if logins are a problem is to go to the subscription server and turn on the Audit Logins option in the server configuration dialog box. To get to this dialog box, right-click on the subscription server and choose Configure. When the dialog box appears, click the Security options tab. Near the bottom are the two choices in the Audit Level box. Turn on both options. All output from logins appears in both the SQL Error Log and the Windows NT event log.

See if the table has appeared in the subscriber database. The table is created before BCP can copy the data in the table (see the next section for more details about BCP). If the table exists, see if it has any rows. If not, BCP can't insert rows. Check the task history for a specific error message.

Background Information

The following description of the steps involved in synchronizing tables between the publisher and subscriber assumes that the synchronization option was left on while creating the publication. You do have the option of choosing no synchronization.

The BCP extracts data from the publisher tables and copies it to the subscriber tables. The BCP scripts are saved in the directory you specified when you added this subscriber. Before BCP can run, the table must be created in the subscription server. The synchronization task makes a Create Table script from the publishing database and executes it on the subscriber database. When the table is created, BCP extracts the data from the publisher to a data file in the synchronization directory. BCP then runs again to read that file and insert the rows into the subscriber table. When this insert operation is completed, the synchronization status is updated on the publisher.

Fixing the Problem

If no history is available, the sync task has not yet run. Click the Run Now button (the green arrow on the toolbar).

Check whether SQL Executive has the appropriate permissions on the directory for the BCP scripts. Use the Windows NT directory permissions to review and modify the permissions.

Text and Image Replication

When used in a database, text and image datatypes can have a maximum size of more than 2 billion bytes. The expense of replicating these large amounts of data is not practical. A new configuration parameter, max text repl size, lets the administrator set the largest block of text or image data that can be replicated. The default size of the block is 64K. Trying to replicate a larger block will fail.

When you delete a row with one or more text/image fields, the transaction is logged and replicated. Insert and Update statements acting on text and image fields are also logged and replicated. However, the Updatetext and

Writetext commands are replicated only when they are used with the With Log extension. As noted before, the log reader process is responsible for taking data marked for publication from the transaction log and sending it to the distribution database. When the With No_log option is used with Writetext and Updatetext, replication does not occur.

When you use the Writetext and Updatetext commands, you must set the pointer to be retrieved in the same transaction. These two commands work on one row or column at a time and cannot be used to modify a set of records. The correct order of tasks in a Writetext or Updatetext transaction is

1. Begin the transaction
2. Read the text or image pointer
3. Use the text pointer in the Writetext or Updatetext operation
4. Commit the transaction

Subscribing databases that receive text or image columns must be sized to allow a minimum of 2K per row, even if the publishing table does not contain text or image data in every row. A Null value in the row of the publishing table is sent to the subscriber as one space, which causes a page to be allocated.

In detail, a text or image field takes 16 bytes in the main record, which is just a pointer to the first 2K page. When the publishing table has a Null value in the text or image column, the pointer is Null and no extra pages are allocated. When this row is published, it sends one blank space (" ") as the text or image value, which causes one 2K page to be allocated on the subscribing database.

For example, imagine a table with one text field that has a row size of 50 bytes (34 bytes, including normal overhead plus 16 bytes for the pointer). If you add 10,000 rows with Null values for the text field, the table will be 500K, or approximately 0.5 MB. When this table is replicated, it will be the original 500K plus 20,480,000 bytes, or more than 20 MB.

If you use the Advanced button to use stored procedures in replication, you usually get better replication performance. However, the stored procedure is not used if multiple text or image columns are modified in the same statement. If you have a text or image column, the publication database's log reader creates an Update statement to send to the distribution database.

ODBC subscribers probably are not able to subscribe to articles with text or image fields. Although the Writetext command is replicated as an Update statement, which lets ODBC subscribers get the text or image field, the Updatetext command is replicated as an Updatetext command, which is not supported by ODBC. If you have a table with text or image fields and you use only Writetext commands, an ODBC database could subscribe to this article. However, if you use an Updatetext command when an ODBC database is subscribing to an article with a text or image field, the transaction on the publisher will fail and roll back.

Tip

When you plan the size of a subscribing table that will receive text or image data, calculate the row size without the text or image columns, then add a minimum of 2K to the row size for each text or image column being replicated. If you know that your average text or image value is more than 2K, round to the next highest 2K value and add it to the normal row length, up to the size of the max text repl size configuration parameter.

Summary

Replication is difficult to master, not because it is conceptually hard, but because you have so many options, features, and dialog boxes that it takes time to find the right place to set up your process. Replication may be difficult to get right the first time, but it runs well and quickly when all the pieces are finally in place.

Chapter 12

Database Backup

In most situations, creating and implementing a backup plan is one of a DBA's most important jobs. Without a well-planned, well-executed backup strategy, database failures can be catastrophic, resulting in lost revenue, customers, and jobs (particularly the DBA's). In fact, most IS managers will say that the two most important requirements for a database are

1. It must be up and running whenever it is required by the users.
2. It must be fully recoverable in the event of any problems.

To formulate a reliable and suitable backup plan, you must take into account many variables, including transaction volume, data volatility, acceptable loss of data (some data will always be lost), acceptable time for recovery, and data security. Unfortunately, some events can't be anticipated, but a good backup system can certainly minimize the impact of the events that can be anticipated and perhaps even those that can't be.

In this chapter, we examine

- backup devices
- the kinds of database dumps: database, log, and table
- the commands and menus you use to back up a database
- database options that affect backups
- the questions to ask and issues to consider when you're developing a coherent backup strategy

Although we defer a thorough discussion of database recovery to Chapter 13, backing up databases and recovering the data are two sides of the same coin, so we mention data recovery occasionally throughout this chapter.

Backup Devices

SQL Server backs up databases by dumping data (from a database, a transaction log, or a table) into backup devices it creates and maintains. A backup device can be a disk file, a tape drive, or even a null device.

Special Note

A *null device* is an output device with no output location, also known as the bit bucket, the vast unknown, or the recycle bin.

You can create a backup device in two ways: through the New Backup Device dialog box (Figure 12.1) or with a Transact-SQL command. You access the Enterprise Manager's New Backup Device dialog box by clicking the Backup Devices item on the Server Manager or through the Backup/Restore menu.

Figure 12.1
The New Backup Device Dialog Box

The following Transact-SQL command also creates backup devices.

```
sp_adddumpdevice {'disk' | 'diskette' | 'tape'},
    'logical_name', 'physical_name' [, {{cntrltype [, noskip |
    skip [, media_capacity]]} | {@devstatus = {noskip |
    skip}}}]
```

The logical_name parameter is the name of the backup device (also called *dump device*) used in the Dump statements. Physical_name is the location of the file to create or the name of the tape device to address. The parameters cntrltype and media_capacity are included for backward compatibility. The noskip|skip option tells SQL Server whether to recognize ANSI tape labels that mark expiration dates and permissions for the tape.

Using either the Enterprise Manager or the Transact-SQL command, you can specify what kind of device to create. Notice that you can create a backup device on a diskette with the Transact-SQL command; however, this option is not available through the Enterprise Manager.

You create a Null dump device by adding a disk dump device and assigning it the physical name NUL. When SQL Server is installed it has a default Null dump device named Diskdump. If you dump to this or any other Null device, you won't be able to recover the data later. You should use Null dumps only to mark a database or transaction log as having been dumped. For example, to empty the transaction log, you can dump the transaction log to a Null device. However, if you want to recover a database, you should always follow a dump to the Null device by a database dump, because you can't dump the transaction log again if the last dump was made to a Null device without first dumping the database.

Before you can dump data to a device the first time, you must initialize the device. After you dump to a device, you can choose whether to initialize the device again. If you initialize a backup device after a dump is made to it, the current contents are erased. If you do not initialize a device that has been used for a dump, any new dump will be appended to the previous contents.

Information about backup devices is kept in the sysdevices system table, along with the database device definitions. The backup devices have a cntrl-type (or device type) of 2, 3, 4, or 5 representing disk, diskette A, diskette B, or tape devices, respectively. When a backup device is created as a disk file, SQL Server stores the name of the file to use but does not create or open the file until the device is initialized. Be sure to remember that the file has not been created when you're attempting to do a data dump, because lack of disk space will cause a backup to fail. However, dump files are usually smaller than the database because only those pages that have been allocated are actually backed up.

You can remove backup devices by right-clicking the backup device in the Server Manager and choosing Delete from the menu or by clicking Delete on the Backup/Restore dialog box discussed later in this chapter. They can also be removed using the system procedure

```
sp_dropdevice logical_name
```

where logical_name is the device name.

Types of Dumps

SQL Server creates dumps from which data may be recovered. These dumps come in three forms: database dumps, transaction dumps, and table dumps.

When the whole database is dumped, the current structure, which is contained in the system tables within each database, is saved with the data. Because the structure is saved, the recovery process can be performed starting from a blank database, without the separate step of creating the database structure. Sometimes database dumps are impractical. Databases can be very large, and dumping the complete structure and all the data regularly can become time-consuming and unwieldy.

To avoid complete database dumps, you can also dump only the transaction log, which dumps the list of changes to the database since the last database dump or transaction log dump. Besides being a shorter process than dumping the entire database, transaction dumps have the added advantage of helping you keep the transaction log a manageable size. After a transaction dump, the inactive portions of the log are *truncated,* or deleted. Inactive portions of the log are completed transactions that have been written to the database at specified checkpoints.

The first two types of dumps are often used together to restore failed databases. In general, recovering a database has two steps. The first step is to restore the structure and initial data from the last database dump. Because this dump might be several hours old, you then need to use the transaction dumps to restore the transactions to the database up to the point of failure.

The third type of dump is for table data only. A table dump stores the current data, but not the structure, of a single table. Table dumps can be useful when one table needs to be kept more current than the rest of the database. For example, if you are managing a sales system, you might want to dump the order table every 15 minutes and dump the rest of the database every two hours. In this way, sales information could be restored up to the last 15 minutes by recovering the database from the last dump, loading the transaction dumps up to the most recent one, and then loading the sales table dumps. The orders could then be reprocessed for shipping or material requirements.

Dumping tables is a new feature to SQL Server 6.5, and you should exercise caution when you use this option. Before dumping a table, be sure to analyze all the dependencies of the table. You must ensure that you will not create stranded records in other tables or references within the recovered table to records that no longer exist when you recover the table. It is very important to ensure that referential integrity can be maintained if individual tables are dumped.

You can dump directly to tape or to disk. Direct tape dumps are often not necessary and, in fact, are often not as useful as disk dumps. Tape dumps usually take longer to perform, and recovery time is longer because tape media devices have slower read and write times. For backing up both databases and transaction logs, we recommend performing a disk dump followed by an external tape backup. This strategy creates the minimum effect on the database and allows very fast recoveries in cases where the failure is not caused by hardware. Backing up the disk dump to tape immediately after the dump makes it possible to recover from hardware errors as well. Disk dumps can be impractical if the database is very large. You need to use different strategies when dealing with very large databases (VLDBs).

When dumping and recovering VLDBs, the optimum strategy is to create a multiple device backup with several tape drives running in parallel on multiple threads. Configuring threads is discussed in Chapter 16, "Performance Tuning," where we cover SQL Server configuration options. Using multiple devices for stripe or parallel-output backups is discussed below.

Performing Dumps

SQL Server provides two ways of controlling dumps — through the Enterprise Manager and through a Transact-SQL command. Because the Transact-SQL command gives you more options, we will discuss it first.

TransactSQL Statement

You can dump databases and transaction logs with the following Transact-SQL commands:

```
DUMP DATABASE {dbname | @dbname_var}
     TO dump_device [, dump_device2 [..., dump_device32]]
   [WITH options [[,] STATS [ = percentage]]]

DUMP TRANSACTION {dbname | @dbname_var}
     [TO dump_device [, dump_device2 [..., dump_device32]]]
   [WITH {TRUNCATE_ONLY | NO_LOG | NO_TRUNCATE} {options}]
```

Both dump commands let you specify multiple dump devices. When you specify more than one dump device, the dump is striped across the devices, which decreases both dump time and recovery time. Stripe backups have benefits and drawbacks. They can be useful when you are dumping to slow devices. In addition, they are the only feasible option for dumping large databases.

However, stripe backups increase the number of variables that you need to keep track of, and they require more equipment and administration. If you lose one tape of a stripe set, you will not be able to recover from that backup, so you must control your environment very carefully to ensure that you keep a recoverable backup.

You can stripe backups across different types of backup devices, which may be a useful feature if security is an issue, because striping data across a combination of disks and tapes limits recovery to only those machines that have access to those specific disk devices. However, striping across different types of devices prohibits using a set of tapes to build a copy of the database. Relying on disk storage alone for backup is generally a poor idea, because restoring damaged disks and computers is usually the primary motivation for performing backups. If your strategy incorporates the recommended dump to disk followed by a tape backup, you should be aware of the exposure that exists during the time between the disk dump and the tape backup. Making this time span as short as possible helps to minimize the chances of failure occurring while no feasible backup exists.

As you can see from the Transact-SQL statement, you can use one of three options to dump transaction logs: Truncate_Only, No_Log, and No_Truncate. However, for most transaction dumps in production environments, you don't need to specify an option.

The Truncate_Only option truncates the inactive part of the log without backing it up and logs the transaction dump in the active portion of the log. This option is used to clean the log file of databases that are created on a single device instead of having the data and log on separate devices.

In cases where the log has become full and no logged events can take place until log space is freed up, you can specify the No_Log option. This option truncates the inactive portion of the log without logging the truncation. This dump does not create a backup, either, so neither of these options is useful for creating backups. They should only be used in special circumstances, when you want to clear the log. If the data is important, you should immediately follow one of these dumps with a full database dump.

The third option is No_Truncate. This option was created as a solution for a special problem — the database and log are on different devices, and the data device is lost but the log device is not. In this situation, you have good backups up to a point, and the log file contains the data changed since the last backup, but you cannot get to the log file because the data portion is missing. This condition is known as an *orphaned log file* and it caused a lot of unhappiness in earlier versions of SQL Server. You can now use the No_Truncate option to dump the transaction log before you drop and re-create the database and restore all of your backups in order. In effect, this option tells SQL Server, "I know the database is broken, but give me this important data before I fix it."

The other parameters in the Dump command specify whether tapes are to be ejected after dumps, whether the dump devices are to be initialized before dumps, and whether to record a creation date and the number of days the tape is to be retained.

As part of the Dump command, you can also create a temporary device to contain the dump by using the following parameter in place of a device name in the To parameter:

```
{DISK | TAPE | FLOPPY | PIPE} = {'temp_dump_device' |
@temp_dump_device_var}}
```

These temporary devices are not recorded in the sysdevices system table, as permanent devices are, and exist as devices within SQL Server only for the duration of the dump that specifies them. You can use dumps to temporary devices to recover data in the same way you can use dumps to permanent devices. However, dumps to temporary devices are used typically to support external backup agents using a Pipe device type. (A *pipe* is a mechanism that communicates across processes. External agents use named pipes and pipe dump devices to perform dumps out of SQL Server into an externally managed backup device.)

Enterprise Manager

You can also use the Enterprise Manager's Backup/Restore dialog box to perform dumps. You activate the Database Backup/Restore dialog box, shown in Figure 12.2, by right-clicking the database in the Server Manager and choosing Backup/Restore or by going to the Tools menu and choosing Database Backup/Restore. Notice that the default Null device diskdump has a trash can as its icon in the Backup Devices list box.

You can also truncate the log with the No_Log option from the Edit Database menu.

Tip

The Enterprise Manager's Backup/Restore interface does not give you all the functions you have with the Transact-SQL statements. You cannot create a temporary backup device, and you can dump the transaction log only with the default truncate option.

Figure 12.2

Database Backup/Restore
Dialog Box

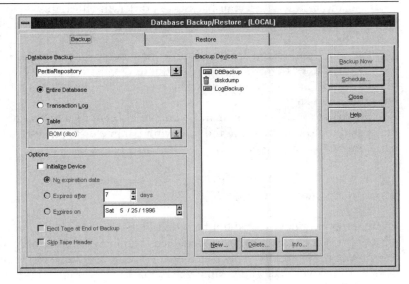

The Database Backup/Restore dialog box gives you easy access to the most common backup settings. You can choose a database, transaction log, or a table to back up. You can set options for initialization, tape ejects, and header information and you can specify one or more backup devices to receive the dump, thereby striping the backup set. By clicking the New button in the Backup Devices window, you can create new devices. Clicking Backup Now or Schedule brings up the Backup Volume Label dialog box (Figure 12.3). Here you can specify a volume label; however, volume labels are not required. In most cases, you gain little benefit from assigning a volume ID, although they can help ensure that a given tape actually contains the backup you think you are restoring.

In most situations, you want to back up regularly. Scheduling automatic backups is preferable to devoting a person to the task, especially if the notification of the success or failure of the backup can be sent to the appropriate person. To get to the Schedule Backup dialog box, click Schedule in the Database Backup/Restore dialog box (Figure 12.2). First, you will see the Backup Volume Label dialog box mentioned in the previous paragraph. After you set the volume ID, click OK to bring up the scheduling dialog box in Figure 12.4.

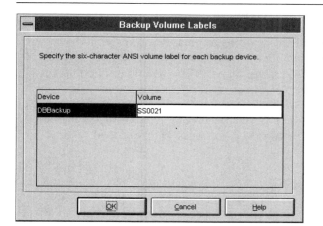

Figure 12.3
*Backup Volume
Labels Dialog Box*

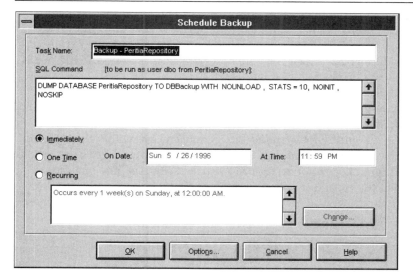

Figure 12.4
*Schedule Backup
Dialog Box*

This dialog box performs the same functions as the New Task dialog box but does not let you specify the type of task that is being performed or the database, because all these options are already set. The Schedule Backup dialog box contains the Dump statement that is generated from the input on the previous screens and lets you create a task to execute the statement on some schedule.

If you use this Schedule option and choose Immediately for the execution time, you can use the Transact-SQL options that aren't available on the base backup screen by simply editing the command and inserting the desired options. Choosing Immediately also lets you execute a long backup and still have access to the Enterprise Manager, because the scheduled task is started as another process in SQL Server. The Options button in Figure 12.4 brings up the TSQL Task Options dialog box, which lets you set up e-mail confirmation that the task has been completed; this screen is the same one that is also available from the Edit Task and New Task dialog boxes.

Database Options

When you configure a database, you can choose two options that can affect your backups.

You can set databases to dump a transaction log when checkpoints are reached. Setting on the "Truncate log on checkpoint" option in the database configuration dumps the log with the Truncate_Only option whenever a checkpoint is executed. This setting can be useful in development environments and when you want to perform a lot of corrections and the log needs to be kept clear during execution.

You can also select the database option Select Into/Bulkcopy. This option lets you perform actions on the database that make it impossible for the log to be dumped and used in a recovery process, because both Select Into and BCP commands perform non-logged insertions. Without log entries, a dump of the log after one of these operations has occurred does not contain sufficient information to restore the database to its previous state. You should not turn on this option in most production environments. Remember that you should always dump the database after performing these types of operations if you want to be able to recover it later.

Developing a Backup Strategy

Before discussing ways to choose a backup strategy, we will consider backup options. Then we can look at the steps in developing a plan for backing up your data. And although having a backup plan may make you feel more secure, you will still be left without data at critical times if you don't set up tasks to carry out your plan.

Basic Backup Options

To recover from the complete loss of a server, you can choose from two methods of backup. The first method is to use an external backup facility to back up the directory where SQL Server is installed, including the Master.dat device and the devices that contain the rest of the databases, and the Windows NT registry. (You can use the Emergency Repair Disk for the registry backup.)

Although you can use the Windows NT tape backup utility to back up the directory where SQL Server is installed, you must first stop SQL Server if you want the backup to include the disk devices directly, because the backup facility cannot back up files that are opened and locked. Third-party backup utilities have been developed that let you back up disk devices while SQL Server is running and let you perform backups across the network.

The second method of creating a complete backup that will restore a lost SQL server is to dump all the databases from the server, back to back. Databases that have interdependencies should be dumped together, preferably in single-user mode.

To recover using this method, SQL Server must first have disk devices already installed that have the same names as the devices stored in the Master database. Then the Master database is restored, followed by the rest of the databases. This method is much less desirable than the first one, and recoveries performed this way can be very difficult. Recovering lost or damaged databases will be covered in detail in the next chapter.

Analyze Your Recovery Requirements

To create a reasonable plan for backing up production databases, you need to consider a number of variables. The order and degree of importance of each of these variables is different in any given situation, and every situation has unique requirements. However, you should ask three questions to help determine your backup strategy.

How Much Data Can Be Lost?

Generally, the frequency with which you want to dump the transaction log is governed by the number of transactions that occur on the database and the acceptable amount data that can be lost if the system has a critical failure. The upper limit of data lost from failure is proportional to the number of transactions that occur on the database in the length of time between the dumps. For example, if a sales system logs 10 orders an hour and you are willing to risk losing up to five sales, then dump the transaction log every half-hour and chances are good you won't lose more than five sales.

How Quickly Must You Complete the Backup and Recovery?

This question affects the medium that may be used for the backup and determines whether you need to stripe your backup. Very fast recoveries are best performed from disk dumps. Keeping the daily transaction dumps on separate physical drives or even on another server provides some protection against critical failures and allows for fast recoveries.

However, for large databases and databases with high transaction rates, this setup may use an unrealistic amount of disk space. In these cases, an alternative is to stripe tape backups. Generally, a two-phase backup — first to disk, then to tape — lets you recover the data very quickly and safeguards the backups against catastrophe. With the low price of a megabyte of disk storage, this method can be used reasonably on databases with gigabytes of data and transaction log. This method also requires less-expensive tape devices, because the speed of the copy to tape is not as critical as the speed of a direct tape backup.

The frequency of full database dumps also has some bearing on the length of time it takes to recover from failure. If a database with a high rate of transactions is dumped only once a week, it can take hours to load its transaction log (or logs) to recover from a crash late in the week. If your database has a high rate of transactions, you should dump it more frequently — for example, nightly.

The number of tapes that you must use to recover a database also influences recovery time. If you stripe the backup, the more tapes you use, the faster the backup and recovery. If you use a single tape drive, using more tapes makes the recovery take longer. Dumps should be appended to a single device or tape whenever feasible so the recovery process does not require tape changes in the middle.

Before setting up the schedule for dumps, you should perform tests to determine the length of time it takes to perform a dump. Be aware that although sessions can remain active during dumps, dumps can severely degrade system performance. The longer the dump takes, the longer users will be inconvenienced. Ideally, your tests should be conducted on data sets that mirror the size and consistency of the expected production data. You can also use smaller sets and scale the results to the expected size of the database; although this method does not always provide a completely accurate measure of the dump time, it should give a good estimate to build upon.

How Big is the Database and How Fast Does the Transaction Log Grow?

If you are going to use a tape drive as part of your backup, the size of the medium and the speed of the drive affect the frequency of both database and transaction log dumps. If the tape drive is small, you should dump the transaction log more frequently to reduce its size so it fits on a single tape. In general, backups that are several tapes long take longer to dump and recover because the tapes need to be changed, so you should dump the full database less frequently if the storage medium is small. A very large database can take several hours to dump onto a single device. You may be able to do a full dump of the database only on weekends or during some extended period of downtime. If the transaction log grows quickly, the database can be dumped more frequently to reduce the size or number of transaction logs that need to be loaded to recover the database.

You can also use some advanced methods of increasing the fault tolerance of your SQL server. First, mirroring and RAID technologies give you some protection against failure. Although these technologies make recovery much less time-consuming, they really can't be recommended as a substitute for tape backups, because they do not create offsite storage and therefore leave holes in the recovery plan if you lose the server completely.

Another advanced way to increase your server's fault tolerance is to create a hot-swap server — sharing an external storage system between two SQL servers, with one accessible and the second in reserve. As long as the data devices are not lost, this setup provides immediate recovery from server failure. A completely independent server can be run and loaded with transaction log dumps from the production server, thus keeping the data on the second server up-to-date. Initially, you synchronize the two databases, and during the course of operation, you load the transaction log created on the production server into the backup server. The backup server should be set so that it doesn't perform checkpoints on recovery, so the transaction count doesn't vary between the production server and the backup server.

Formulating the Plan

After you have analyzed the restrictions and requirements, you can lay out a backup plan. By taking into consideration the answers to the above questions and factoring in any unique requirements of your situation, you can generate a rough schedule that lays out the number of times in a day or week the transaction log and database should be dumped. Next, you need to decide the exact times you should conduct these dumps.

Before you dump a database, we recommend that you run DBCC CHECKDB, DBCC CHECKALLOC or DBCC NEWALLOC, and DBCC CHECKCATALOG. These consistency checks will detect and in some cases fix physical and logical errors. If a database contains errors when it is dumped, it is often impossible to recover the dump. These consistency checks can take a significant amount of time if the database is large. They are best performed when the database is in single-user mode, because they can have a detrimental effect on database performance and may report spurious errors if the database is changed while they run. The results from these checks need to be monitored by an operator and the success of backups should be determined in part by success of these checks. Remember that the SQLMAINT utility lets you perform a backup that depends on the result of the consistency checks, which is a great feature.

You need to approximate the time it will take to check and dump the database to determine when the backup procedure should start. It is at this point in the plan that hardware inadequacies will surface. For example, you may find that a database dump will take six hours given the parameters laid out and you only have a four-hour window to perform the backup. In this case, you need to either upgrade the hardware or change the schedule to fit the capabilities of the hardware.

Enacting the Plan

After the exact times have been determined, you need to set up the tasks that SQL Executive will run. As mentioned above, you can use either the Manage Scheduled Tasks dialog box or the Database Backup/Restore dialog box. You should schedule the consistency checks to occur before the database dumps, and an operator should receive notification that these events occurred and what the results were. These DBCC tasks can be scheduled as CmdExec tasks using ISQL to execute the DBCC commands through a batch file and specifying a log file that can be examined by an operator. You can schedule the database and transaction log dumps as Transact-SQL tasks using the Dump commands and send a notification concerning their exit status to an operator through e-mail. As discussed in Chapter 7, "Scheduling and Performing Administrative Tasks," the SQLMAINT utility lets you run backups and consistency checks in a single command.

You should run all the tasks manually to be sure that they are configured properly. Once the schedule is fixed and has been tested, you should try a test recovery. To verify the backup process in various test emergencies, you should attempt the whole recovery process. In production environments, the backups should be recovered onto another server regularly to test that the process still works and is up-to-date.

Summary

Recovering damaged databases is of primary importance in most production environments, and recovery depends on your backup strategy. Setting up a backup strategy is a three-step process: creating dump devices, formulating requirements, and setting up tasks. The dump devices are the location to which the dumps will be written. The requirements for the backups and recovery are determined by analyzing system usage and acceptable loss of data. The tasks can be scheduled through SQL Executive or executed manually.

Using DBCC, databases can be checked to determine whether they will be recoverable from the dumps. Although all emergencies cannot be anticipated, a backup strategy that ensures complete restoration of a database on a new server will cover almost any contingency. Backups can be time-constrained in many circumstances, and faster hardware or striped backups can sometimes reduce these constraints.

By testing the backup and recovery plans regularly, DBAs can rest assured that their current procedure is adequate and that they will be prepared to perform the necessary tasks under pressure.

Chapter 13

Database Recovery

After you have implemented and tested a backup procedure, your next tasks are formulating and testing a recovery plan. In this chapter, we first give you ideas for your own recovery plan and then discuss various ways you can recover data. SQL Server performs an automatic recovery at startup, but you can also manually recover databases and logs. Using the backups we discussed in Chapter 12, you can recover from three basic types of problems: user error, software failure, and hardware failure. In considering hardware failure, we will discuss the Master database's unique position in backup and recovery — losing the Master database can make other devices unusable even though these devices are not damaged.

The Recovery Process

To ensure that you will successfully recover from a database failure, you should formulate a plan of attack in advance. The basic steps in performing a recovery are

1. Isolating the database from other users. Occasionally, you may need to drop and re-create the database to continue the recovery.
2. Restoring the database from the most recent useable dump.
3. Applying transaction log dumps, in the correct sequence, to the database to make the data as current as possible.

It is a good idea to test your backup and recovery plans periodically by loading the backups and transaction logs into a test database and verifying that your procedure really works.

When you recover a database, you will need to have some information at hand, including the layout of the data segments, devices, and database. It is also vital to know which backup media correspond to which backups, so you need to establish a system to organize your backups and keep records long before you need to recover a database. You also need some kind of documentation that describes the sort order and code page that the SQL server is running. Without this information it may be impossible to recover from catastrophic failures that require rebuilding the Master database.

Recovery at Startup

SQL Server performs an automatic recovery at startup to write committed transactions into the database. This automatic recovery records actions on the database that may have been left in cache memory when SQL Server stopped. SQL Server's two-phase commit model guarantees that transactions are recorded in the database only when they are completed successfully and a log is created. Although this model inhibits data corruption, it also means that when the database is terminated abnormally, you might lose work and wait through a long recovery period.

Because the two-phase commit model can leave large amounts of work in memory while a particular transaction is completing, the transaction log and the data pages in the database can be substantially different. As a large transaction is being processed, the component transactions can be flushed from memory and written to the transaction log as the first step of the two-phase commit. However, if SQL Server fails in the middle of this transaction, and the component transactions have been flushed to the transaction log but the database changes have not yet completed, no Commit is recorded in the transaction log for the second phase of the data change. When you restart SQL Server and the automatic recovery begins, the transaction log information is executed against the database in order from the beginning of the transaction. The time this recovery takes depends entirely on the number of outstanding transactions existing in the transaction log. The two-phase commit model is covered in more detail in Chapter 11, "Replication."

The SQL Server configuration value for Recovery Interval gives the length in minutes a recovery like this should take. The default is 5 minutes per database. However, the actual recovery time depends on the size and number of transactions open at the time of failure.

"Dirty" pages are left in memory only in the event of an abnormal termination. During a normal shutdown, a checkpoint is issued and the committed transactions stored in memory are flushed to disk. In cases of abnormal shutdown, the recovery process locates the last checkpoint in the log and re-executes the transactions, rolling forward in time. The startup recovery does not leave the uncommitted transactions in the state they were in before failure, so they cannot be continued when SQL Server restarts. Instead, the uncommitted transactions are cleared from the log. The recovery does restore committed transactions that were not written to disk by the lazy writer process or a checkpoint. The recovery continues until the end of the log is reached. When the server configuration flag No Checkpoint on Recovery is turned off, a checkpoint is executed at the end of the recovery.

Restoring from Dumps

You can restore databases and log files through the Enterprise Manager by going to the Tools menu and choosing Database Backup/Restore or by right-clicking the database to be restored in the Server Manager and choosing Backup/Restore from the menu. The Backup/Restore dialog box in Figure 13.1 will appear. At the bottom is the backup history of the specified database. The restore process can be specified for the whole database or for a table within the database. The Select Into/Bulk Copy SQL Server configuration flag must be set to True in the database to restore a single table from a backup.

The system administrator must have complete control over the database before a recovery can be performed. You can see who is connected from the current activity window, send messages to users that they need to log off, and terminate (kill) their sessions if they do not respond. The database can be paused to stop any additional connections, and current connections will still be allowed to finish processing. When all the user connections have been

Figure 13.1
*Backup/Restore
Dialog Box,
Restore Tab*

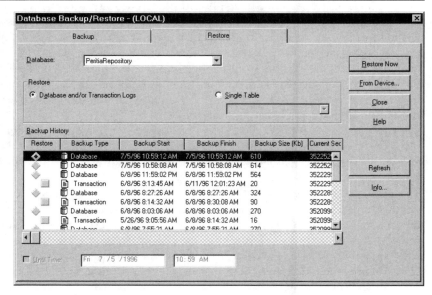

discontinued, the database flag DBO Use Only and server configuration Single User Mode can be set to True. Once a recovery has started, no other connections are allowed in the database until the recovery is finished, regardless of the status of these two flags. Normally a warning message is sent out before connections are dropped and the NT Server Manager can send a message to all currently connected users.

In cases of severe failure, an even better way to ensure that only the administrator connects to SQL Server is to bring it up in single-user mode. If the server has been brought down, use the -m option with Sqlserver.exe and SQL Server will come up in single-user mode, guaranteeing that no connections to any database will be made between recovery steps.

The Backup History window can be used to pick any of the backups recorded for the database. The list does not guarantee that the backup can be restored from the device specified or that the backup contained on the device is the same as the backup listed in the Backup History list. If the ANSI volume label is duplicated when a backup is made to a device already containing a dump and the device is re-initialized, the history list will still show the two backups. However, the backup device will contain only the most recent dump. We highly recommend that the default ANSI label not be changed unless a new unique identification scheme is in place. Unique labels help avoid the possibility of performing a recovery that restores the database to an unexpected state.

New system tables in the Msdb database keep track of all backup and restore operations. The information in the Backup History list comes from these tables. The Backup History list is not reading the file or tape header to see what is on a particular dump device. This list can be confusing at first, especially if you are used to the screen in version 6.0.

The Backup History list shows database dumps and the associated transaction log dumps in a parent-child relationship. The "child" log dumps occurred after the database dump and can be used to recover transactions that were made after the database was dumped. You can select more than one item in the history list, which lets you recover one full database dump and many transaction log dumps in one step. When you select a database for recovery, log dumps are automatically chosen for recovery, too.

If a specific log dump and the database are chosen for recovery, the history list automatically checks all the transaction logs from before the currently selected dump. The history list will not allow nonsequential recovery of transaction logs when the database is selected. If only a transaction log is selected, the history list will allow any of the log dumps to be selected but will not allow multiple log dumps to be chosen if they are not sequential. Thus, you can load transaction dumps one at a time for troubleshooting, but you can't skip transaction log dumps or restore dumps out of sequence. Attempts to restore nonsequential log files will fail.

Stripe backups look just the same in the Backup History list as backups made to single devices. The Enterprise Manager initiates the load off the stripe set and the ANSI labels provide the same sort of identification as discussed above. You can see the Backup History Information dialog box shown in Figure 13.2 by double-clicking a history entry or clicking the Info button. This dialog box displays the device names and ANSI labels of all of the devices involved in the backup. Stripe sets can be assembled using this information and their headers.

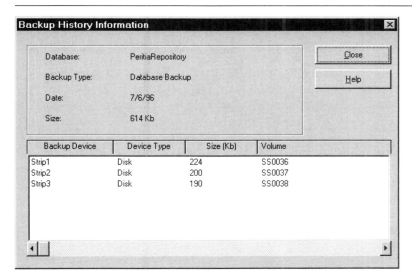

Figure 13.2
Backup History Information Dialog Box

You can use the Until Time check box and the date and time edit boxes in Figure 13.1 to specify a time up to which to restore the transaction logs. In this way, you can eliminate some period of time from the end of a dump if transactions in that timeframe are suspected to have caused the failure of the database. If a time is specified in a recovery, transaction log dumps after that time cannot be used to continue the recovery. This feature prevents you from losing a block of time from the middle of the log dumps.

Clicking the From Device button in Figure 13.1 brings up the Restore From Device On Server dialog box in Figure 13.3. This dialog box lets you choose a backup device that is not listed in sysdevices.

Figure 13.3
Restore From Device On Server Dialog Box

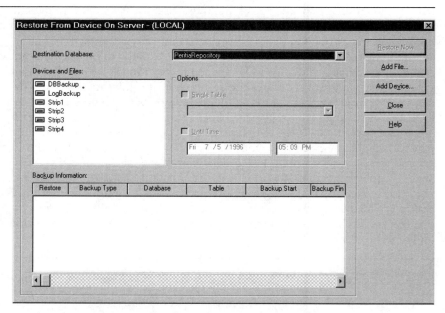

Choosing Add Device in Figure 13.3 brings up the New Backup Device dialog box (Figure 13.4). At this dialog box, you can create a new backup device that writes the backup device information into sysdevices.

Special Note

Creating a backup device, unlike creating a data device, does not initialize the space on disk. In fact, creating a backup device only registers the location and existence of the device in the system tables. The backup initialization creates the file and the dump alters the content of the device. This feature means a backup device file can be copied from one SQL server to another and restored to the second machine without creating the backup device first.

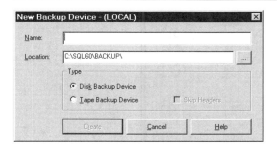

Figure 13.4
*New Backup Device
Dialog Box*

Clicking the Add File button in Figure 13.3 brings up the Add Backup Disk File dialog box (Figure 13.5). Here, you can recover from a disk file that was used as a temporary device, either by using the SQLMAINT utility or the device = disk = *<filename>* option in the Dump command. You can also use this feature to load a transaction dump from another SQL server without creating a record in the sysdevices table.

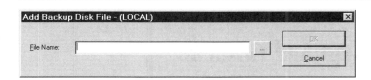

Figure 13.5
*Add Backup Disk
File Dialog Box*

You can also use the Transact-SQL commands below to perform a recovery.

```
LOAD DATABASE | @dbname_var}
    FROM dump_device [, dump_device2 [..., dump_device32]]
    [WITH options
    [[,] STATS [ = percentage]]]

LOAD HEADERONLY
    FROM dump_device

LOAD TRANSACTION {dbname | @dbname_var}
    FROM dump_device [, dump_device2 [..., dump_device32]]
    [WITH options]

LOAD TABLE [[database.]owner.]table_name
    FROM dump_device [, dump_device2 [..., dump_device32]]
    [WITH options]
```

```
WHERE
dump_device =
{dump_device_name | @dump_device_name_var}
|{DISK | TAPE | FLOPPY | PIPE} =
      {'temp_dump_device' | @temp_dump_device_var}
[VOLUME = {volid | @volid_var}]
options =
[[, ] {UNLOAD | NOUNLOAD}]
[[, ] {SKIP | NOSKIP}]
[[, ] FILE = fileno]
[[, ] STOPAT = {date_time | @date_time_var}]
[[, ] SOURCE = source_name]
[[, ] APPEND]
[[, ] STATS [= percentage]]
```

The Load command is self-explanatory, and all of the command's options correspond directly to the Enterprise Manager's screens. The new option Stopat in the Load Transaction statement supports the Enterprise Manager's Until Time recovery option. The Load Headeronly option lets you examine the information of the header without trying to load the whole dump.

Different Types of Failures

You can recover databases after three basic types of problems: user error, software failure, and hardware failure. We will consider each type of problem in depth.

Recovering from User Error

Occasionally (every other day), users will want bits and pieces of data restored that they accidentally changed or deleted. Although backups are generally not created with this function in mind, the best way to get on somebody's good side is to save that person five hours of recovery work.

If the database is backed up regularly, you can recover from user accidents by restoring the database or the needed tables into a secondary database. The lost data can then be loaded into the production database. You should exercise care to ensure that this process doesn't insert duplicate data. As long as the delete or update operation was not cascaded in the database, these sorts of recoveries can be very simple to perform. However, databases with more complicated triggers can pose a significant challenge. Not every DBA will want to shoulder this responsibility, but you should be aware that this sort of selective recovery can be done.

Recovering from Software Failure

Software failure includes problems such as missing extents, pages, or rows in the database. In many of these cases, SQL Server will mark the database as suspect in the Master sysdatabases table on startup by setting on the bit-mask value of 256 in the status column. If a database is marked suspect, the automatic recovery that's performed on startup will not be performed and an error will be logged.

A database will be marked suspect on recovery for a variety of reasons. For example, if SQL Server cannot locate a device used by the database, the database will be marked suspect. Re-establishing the device and resetting the suspect bit in the status field should correct the problem.

At startup, if a database is found to have missing pages, an out-of-bounds row identifier (RID), or corrupt indexes, it will be marked suspect and no other transactions will be allowed in the database. If these types of errors occur during normal database operation, they almost always indicate a serious problem, and you should correct these problems immediately.

To update the status field, the Allow Updates configuration flag must be set on. Remember that this status field is a bit-masked set of values. To update the appropriate bit, use the bitwise OR(|) and AND(&) operators.

Special Note

The first step in correcting these problems is to shut down SQL Server and bring it back up. Occasionally, the startup recovery process will eliminate the errors if they were generated through hardware glitches.

Once SQL Server is running again, examine the error log and note the errors. If the suspect flag was removed at start up, set the database into single-user mode and run consistency checks. By manually updating the status field to remove the suspect flag and running the DBCC NEWALLOC command, you can remove any internal logical problems that were generated, such as incorrect allocation linkages.

You can also update the status field in the sysdatabases table with the bitmask value of −32768 to place the database in Emergency Mode. Emergency Mode turns off the startup recovery for the database and gives you a chance to address problems that are associated with the startup process.

Occasionally, the status field in sysdatabases will not be reset, and the database will stay marked as being in recovery or as still not recovered (bitmasks 64 and 128). Sometimes simply resetting these bits and restarting SQL Server will correct this problem, though you should conduct detailed troubleshooting whenever these flags are set incorrectly during the recovery process.

If the DBCC command fails to identify and remove incorrect linkage problems, and the error messages it generates indicate a problem with an index on a table, dropping and rebuilding the index will usually fix the problem. If the object that caused the error is a user table, sometimes unloading the table, dropping it, and re-creating it will eliminate allocation problems. If all of these actions fail to give you a clean startup, you need to load the database from the most recent clean dump. It is important to note that if a database is marked suspect by the recovery process, the database can not be dropped using the Drop Database command. Instead, you must use the sp_dbremove stored procedure or DBCC DBREPAIR (dbname, dropdb) to drop it.

Special Note

As discussed in Chapter 12, "Database Backups," it is very important that the internal consistency of a database be checked before a dump is made. Dumping a database that has inconsistencies will give you a database that cannot be loaded. Always run consistency checks before and after dumping and loading a database.

Recovering from Hardware Failure

Hardware failure is usually more complicated than software corruption, and it takes three general forms: corruption of the Master device, corruption of data devices, and complete loss of a server.

Master Device Failure

When a Master device is corrupt, you need to completely rebuild the Master database. Running the setup program and choosing Rebuild Master Database (see Figure 13.6) will lead you through the same screens you use during installation to create the Master device.

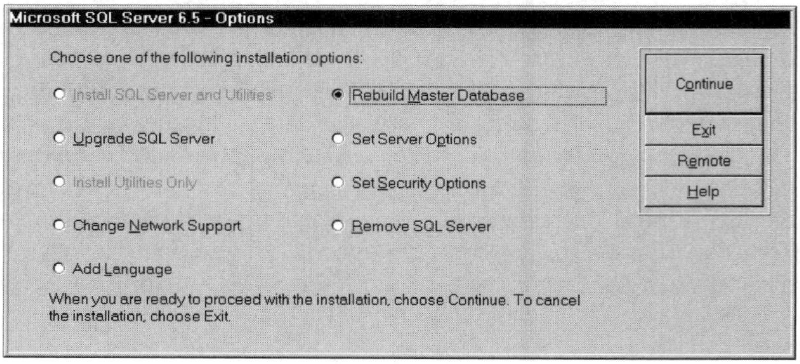

Figure 13.6

SQL Server Setup Options

Rebuilding the Master database eliminates all system table entries and sets the character set and sort order. It also rebuilds the Msdb database. The logins and remote server information will be lost, as well as the list of the devices and databases that existed in the Master database when it failed. All task scheduling is also lost, as well as any replication information. If an up-to-date dump exists for the Master database, you can load this dump into the rebuilt Master device to recover the system information. (SQL Server must be started in single-user mode to load the Master database from a dump.) Loading a backup of Msdb restores the tasks and the basic information for the replication setup, but replication often needs to be re-established. For this reason, you should always back up Msdb when you back up the Master database.

It is critical that the Master database be rebuilt with the same sort order and code page that the original installation used. Databases created under one code page or sort order will not function if the Master database has different ones.

Failure of the Master device can cause the loss of other devices if changes affecting the Master database were made since the last clean dump. If only the Master device is lost and a recent, clean dump of the Master database is not available, the data devices can be added to the sysdevices table, and the databases that existed in sysdatabases can be re-created using Disk Reinit and Disk Refit, as shown below.

The Transact-SQL statement below adds a device to sysdevices and opens the file without initializing it. The file specified by Physname must exist and be a valid SQL Server device.

```
DISK REINIT
NAME = 'logical_name',
PHYSNAME = 'physical_name',
VDEVNO = virtual_device_number,
SIZE = number_of_2K_blocks
[, VSTART = virtual_address]
```

Once all the devices are re-established in this way, you can run Disk Refit to try to recover the database structure of these devices. Running Disk Refit creates records in the sysdatabases and sysusages system tables that define a database and the devices it has allocations on. To successfully recover SQL Server this way, you must know the virtual device number and the allocated size of all of the devices that were on the server. It is a good idea to keep an up-to-date copy of these values.

We strongly recommend that every change to the Master database be followed by a complete dump to ensure that the Master database can be recovered quickly and easily.

Data Device Failure

If the Master device is on a separate physical device from the data devices, and if the data devices are lost through hardware failure, the recovery process is completely different. First, drop from the Master database those databases that resided on the separate devices. Then drop the lost devices and re-create them; you can use Disk Init to re-create the device, as shown below.

```
DISK INIT
NAME = 'logical_name',
PHYSNAME = 'physical_name',
VDEVNO = virtual_device_number,
SIZE = number_of_2K_blocks
[, VSTART = virtual_address]
```

This command initializes the disk file and adds a record to the sysdevices table. After the devices are re-created in the Master database, you can re-create and restore the lost databases from the last clean dump. You do not have to re-create an identical device structure, although you will get errors when the databases are recovered if they are restored into a database with different segment allocations. In fact, you might have serious problems if the system tables have allocation pages that were on segments that no longer exist. For example, let's say you extended a database and the sysprocedures table expanded onto pages in this second allocation segment. If a dump of this database is loaded into a database of the same size as the original database but with only a single segment, then the new pages that sysprocedures used will have incorrect allocation information — the data pages are no longer on a second segment.

In the cases where the affected system tables contain information about the other database objects, the allocation problems can be fixed by dropping and creating all the user objects. For example, rebuilding all the table objects in the database fixes segment allocation mismatches in the sysindexes table, while dropping and re-creating all the stored procedures and triggers fixes the allocation problems in the sysprocedures table.

Server Failure

If you completely lose a server, including both the Master and data devices, you need to perform both recoveries described above. If a recent system-level backup exists (that is, a backup of the complete disk structure through an agent outside of SQL Server), you can load the new disks from the system-level dump and restore recent database dumps as appropriate. If no system-level dump exists, you need to install SQL Server and restore the Master database from backup if one exists.

At this point, you do the same recovery that you would when you lose the data devices. If no current backup of the Master database exists, you need to re-create all the devices and databases and then load them from recent database dumps.

Having a recent system-level backup of the drives on which SQL Server resides can eliminate some of the complexities of recovering from catastrophic failures. It is important to recognize that the registry information is fundamentally important to the operation not only of SQL Server but of Windows NT. Any system backup must include the registry database to provide a reliable backup. If a system-level backup is available for the data devices that fail, you do not need to initialize the devices and databases; all you need to do is restore the last system-level dump onto the replacement drives and load the databases from the most recent dumps. If system dumps are performed regularly, the Master database usually does not need to be rebuilt, because changes happen infrequently in the Master database on production systems.

Summary

SQL Server's startup recovery processes any transactions that may have been left in memory. In the case of software corruption, dropping and re-creating database objects will sometimes fix errors. The status field in the sysdatabases table indicates the current condition of the databases. It is possible for this field to be left in an incorrect state, which makes the database inaccessible; however, this problem can be resolved by manually resetting the bit. System-level backups can make recovery from catastrophic failure much easier. You should always keep available a current clean backup of the Master database and a list of devices and databases. In some cases, you can recover information lost through user error, which saves the user a lot of time and effort and enhances the DBA's prestige.

Chapter 14

Importing and Exporting Data

Many organizations using SQL Server find that they routinely import
and export data from various sources. Data transfers can take many
forms. For example, if you are implementing a replacement system, you
may need to use legacy data to initialize the database. Or your routine
operations might require you to update information regularly, such as
price lists or mailing lists. In these cases, you will be importing data.

Exporting data is a crucial part of many tasks. In a development
environment or when you're troubleshooting problems, it can be very
useful to copy the structure and data from an application while preserving the database state. By working directly with the output of a
query, you can generate quick reports without a report writer or a
custom program. All of these activities are crucial for much of the day-
to-day operation of a database.

Transferring data, whether into or out of a database, can be a
complex process. SQL Server provides several tools that help you in a
variety of situations, including

- The Bulk Copy Program (BCP)
- The Select statement
- The Transfer Manager
- Query results

We consider these options, and times when each option is particularly
useful, in this chapter.

The BCP Utility

When you need to load a large amount of data from or into an external file, the BCP utility can be helpful. BCP is a command-line utility that can read and write files in both ASCII format and in *native* format. (Native format uses variable-length records with field type and length descriptors embedded in them.) BCP using native format is the fastest way to transfer data between databases in SQL Server or Sybase SQL Server. If you use BCP with ASCII files, the ASCII files can be generated as fixed-length records or delimited files, and you can choose the delimiters.

Although BCP has been supplanted in many of its SQL Server data transfer roles, it still is an efficient way to load data generated from any one of a variety of platforms and provide output that can be used on nearly every platform. BCP can quickly load a table without activating triggers and, under the right conditions, can operate without transaction logging. The Transfer Manager, which was added in SQL Server 6.0, eliminated the need to use BCP when transferring data between two SQL Servers connected by a network or between two databases on the same server. (Our discussion of the Transfer Manager begins on page 272.) However, until the addition of removable media databases to SQL Server, BCP was the only standard way to get data to remote locations (locations with no wire connection).

BCP Parameters

The command line for BCP is complicated. Improper use of the options can cause BCP to fail and create significant headaches. BCP runs in an interactive command-line mode, which lets you specify the format of the table to dump if a format file is not provided for export, but other options default unless they are specified on the command line. Knowing when an option can be left out is as important as knowing what the defaults are for other values. We describe the command line in detail here to try to prevent your frustration when you first attempt to use it. Be aware that the options are case-sensitive. Note also that the login information comes at the end, whereas in most other utilities it is the first thing you supply.

```
bcp [[database_name.]owner.]table_name {in | out} datafile
[/m maxerrors] [/f formatfile] [/e errfile]
[/F firstrow] [/L lastrow] [/b batchsize]
[/n] [/c] [/E]
[/t field_term] [/r row_term]
[/i inputfile] [/o outputfile]
/U login_id [/P password] [/S servername] [/v] [/a packet_size]
```

- [[database_name.]owner.]table_name — The table that data will be imported to or exported from. If the user's ID does not have the desired database as its default, the database name must be specified. If the user ID supplied does not own the table, the owner must be specified and the user must have the appropriate permission. To import data into a table, the user must have Insert permission on the table. To export data from a table, the user must have Select permission on the table and on several of the system tables (sysobjects, sysindexes, and syscolumns). Usually the DBO or SA performs this task, in which case, permissions are not an issue.

- {in | out} — Specifies the direction of the data transfer, into the database table (in) or out of the database table (out).

- datafile — The physical location of file to import or export to. This location must be in the path on the machine executing the BCP or you must specify the file with a complete path.

- [/m maxerrors] — The number of errors per batch to ignore before stopping. The default value is 10. If you expect errors, you can raise the maximum number of errors to ignore to let the non-error data load completely.

- [/f formatfile] — The physical location of a BCP format file to be used for export or import. You must use a format file if you are not using a native format or default character format (see the /n and /c parameters, below). This parameter must be supplied with a complete path. When you export data, the format file is used to create the required format. When you import a file, the format file specifies the fields in the data file and the columns that the data fields are to be imported into. If you do not specify the file when you're exporting data, BCP will run interactively and create the format file you describe. If a format file is specified during import and the file does not exist, BCP will generate an error.

- [/e errfile] — The physical location of a file to which BCP should write error messages and records with errors. You should specify the complete path. The default path is the directory from which the BCP executable is run.

- [/F firstrow] — The row on which the import or export is to start. This parameter is particularly useful if you want to skip headers or break up large files into smaller batches.

- [/L lastrow] — The row on which to stop the import or export. This parameter is useful for very large loads that need to be broken up.

- [/b batchsize] — The number of records to load between committing transactions. The default value is all the records being inserted in one transaction. If this parameter is not set appropriately for the job, the load can cause transaction logs to become full (see the discussion about fast and slow BCP on page 266). It works with the number of errors to determine when it will abort.

- [/n] [/c] — Native format or character format. These two options are mutually exclusive; you can specify a format with the /f parameter instead of using either. They are discussed in more detail on page 265.

- [/E] — Turns off the identity insert, allowing files containing rows with identity column information to be inserted with their current identity value. Otherwise, the identity column is set according to the seed and increment defined at the time of creation. If you don't want to preserve the identity column, it is best to use the format file to leave it out of the data export.

- [/t field_term] — The field delimiter indicator; tab (\t) is the default. The most common delimiter is the double quote ("x") or the comma (,), but be aware that comma-delimited data will fail if the data records include commas. We recommend that you choose a character that you are sure is not in the data, such as the pipe (|) or tilde (~), if the source of the data supports it.

- [/r row_term] — The row terminator, typically a carriage return/linefeed (\r \n).

- [/i inputfile] — A file to replace standard input. You can use the file to provide the information BCP requests interactively.

- [/o outputfile] — The physical path to the file to which standard output should be redirected. The file logs information such as the number of rows and other non-error output.

- /U login_id — A valid login ID and user ID for the database(s) the tables are being imported to or exported from. The system administrator login and ID are used by default.

- [/P password] — The correct password for the above user ID. The BCP utility will prompt for a password if none is provided.

- [/S servername] — Server name to connect to. The default is the local server. BCP is faster if you use it locally instead of across the network.

- [/v] — Gives the current version information for BCP. This information is important for the format files.

- [/a packet_size] — Network packet size to be used in transferring data. Values can be between 512 and 36635. Larger packets can improve performance for larger BCP data transfers. Defaults for SQL on Windows NT are now 4096. This parameter can be set for SQL Server under the Configurations menu and overridden on a case-by-case basis through BCP. BCP reports information concerning the network packet size, number of rows processed, and the rate of processing. Microsoft recommends using a value of between 4096 and 8192 for SQL Server running on Windows NT.

The BCP Format File

The most important aspect of using BCP is the format file. The format file defines how data is stored outside the database and in which columns it belongs when it is loaded back into the database. BCP always needs format information even if you don't want to save the format afterward.

If no format file is specified, neither /n nor /c is indicated, and you're exporting data, BCP will query you for field types, prefix lengths, and the field delimiter. These questions are followed by the default value in brackets. These default values represent the default character format dump, which writes numeric data as binaries. If you prefer an ASCII dump so that numeric data is exported as strings, you should specify character ("c" or char) as the type and a 0 prefix length. If the type is given as "c," BCP will ask for the length of the field in characters for all of the fields, including those fields holding numbers.

The BCP format file is itself an ASCII character file with a very specific layout, as shown in Figure 14.1. The version number appears on the first line of the file. This version number should match the version of SQL Server that you're loading data into (you still use 6.0 as the value if you're using either 6.0 or 6.5). You can load data from version 4.21 to version 6.5 in most cases and, using ASCII files, usually into 4.21 from either 6.0 or 6.5. The number of columns appears on the next line of the BCP format file.

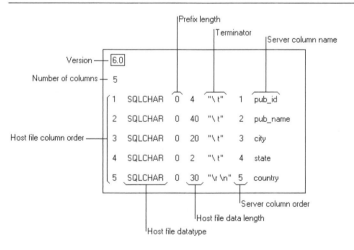

Figure 14.1
Format File Layout

The rest of the file contains the description for each column in the data file. It gives the order the columns appear in the data file, the host file data type, the prefix length (0 for ASCII files and fixed-length binary files), the host file data length, the field terminator, and the number and name of the column in the table the field is to be inserted into. You can change the order of the columns on output, on import by editing this file, or during input, as long as the data types described in the format file are accurate representations of the data types of both the data file and the database table. The column name does not need to match the column name in the database but it cannot be left blank.

For example, the following format file exports data from a table, interchanging the second and third columns.

```
6.0
4
1       SQLDATETIME   0   8      "\t"    1       ErrorDate
2       SQLCHAR       0   255    "\t"    3       ErrorMsg
3       SQLCHAR       0   255    "\t"    2       ErrorCaption
4       SQLCHAR       0   255    "\n"    4       ErrorClass
```

If the same format file is used on import, the columns show up in the correct order in the table. If the format file is changed to the following file for the import, the columns will be interchanged on the load; resulting rows will have the second and third columns interchanged.

```
6.0
4
1       SQLDATETIME   0   8      "\t"    1       ErrorDate
2       SQLCHAR       0   255    "\t"    2       ErrorMsg
3       SQLCHAR       0   255    "\t"    3       ErrorCaption
4       SQLCHAR       0   255    "\n"    4       ErrorClass
```

Fast BCP

BCP operates in one of two ways, depending on the options set in the database and whether you have indexes in the table. If the Select Into/Bulk Copy database option is set to true and the table being loaded with BCP has no indexes, BCP will run in fast mode, which means that BCP will not log transactions. Not logging transactions not only increases performance but also eliminates the need to break up large data loads so the transaction log can be cleared. (However, large batches can fail if the file causes too many errors, so breaking the data into smaller batches is still recommended if problems are encountered during the load.) If the table has indexes, BCP will operate in slow mode even when the Select Into/Bulk Copy database option is set to true. In slow mode, the transactions for the inserts are logged as normal inserts.

If it is not feasible to perform non-logged BCP, you have an option besides using BCP command-line options to break up your data loads. First, perform a non-logged insert into a separate database and table, then use those inserts to load the data in ranges. You may need to dump the transaction log during the load operation. However, remember that a normal transaction log dump writes only completed transactions to the disk dump. If you are loading a large amount of data in one batch, dumping the transaction log while loading the data does not guarantee that the log will not fill up and kill the load. To execute a large data load and still log the transaction, break the load into batches using the first and last row options on the BCP command line and dump the transaction log between the execution of the copy.

Generally speaking, in cases of mass data transfer between SQL Servers it is faster and less problematic to drop the table indexes, set the Select Into/Bulk Copy flag to true, and load the data using fast-mode BCP. You can then reset the flag, dump the database, and rebuild the indexes once the load has been performed.

Defaults, Datatypes, Rules, Constraints, and Triggers

Several unique cases can present problems when using BCP. Using BCP to transfer data between SQL Server tables that have defaults bound to columns can present a problem. When BCP loads fields that have defaults, it replaces null values with the default value, which is often what you want. However, in cases where a default exists to supply a value when none is given and the column is expected to hold the null value when it is explicitly set, BCP will substantially change the data. If you want the column to hold the null value, drop the default value and add it again after the load.

Loading a table with BCP will not execute triggers or apply any rules or foreign key constraints. If you want data in the table to conform to constraints or triggers, you might want to load a secondary table and then validate that the data satisfies the constraints. You can then use Insert statements to insert the data, which will execute the relevant triggers.

Common BCP Mistakes

The most common mistake when using BCP is to use slow-mode loads on very large data sets. Not only does a slow-mode load take a lot longer than a fast-mode load, but the transaction log often fills and causes the load to fail. For large loads, dropping indexes and re-creating them at the end of the BCP is usually faster than updating them during the load. However, it takes time and space within the database to recreate indexes, so you should monitor which method is faster. If you are continually adding data to your table, at some point it is just as fast to do the logged version as the fast-mode load. You need to keep track of the times and resources involved to see if this happens to you. (And then don't forget to update the index statistics if you are not rebuilding the indexes.)

Another common mistake is failing to preserve or create the format file when the data is dumped. Trying to create a valid format file from scratch can be tricky. If the original source exists, performing a second dump on a very small number of rows (say, one row, by setting the last row command-line option to 1) is an excellent way to generate a format file. If you're loading a file from an external source, it is often best to load the complete record layout into a secondary table designed to match the record structure and then use SQL to manipulate the data, eliminating values or certain fields as desired. This approach is usually easier than trying to use the format file to selectively load fields.

Some examples of BCP command lines and the resulting data files are below.

BCP Example 1

The following command line specifies a default character-mode dump using tabs to delimit the fields and carriage return/line feeds to terminate the rows. The resulting data file is shown below.

```
bcp pubs..publishers out publ_out /c /Sservername /Usa /Ppass-
word
```

```
0736    New Moon Books          Boston        MA    USA
0877    Binnet & Hardley        Washington    DC    USA
1389    Algodata Infosystems    Berkeley      CA    USA
1622    Five Lakes Publishing   Chicago       IL    USA
1756    Ramona Publishers       Dallas        TX    USA
9901    GGG&G                   München             Germany
9952    Scootney Books          New York      NY    USA
9999    Lucerne Publishing      Paris               France
```

BCP Example 2

This command line produces a character file with comma-delimited fields and a linefeed at the end of each row. The resulting data file is shown below.

```
bcp pubs..publishers out publ_out /c /t , /r \n /Sservername
/Usa /Ppassword
```

```
0736,New Moon Books,Boston,MA,USA
0877,Binnet & Hardley,Washington,DC,USA
1389,Algodata Infosystems,Berkeley,CA,USA
1622,Five Lakes Publishing,Chicago,IL,USA
1756,Ramona Publishers,Dallas,TX,USA
9901,GGG&G,München,,Germany
9952,Scootney Books,New York,NY,USA
9999,Lucerne Publishing,Paris,,France
```

The Select Statement

In many cases, it is not necessary to use BCP to transfer data between SQL servers. The Into option of the Select statement and the Insert statement used in conjunction with the Select statement are two powerful methods of transferring data and structure between databases and servers.

Adding the Into clause to a Select statement lets you create a new permanent or temporary table. This method is good for straightforward table replication. This syntax creates the table and then inserts the data specified in the Select statement into the newly created table. The table you create with the Select Into statement must not currently exist in the database.

You can also write more complex queries to create a new structure using fields from various tables. You can add fields to the structure by creating variables of the correct type and using them to augment the Select field variables.

You can insert the values into the new table either when you specify the new structure or later by using the Insert statement with the exact Select statement used to create the structure.

The Select statement and its parameters are explained below.

```
SELECT [ALL | DISTINCT] select_list
    [INTO [new_table_name]]
[FROM {table_name | view_name}[(optimizer_hints)]
    [[, {table_name2 | view_name2}[(optimizer_hints)]
    [..., {table_name16 | view_name16}[(optimizer_hints)]]]]
[WHERE clause]
[GROUP BY clause]
[HAVING clause]
[ORDER BY clause]
```

When you use variables to add fields in a Select Into statement, the added fields must be given explicit column headers if more than one variable is to be used. If no column header is given, the column is created with a null name.

Because each of the columns within a table must have a unique name, using two or more variables without assigning column headers to them will cause the Select Into statement to fail. Generally speaking, creating a table with a null column name is a bad idea and is not recommended.

Using Select Into to replicate data is a two-step process. First the table is created, then any rows that qualify are inserted. You can insert a phony Where clause to create only the table, which is a useful strategy if you want to transfer the data at some other time. For example:

```
SELECT T1.field1, T2.field2, T3.field3, field4 = @variable1 into
NewTable
FROM Table1 T1, Table2 T2, Table3 T3
WHERE 1 = 2
```

You can create permanent objects with Select Into if the database configuration option Select Into/Bulk Copy is set to true. This option is required because, like a fast BCP, the Select Into statement is a non-logged operation. Once a Select Into has been performed on a database, you should do a full database dump if you want to recover the data.

The Select Into statement can also create global and local temporary tables if you specify a temporary table that is not currently defined. They can be created regardless of the value of the Select Into/Bulk Copy flag.

The ability of the Select Into statement to copy and preserve data structure on the database is very useful when you're developing or fixing a database. In cases where you need to save test data in its original state to be used again, the Select Into option saves time setting up the test. If you are performing large updates to correct a problem, you can preserve the current state and revert to it if the update does not resolve the problem. In general, you should precede any data adjustment to a database on a production system by creating a duplicate of all current data, either through a data dump or through Select Into and Insert statements.

Using the Insert statement with the Select statement lets you copy data from one table to another and have defaults, rules, triggers, and constraints executed during the copy. This feature is very useful for testing and for data loads. The fields in the Insert and Select statements must match in number and type, but the names of the fields do not need to be the same. Note that the table you're inserting data in must already be defined for this to work, whereas with the Select Into statement, the table CANNOT be defined for it to work.

The Insert statement can assume two formats. The first format allows inserts with stated values. These values can be forced to defaults or can be specified using a Values statement. The second format lets you use a query to specify the data to be inserted. The two formats are as follows:

```
INSERT [INTO]
    {table_name | view_name} [(column_list)]
{DEFAULT VALUES | VALUES(values_list) | select_statement)

INSERT [INTO]
{table_name | view_name} [(column_list)]
SELECT {field_list}
[FROM {table_list}]
[WHERE {where_clause}]
```

If the (column_list) parameter is left out of the Insert statement, SQL takes the whole table, in column ID order, as the default. The Default Values option is used to insert the default values in the columns of the insert table. Type, time-stamp, and identity fields take on their next appropriate value. Fields that accept nulls and have no default defined are set to null. If a field in the table does not have a default and does not accept nulls, the Insert statement will fail. The Values clause lets you insert variables and fixed values and can be used in scripts to load data. The Default keyword can be used in the Values list in place of an actual value if the column has a default or allows nulls.

Stored Procedures

Instead of using a Select statement directly, you can use a stored procedure containing a Select statement to insert data into a table. When Select is used in this way, the result set generated by the stored procedure's Select statement is loaded into the table. The number and type of the returned fields must match the layout of the table given in the Insert statement, as shown below.

```
INSERT [INTO]
{table_name | view_name} [(column_list)]
    EXECute { procedure_name | @procedure_name_var}
    [[@parameter_name=] {value | @variable [OUTPUT] | DEFAULT}
    [, [@parameter_name =] {value | @variable [OUTPUT] |
DEFAULT}]...]
```

The stored procedure can have multiple Select statements in it, as long as all of them have the same result format. The parameters provided to the stored procedure can be specified as output types, which allows the stored procedure to return additional information.

You can use remote stored procedures to load or pull data from a remote source either by taking the field values as arguments and executing the Insert statement on the remote machine or by returning result sets and using the remote procedure in the Insert statement. With these methods, you can perform transfers across servers, which can be very useful in distributed systems.

Transfer Manager

If you don't need to manipulate data during a transfer between two SQL Servers, the Transfer Manager is the easiest way to do transfer data. Go to the Enterprise Manager's Tools menu and choose Database/Object Transfer to display the Database/Object Transfer dialog box in Figure 14.2. From this dialog box, you can transfer data and structure between any two SQL Server databases.

Figure 14.2

Database/Object Transfer Dialog Box

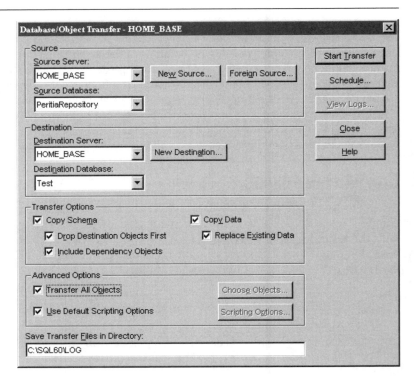

Clicking the Foreign Source button displays the Foreign Source dialog box, where you enter the server name, user ID, and password required to make the connection. The source server can be any SQL server that you can connect to from the destination server. The specified user account must have Select permission on the objects to be transferred. The destination server must be a registered server; you can access the Register Server dialog box with either the New Source or the New Destination button.

From the dialog box in Figure 14.2, you can choose to transfer data, schema, or both. You can generate schema to include Drop statements to guarantee that the new schema will replace any objects that currently exist. Remember that this process will eliminate all the data in destination tables, so if you aren't transferring the data at the same time or if you need to preserve the data on the destination objects, you should use some sort of storage. If the schema contains Drops and objects in the schema don't exist in the destination database, errors will be generated, but the transfer process will ignore these errors and transfer the remaining objects. If the schema doesn't contain Drops, errors will be generated if the object is already present in the destination database. The schema can also be generated to include all the dependencies of the objects specified, thereby ensuring that if the entire database isn't transferred at once, all the necessary dependent objects are generated at the time the transfer is performed. The data can be transferred either preserving the current data or overwriting it. Data rows that violate constraints or rules will not be transferred. The data transfer aspect of the transfer manager follows the same rules as the BCP application in terms of triggers, rules, defaults, and DRI.

All the objects in the source database are transferred by default. By clearing the Transfer All Objects check box and clicking Choose Objects, you can see the Choose Objects to be Transferred dialog box (Figure 14.3). You can choose categories or individual objects.

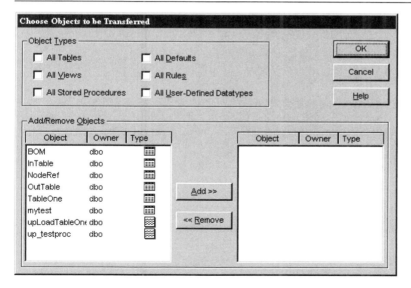

Figure 14.3

Choose Objects for Transfer

You can customize scripting options from the Database Object Transfer dialog box (Figure 14.2) by clearing the Use Default Scripting Options check box and clicking Scripting Options. The Transfer Scripting Options dialog box (Figure 14.4) will appear. At this dialog box, you can specify scripts to include referential integrity, triggers, and column bindings. The user-defined types can be forced to their base values and the field identifiers can be specified in quotes so that fields that have key words for names will be interpreted correctly.

Figure 14.4

Transfer Scripting Options

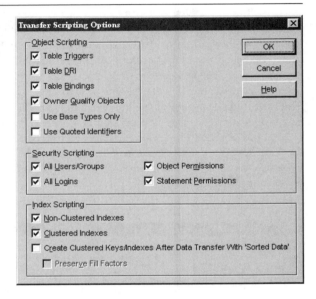

You can also customize the security generated with each script, which controls users, logins, and permissions on transfer. You can also selectively include the clustered and non-clustered indexes in the script. By default, the clustered indexes are created before the data transfer and the non-clustered indexes are created after the transfer, requiring the index pages to be updated during the data load. When you select the Create Clustered Keys/Indexes After Data Transfer With 'Sorted Data' option, the clustered indexes are built with the SORTED_DATA option after the data is transferred. This option causes the statistics to be generated correctly and significantly improves the performance of large data transfers. By specifying this option, the fill factor for the index can be retained in the destination table.

The transfer process generates storage files containing the scripts for the transfer. These files are stored in the <SQLRoot>\Log directory. Many files are generated, each corresponding to one of the object type categories. After the scripting is complete, if any errors were encountered, the View Logs button is enabled and you can review the list of errors. If the whole database is not transferred, errors in transferring rights and owners often occur. The object is not transferred if the user does not exist in the database that the object is transferred to and the scripting options are set not to transfer the users.

Saving Query Results

The query interface can be a fast and efficient method of exporting data. After executing a query or stored procedure, you can save the output to a file by clicking the File Save button. The Save option in the Enterprise Manager's File menu also presents the dialog box. When you use this method, you should generally limit the output to a single result layout; you can use multiple queries easily if all of the result sets have the same number of fields. You can display the Query Flags tab of the Query Options dialog box (Figure 14.5) by clicking Query Options on the tool bar in the Query window or by selecting Set Options from the Enterprise Manager's Query menu.

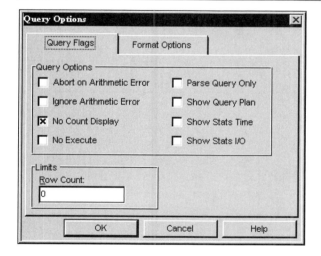

Figure 14.5
Query Flags Tab of Query Options Dialog Box

The second tab of the Query Options dialog box is the Format Options tab (Figure 14.6); from this tab, you can set the characteristics of the output format. The output from a query can be returned as a standard, column-aligned result set or as text delimited with a comma, tab, or with any other single character. The numeric fields in a column-delimited file can be right-aligned, which helps some import programs recognize them as numeric. The output format can be adjusted to perform Verbose Prints to include print statements in Showplan and I/O statistics analysis. You can suppress column headings by clearing the Print Headers check box. Selecting the Output Query box inserts the query that was executed to produce the results at the top of the result set. After the data is saved, the file can be loaded into any application capable of processing the format the query was generated in.

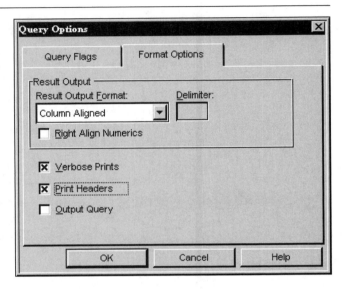

Figure 14.6
Format Options Tab
of Query Options
Dialog Box

Using query results to transfer data lets you gather specific data quickly with very little preparation. It can also be very useful in troubleshooting. You can create one-time reports and perform very specialized data analysis with this technique, saving hours of development time.

Summary

You can move data and the structure of a database into and out of SQL Server in many ways. Some of the older methods can still be used effectively in appropriate circumstances. When you transfer database information between SQL servers, using the SQL object identifier extensions makes writing the transfer as easy as writing the Select statement. The Transfer Manager lets you load remote, connected servers with data from a variety of sources, which is very useful when you create a new database on a registered server. The results window of the query tool provides a quick and easy way of exporting character data for other applications from any registered server.

Table 14.1 summarizes your data transfer options.

TABLE 14.1 RECOMMENDED DATA TRANSFER METHODS		
Source	**Destination**	**Type of Transfer**
SQL Server	SQL Server	Transfer Manager or BCP native mode (Insert statements using RPC calls can also be used)
SQL Server database	Database on same server	Transfer Manager or Insert statements
SQL Server	Third-party database	BCP character mode
SQL Server	Secondary application	BCP character mode or Query window

Chapter 15

Performance Monitoring Guidelines

Learning how to use Performance Monitor and deciding what aspects of performance to monitor are two very important parts of improving SQL Server's performance. Besides taking you on a brief tour of SQL's Performance Monitor, this chapter will discuss the most important counters to monitor (in both Windows NT and SQL Server), consider time intervals, and recommend a long-term strategy for monitoring performance. A final table summarizes which counters to consider for particular problems.

Performance Monitor

Performance Monitor collects data about different counters, such as memory use. Performance Monitor can show you data in graphical format in real time, or you can save the data to log files. Pay particular attention to the discussion of log files in this section, because you will also use log files for long-term performance monitoring, which we will discuss in detail later. Working with a log file can be difficult to learn on your own because the options are not intuitive and are hidden on different screens.

You can choose between two Performance Monitors: one in the Administrative Tools group and one in the SQL Server group. They are the same basic program, but you need to run the one in the SQL Server group because it automatically loads the SQL Server-related counters. You run this version of the program with the following command: Perfmon.exe C:\Mssql\Binn\ Sqlctrs.pmc, where the .pmc file is the Performance Monitor counter file that contains the SQL counters. You can write applications that provide your own counters, and you can modify the new system stored procedures called sp_user_counter1 through sp_user_counter10 and track them, too.

When you run the program from the SQL Server group, the window in Figure 15.1 appears. Because you started the program that includes the set of SQL counters, five counters appear at the bottom of the window when Performance Monitor starts. The five counters are

- Cache Hit Ratio
- I/O — Transactions per second
- I/O — Page Reads per second
- I/O Single Page Writes per second
- User Connections

Figure 15.1

Performance Monitor Window with Tool Bar, Status Row, Watch List, and Status Bar

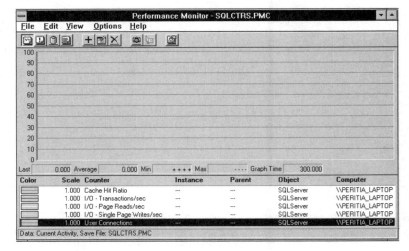

These counters will be explained in more detail later, but first, let's learn how to navigate in Performance Monitor.

Changing Menu Options

The first set of buttons on the tool bar at the top of the window corresponds to the four views of the monitor: chart, alert, log, and report views. You can get to the same options using the View menu.

The menu options change depending upon which view is currently active. Without going into too much detail about the View menu options, their basic purpose is to let you set up and save standard viewing templates for each of the four views.

Understanding Counters

Windows NT lets you watch the performance of the system by "counting" the activity associated with any of its objects. Examples of objects in Windows NT are processors, disk drives, and processes. Each object has specific counters associated with it; for example, the % User Time counter is associated with a CPU or processor to designate what percent of the CPU is taken up by user programs (as opposed to system processes). This chapter gives you enough information to help you choose the right counters at the right time.

SQL Server includes many predefined counters, most of which you aren't likely to use except in special cases. It can be difficult to know which counters are the basic ones to watch. If you have chosen the SQL Server Performance Monitor, several counters have been set up as default counters, such as Cache Hit Ratio and User Connections. You can create your own defaults by creating a .pmc file.

The counters are *hooks* into the operating system and other programs, like SQL Server, that have been built into the software to let Performance Monitor get data. Data collection is performed efficiently so that the additional load on the system is minimized. Windows NT needs most of the information gathered for managing memory, processes, and threads, and Performance Monitor is a good program to display the results.

On the tool bar in Figure 15.1, the button next to the four view buttons at the top of the window is a big plus sign, which you use to add counters to monitor. Click the + button, and the window in Figure 15.2 will appear. The first field, Computer, has a search button at the end of the field. You can click on this field to bring up a list of all computers in your domain and choose a computer from the list, or you can type the name of a server you want to monitor. To monitor other servers, you need Windows NT administrative privileges on them.

In the next field, Object, you choose an object to monitor. The default is Processor, and the default counter shown in the field below is % Processor Time. The box on the right is the Instance. Any particular resource may have more than one *instance*; that is, more than one of that particular resource — in this case, processors — may exist. This computer has only one processor (CPU) because the instance in the box is 0. Instance 3 refers to the fourth CPU.

From the fields along the bottom, you can pick the color, scale, line width, and line style of the information that will be displayed about the counter you are adding. These options let you choose a different look for each counter you add to the window. The only display choice that may need explanation is scale. The scale field is a multiplier that helps you fit the values on the screen in the range you have set on the y-axis, which by default is 0–100.

After you choose the Object, Counter, and Instance you want to monitor and determine how you want the information to appear, click Add. The counter is added at the bottom of the list on the main window (Figure 15.1) and starts graphing the next time your data is refreshed.

If you click the Explain button in Figure 15.2, a brief explanation of the counter you specified will appear (Figure 15.3). Sometimes, though, it uses abbreviations and acronyms that require further research, unless you are a Windows NT internals guru.

Figure 15.2

Adding a Counter

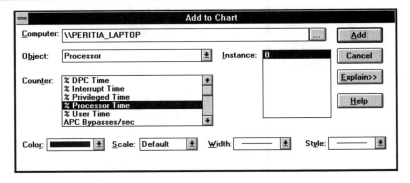

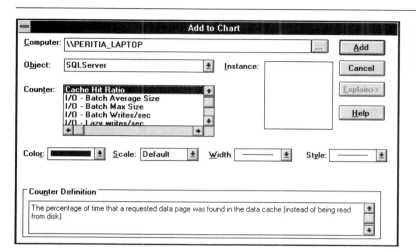

Figure 15.3
*Sample Counter
Explanation*

Setting Up Alerts

An *alert* is the warning the computer sends you when a resource such as
memory or the network becomes a bottleneck. When an alert occurs, it is
written to a log file, along with the date and time it occurred. The log file is a
circular file, allowing at most 1,000 entries before it starts overwriting the
oldest alerts. The alert can also be written to the Windows NT event log.

To add a new alert, click the second button on the toolbar in Figure 15.1,
then click the + button. The dialog box shown in Figure 15.4 will appear.
Choose the counters you want to create alerts for, then click Add. The
example on the screen will create an alert when the Cache Hit Ratio drops
below 85 percent.

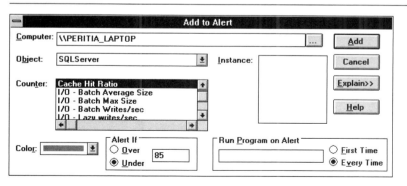

Figure 15.4
Adding Alerts

Notice the Run Program option in the lower right portion of the screen. You can use it to execute a program when the alert occurs. For example, you can choose SQL Server — Log in the Object field, Log Space Used (%) for the Counter, and the database you want to monitor from the Instance list. When the log file for that database gets above 90 percent, you can execute a batch file that runs an ISQL script to dump the transaction log. In this way you can reduce your chances of running out of log space.

Starting Log Files

Learning how to establish log files is very important, because log files are a critical part of the long-term strategy recommended later in this chapter. It can be a bit confusing, so let's go through the steps.

1. Click the third button on the toolbar — View Output Log File Status. Notice that the Log File entry at the top is blank, the status is closed, the file size is zero, and the log interval is 15.00 (seconds).

2. Click +, and the list of objects shown in Figure 15.5 will appear. Select the ones you want to add to the log and click Add. If you hold down the Ctrl key while selecting, you can choose more than one counter, and holding down Shift lets you highlight all the items in a range. All counters in the objects you pick will be tracked in the log file. We will discuss what to monitor later.

Figure 15.5

Adding Counters to Log

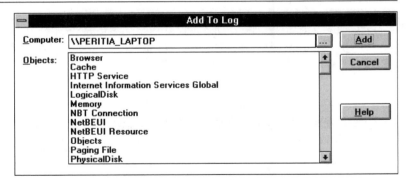

3. Now we need to specify a log file. From the Options menu, choose Log. The dialog box shown in Figure 15.6 will appear.

4. This dialog box looks almost like the standard file dialog box, but it has two very important additions. At the bottom of the screen, the Update Time section shows the refresh interval. For short-term tracking, keep it at 15 seconds. For long-term tracking, set it at 300 seconds

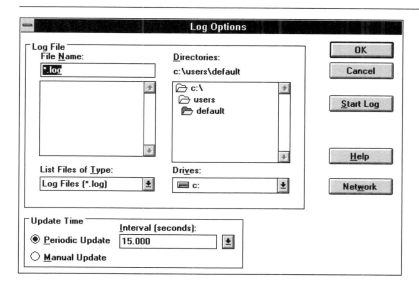

Figure 15.6

*Specifying a Log File —
Options*

(5 minutes). The other important difference between this dialog box and the standard file name dialog box is the Start Log button. Nothing happens until you click this button to start collecting data. Once you do, the text of the button will change to Stop Log.

Type a log file name in the File Name box at the top. Then click Start Log.

5. Click OK to close this dialog box, then minimize the window and let the log run for a while.

6. Maximize the window and click the Stop Log button. Then switch to the Chart view by clicking the first button on the toolbar.

7. From the Options menu, choose Data From. Select the log file you named earlier. You can then choose the counters you want to view from the log.

The best part about using log files is that you can view a few counters at a time to avoid overcrowding the window. You can also mix and match the counters you want to analyze at the same time. This feature is important because many of the counters depend on other counters.

The log file does not do anything until you click the Start Log button in the Log Options dialog box (also available by choosing Log in the Options menu).

Special Note

Reports

The fourth button on the toolbar, the Reports button, lets you print customized reports of the data collected in your log file. Experiment with the available reports when you have a chance; we won't cover this option here.

Time Intervals

The default refresh interval for Performance Monitor is one second. Every second, you get new information about your system's performance. This interval is good for a very short-term examination of the system, but it can be a drain on the server. A five-second interval causes much less overhead, probably in the neighborhood of five percent extra activity. However, for long-term monitoring, 5 seconds produces a very large log file.

Setting the interval to 5 minutes creates a reasonable size log file, but this large an interval can mask performance peaks. However, because each entry in the log file stores the minimum, average, and maximum values for each *counter*, or aspect of SQL Server you want to monitor, you can discover the peaks with a little extra analysis. Five minutes is a good setting for long-term logging. You can always fire up another copy of Performance Monitor and look at one- to five-second intervals if you want a short-term peek into the system's performance.

To determine the amount of drain on the system from Performance Monitor, shut down all the services and start the Monitor again. Add the CPU usage and watch it for about 30 seconds at the default interval of one second. Then change the interval to 0.1 seconds. Your CPU usage will jump dramatically. One odd observation is that the effect of changing from one second to 0.1 seconds is different on different computers, and it is different between Windows NT 4.0 and Windows NT 3.51. For example, when changing the interval on two 133 MHz computers — a laptop and a tower box — the tower machine has the better performance at the shorter interval, showing about 55 percent utilization, while the laptop shows about 60 percent utilization.

Special Note

The faster your refresh option, the more the drain on the system. The default one-second refresh interval creates less than 5 percent overhead on a single-processor machine. For multiprocessor machines, the overhead is negligible. With the refresh interval set to 0.01 seconds, Performance Monitor takes about 60 percent of the resources. At 10 seconds per refresh, the drain is almost too small to measure, even with a lot of counters turned on.

What to Monitor

Now that you know how to use the program, let's get to the section you've been waiting for: How do you know what to monitor? Of the hundreds of Windows NT counters and 50 or so SQL counters, how do you choose? Should you monitor everything? How long should you monitor the system?

Monitoring performance helps you perform two related tasks: identifying bottlenecks and planning for your future hardware and software needs (capacity planning). Learning about the important counters will help identify potential bottlenecks. The strategy section later in this chapter will help you put together a good plan for creating a general monitoring strategy.

What do you want to monitor? Everything! Well, monitoring everything may be a good idea for a short period, but the results will show that many of the counters are always at or near zero; monitoring them all the time may be a waste of time and resources. You need to establish a baseline for your system. This baseline lets you know what results are normal and what results indicate a problem. Once you establish a baseline, you don't need to track everything.

The key categories to monitor can be split into two major sections: Windows NT categories and SQL Server categories. *Categories* in this sense are groups of objects that contain counters.

- Windows NT
  - Memory
  - Processor
  - Disk I/O
  - Network
- SQL Server
  - Cache
  - Disk I/O
  - Log
  - Locks
  - Users
  - Other Predefined Counters
  - User-Defined Counters

When monitoring both categories of data, look for trends of high and low activity. For example, particular times during the day, certain days of the week, or certain weeks of the month might show more activity than others.

After you identify highs and lows, try to redistribute the workload. These peaks and valleys are especially good to know when something new is added to the schedule. If the peak loads are causing problems, identify which things can be scheduled at a later time when the system is not so busy. Knowing the load patterns is also helpful when problems occur, so that you can re-run a particular job or report when the load is low.

Get to know your users — find out which reports they need first thing in the morning. Perhaps you can schedule these reports to run at night in a batch mode, instead of having the user starting them during a busy time.

Monitoring Windows NT

The purpose of monitoring the Windows NT categories is to answer one of two questions: "What resource is my bottleneck?" or "Do I see any upward usage trends that tell me what resource I might run low on first?" SQL Server 6.5 introduced several highwater markers, such as Max Tempdb space used, which make it easier to identify potential long-term problems.

Memory

The Memory: Pages/sec counter is the number of pages read or written to the disk when the system can't find the page in memory. This page management process is referred to as *paging*. If the average value for this counter is five, you need to tune the system. If this value is 10 or more, put tuning the server high on your priority list. Before SQL Server 6.0, the value for this counter was an important flag to tell you whether memory was the bottleneck. Now, with SQL Server's parallel read-ahead feature, this counter will give you only an indication of how busy the read-ahead manager is. However, we will discuss other counters that are better at tracking the read-ahead manager. In other words, this counter may have been one of the most significant counters to track in the past, and it still is on machines without SQL Server, but better ones are available to track memory.

The Memory: Available Bytes counter displays the amount of free physical memory. If the value for this counter is consistently less than 10 percent of your total memory, paging is probably occurring. You have too much memory allocated to SQL Server and not enough to Windows NT.

Processor

Before we start talking about the counters in the processor category, it is important to know that Windows NT assigns certain responsibilities to certain processors if you have four or more CPUs. Processor 0 is the default CPU for the I/O subsystem. Network Interface Cards (NIC) are assigned to the remaining CPUs, starting from the highest-numbered CPU. If you have four processors and one NIC, that card is assigned Processor 3. The next NIC gets Processor 2. Windows NT does a good job of spreading out processor use. You can also set which processors SQL Server uses. See Chapter 16, "Performance Tuning," particularly the notes on the Affinity Mask, for more information about allocating processors.

You can monitor each processor individually or all the processors together. For monitoring individual processors, use the Processor: % Process Time counter. This counter lets you see which processors are the busiest.

A better counter to monitor over the long term is the System: % Total Processor Time counter, which groups all the processors to tell you the average percentage of time that all processors were busy executing non-idle threads.

Who (or what) is consuming the CPU time? Is it the users, system interrupts, or other system processes? The Processor: Interrupts/sec counter will tell you if it is the system interrupts. A value of more than 1,000 indicates that you should get better network cards, disk controllers, or both. If the Processor: % Privileged Time is greater than 20 percent (of the total processor time) and Processor: % User Time is consistently less than 80 percent, then SQL Server is probably generating excessive I/O requests to the system. If your machine is not a dedicated SQL Server machine, make it so. If none of these situations is occurring, user processes are consuming the CPU. We will look at how to monitor user processes when we consider SQL Server-specific counters in the next section.

Disk I/O

As discussed in Chapter 16, "Performance Tuning," having many smaller drives is better than having one large drive for SQL Server machines. Let's say that you need 4 GB of disk space to support your application with SQL Server. Buy four 1-GB drives instead of one 4-GB drive. Even though the seek time is faster on the larger drive, you will still get a tremendous performance improvement by spreading files, tables, and logs among more than one drive.

The single best performance increase on a SQL Server box comes from spreading I/O among multiple drives (adding memory is a close second).

Special Note

Monitor the disk counters to see whether the I/O subsystem is the bottleneck, and if it is, to determine which disk is the culprit. The problem may be the disk controller board. The first thing to know about monitoring disk I/O is that to get accurate readings from the Physical Disk counters, you must go to a command prompt window and type **DISKPERF -y**, then reboot. This procedure turns on the operating system hooks into the disk subsystem. However, this setup also causes a small performance decrease of 3 to 5 percent, so you want to turn this on only periodically and only for a short period. Use the Diskperf -n command to turn it off, then restart your system.

Track Physical Disk: % Disk Time to see how much time each disk is busy servicing I/O, including time spent waiting in the disk driver queue. If this counter is near 100 percent on a consistent basis, then the physical disk is the bottleneck. Do you rush out and buy another disk? Perhaps that is the best strategy if the other drives are also busy, but you have other options. You may get more benefit from buying another controller and splitting the I/O load between the different controllers. Find out what files or SQL Server tables reside on that disk, and move the busy ones to another drive. If the bottleneck is the system drive, split the virtual memory swap file to another drive, or move the whole file to a less busy drive. You should already have split the swap file, unless you only have one drive (which is very silly on a SQL Server machine).

LogicalDisk: Disk Queue Length and PhysicalDisk: Disk Queue Length can reveal whether particular drives are too busy. These counters track how many requests are waiting in line for the disk to become available. Values of less than 2 are good; if the value is any higher, it's too high.

Network

Redirector: Read Bytes Network/Sec gives the actual rate at which bytes are being read from the network. Dividing this value by the value for the Redirector: Bytes Received/Sec counter gives the efficiency with which the bytes are being processed.

If this ratio is 1:1, your system is processing network packets as fast as it gets them. If this ratio is below 0.8, then the network packets are coming in faster than your system can process them. To correct this problem on a multiprocessor system, use the Affinity Mask and SMP Concurrency options in the SQL Configuration dialog box to allocate the last processor to the network card, and don't let SQL Server use that processor. For example, if you have four CPUs, set the Affinity Mask to 7 (binary 0111) and SMP Concurrency to 3. This setup gives three CPUs to SQL Server and the fourth processor to the network card, which Windows NT assigns to that processor by default. If I/O is also a problem, set the Affinity Mask to 6 (binary 0110) and SMP Concurrency to 2, because Windows NT assigns the I/O subsystem to the first processor by default.

Monitoring SQL Server

The questions to ask yourself when monitoring the SQL Server categories are "Do I have the optimal configuration values for SQL Server?" and "Who is consistently using the most resources?"

If any of the counters considered in this section indicate a problem, the problem is somewhere related to SQL Server. If the problem is I/O, memory, CPU, or locks, you can dig deeper and find out who the culprits are. However, if you are using a long-term logging strategy for monitoring, you must monitor every session to be sure you have the necessary historical data when you want to see what was happening at a particular time.

If you are watching the monitor when a problem occurs, go to the SQL Server-Users object and turn on the counter for all instances. The instances in this case are the sessions currently logged on. You can see the login ID and the session number. If you see one or more sessions causing the problem, you can spy on them to find the last command sent. Go to the Enterprise Manager, click the Current Activity button on the toolbar, and double-click the line in the display corresponding to the session number. You will see the last command received from the session. To trace commands in more depth, use the SQLTrace utility that is new with version 6.5. (See Chapter 3, "Administrative and Programming Tools," for details.)

The five main categories of SQL Server counters to monitor are cache, disk I/O, log, locks, and users. We will consider each of these categories separately as well as a mix of other important predefined counters. The final part of this section discusses the new user-defined counters.

Cache

To monitor your cache, watch SQL Server — Cache Hit Ratio. It monitors the rate at which the system finds pages in memory without having to go to disk. The cache hit ratio is the number of logical reads divided by the total of logical plus physical reads. If the value for this counter is consistently less than 80 percent, you should allocate more memory to SQL Server, buy more system memory, or both. However, before you buy more memory, you can try changing the read-ahead configuration options. Also look at the discussion of free buffers in the next chapter to determine whether the number of free buffers is approaching zero. Changing the free buffers configuration parameter may increase the cache hit ratio.

To find out if you have configured SQL Server properly, you should monitor SQL Server-Procedure Cache: Max Procedure Cache Used (%). If this counter approaches or exceeds 90 percent during normal usage, increase the procedure cache in the SQL Server configuration options. If the maximum cache used is less than 50 percent, you can decrease the configuration value and give more memory to the data cache. Rumor has it that SQL Server 7.0 will have a floating-point number for the procedure cache configuration parameter so that you can give the procedure cache less than 1 percent of your SQL Server memory. For a super server with gigabytes of memory, even 1 percent is too much for procedure cache.

If a 2K data page has been swapped to the Windows NT virtual memory file and read in again later, SQL Server still counts the page as already in memory for the purposes of the Cache Hit Ratio counter. Therefore, a system bogged down by heavy swapping to virtual memory could still show a good cache hit ratio. To find out if your system is in this category, monitor the Memory: Page Faults/Sec counter.

The Memory: Page Faults/Sec counter watches the number of times a page was fetched from virtual memory, meaning that the page had been swapped to the Windows NT swap file. It also adds to the counter the number of pages shared by other processes. This value can be high while system services, including SQL Server, are starting up. If it is consistently high, you may have given too much memory to SQL Server. The network and operating system may not have enough memory to operate efficiently.

Warning: This counter is a strange one to figure out. Running this counter on four different types of machines gave widely different results. To try to get a baseline value, we turned off all services, including SQL Server, unplugged the boxes from the network, and ran Performance Monitor with only the Memory: Page Faults/Sec counter turned on. The lowest measurement of page faults per second was from the system we least expected — a 50 MHz 486 with 16 MB of memory and one disk drive. It settled in at about five to seven page faults per second. The DEC Alpha with 4 processors, 10 GB RAID 5 striping on 5 drives, and 256 MB of memory was up in the 35 to 40 page faults per second range. So was a similarly configured Compaq ProLiant. The laptop performed in the middle, at about 15 page faults per second. It is a 90 MHz Pentium with 1 disk drive and 40 MB of memory. All were running Microsoft Windows NT version 3.51 service pack 4. All services except Server and Workstation were turned off. Running the same experiment with Windows NT 4.0 service pack 1 showed approximately the same results, except that the page faults per second numbers ran consistently 10 percent less than in Windows NT 3.51.

The result of this experiment is that we can't recommend a range to gauge the performance of your machine. The best you can do is turn off all services for a brief period to get a baseline measurement on your machine, then use this value as a guide for your regular usage.

Disk I/O

Several counters measure how busy your disk drives are and which disk drives are the busiest. Remember that for any I/O measurements to be effective, you must run the Windows NT Diskperf -y command and reboot the system.

Even though the SQL Server: I/O Transactions Per Second counter is a bit misleading, it is still good, especially for capacity planning. This counter measures the number of Transact-SQL batches processed since the last refresh period. You should not use these results against any standard TPC benchmark tests that give results in transactions per second — it is not referring to a Begin/Commit transaction, just to batches of commands. Watch this number over a span of several months, because an increase in this counter can indicate that the use of SQL Server is growing.

The SQL Server: I/O — Lazy Writes/Sec counter monitors the number of pages per second that the lazy writer is flushing to disk. The lazy writer is the background Windows NT process that takes the data from cached memory and writes it to disk, although sometimes a lazy writer is hardware that reads the cached memory on the disk drive and is managed by the disk controller. A sustained high rate of lazy writes per second could indicate any of three possible problems:

* the Recovery Interval configuration parameter is too short, causing many checkpoints
* too little memory is available for page caching
* the Free Buffers parameter is set too low

Normally this rate is zero until the least-recently used (LRU) threshold is reached. LRU is the indicator by which memory is released for use by other processes. Buying more memory may be the best solution if the configuration parameters seem to be in line for your server size.

The SQL Server: I/O Outstanding Reads counter and the I/O Outstanding Writes counter measure the number of physical reads and writes pending. These counters are similar to the PhysicalDisk: Disk Queue Length counter. A high value for this counter for a sustained period may point to the disk drives as a bottleneck. Adding memory to the data cache and tuning the read-ahead parameters can decrease the physical reads.

The SQL Server: I/O Page Reads per Second counter is the number of pages not found in SQL Server data cache, which indicates physical reads of data pages from disk. This value does not count pages that are read from the Windows NT virtual memory disk file. There is no way to watch only the logical page reads per second. According to sources in the SQL development team, counters for logical pages reads are hidden in a structure that is not available in this version of SQL Server. However, you can figure out the logical page reads per second by taking the total page reads per second and subtracting the physical page reads per second.

You should occasionally turn on the I/O Single Page Writes counter. A lot of single page writes means you need to tune SQL Server, because it is writing single pages to disk instead of its normal block of pages. Most writes consist of an entire extent (eight pages) and are performed at a checkpoint. The lazy-writer handles all the writing of an extent at a time. When SQL is forced to hunt for free pages, it starts finding and writing the LRU pages to disk — one page at a time. A high number of single page writes means that SQL Server does not have enough memory to keep a normal amount of pages in data cache. Your choices are to give more memory to SQL Server by taking memory away from the static buffers, by decreasing the procedure cache, or decreasing the amount of memory allocated to Windows NT.

Log

Tie the SQL Server — Log: Log space used (%) counter to an alert. When the value goes over 80 percent, send a message to the administrator and to the Windows NT event log. When it goes over 90 percent, dump the transaction log to a disk file (not the diskdump device), which will back up the log and truncate it. You want to track this counter for all your application databases, for Tempdb, and for the Distribution database if you are running replication.

Locks

To check out locking, turn on the SQL Server Locks: Total Locks and Total Blocking Locks counters. If you notice a period of heavy locking, turn on some of the other lock counters to get a better breakdown of the problem. The value for Total Blocking Locks should be zero or close to it as often as possible.

One counter to turn on to see if you have configured the system correctly is SQL Server Licensing: Max Client Count. Once you have established that your licensing choice is correct, turn it off. You should turn it back on occasionally to check the connections. If you do exceed the license count, you will know because users will be denied access.

Users

When you suspect that one particular user is the cause of any performance problems, turn on the counters in the Users section. However, with many users on the system, it is difficult to guess which counters to use, and it is difficult to turn on all counters for all sessions. One shortcut is to go into the Current Activity screen of the SQL Enterprise Manager and look at the locks in the Locks tab as well as the changes in CPU and Disk I/O activity in the Detail tab.

Monitor the SQL Server — Users: CPU Time counter for each user. Users for whom this counter returns high values may use inefficient queries. If the query appears reasonable, a high value may indicate an indexing problem or poor database design. Use Showplan to determine if the database's indexes are optimal. Look for wide tables (long row sizes), which indicate a non-normalized database. Wide tables and inefficient indexes can cause more I/O than table scans.

Other Predefined Counters

A new counter in SQL Server 6.5, SQL Server: Max Tempdb Space Used, indicates how well you have estimated the size of Tempdb. If the value for this counter is very small, you know you have overestimated the size of Tempdb. Be sure to watch this counter frequently, especially during the busiest times and when your nightly jobs run. If it approaches the size of Tempdb, then you should probably increase Tempdb's size.

Compare SQL Server: NET — Network Reads/Sec to SQL Server: NET — Bytes Received/Sec (or Network Writes/Sec compared to Bytes Transmitted/Sec). If the SQL Server network counters are significantly lower than your server counter, your server is busy processing network packets for applications other than SQL Server. This reading indicates that you are using the server for uses other than SQL Server, perhaps as a primary or backup domain controller, or as a print server, file server, Internet server, or mail server. To get the best performance, make this server a dedicated SQL server and put all the other services on another box.

If you are using replication, you should focus on the publishing machine. You should monitor the distribution machine and the subscriber as well, but the publisher will show the first signs of trouble. Turn on all counters in the SQL Server Replication-Publishing DB object. The three counters will tell you how many transactions are held in the log waiting to be replicated, how many milliseconds each transaction is taking to replicate, and how many transactions per second are being replicated.

User-Defined Counters

Last but not least, you can define counters. The user-defined counters are in the SQL Server User-Defined Counters object in the Master database. The 10 counters correspond to 10 new stored procedures called sp_User_Counter1 through sp_User_Counter10. These stored procedures are the only system stored procedures you should change. If you look at the code of the procedure, they all perform a Select 0, which, when tracked on Performance Monitor, draws a flat line at the bottom of the screen. Replace the Select 0 with a Select statement that returns one number; an integer is preferable, but float, real, and decimal numbers also work. These queries should be quick, not ones that take minutes to run.

Please note that these counters are different from the user counters mentioned earlier, which track the specific activity of a particular person logged in to SQL Server.

The current version of Performance Monitor contains a bug. If User Counter 1 contains an error, none of the 10 counters will show up in Performance Monitor. However, this bug is not the only reason that you might not see these user defined counters in Performance Monitor. The Probe login account, added when you install SQL Server, must have both Select and Execute permission on these 10 stored procedures for them to appear.

It would be nice to be able to change the names of these stored procedures so you could more easily remember what you are tracking. Maybe this feature will be included in version 7.0.

Here is a trick: Suppose you want to count the number of transactions you have in a table. You could put the following statement in sp_User_Counter1:

```
SELECT COUNT(*) FROM MyDatabase.dbo.MyTable
```

If MyTable had 40 million rows, the stored procedure would take a lot of time to execute, even though it scans the smallest index to get an accurate count. Instead, you could get an approximate number by using the following command:

```
SELECT rows
FROM myDatabase.dbo.sysindexes
WHERE id=OBJECT_ID('MyTable')
AND indid in (0,1).
```

This way is much faster, even though SQL Server does not keep the value in sysindexes up-to-date. Sometimes the counters tracked in sysindexes get out of sync with the actual table, and the only way to get them updated accurately is with DBCC. But most of the time the value in sysindexes is accurate enough.

Long-Term Performance Monitoring

The concept behind a good long-term strategy for monitoring performance is simple to explain: Use log files to track as many items as you can without affecting performance. We break this discussion into three sections: establishing a baseline, monitoring performance over the long term, and tracking problems.

Establishing a Baseline

First, go to a command prompt and turn on the disk counters using the command Diskperf -y, then reboot. Then establish a new log file, click the + button, add all the options, and start the logging process. Choosing all the options tracks every instance of every counter in every object. You are tracking a lot of information, especially with the physical disk counters turned on.

Run Performance Monitor with this setup for a week; if you wish, you can manually stop and restart the log file every night so that each day is contained in a different log file. These measurements become your baseline; all your trend measurements will be based on this baseline. This method is not a perfect way to establish a baseline if you have very many special activities taking place on your server that week. But you may never experience a "typical" week, and it's better to get some baseline measurement than wait.

We also recommend that you start a performance notebook. In this notebook, keep a page where you log special activities and events. For instance, an entry in your log might say, "Ran a special query for the big boss to show what a Cartesian product between two million-record tables does to the system." In your performance notebook, be sure to record changes to the hardware, along with dates and times. You should also schedule actions like backups and transaction log dumps regularly so that when you look at system performance for one night last week, you do not have to wonder whether the backup was running.

We recommend that you run your long-term monitoring from another computer on the network. This way, you are not skewing the results by running it on the server you are trying to monitor. Also, avoid running Perfmon.exe to capture the long-term baseline, because someone must be logged on for it to run, and leaving an administrator machine logged on for long time periods is not a good idea. Instead, run the command-line version of Performance Monitor, called Monitor.exe. It is essentially the same program as Perfmon.exe without the screens. All output can be directed to the log files. To further simplify your life, get Srvany.exe from the Windows NT resource kit and make Monitor.exe into a Windows NT service. This way you can manage Monitor.exe like any other network service.

Periodically, perhaps once every six months, repeat this baseline process with all the counters turned on. Then compare your baselines to establish a trend.

Monitoring Performance over the Long Term

Once you have established your baseline, start another series of log files for your everyday use. First, turn off the physical disk counters with the Diskperf -n command from a command prompt and reboot the system. You can still track everything else if you want to because turning off the physical disk counters reduces the performance problems caused by monitoring. However, it is not necessary to track all the counters. We recommend you track the following objects:

- Logical Disk
- Memory
- Paging File
- Processor
- Server
- SQL Server
- SQL Server — Replication (only if you are running replication)
- SQL Server — Locks
- SQL Server — Log
- SQL Server — Procedure Cache
- SQL Server — Users
- System

Tracking Problems

When you experience performance problems, leave your Performance Monitor running with the log file so you continue to collect long-term data. Then start Performance Monitor again to track the particular problem. Turn on whatever counters you need to look at, using this chapter as a guide for the key counters to monitor in the disk, memory, network, and processors categories.

Start with the high-level counters — look for the words "total" or "percent" (or the % sign). When one of these counters indicates a problem, you usually have the option of watching counters that give you more detail. Learn which counters in different sections are related to each other. The relationships can tell you a lot. For example, the I/O Transactions Per Second counter in the SQL Server section is closely related to the CPU % counter in the processor section. If the number of I/O transactions per second goes up, so does the processor usage.

Concentrate on finding out which resource is causing the problem. Is it the system or a user process? Is it Windows NT or SQL Server? Before you purchase more hardware, try to find a configuration option related to the problem. Don't hesitate to change hardware configuration or move data to different servers to balance the work among the available resources.

For specific examples of tuning performance, see Chapter 16, "Performance Tuning."

Use log files to track as many items as you can without affecting performance.

Special Note

Monitoring with Transact-SQL

You can also use three Transact-SQL commands to do your own monitoring:

- DBCC MEMUSAGE
- DBCC SQLPERF — cumulative from the start of SQL server; use iostats, lru stats, and netstats parameters
- DBCC PROCCACHE — six values used by Performance Monitor to monitor procedure cache

The output from these commands can be inserted into a table for long-term tracking and customized reporting. Tracking the MEMUSAGE output calls for some tricky programming because different sections have different output formats. The other two commands are more straightforward.

The example below shows how to capture the DBCC PROCCACHE output. This command displays the same six values that you can display in Performance Monitor to watch the procedure cache usage in SQL Server.

```
CREATE TABLE PerfTracking
(date_added datetime default (getdate()),
num_proc_buffs int,
num_proc_buffs_used int,
```

```
num_proc_buffs_active int,
proc_cache_size int,
proc_cache_used int,
proc_cache_active int)
go
INSERT PerfTracking (num_proc_buffs, num_proc_buffs_used,
num_proc_buffs_active,
    proc_cache_size, proc_cache_used, proc_cache_active)
EXEC ("dbcc proccache")
go
```

After running this command, you can use any SQL Server-compliant report writer or graphing program to create your own fancy graphs.

Counters: A Summary

The list below is a quick reference to the information about counters we've presented in this chapter. After the performance questions you may ask, we list related counters.

Is CPU the bottleneck?
- system: % total processor time
- system: processor queue length

What is SQL Server's contribution to CPU usage?
- SQL Server: CPU Time (all instances)
- process: % Processor Time (SQL Server)

Is memory the bottleneck?
- memory: page faults/sec (pages not in working set)
- memory: pages/sec (physical page faults)
- memory: cache faults/sec

What is SQL Server's contribution to memory usage?
- SQL Server: cache hit ratio
- SQL Server: RA (all read ahead counters)
- process: working set (SQL Server)

Is disk the bottleneck? (Remember that disk counters must be enabled for a true picture.)
- physical disk: % disk time
- physical disk: avg disk queue length
- disk counters: monitor logical disk counters to see which disks are getting the most activity

What is SQL Server's contribution to disk usage?
- SQL Server-users: physical I/O (all instances)
- SQL Server: I/O log writes/sec
- SQL Server: I/O batch writes/sec
- SQL Server: I/O single-page writes

Is the network the bottleneck?
- server: bytes received/sec
- server: bytes transmitted/sec

What is SQL Server's contribution to network usage?
- SQL Server: NET — Network reads/sec
- SQL Server: NET — Network writes/sec

Did I make Tempdb the right size?
- SQL Server: Max Tempdb space used (MB)

Is the procedure cache configured properly? (The highwater marks for the percentages are more important than the actual values.)
- Max Procedure buffers active %
- Max Procedure buffers used %
- Max Procedure cache active %
- Max Procedure cache used %

Summary

SQL Server 6.5 gives you new configuration and tuning options. It also adds new counters to help you track the use of SQL Server on your system. Use Performance Monitor to see if your system is configured properly. Performance Monitor is one of the best tools you can use to identify current bottlenecks and prevent future problems.

Chapter 16

Performance Tuning

In this chapter, we discuss how to tune SQL Server, the Windows NT Server, and your network options so your server can achieve optimal performance. Notes and documents we have collected over years of working with SQL Server have been used as background for this chapter.

Any discussion of performance tuning must consider the following four topics:

- configuring SQL Server
- tuning the operating system
- designing databases
- optimizing queries

This chapter covers the first three topics. The next chapter is devoted to an in-depth coverage of indexing, and Chapter 18 deals exclusively with optimizing queries.

Configuring SQL Server

Almost all the configuration options in SQL Server directly or indirectly affect the performance of the machine. Most of the minimum and maximum values for these configuration settings are kept in a table in the Master database called spt_values. We describe each configuration parameter, the reason it exists, and (when applicable) its effect on performance.

If you find yourself in a situation where you cannot start SQL Server because of configuration settings, start SQL Server with the -f option, which gives it the minimum configuration values. Then fix the problem and restart SQL Server without the -f option.

As always, you have two options for configuring SQL Server: a command and a dialog box. The command is the sp_configure system stored procedure. To get to the dialog box option, at the Enterprise Manager right-click on a server name and choose Configure from the menu. Click the Configure tab, and the Server Configuration/Options dialog box in Figure 16.1 will appear.

Figure 16.1
*Server Configuration/
Options Dialog Box*

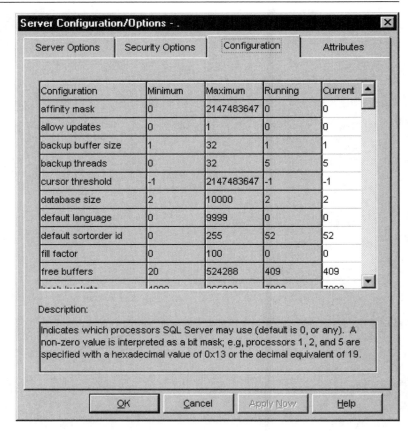

Configuration	Minimum	Maximum	Running	Current
affinity mask	0	2147483647	0	0
allow updates	0	1	0	0
backup buffer size	1	32	1	1
backup threads	0	32	5	5
cursor threshold	-1	2147483647	-1	-1
database size	2	10000	2	2
default language	0	9999	0	0
default sortorder id	0	255	52	52
fill factor	0	100	0	0
free buffers	20	524288	409	409

Description:

Indicates which processors SQL Server may use (default is 0, or any). A non-zero value is interpreted as a bit mask; e.g., processors 1, 2, and 5 are specified with a hexadecimal value of 0x13 or the decimal equivalent of 19.

The note at the bottom of the screen is a quick reminder of what the parameter is used for, not an in-depth explanation. It assumes that you know something about the values from reading SQL Server *Books Online* or other valuable resources like this book.

Table 16.1 lists the configuration options. We added the last two columns, but the rest of the information is available either through the GUI or from the command. We will consider each option in the table individually in the next sections.

TABLE 16.1 OPTIONS FOR CONFIGURING YOUR SERVER

Name	Minimum	Maximum	Running	Current	New In Version	Dynamic
affinity mask	0	2147483647	0	0	6.5	N
allow updates	0	1	0	0		Y
backup buffer size	1	10	1	1	6.0	Y
backup threads	0	32	5	5	6.0	N
cursor threshold	−1	2147483647	−1	−1	6.0	Y
database size	2	10000	2	2		N
default language	0	9999	0	0		N
default sortorder id	0	255	52	52		N
fill factor	0	100	0	0		N
free buffers	20	524288	409	409	6.0	Y
hash buckets	4999	265003	7993	7993	6.0	N
language in cache	3	100	3	3		N
LE threshold maximum	2	500000	200	200	6.0	Y
LE threshold minimum	2	500000	20	20	6.0	Y
LE threshold percent	1	100	0	0	6.0	Y

continued

TABLE 16.1 OPTIONS FOR CONFIGURING YOUR SERVER, CONTINUED

Name	Minimum	Maximum	Running	Current	New In Version	Dynamic
locks	5000	2147483647	5000	5000		N
logwrite sleep (ms)	−1	500	0	0	6.0	Y
max async IO	1	255	8	8		N
max lazywrite IO	1	255	8	8	6.0	Y
max text repl size	0	2147483647	65536	65536	6.5	N
max worker threads	10	1024	255	255		Y
media retention	0	365	0	0		N
memory	2800	1048576	8192	8192		N
nested triggers	0	1	1	1		Y
network packet size	512	32767	4096	4096		Y
open databases	5	32767	20	20		N
open objects	100	2147483647	500	500		N
priority boost	0	1	0	0	6.0	N
procedure cache	1	99	30	30		N
RA cache hit limit	1	255	4	4	6.0	Y
RA cache miss limit	1	255	3	3	6.0	Y
RA delay	0	500	15	15	6.0	Y
RA pre-fetches	1	1000	3	3	6.0	Y
RA slots per thread	1	255	5	5	6.0	N
RA worker threads	0	255	3	3	6.0	N

continued

TABLE 16.1 OPTIONS FOR CONFIGURING YOUR SERVER, CONTINUED

Name	Minimum	Maximum	Running	Current	New In Version	Dynamic
recovery flags	0	1	0	0		N
recovery interval	1	32767	5	5		Y
remote access	0	1	1	1		N
remote connections timeout	−1	32767	10	10	6.5	N
remote login timeout	0	2147483647	5	5	6.0	Y
remote procedure transaction	0	1	0	0	6.5	N
remote query timeout	0	2147483647	0	0	6.0	Y
remote sites	0	256	10	10		N
resource timeout	5	2147483647	10	10		Y
set working set size	0	1	0	0	6.0	N
show advanced options	0	1	1	1	6.0	Y
SMP concurrency	−1	64	0	1	6.0	N
sort pages	64	511	64	64	6.0	Y
spin counter	1	2147483647	10000	0	6.0	Y
tempdb in RAM (MB)	0	2044	0	0		N
time slice	50	1000	100	100		N
user connections	5	32767	20	20		N
user options	0	4095	0	0	6.5	N

The data in the Running column usually matches the data in the Current column. However, when you change parameters that have an N in the Dynamic column, the data in these two columns will be different. A Y in the Dynamic column means that any change to the parameter will take place immediately; you do not have to restart SQL Server. When you change an option that is not dynamic, the change will not take place until you issue a Reconfigure command and restart SQL Server. That's when the values in the Running and Current columns will be different. If you change a value from the configuration screen, the Reconfigure command is executed for you. If you change it using the sp_configure stored procedure, you must also type and execute the Reconfigure command.

The Running and Current columns appear when you use the configuration dialog box in SQL Enterprise Manager. When you use the sp_configure stored procedure in a query window, these columns are called Run Value and Config_Value.

Several advanced options became available with version 6.0. You won't see those options until you change the value for the Show Advanced Options parameter from 0 to 1 and then re-execute the sp_configure command.

Affinity Mask

The Affinity Mask parameter configures SMP (Symmetric Multiprocessing) machines that have four or more CPUs. This bitmask lets you assign SQL Server to use one or more of the CPUs. Assigning SQL Server to particular CPUs lets the network and Windows NT operating system use a restricted set of CPUs, thereby cutting down on the movement of thread structures and thread data between CPUs.

Windows NT automatically uses the first processor for its I/O subsystem and the last processor(s) for the network (NIC) controllers. For example, on a system with eight processors, the last one, processor 7, is used for the first NIC card, and processor 6 is used for the second NIC card. Processor 0 is the first processor. In this example, it would be a good idea to give SQL Server processors 1 through 5, and leave 0, 6, and 7 for Windows NT. This setup defaults the I/O subsystem to processor 0, the first NIC card to 7, and the second processor card to 6; it improves performance by keeping some of the NT processes separate from the SQL Server processes. This configuration would be a binary value of 00111110, or 62 decimal. The binary numbers start right to left, so the bit on the right is processor 0.

Allow Updates

This flag is potentially dangerous because it lets you insert, update, and delete rows in the system tables. You should not turn it on unless you know what you are doing or unless you are instructed to use it by Microsoft support. You will perform most routine updates to system tables with screens or system stored procedures. The Allow Updates flag, like several other configurable parameters, does not affect performance.

A little-known fact is that this flag can cause a security hole. If you turn on the Allow Updates flag and someone compiles a stored procedure that can update the system tables, that stored procedure will still be able to update the system tables even when you turn the flag off. The system stored procedures were designed to work this way; they were originally compiled with Allow Updates set on during the installation or upgrade of SQL Server. If you do elect to turn on this flag, be sure you are the only one on the system and reset it as soon as you finish what you're doing.

Backup Buffer Size

This flag lets you increase or decrease the buffer size used in backup and reloads. This option is measured in 64K chunks (thirty-two 2K pages), so a configuration of 10 increases the normal buffer size by 640K.

Backup Threads

Usually referred to as stripe backups, this option makes parallel backups and reloads possible. With this flag turned on, you can dump the same database to multiple devices at the same time. The devices can be a mixture of tape and disk devices. Stripe backups are useful when your database is too large to back up in the window of availability.

Setting this value to 0 turns off your ability to do stripe backups. Any number greater than 0 represents one less than your number of backup devices. For example, setting this configuration value to 5 lets you have up to six devices.

Cursor Threshold

To understand the meaning behind this parameter, you need to know the basic definition of synchronous and asynchronous queries. A *synchronous query* is one in which the client waits until the query is completed before returning control to the program. An *asynchronous query* lets the calling program continue with other tasks while the query is running. The programming for asynchronous queries can be complex.

The default setting for the cursor threshold parameter is −1, which makes all queries synchronous. When set to 0, all queries are asynchronous and on a separate thread. For any other positive value, SQL Server uses the index distribution page to estimate how many rows will be returned from any particular query. If the estimate is greater than the number specified in the cursor threshold, the query will be asynchronous and run on another thread. For example, if the cursor threshold is set to 100, the query will be asynchronous when the optimizer estimates it will return more than 100 rows.

Don't set this value too low, because small queries are best run synchronously. It is probably best to leave this value alone because it affects the whole server. Front-end clients give you ways to perform asynchronous queries, and using a front-end client such as a Visual Basic application will only affect one session or one query.

Database Size

This option specifies the default size of a database in megabytes if a size is not given during a Create Database command. The default is 2 MB or the size of the Model database, whichever is larger. Incidentally, the Model database used to be 2 MB but was reduced to 1 MB in version 6.0 so that databases could be created for distribution on removable media, like floppy disks. If you add many items to the Model database, you will need to increase the value for this option to avoid getting the error "No more room in database" during a Create Database statement.

Default Language

This flag controls the default language for displaying system messages. U.S. English is always 0, and each language added to the server gets the next available number. You must run the SQL Server Setup program to add another language. The languages are added to the syslanguages table in the Master database. Even though it does not appear in the syslanguages table, U.S. English is always available. You can set the default language for one user with the sp_defaultlanguage system stored procedure.

Default SortOrder ID

The value for this parameter is the number assigned to the currently installed sort order. For example, if you keep the default sort order of "Dictionary

Order, Case Insensitive" during SQL Server installation, then the sp_configure value is 52. To get a list of numbers, their definition, and the corresponding sort order file from the MSSQL\Charsets folder, look in SQL Server *Books Online* under Appendix A/Sort Orders/Sort Order Ids. Do not use sp_configure or the configuration screen to change this number; instead, use Setup.exe in the MSSQL\Binn folder. Get this number right the first time, because if you have to install a new sort order, you must completely rebuild the Master database, which renders all your user databases useless.

Fill Factor

The Fill Factor flag indicates how full the index pages will be after creating an index. For example, a value of 75 means the index pages will be 75 percent full after the creation of the index. For more information about indexes, see Chapter 17, "Indexing."

SQL Server does not maintain the fill rate as records are added and deleted. You must occasionally repack the indexes for optimal performance. The default is 0, which will leave room in the nonleaf pages for one entry on the non-clustered indexes and two entries on the clustered indexes, and the leaf pages will be 100 percent full. Using 100 as a fill factor lets the leaf and nonleaf pages become 100 percent full, which is a good idea for static lookup tables. Refer to the discussion on hot spots and page splits in Chapter 18, "Optimizing Queries," to see the fill factor used to solve a specific performance problem.

Free Buffers

Free buffers are available for buffering I/O. Running out of free buffers can use a lot of system resources. The lazy writer makes sure that the number of free buffers does not fall below the value set for this flag. This parameter can be tracked with Performance Monitor by watching the Cache - Number of Free Buffers counter. If you are getting close to or exceeding the configured value, you can increase the Free Buffers, Max Async. I/O, or the Max Lazy-write I/O parameters. You can also track free buffers with the DBCC SQLPERF (LRUSTATS) command.

Every time you change the memory parameter, the free buffers are recalculated from the amount of memory allocated to SQL Server: free buffers are equal to SQL Server memory multiplied by 0.05. The minimum buffer space is 20 pages. SQL Server does not let you specify more than one-half the amount of memory available to SQL Server when it starts. If you try to set this flag to a higher number, SQL Server will ignore your entry and give you the maximum calculated amount.

Hash Buckets

The Hash Buckets option tells SQL Server how many pages to keep track of at one time. *Hashing* refers to the calculation used to place data pages in memory buffers. Data pages are assigned a number that is calculated (hashed) from some of the data in the pages. The calculated number results in a page number that the data is copied into. If the resulting page is already in use, the algorithm will find and use the next available one. The calculation depends upon setting the value for Hash Buckets to a prime number. But don't worry; if you get close, SQL Server uses the nearest prime number.

For systems with less than 160 MB of memory, this number does not need to be changed; the configured value of 7,993 is adequate. Increase it by a proportional amount for larger systems, but don't make it too large. For example, for a system with 256 MB of memory, around 11,000 is adequate. If you have a system with a very heavy write load, increase the value to 12,000 or 13,000.

Language in Cache

This option determines how many languages can be held in the language cache simultaneously. The default is three languages. We're talking about languages like French and German, not programming languages like Algol and Pascal.

LE Threshold Maximum

The Lock Escalation (LE) Threshold Maximum parameter can help mitigate potential locking problems for extremely large tables. The term *large tables* can mean different things to different people, so read on to find out if tuning this parameter will help you.

The SQL Server Lock Manager escalates a page lock to a table lock when it finds too many page locks on one table. Before version 6.0, when 200 pages were locked, the tables locked, thereby preventing other users from using the tables. The setting of 200 pages could not be changed. On a very large table, 200 pages is a very small percentage of the table, and this upper limit was a significant problem. This parameter now lets you set the number of page locks SQL Server will manage before escalating the lock to a table lock.

If you have a problem with replication deadlocks between the log reader and the distribution process, increasing this parameter will help get rid of the problem. It will minimize table locks during replication.

This parameter and the next two lock escalation parameters apply per SQL statement, not per transaction. Lock escalation applies to any of the four basic SQL statements: Insert, Update, Delete, and Select. These thresholds apply to the system as a whole but can be overridden using these optimizer hints in the Select statement: Paglock, Tablock, Tablockx, and Updlock.

LE Threshold Minimum

The LE Threshold Minimum option prevents table locks on small tables where the next parameter, LE Threshold Percent, is reached too quickly. See also LE Threshold Maximum, above.

LE Threshold Percent

The LE Threshold Percent value tells the lock manager to escalate to a table lock when a percent of the table has been locked. A value of 0 works in conjunction with the LE Threshold Maximum parameter, causing a table lock only after the value in the Maximum parameter is exceeded.

Locks

With this parameter, you set the total number of available lock entries that the lock manager can handle. In other words, this value represents the maximum number of rows allowed in the syslocks table. Be aware that each lock takes 32 bytes, and the syslocks table resides in memory after SQL Server is started. The memory block that manages locks is fully allocated as soon as SQL Server is started. For example, the default of 5,000 locks takes up 160,000 bytes (32 multiplied by 5,000) of the memory allocated to SQL Server.

How do you know if you need to make this value larger? An error message tells you that you have run out of locks. If you are running a very large transaction when this occurs, you may need to break the transaction into smaller pieces. Monitoring the total locks in Performance Monitor during medium and high loads is the best way to determine whether you are getting close to the limit. You will find the Total Locks counter in the SQL Server Locks section of the counters.

Logwrite Sleep (ms)

This option lets the SQL Server log writer delay a certain number of milliseconds before writing the log buffer to disk if the log buffer is not full. The purpose of this option is to give the buffer time to fill up before it writes. A value of −1 means that delays never occur, and a value of 0 means that the server will wait only if current active transactions are open. If you have performance problems on a system with very heavy write loads, this value is one of your many performance tuning options. Try setting it to −1.

Max Async I/O

This parameter tells SQL Server how many asynchronous I/Os can be issued simultaneously. You should use this option if you are using disk striping (any RAID level) and your server has multiple disk controllers or a smart disk controller, such as the Compaq Smart Array. You can also use this option if your database is on multiple physical drives with multiple controllers. Max Async I/O controls batched asynchronous I/Os such as Bulkcopy commands and checkpoints.

Max Lazywrite I/O

The Max Lazywrite I/O option controls the priority of batched asynchronous I/Os for the lazywriter. The lazywriter caches writes to disk in a background thread so that the originating thread does not have to wait until the writes are completed. The maximum value is the current setting for the Max Async I/O. Do not change this parameter unless told to by Microsoft support.

Max Text Repl Size

SQL 6.5 now supports replication for text fields. This parameter specifies the largest text block that can be replicated. The default value is 64K, and the maximum is the largest possible size of a text field (2,147,483,647 bytes).

Max Worker Threads

This parameter sets the maximum number of threads that can be open at one time. Each user connection, including the standard SQL Server connections, gets a thread. SQL Server checkpoints get their own threads. Each network supported simultaneously by SQL Server gets its own thread. Each task get a new thread when it runs, and so on. If the number of concurrent connections is greater than the value of Max Worker Threads, a thread pool is established. When the thread pool is full, the next user attempting to connect to SQL Server will be rejected.

Media Retention

With this option, you specify the number of days SQL Server will keep backups before it lets you write over media. Attempts to reuse media before the expiration date result in a warning message and the option to overwrite.

Memory

This parameter may be the first one you change after installing SQL Server. It tells SQL Server how much of the total memory on the system it gets to use. The hard part of setting this option is that the number is in 2K pages, so if you want to give SQL Server 16 MB, enter 8192. Although this option lets you give SQL Server an odd number of pages, it seems that most examples — articles and documents — use a value that is a power of two. The easiest way to figure it out is to remember that 512 multiplied by 2K is 1 MB. Just multiply 512 by the number of megabytes you want to use and the result is the number of pages you should enter here.

Adding memory to SQL Server will generally increase the performance of your system. However, it is possible to give it too much memory, which can cause excessive paging. In Performance Monitor, watch the Page Faults/Sec counter. If many page faults are occurring regularly, you have taken too much memory away from Windows NT. Reduce the amount of memory allocated to SQL Server, restart the system, and monitor it again. You should always leave a minimum of 12 MB for Windows NT, and if your system has a high number of logins, network traffic, or both, give even more memory to Windows NT. Be aware that the number of page faults per second is a strange item to track in the Performance Monitor and that the counter may not give you the results you expect. See Chapter 15, "Performance Monitoring Guidelines," for a detailed explanation and suggested counters to monitor instead.

In earlier versions of SQL Server, setting this Memory parameter higher than the physical memory of the system put you in big trouble. Now if SQL Server 6.5 detects this situation, it will start with the minimum number of 2,800 pages. This fact is not mentioned in any of the documentation, but a trial run proved it to work fine.

The Windows NT virtual memory manager lets you run the system with the ratio of virtual to physical memory greater than 1:1, but this configuration will result in poor performance. If you experience Out of Memory errors in the Windows NT event log, you have either given SQL Server too much memory or put Tempdb in RAM when it shouldn't be. See page 330 for more information on putting Tempdb in RAM.

It is possible to set this value too low. Other configuration settings, such as users, locks, open databases, and open objects, are all assigned to the static portion of SQL memory allocation. If the total of these settings plus the base requirements of the SQL program itself exceeds the memory configuration, SQL Server will not start. You can see how much each portion of the static memory is used by different options from the first part of the output from the DBCC MEMUSAGE command.

Tables 16.2, 16.3, and 16.4 show the output from the DBCC MEMUSAGE command. The first section, shown in Table 16.2, is the memory usage for SQL Server and its components. The largest portion is the page cache (6.86 MB), followed by the procedure cache and the code size, which is the SQL Server code loaded in memory. Because the number of user connections is configured at 100, they use 2.94 MB.

TABLE 16.2 DBCC OUTPUT, MEMORY USAGE

	MB	2K Blocks	Bytes
Configured Memory	16.00	8192	16777216
Code size	2.45	1254	2568192
Static Structures	0.25	128	261024
Locks	0.29	147	300000
Open Objects	0.11	59	120000
Open Databases	0.02	13	26080
User Context Areas	2.94	1505	3081420
Page Cache	6.86	3513	7193312
Proc Headers	0.17	85	173240
Proc Cache Bufs	2.78	1421	2910208

The second section of the output, shown in Table 16.3, displays the tables occupying the buffer cache, which is usually referred to as the data cache. It shows the database ID, where 1 is always the Master database, and the object ID, where 5 is sysprocedures. You can easily obtain the name of an object from the number (for example, object 5) by executing the following query: Select object_name(5). The table also shows the index ID, where 0 is a table without a clustered index and 1 indicates the clustered index. Any number greater than 1 is the index number for that table.

TABLE 16.3 BUFFER CACHE, TOP 20			
DB ID	**Object ID**	**Index ID**	**2K Buffers**
1	5	0	147
1	3	0	55
1	1	0	28
1	99	0	10
1	1	2	8
1	2	0	7
1	5	1	6
1	6	0	6
1	6	1	3
1	36	0	3
2	2	0	3
1	36	1	2
1	45	255	2
1	704005539	1	2
2	99	0	2
3	2	0	2
4	1	2	2
4	2	0	2
5	1	2	2
5	2	0	2

Table 16.4 shows the third section, which lists the top 10 items in procedure cache. These items are usually stored procedures, although triggers, views, rules, defaults, and constraints also occupy this space. When a

procedure is first created, all the objects in the code are recognized and stored in the sysprocedures table as a *tree*. When someone executes the procedure, it is loaded into memory where an optimized plan is produced. Thus a tree is a precompiled, or perhaps a better word to use is semi-compiled, version of a procedure. This section shows the number and size of the trees, as well as the number and size of plans. The important value is the size of the plan, because it shows the number of 2K pages for the optimized version of the procedure.

TABLE 16.4 PROCEDURE CACHE, TOP 10	
Procedure Name	sp_MSdbuserprofile
Database Id	1
Object Id	1653580929
Version	1
Uid	1
Type	stored procedure
Number of trees	0
Size of trees	0.000000 MB, 0.000000 bytes, 0 pages
Number of plans	2
Size of plans	0.171600 MB, 179936.000000 bytes, 90 pages
Procedure Name	sp_helpdistributor
Database Id	1
Object Id	1717581157
Version	1
Uid	1
Type	stored procedure
Number of trees	0
Size of trees	0.000000 MB, 0.000000 bytes, 0 pages
Number of plans	1
Size of plans	0.021484 MB, 22528.000000 bytes, 12 pages
Procedure Name	sp_helplanguage
Database Id	1
Object Id	1680009016
Version	1
Uid	1
Type	stored procedure
Number of trees	0
Size of trees	0.000000 MB, 0.000000 bytes, 0 pages
Number of plans	1
Size of plans	0.014807 MB, 15526.000000 bytes, 8 pages

continued

TABLE 16.4 PROCEDURE CACHE, TOP 10, CONTINUED

Procedure Name	sp_server_info
Database Id	1
Object Id	361052322
Version	1
Uid	1
Type	stored procedure
Number of trees	0
Size of trees	0.000000 MB, 0.000000 bytes, 0 pages
Number of plans	1
Size of plans	0.003166 MB, 3320.000000 bytes, 2 pages
Procedure Name	xp_sqlregister
Database Id	1
Object Id	953054431
Version	1
Uid	1
Type	stored procedure
Number of trees	0
Size of trees	0.000000 MB, 0.000000 bytes, 0 pages
Number of plans	1
Size of plans	0.000578 MB, 606.000000 bytes, 1 pages
Procedure Name	xp_msver
Database Id	1
Object Id	1036530726
Version	1
Uid	1
Type	stored procedure
Number of trees	0
Size of trees	0.000000 MB, 0.000000 bytes, 0 pages
Number of plans	1
Size of plans	0.000578 MB, 606.000000 bytes, 1 pages
Procedure Name	xp_regread
Database Id	1
Object Id	585053120
Version	1
Uid	1
Type	stored procedure
Number of trees	0
Size of trees	0.000000 MB, 0.000000 bytes, 0 pages
Number of plans	1
Size of plans	0.000578 MB, 606.000000 bytes, 1 pages

continued

TABLE 16.4 PROCEDURE CACHE, TOP 10, CONTINUED	
Procedure Name	sp_sqlregister
Database Id	1
Object Id	985054545
Version	1
Uid	1
Type	stored procedure
Number of trees	0
Size of trees	0.000000 MB, 0.000000 bytes, 0 pages
Number of plans	1
Size of plans	0.000822 MB, 862.000000 bytes, 1 pages
Procedure Name	xp_snmp_getstate
Database Id	1
Object Id	921054317
Version	1
Uid	1
Type	stored procedure
Number of trees	0
Size of trees	0.000000 MB, 0.000000 bytes, 0 pages
Number of plans	1
Size of plans	0.000578 MB, 606.000000 bytes, 1 pages
Procedure Name	sp_MSSQLOLE65_version
Database Id	1
Object Id	1685581043
Version	1
Uid	1
Type	stored procedure
Number of trees	0
Size of trees	0.000000 MB, 0.000000 bytes, 0 pages
Number of plans	1
Size of plans	0.001543 MB, 1618.000000 bytes, 1 pages

Reconfiguring the memory option causes the free buffers option to be reconfigured to a value of 5 percent of the memory allocated to SQL Server (see the explanation of free buffers on page 311). Also, this memory value does not take the Tempdb in RAM setting into consideration.

After the static memory is reserved and the free buffer space is allocated, the rest of the memory is split between data pages and the procedure cache. The procedure cache setting determines the percentage of total SQL Server memory given to code objects (procedures, views, triggers, defaults, and rules). See page 323 for more information about procedure cache.

Table 16.5 gives recommended memory settings for SQL Server, based on how much memory you have. A similar table in the SQL Server *Books Online* has different figures. Neither table is right or wrong; they probably use different assumptions. Table 16.5 is based on the following assumptions:

- Tempdb is not in RAM.
- Windows NT requires a minimum of 12 MB of RAM (except on the lowest setting, because the new minimum for SQL Server is 2,800 pages, or approximately 5.5 MB).
- The user configuration parameter is set as low as you can get it.
- The other parameters for locks, open objects, and open databases are set to optimal values for your size server and application needs.

TABLE 16.5 RECOMMENDED MEMORY SETTINGS

Machine Memory (MB)	Approximate SQL Server Memory Allocation (MB)
16	5.5
24	12
32	20
48	32
64	48
128	108
256	216
512	464

SQL Server does a good job of supporting a small development team of five to eight people on 16 MB of memory. Sometimes it seems exceedingly slow, but overall performance is generally acceptable.

Monitoring the cache hit ratio with Performance Monitor will usually give you the first indicator of how well your memory is configured. A cache hit ratio that is more than 90 percent means you have a memory-resident database (at least the pages you use most often are usually resident in cache). Adding more memory will not bring better performance in this case.

If the cache hit ratio occasionally drops, it usually means that a certain query or job is causing a lot of disk I/O. Tweaking the read-ahead values may help these jobs. If the cache hit ratio is constantly below 85 percent, adding more memory to the system and allocating more to SQL Server is probably a good idea.

Nested Triggers

When the value of this option is 1, triggers can call other triggers, which is the normal behavior for SQL Server. The 0 value is provided for backward compatibility to the earliest versions, which did not support nested triggers. It is recommended that you leave this option set to 1, unless you have a very specialized database.

Network Packet Size

You use this parameter to improve performance when you are running a network protocol that supports larger buffer sizes. The default value for this option is 4096 bytes; the value you assign should be divisible by 512, because most network management systems use multiples of 512 for buffer sizes. You should set this value to be the most common buffer size if you are running multiple network protocols. Large network copies involving Tabular Data Stream (TDS) packets can improve with a setting of 8192. Individual client applications can override this setting for one session.

Open Databases

This parameter sets the maximum number of open databases allowed on the server. This value is for the entire server, not per session. Each open database uses approximately 4K per configured database, so 20 databases use 80K. When 40 people are logged on to the same database, only one entry is counted toward this parameter. You may be tempted to reduce this value, but remember that SQL Server has several databases of its own: Master, Tempdb, Model, Msdb, and Distribution (if you are running replication). It is OK to set this value to 10, but reducing the value to 10 has very little effect, so it is best to leave it alone.

Open Objects

With this parameter, you control the maximum number of objects that can be opened simultaneously on the server. This number is objects per server, not per database. All open objects in all databases count toward the total. However, 10 people accessing the same table increase the open object count only by one (the table). The following SQL Server objects contribute toward the object count: tables, views, triggers, stored procedures, rules, defaults, and constraints. Indexes do not count toward the total.

Priority Boost

This option determines when SQL Server should be run at a higher priority than other processes. Although setting this parameter to 1 gives SQL Server a higher priority in the Windows NT processing scheme, we recommend that you leave it at 0. Do not change this setting unless you know what you are doing or are instructed to do so by Microsoft support. Changing it affects everything else running on the server, including the ability of the client machines to send anything over the network to SQL Server. Even the shutdown process will be affected. Other tools run on the server will be agonizingly slow. SQL Server runs just fine in the normal Windows NT priority scheme.

Procedure Cache

The memory allocated to SQL Server is divided between data cache and procedure cache. The procedure cache is used by the code objects such as stored procedures, triggers, views, defaults, and rules. SQL Server keeps the code objects in memory as long as possible. The SQL cache manager uses a Least Recently Used (LRU) algorithm to determine which objects are removed from the procedure cache first.

Use the DBCC MEMUSAGE command to view the system memory breakdown, the top 20 table objects, the 12 largest code objects, the number and size of trees, and the number and size of plans. Tables 16.2, 16.3, and 16.4 show output from the DBCC MEMUSAGE command. Plans are compiled/optimized procedures and are kept in memory. If multiple copies of the object are in memory, it will show in the total. Multiple copies are necessary when more than one session is running the same procedure, view, or trigger at the same time. The code objects are not re-entrant, meaning that each person gets his or her own copy of the optimized code.

Keep the procedure cache at between 10 and 30 percent. Don't make this value too big, however, because SQL Server runs faster when the largest memory block is allocated to the data cache. The more memory you give to SQL Server, the lower the proc cache value should be. For very large memory servers, even 1 percent is too much for the proc cache, which is why this option is changing to a floating-point value in SQL Server 7.0.

You can use Performance Monitor to track the usage of the procedure cache. The Total Procedure Buffers is a good statistic to track on a long-term basis, but it is also a good idea to turn on the other nine options in the procedure cache section for a short period during a time of normal usage to get an idea of how your system is acting. See Chapter 15, "Performance Monitoring Guidelines," for more details.

RA (Read-Ahead) Cache Hit Limit

The Read-Ahead Manager, sometimes called the *pre-fetch manager*, handles queries. The Read-Ahead Manager checks page requests to see whether the pages are already in cache; if they are, the Read-Ahead Manager won't start a new read-ahead activity. When the number of times the Read-Ahead Manager finds the page in cache matches the value set for this parameter, the Read-Ahead Manager is canceled for this thread. When the parameter described below, RA Cache Miss Limit, is reached, the Read-Ahead Manager starts again.

You should not have to change this option unless instructed to by Microsoft support. Use the Cache Hit Ratio counter in Performance Monitor to watch how many page requests are fulfilled by pages already in memory.

RA Cache Miss Limit

The Read-Ahead Manager, which handles queries, will not start a new read-ahead (or *pre-fetch*) activity until the value set in this parameter matches the number of page requests that are not fulfilled by cached pages. The default setting is 3, which means that after three page requests are read from disk, the fourth request will start a read-ahead task. Each read from disk will then load one extent (eight pages). How many extents are read before the task idles again? See the RA Pre-Fetches parameter, below, for the answer.

RA Delay

The read-ahead task pauses the length of time set in this parameter to let the disk latency complete so the controllers don't get overloaded with pre-fetches. (*Disk latency* is the time it takes a disk drive to spin one complete revolution.) The delay established in this option also lets the Read-Ahead Manager complete its initialization before continuing. The default value is 15 milliseconds and should not be changed, especially for multiprocessor machines.

RA Pre-Fetches

Once a read-ahead activity has started, this parameter, measured in extents, determines how far ahead of the current query position the pre-fetch manager stays. The default value of 3 means that the Read-Ahead Manager stays 3 extents in front of the query. A long-running query gets the most benefit out of the read-ahead process.

RA Slots per Thread

This parameter sets the maximum number of slots that one thread can handle in a read-ahead activity. Each thread can handle several read-ahead requests, one for each table or range scan. Any query with an Or clause uses more than one range scan. If each part of the Or clause generates enough expected reads to cause the system to read ahead, then one thread gets multiple slots.

RA Worker Threads

This option determines the number of read-ahead threads that the system handles at one time. Each session can get one thread, so the best configuration value for this parameter is the number of concurrent connections on the system. Each thread can handle several read-ahead requests (see RA Slots Per Thread, above).

The SQL Server error log and the Windows NT event log (applications section) contains warnings when this parameter is set too low. The warning message tells you that the number of read-ahead requests exceeds the number of threads available. It is best to leave this parameter alone unless you find this warning in the error log.

Recovery Flags

The default value of 0 for this option displays minimal information during the recovery process at startup. When this option is set to 1, information about each transaction is displayed, along with a message stating whether a commit or rollback occurred. This feature can be especially helpful if you name your transactions. You can tell at least which transaction was rolled back, even if you don't know what the data was.

Recovery Interval

The value for this parameter tells SQL Server the amount of acceptable time, in minutes, it has to complete a database recovery during startup. The default is five minutes, and if three user databases are on your server, SQL Server could take 15 minutes to start if it must fully recover all the user databases. Add to this 15 minutes the time it takes to recover the system databases. Most of the time, a normal recovery is about 15 to 30 seconds per user database, but some circumstances (discussed later) can cause recovery to take hours.

A full understanding of the recovery interval requires an explanation of several concepts. The first concept is *dirty pages*. A dirty page is a page that has been modified in cache but not yet flushed to disk. These pages are flushed to disk during a process called a *checkpoint,* another complicated concept to explain. A lot of actions occur during a checkpoint, even though the whole process takes about 1 second, on average. The recovery interval does **not** set the amount of time between checkpoints; it sets the expected time for recovery for each database.

In a checkpoint, SQL Server first checks every database on the server once every minute to determine whether enough activity has occurred to warrant a checkpoint. If enough activity has taken place, the second action occurs — the dirty pages are flushed to disk. SQL Server is the judge of how much activity is "enough activity." The third action occurs after the dirty pages are written to disk: A checkpoint mark is made in the log file for that database. SQL Server rolls forward to this checkpoint mark on recovery of the database.

The fourth action happens only if the Truncate Log on Checkpoint flag is set to true for this database. This option clears all the committed and replicated transactions from the log file. Very large transactions that have filled up the log file are cleared by a checkpoint because they have not completed. In this case, you use the command Dump transaction *myDB* with no_log (substituting the appropriate database name for *myDB*) to clear the log file. Also, only system checkpoints will clear the log, not user checkpoints entered from query screens or with other mechanisms. The checkpoint process attempts to truncate the log every minute even if it does not have dirty pages to write.

Special Note

The Truncate Log on Checkpoint option is recommended for development databases only — definitely not for production databases.

Special Note

The logs in the Tempdb system database are truncated every minute, even if you turn off the Truncate Log on Checkpoint option.

Now that we understand dirty pages and checkpoints, we can return to the circumstances that cause SQL Server to take hours to recover. One example is when SQL Server is interrupted by a power outage during a very large transaction. Here is the short version of the sequence of events on startup: SQL Server goes through the log files of every database, attempting to roll all the transactions forward from the last checkpoint. A long-running transaction has lots of entries in the log file, and the recovery process starts from the beginning of the transaction. When SQL Server gets to the end of the log file, it doesn't find a Commit command, so it rolls back the entire transaction, which takes slightly longer than the original transaction. To make a long story short, a transaction that had been running for an hour can take longer than two hours to recover.

If you set the recovery interval very short, the system will always be doing checkpoints. If you set it too long, it may take an extraordinarily long time to start SQL Server. As a rule of thumb, if your databases are update-intensive, you should set shorter recovery intervals.

Remote Access

When this option is set to 1, users from other SQL servers have access to this server. This Remote Access configuration option is not the same as the RAS (Remote Access Services) for Windows NT dial-in access. If you are trying to get two servers to talk to each other via remote stored procedures or remote sessions, check the value of this parameter. Nothing can come in from a remote server when this value is set to 0.

Remote Connection Timeout

Connections to remote servers are kept open for the timeout period specified in this option instead of disconnecting after every remote procedure call. Keeping the connections open is a significant improvement in performance between two SQL Servers. Those of you who had given up on remote stored procedures because of lack of speed shouldn't hesitate to try them again. Perhaps more significant than the connection improvement, remote procedures can now return result sets into a temporary table.

This timeout value starts when the connection becomes inactive. The connection will not be broken as long as it is active. The connection will be dropped as soon as the originating session is gone.

Remote Login Timeout

The timeout period specified in this parameter indicates how long an attempt to log on to a remote server waits until timing out. A value of 0, which is the default, specifies an infinite timeout period. Leaving it at 0 is OK for most applications.

Remote Procedure Transaction

This parameter is new in SQL Server 6.5 and lets you use the DTC in remote procedures. If this parameter is set to 1, all remote procedures will be managed by the DTC. This setting protects the ACID properties of the transactions. *ACID* (Atomicity, Consistency, Isolation, Durability) is an industry-standard term that defines how a database guarantees the safety of your data.

Sessions that have already begun before this option is set are not affected. Also, programs and procedures can implicitly start a distributed transaction, even if this parameter is turned off.

Remote Query Timeout

This value determines how long the server waits after starting a remote query until it times out. A value of 0, which is the default, sets an infinite timeout period. Leave it at 0 for most applications.

Remote Sites

This parameter sets the maximum number of remote sites that can be configured. The default is 10.

Resource Timeout

Here, *resources* refers to items such as disks, memory, log files, and buffers. This parameter indicates how long a thread waits for a resource before relinquishing its turn to another thread. The default value is 10 seconds. If you are seeing a lot of "logwrite" or "bufwait timeout" entries in the SQL error log, you should increase this parameter.

Set Working Set Size

The value here reminds Windows NT to reserve the amount of memory SQL Server needs. This parameter comes into effect when Windows NT has been running before SQL Server is started. Windows NT does not use the memory that SQL Server needs. If you have SQL Server and SQL Executive configured to start when Windows NT starts, you do not need to change this parameter.

Show Advanced Options

The advanced options are displayed when you bring up the configuration dialog box in Figure 16.1 or when you run the sp_configure query. If you set this parameter to 1 with the user interface, then click Apply Now, the advanced options do not show up until you close the screen and come back in.

SMP Concurrency

This parameter limits the number of CPU chips SQL Server can use. This option works in conjunction with the Affinity Flag option, which tells SQL server which CPUs it can use. The default value of 0 for SMP Concurrency means the system auto-configures; that is, SQL Server figures out how many CPUs are installed when it starts and lets SQL Server use all but one. SQL Server plays nicely enough with the other kids because it still lets them use one CPU. In informal testing, letting Windows NT and the networking services use one CPU has proved to be a good setting.

The appropriate setting for this parameter depends on whether your server is a dedicated SQL Server machine, which is the recommended way to set up your server. You should move file and print services to another server. Do not make your SQL server a primary or backup domain controller.

When this parameter is set to −1, the number of CPUs that SQL Server uses is not limited. It will spread itself over all the available CPUs. Processes switching in and out of active context move their buffers when they change CPUs. In informal testing, this setting has shown a slight decrease in performance.

You can also set this value equal to the number of CPUs. When you have a uniprocessor (single CPU) machine, we recommend that you set this parameter to 1. That way, SQL server will not even attempt to try any dynamic CPU usage. The best setting for servers with more than one CPU is $n-1$, where n is the number of processors on the machine. If you have four or more processors, use this in conjunction with the Affinity Flag configuration setting.

Sort Pages

This parameter determines the maximum number of memory sort pages each user is allocated. If you have very large queries that run occasionally, increasing this number improves these sorts. When a user runs out of sort pages, Tempdb continues the sort in conjunction with memory. On single-CPU machines, the default value for this parameter is 64.

Spin Counter

This parameter sets the maximum number of times SQL Server tries to obtain a resource. The default value is 10,000. Notice that the run value is set to 0.

SQL Server automatically sets the run value to 10,000 for SMP (multiprocessor) machines and to 10 for single-CPU machines.

Tempdb in RAM

Tempdb is a system table that stores temporary tables created by either a user application or the system. Using the SHOWPLAN utility, you can tell if a query is using Tempdb by spotting the words "work table" in the output.

Tempdb is installed with 2 MB in the Master device. Most production systems need a much larger database than the initial value. The recommended size for Tempdb is about 40 percent of the total size of all your production databases. You should increase the size of the Tempdb log to 40 percent of the size of Tempdb. This setting gives you a safe comfort margin to ensure that you do not run out of Tempdb space. It is also best to place Tempdb and its log on separate devices.

The option of putting Tempdb in RAM has been widely misused since it was introduced. Most of the time it is not necessary to put Tempdb in RAM, because by default the pages start in memory. The physical I/O rate on Tempdb is usually very small and starts to increase only when larger transactions are active.

Tempdb can be altered to increase or decrease the database size while it is in RAM. You can alter the database about 10 times before you need to shut down and restart SQL Server. Although it is recommended that you not put Tempdb in RAM, you should certainly set up some performance tests.

Here are our recommendations: Don't put Tempdb in RAM on development machines; they usually run more slowly. Don't put Tempdb in RAM unless you have 64 MB or more of memory. Don't have Tempdb in RAM when upgrading to a new version of SQL Server — too many things can go wrong when the upgrade process automatically takes Tempdb out of memory.

The documentation says that the maximum value for Tempdb in RAM is 2044. Because this value is in megabytes, 2044 here really means 2 GB of memory. A value of 0 for the parameter means that Tempdb is not in RAM.

Time Slice

Each process gets a certain amount of CPU time before the system forces it to yield to another process in the queue. The time slice parameter is the maximum number of times a user process can ignore a yield request. If this parameter is set too low, SQL Server can spend too much time switching processes. This option is rarely changed.

User Connections

This option sets the maximum number of user connections that can exist simultaneously on a server. This value is not the same as the number of users, and it is also not the same as the license limit. If you have an application that requires two connections, they both count toward the limit of this parameter, but only one counts toward the license limit.

The buffer space needed for user connections is pre-allocated from SQL Server's memory, so setting this value too large reduces the amount of memory available for data and procedure cache. Making it too small means that your users will be denied a connection.

This parameter is important. Using Performance Monitor, watch the SQL Server: Max User Connections counter. If it approaches 10 percent of your configured value for the user connections, you may want to increase the value of this parameter. You know you have set this too high, thereby wasting space, if the Max User Connections doesn't even come close to this configuration value. SQL Server needs to be shut down and restarted when this value is changed.

User Options

You can apply a number of options to your session with the Set statement. Until now, you couldn't apply these options on a global default basis, but this parameter was designed to do just that. This parameter is a bitmask. The values are listed in Table 16.6.

TABLE 16.6 VALUES FOR USER OPTIONS	
Value	**Description**
1	DISABLE_DEF_CNST_CHK — Controls interim constraint checking.
2	IMPLICIT_TRANSACTIONS — Controls whether a transaction is started implicitly when a statement is executed.
4	CURSOR_CLOSE_ON_COMMIT — Controls behavior of cursors once a Commit has been performed.
8	ANSI_WARNINGS — Controls truncation and Null values in aggregate warnings.

continued

TABLE 16.6 VALUES FOR USER OPTIONS, CONTINUED	
Value	**Description**
16	ANSI_PADDING — Controls padding of variables.
32	ANSI_NULLS — Controls Null handling by using equality operators.
64	ARITHABORT — Terminates a query when an overflow or divide-by-zero error occurs during query execution.
128	ARITHIGNORE — Returns Null when an overflow or divide-by-zero error occurs during a query.
256	QUOTED_IDENTIFIER — Differentiates between single and double quotation marks when evaluating an expression.
512	NOCOUNT — Turns off the message returned at the end of each statement that states how many rows were affected by the statement.
1024	ANSI_NULL_DFLT_ON — Alters the session's behavior to use ANSI compatibility for nullability. New columns defined without explicit nullability will be defined to allow Nulls.
2048	ANSI_NULL_DFLT_OFF — Alters the session's behavior to not use ANSI compatibility for nullability. New columns defined without explicit nullability will be defined not to allow Nulls.

Users can view the options set for their session with the Select @@OPTIONS command. The @@OPTIONS parameter is a global variable that corresponds to all the choices configured either with this User Options parameter or with the Set command. In effect, this parameter is a global default for every session.

For example, if Select @@OPTIONS returns a value of 11, 11 breaks down to 8 + 2 + 1, which indicates that ANSI_WARNINGS, IMPLICIT_TRANSACTIONS, and DISABLE_DEF_CNST_CHK are turned on.

Configuring Windows NT and the Network

Now that we have gone through the myriad options for configuring SQL Server so that it performs well, we need to tune the operating system. We consider the following tasks:

- Paring down
- Spreading and resizing the system paging files
- Changing the system tuning parameters
- Changing the size of the event log files
- Changing the server's resource allocation
- Redesigning disks

Paring Down

Turn off unnecessary Windows NT services and uninstall any unnecessary device drivers. Both CPU and memory will be freed up.

Spreading and Resizing the System Paging Files

One of the most important ways to tune your operating system setup is to spread system paging files across multiple disk drives and controllers. This setup improves overall system performance, because multiple disks can then process I/O requests concurrently. Up to 16 separate page files are allowed. Whenever possible, you should locate paging files on drives other than those that contain the operating system and SQL Server devices. Page file I/O and application file I/O can occur concurrently when the disk drive and controller can accommodate asynchronous I/O requests.

Always use the fastest disks for all your paging files. Set the page file to a size that is least likely to require an extension — the number of megabytes of system memory plus 12.

You change the size of the system paging file at the Virtual Memory dialog box. Open the Control Panel, click the system icon, and click the virtual memory button. The dialog box shown in Figure 16.2 will appear. Change the Initial Size and Maximum Size settings and click Set. The next time you restart the machine, the new settings will take effect.

Figure 16.2

*Changing Paging with the
Virtual Memory Dialog Box*

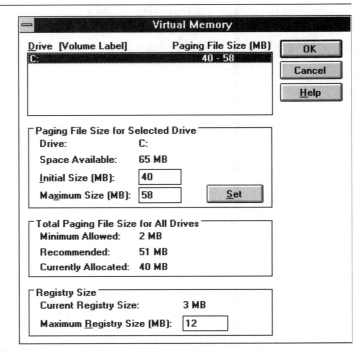

Changing System Tuning Parameters

Each application (as well as each thread) in the system has a set priority. You can control the system-wide priority by changing the operating system's tasking instructions. Changing the tasking changes the relative responsiveness of applications that are running at the same time.

If you are running Windows NT 3.51, you change tasking from the Control Panel by choosing the System icon and clicking Tasking. The dialog box in Figure 16.3 will appear. Choose the last option to give your background applications the best response. If you are running Windows NT 4.0, go to the Control Panel, System icon, and click the Performance tab. Then slide the bar to the left so that the foreground (screen) applications get no performance boost.

Following these instructions gives the network and SQL Server processes the best response. It does make your screens run slower while you are working on the server.

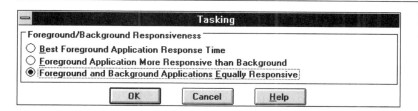

Figure 16.3
Changing Tasking

Changing the Size of the Event Log Files

To check the size of the event log files, go to the File Menu from the Event Viewer and select Log Sizing. The dialog box shown in Figure 16.4 appears.

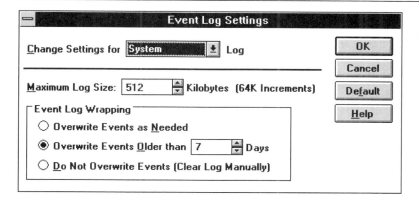

Figure 16.4
Event Log Settings

It is OK to leave these setting as they are, because the system will overwrite the start of the file after seven days, preventing the file from growing too large. If you change this setting to Do Not Overwrite Events (Clear Log Manually), you need to establish a regular procedure to save the log under a different file and clear the event log. Be sure to check the settings for all three logs — system, security, and application — and establish a schedule for clearing them if necessary.

Changing the Server's Resource Allocation

The reason for changing this configuration is to find the optimal Windows NT configuration on a SQL Server machine. Configure the server's resource allocation (and the associated non-paged memory pool usage) by clicking the Network applet in the Control Panel. Then choose Configure from the Server menu if you are using Windows NT 3.51 or Properties from the Server Menu if you are running Windows NT 4.0. The dialog box in Figure 16.5 will appear.

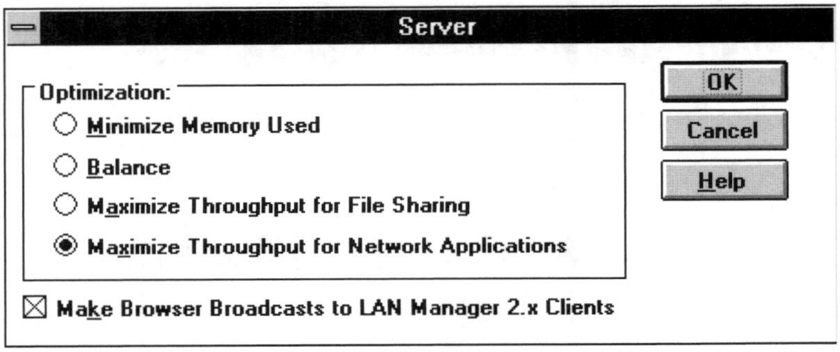

Figure 16.5

Configuring Resource Allocation

The settings in the dialog box are

- Minimize Memory Used — This is the best setting for up to 10 simultaneous users, because the normal memory settings are sufficient for up to 10 users.
- Balance — This option is for up to 64 users.
- Maximize Throughput for File Sharing — This setting is also for 64 or more users. File cache access has priority over user application access to memory. Use this option if you are using the Windows NT server as a file server. This setting is the default.
- Maximize Throughput for Network Applications — Use this option for 64 or more remote users. This option gives user application access priority over file cache access to memory. This setting is the optimal setting for Microsoft BackOffice applications such as Microsoft SQL Server, SNA Server, and Systems Management Server. ***This setting is recommended for SQL Server.***

This dialog box also contains one final option. Be sure to turn off the Make Browser Broadcasts to LAN Manager 2.x Clients option if you have no LAN Manager clients or servers on the same network. It puts an unnecessary drain on network resources.

CPU Usage

If you have four or more processors, take advantage of the SQL Affinity Mask and SMP Concurrency configuration parameters. Let Windows NT have processor 0, which it uses as the default I/O processor. If network performance seems to be a problem, then let Windows NT have the last processor(s), which it uses to control the NIC card(s). For more information, see the Affinity Mask and SMP Concurrency sections above.

Redesigning Disks

To give SQL Server a performance boost, the two most important hardware resources you can add are disk drives and memory. This section discusses the reasons why having many disk drives is important to getting the optimal performance.

The rule of thumb for database servers is that many smaller disk drives give you better performance than a few large-capacity drives because you can spread I/O among the different drives. Unfortunately, it is very difficult to get 512 MB and 1 GB drives for the super servers today because the hardware vendors sell only 2 GB or 4 GB drives with their systems. If you are looking at a requirement of less than 10 GB for a database, you don't have many choices for optimal configurations.

RAID 0 and RAID 5 are the two best choices for drive configurations. RAID 0 is data striping without parity, and although it is the fastest design for database usage, it does not provide any protection against failure. Therefore it is best for data warehouse, read-only databases. RAID 5 provides data redundancy. Even with the extra parity bits being written, performance on RAID 5 drives is still better than performance on non-stripe drives.

You should balance the following files across the different disk drives for optimal performance.

- Master.dat
- Msdbdata.dat
- Msdblog.dat
- ExtendTempData.dat (which you need to build)
- ExtendTempLog.dat (which you need to build)
- Your database devices
- Your log devices
- The operating system files and SQL executables
- The Windows NT virtual memory swap file

If you have only one disk drive, obviously you cannot spread any files across drives. If you have more than one disk drive, check Table 16.7 for recommended configurations to help you spread out the files. The drives listed below give best performance if they are stripe drives, either RAID 0 or RAID 5. The drives should be physical drives, not partitions.

TABLE 16.7 SUGGESTED FILE ALLOCATION		
Number of Drives	**Drive Letter (example only)**	**Files for this Drive**
2	c:	operating system files, system swap file, Master.dat, ExtendTempLog, your log file
	d:	your database, ExtendTempData
3	c:	operating system files, system swap file, Master.dat
	d:	your database, ExtendTempData
	e:	ExtendTempLog, your log file
4	c:	operating system files, split system swap file, Master.dat
	d:	your database
	e:	split system swap file, ExtendTempData
	f:	ExtendTempLog, your log file
5	c:	operating system files, split system swap file
	d:	your database
	e:	split system swap file, ExtendTempData
	f:	ExtendTempLog, Master.dat
	g:	your log file
6	c:	operating system files, split system swap file
	d:	your database
	e:	split system swap file, ExtendTempData
	f:	ExtendTempLog, Master.dat
	g:	your log file
	h:	split system swap file

In Table 16.7, ExtendTempData and ExtendTempLog are both devices that you should add when you install SQL Server. Of course, you can name them anything you want, but the purpose is to give yourself a normal amount of operating room in Tempdb. As mentioned earlier, the default 2 MB in the Master device is not large enough for Tempdb.

Database Design Considerations

Why is database design in a chapter on performance and tuning? Well-designed databases are a necessary starting point for discussing performance-enhancing alternatives. Good database design can create an environment that lets you consider more tuning choices. The database design considerations discussed in this section are

- Logical design (normalization)
  - Benefits and drawbacks
  - Forms of normalization
- Denormalization
  - Redundant data
  - View-to-Table conversion
  - Derived (summary columns)
  - Contrived (identity) columns
  - Data Partitioning

Logical Design

Yes, logical and physical database design are different. Logical design is the process of gathering user requirements and formulating a logical grouping of the data. The process of logical grouping is called *normalization*. Physical design encompasses tasks such as placing the tables in databases on different disk drives, creating indexes, and planning distributed solutions.

Benefits and Drawbacks of Normalization

Normalization provides two primary advantages. First, the tables are narrower and have more records in a page, which results in less I/O. Also, normalization causes less redundant data — any updates will be performed on one record, so updates are generally faster.

The primary disadvantage of normalization is that it increases the number of joins. *Joins* are a mechanism in relational databases that let two tables with matching key values retrieve information from both tables. It is a disadvantage to have too many joins in a query because of the way the query optimizer works and because of the number of I/Os that are required to retrieve all the information.

Forms of Normalization

Of the five forms of normalization, the first three forms are necessary for a complete database design. The fourth and fifth normal forms are extensions to the third normal form and are used to correct specific situations.

Keys are the foundation of normalization. A *key* is a column or a set of columns. There are two types of keys, primary keys and foreign keys. A primary key is a single column or a combination of columns that uniquely identifies each row. A foreign key is a column or combination of columns in tables whose values relate to a certain row in the primary key table. Non-key fields are those columns in a table that do not participate in either a primary or foreign key.

Whoever came up with the shortcuts to the first three forms of normalization deserves a lot of credit. The shortcut is "the key, the whole key, and nothing but the key."

- First normal form — the key. One primary key is used to uniquely identify each row. No groups are repeated. For example, you wouldn't carry fields like HomePhone, OfficePhone, and FaxNumber in a Person table, because you may want to collect more types of phone numbers later. Instead, you create a new table called PersonPhone, with attributes (fields) of Person-Number, PhoneType, and PhoneNumber. The PersonNumber is a foreign key that relates to a record in the Person table.

- Second normal form — the whole key. No non-key field is dependent upon a portion of the key. All non-key fields are dependent upon the entire primary key.

- Third normal form — nothing but the key. Non-key fields cannot be dependent upon other non-key fields.

- Fourth normal form — remove independent multiple relationships. No table can contain multiple one-to-many (1:n) or many-to-many (n:m) relationships that are not directly related to the primary key.

- Fifth normal form — remove semantically related multiple relationships. A common example is closely related record types that collect slightly different data.

     For example, consultants bill their customers for hours and for expenses. You could have one Billing table that carries both record types if the exact same data is collected for both hours and expenses — perhaps you are just recording a description and a total charge. However, you may want to collect more information for each charge; for example, you want to record the time spent on a task for hours-related charges, and you want to record a vendor to whom an expense was paid. A choice that satisfies the fifth normal form for this design is to put this data in separate tables called HoursWorked and Expense.

Denormalization

Denormalization is the art of introducing database design mechanisms that enhance performance. Successful denormalization depends upon a solid database design normalized to at least the third normal form. Only then can you begin a process called *responsible denormalization*. The only reason to denormalize a database is to improve performance.

In this section, we will discuss techniques for denormalization and when they should be used. The techniques are

- Creating redundant data
- Converting views to tables
- Using derived (summary) columns and tables
- Using contrived (identity) columns
- Partitioning data
  - Subsets/vertical partitioning
  - Horizontal partitioning
  - Server partitioning (multiple servers)

Creating Redundant Data

Repeating a column from one table in another table can help avoid a join. For example, because an invoice is for a customer, you could repeat the customer name in the invoice table so that when it is time to print the invoice you do not have to join to the customer table to retrieve the name. However, you also need a link to the customer table to get the billing address. Therefore, it makes no sense to duplicate the customer name when you already need to join to the customer table to get other data. A good example of redundant data is to carry the customer name in a table that contains time-related customer activity; for example, annual or monthly summaries of activity.

You can keep redundant data up-to-date with a trigger so that when the base table changes, the tables carrying the redundant data also change.

Converting Views to Tables

This technique creates redundant data on a grand scale. The idea is that you create a table from a view that joins multiple tables. You need complex triggers to keep this table synchronized with the base tables — whenever any of the base tables change, the corresponding data in the new table must also change.

An example of this technique is a vendor tracking system that contains several tables, as shown in Figure 16.6, an entity-relationship diagram. A vendor can have multiple addresses, one of which is marked "billing"; a vendor can have multiple contacts, one marked "primary"; and each contact can have many phone numbers, one marked "Main."

Figure 16.6
Vendor Tracking System (Vendor, VendorAddress, VendorContact, and ContactPhone)

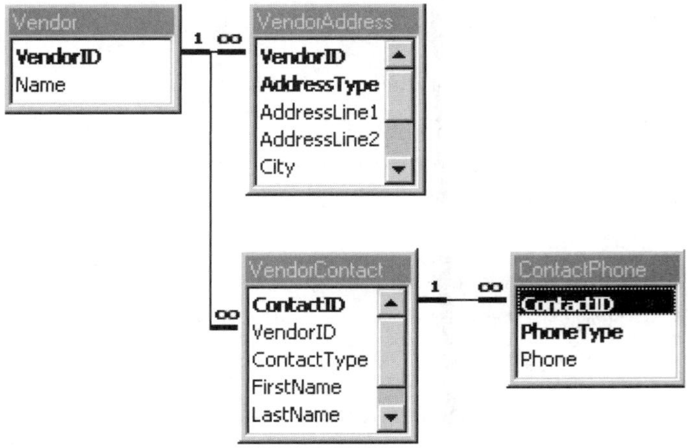

The following Select statement creates a view that joins all the tables.

```
SELECT    V.VendorID,
          V.Name,
          VA.Address1,
          VA.Address2,
          VA.City,
          VA.State,
          VA.PostalCode,
          VA.Country,
          VC.FirstName,
          VC.LastName,
          CP.Phone
FROM      Vendor V,
          VendorAddress VA,
          VendorContact VC,
          ContactPhone CP
WHERE     V.VendorID = VA.VendorID
AND       VA.AddressType = 'Billing'
AND       V.VendorID = VC.VendorID
AND       VC.ContactType = 'Primary'
AND       VC.ContactID = CP.ContactID
AND       CP.PhoneType = 'Main'
```

The above view is often too slow for quick lookup and retrieval. Converting that view to a table with the same columns and datatypes and using a trigger to keep it up-to-date could give you improved performance. More important, creating a table from a view gives developers a choice of retrieving data from either the base tables or the redundant table.

The drawback to this technique is the performance penalty of keeping the table up-to-date. You would use it only if the retrieval speed outweighed the cost of updating the table.

Using Derived (Summary) Columns and Tables

The two main types of derived columns are calculated and summary. *Calculated columns* are usually extensions to the row containing the base field. For example, an invoice detail record has QtyOrdered and ItemCost fields. To show the cost multiplied by the quantity, you could either calculate it each time it is needed (for example, in screens, reports, or stored procedures) or you could calculate the value each time you save the record and keep the value in the database. However, in this particular example you would not use this form of denormalization because calculated fields whose base data is in the same row don't take much time to calculate, and storing the calculation isn't worth the extra storage cost.

Summary columns, on the other hand, are examples of denormalization that can have substantial performance gains. Good examples include adding MonthToDate, QtrToDate, and YearToDate columns in the Account table of a general ledger system. Each of these columns summarizes of data in many different records. By adding these columns, you avoid the long calculation needed for the summary and get the same data from one read instead. Of course, this option is not very flexible, because if you need a total from a certain date range, you still have to go back to the base data to summarize the detail records.

A poor example of using summary fields is carrying an invoice subtotal on the header record when your orders average five lines — for example, in a high-priced, low-volume inventory system, such as a major appliance store. It doesn't take much time or effort for SQL Server to add five rows. But what if you have a low-priced, high-turnover inventory, such as a grocery store, with hundreds of lines per order? Then it would make more sense to carry an InvoiceSubtotal field in the header record.

Summarizing data by time period (day, month, year, etc.) or across product lines and saving the summaries in a table or tables is a good strategy to shortcut the reporting process. This technique is sometimes called a *data warehouse*. It can be expensive to keep up-to-date, because the data collection process must also update the summary tables. One strategy to bypass the cost of the data collection process is to replicate the transaction data to another database on another server where the data warehouse is periodically updated.

Using Contrived (Identity) Columns

Sometimes called *counter columns* and *identity columns*, contrived columns are columns to which the database assigns the next available number. Contrived columns are the primary keys in these tables, but they are not necessarily the only unique indexes. They are usually a shortcut for wide, multi-column keys. The contrived values are carried in other tables as foreign key values and link to the original table.

Data Partitioning

You can partition data vertically or horizontally, depending on whether you want to split columns or rows. You can also partition data across servers. We consider each type of partitioning below.

Subsets/Vertical Partitioning

Also called *subsets*, *vertical partitions* split columns that are not used often into new tables. Subsets are zero- or one-to-one relationships, meaning that for each row in the main table, one record (at most) exists in the subset table. The advantage to vertical partitioning is that the main table has narrower records, which results in more rows per page. When you do need data from the subset table, a simple join can retrieve the record.

Horizontal Partitioning

Horizontal partitioning, also known as *row partitioning*, is a more difficult type of partitioning to program and manage. The table is split so that rows with certain values are kept in different tables. For example, the data for each branch office could be kept in a separate table. A common example in data warehousing — historical transactions — keeps each month of data in a separate table.

The difficulty in horizontal partitioning comes in returning rows from each table as one result set. You use a Union statement to create this result set, as demonstrated below.

```
SELECT * FROM JanuaryTable
UNION
SELECT * FROM MarchTable
```

SQL 6.5 has a major new feature that allows Unions in views. Most systems that use horizontal partitioning build flexible SQL statements on the front-end, which do not take advantage of stored procedures.

Server Partitioning (Using Multiple Servers)

An enhancement in version 6.5 gives you even more incentive to distribute your data and spread the load among multiple servers. Now that you can return result sets from a remote procedure and replicate to ODBC databases, programming and maintaining distributed databases is getting easier. Mixing OLTP and data warehousing has rarely been successful. It is best to have your data collection systems on one server and reporting database(s) on another.

The keys to designing an architecture involving multiple servers are a thorough knowledge of replication and of returning results from remote procedures. For a complete discussion of replication, see Chapter 11.

Here is a simple example of returning a result set from a remote procedure and inserting it into a table.

```
INSERT MyTable (Field1, Field2, Field3)
EXECUTE OtherServer.OtherDatabase.Owner.prProcedure @iParm1,
    @sParm2
```

The remote procedure must return a result set with the same number of fields and the same data types. In the example above, three fields must be returned. If they are not exactly the same data types, they must be able to be implicitly converted by SQL Server. As you can see from the example, you can pass parameters to the remote procedures. You can also insert the results into an existing temporary table by placing the # symbol in front of the table name, as in #MyTable.

Summary

Performance tuning can be a never-ending series of adjustments in which you alleviate one bottleneck only to find another immediately. If your server is performing poorly, you need to answer two basic questions: "Do I add more memory, disk space, or CPU?" and "Do I have enough capacity to handle the anticipated growth of the company?" This book gives you enough information to make informed decisions. Although more can be gained from tuning hardware than ever before, the real gains come from tuning your queries and making good use of indexes, so don't stop reading here.

Chapter 17

Indexing

This chapter gives you an in-depth look at indexing, the foundation for optimizing and tuning queries. Efficient queries can greatly improve your application's performance. In this chapter, we

- walk through all the options in the Manage Indexes dialog box, one of the best improvements in SQL Server 6.0

- consider advanced topics in indexing

- discuss indexing strategies

Using the Manage Indexes Dialog Box

The Manage Indexes dialog box, shown in Figure 17.1, lets you perform almost every function related to indexing. In SQL Enterprise Manager, choose Indexes from the Manage menu. Walking through the options in this dialog box is a good, methodical way to cover many indexing topics.

Figure 17.1
Manage Indexes Dialog Box

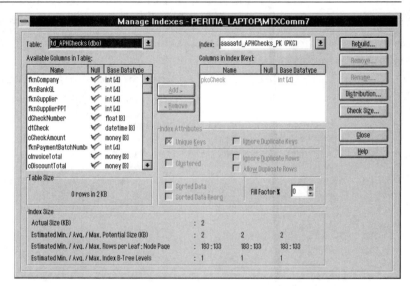

Proper Indexing

One of the most important ways to improve the performance of your applications is to index properly. SQL Server currently allows only b-tree indexing, which you could see as a limitation; however, this specialization also means you must become expert in only one form of indexing to optimize your indexes.

SQL Server's b-tree indexing structure is composed of three parts: a non-leaf level, which has a root page and other levels, depending on the size of the fields in the key; a leaf level, where the key is in sorted order; and the data itself. The non-leaf and leaf levels are allocated their own separate storage areas (in extents, or eight-page blocks).

B-tree indexes have strengths; for example, they are the most flexible kind of index over the widest variety of applications. However, they are not the fastest index for certain data retrieval operations. For example, hashing is considered the fastest algorithm for retrieving records when you have exact matches on key values, but hashing is poor for partial key retrievals.

Index Attributes

The Index Attributes section of Figure 17.1 contains many options that you can use to create the fastest index for any particular situation. We will consider the attributes individually.

Clustered vs. Nonclustered

Although this option is not the first one in this section of the dialog box, we need to consider it first because it's basic to an understanding of some of the other options. SQL Server allows two basic types of indexes: clustered and nonclustered. A clustered index has three fundamental properties.

- the data is kept in sorted order
- the leaf-level rows are the data rows
- the non-leaf level pages and the data are in separate storage areas

Only one clustered index is allowed in each table because you can keep the records in only one sorted order.

Nonclustered indexes have an extra level, with the keys in sorted order and pointers to the actual data rows. This type of index requires three separate storage areas. You can have as many as 250 indexes per table, and they can all be nonclustered. If you have one clustered index, then you can have up to 249 nonclustered indexes.

Unique Keys

This option allows only one instance of each value in the index table. If you try to insert another row with the same value in the field(s) designated with the unique tag, you get an error and the insert will be rolled back. Every table should have one unique index. Although SQL Server does not force this rule, having a table without at least one unique index violates relational theory.

Some front-end products do not work well unless you have one unique index. For example, Microsoft Access does not allow updates to a SQL Server table unless it has a unique index. The only tables without unique indexes in most applications are intermediate work tables, usually used when converting or importing data from legacy systems.

Ignore Duplicate Keys

This attribute controls what happens when an Insert or Update statement attempts to create a duplicate key entry in a table with a unique clustered index. The IGNORE_DUP_KEY parameter of the Create Index command gives you this same option. When this attribute is not set, a warning is generated and the duplicate entry is discarded, which can be disastrous in an Update statement.

However, this option can be very useful because it lets transactions proceed when a duplicate is encountered. It is particularly helpful when you are inserting more than one record at a time; for example, using BCP when you don't want to drop your index and you don't want the entire batch to fail.

Even when this option is turned on, you cannot create a unique index on a table that already has duplicate data. To create a unique index on a table with duplicate data, first use the next option, Ignore Duplicate Rows, which gets rid of the duplicate data. Then come back and create the unique index.

Ignore/Allow Duplicate Rows

These mutually exclusive options control nonunique clustered indexes. The Ignore Duplicate Rows option removes duplicate rows, if any, when the index is created. This option is one way to pull duplicate rows out of legacy data — but note that it removes the entire **row**, not just the **key**. Duplicate rows you try to insert after the index is created are *ignored*, meaning in this case that the row is never inserted in the table.

When you use the Allow Duplicate Rows option, SQL Server generates no errors or warnings if data is duplicated. You should avoid using the Allow Duplicate Rows option because it violates relational theory and you will not be able to create a unique index, which can in turn create other problems.

The IGNORE_DUP_ROW and ALLOW_DUP_ROW parameters to the Create Index statement also give you these options.

Sorted Data

This option avoids resorting the data when a clustered index is created. You should check the box for this option only when you are positive that the data is in sorted order — if it's not, an error is generated and the Create Index statement fails. The SORTED_DATA parameter on the Create Index statement gives you this same option.

Sorted Data Reorganization

When you check this option, SQL Server physically reorganizes the data without doing a sort. The data must already be in sorted order before you can use this option.

This option is particularly useful when you're using the Fill Factor option (discussed below) and when the data needs to be reorganized for better performance. Reorganization is also a good idea when the data becomes fragmented, which you can check by running the DBCC SHOW_CONTIG (table, index) command. This option is also available with the SORTED_DATA_ REORG parameter to the Create Index statement.

Fill Factor

This seldom-used but effective option, also available through the Fillfactor parameter of the Create Index statement, can do more than most people expect. It specifies the initial percentage to which the index leaf-level pages are filled. The key word in the previous sentence is "initial," because the indexes are not kept at this percentage. Over time, index page splits, inserts, and deletes change the average. Although an overall, server-wide option in the system configuration sets the fill factor for all databases, you should not use it. It is better to use this option on individual indexes.

The default setting for this option is 0, which means that only the leaf pages are filled. Space for one row is reserved in the nonleaf pages for nonclustered indexes (either unique or nonunique) and for unique clustered indexes. Space for two entries is reserved in the nonleaf pages for nonunique clustered indexes.

A value of 100 means that all pages, leaf and nonleaf, will be filled to capacity. This value should be used only for read-only tables because inserted data will cause a page split, which makes two of the pages approximately 50 percent full. An Update statement may or may not cause a page split, depending upon whether the update is deferred or direct and whether the length of a value in a variable-length key field increases enough to overflow a page.

When a value from 1 to 99 is specified, nonleaf pages follow the same rule as they do when the value is 0; i.e., space for one row is reserved in the nonleaf pages for nonclustered indexes (either unique or nonunique) and for unique clustered indexes. Space for two entries is reserved in the nonleaf pages for nonunique clustered indexes. Leaf pages are filled to a capacity that is less than or equal to the fill factor value. Because the data pages in a clustered index are the leaf-level pages, the fill factor affects the data pages of clustered indexes.

Table 17.1 shows the effect of the fill factor on index packing. For further discussion of the usefulness of this command, see the discussion of hot spots and page splits in Chapter 18, "Optimizing Queries."

TABLE 17.1 THE EFFECT OF THE FILL FACTOR PARAMETER ON INDEX PACKING		
Setting (%)	**Internal page**	**Leaf page**
0	One free slot*	100 percent full
1–99	One free slot*	≤ Fillfactor percent full
100	100 percent full	100 percent full

*Two free slots for nonunique clustered indexes

Manage Index Buttons

These buttons, which appear down the right side of the Manage Indexes dialog box (Figure 17.1), help you manage your indexes.

Rebuild, Remove, and Rename Buttons

These buttons affect the currently selected index in the ways their names imply. To change the table or the index the buttons will affect, use the Table or Index fields next to these buttons.

The Rebuild button rebuilds the current index. You should regularly rebuild indexes of active tables. You can use the DBCC DBREINDEX command to schedule this task regularly. When you rebuild a clustered index, all the non-clustered indexes will be rebuilt as well. Whether you click the Rebuild button, use DBCC DBREINDEX, or use SQLMaint.exe (the Database Maintenance Wizard) to rebuild the indexes, the actual indexing is done by the DBCC REINDEX command. You can rebuild the indexes on a table without dropping all the constraints associated with the table, which is required if you attempt to drop and rebuild an index that is also a primary key.

The Remove button deletes the index.

The Rename button renames the index. This action affects only one record in the sysindexes table and does not affect any other table, even if the index is referenced by a primary key.

Check Size Button

Clicking Check Size shows you how large an index is and updates the sysindexes table. The figure in the Actual Size field in the Index Size box at the bottom of the dialog box comes from the sysindexes table, which is not kept up-to-date. Clicking Check Size brings up a warning that updating the size can take a long time and the pages could be unavailable for update while it's processing. You can also check the size of all the indexes for this table. If you have an overwhelming need to check the size of an index, you can do it here, but we recommend that you wait until you run the DBCC CHECKDB or DBCC CHECKTABLE commands during your normal nightly or weekly schedule.

Distribution Button

SQL Server has one of the best query optimizers in the database industry. The core of the optimizer is a distribution page, which keeps a statistical distribution of the values in the first field of each index in a table. Every index has one and only one distribution page. The optimizer uses this page to help make its final decision of how to minimize I/O to satisfy a query.

The Distribution button brings up the window in Figure 17.2, which shows the statistical distribution of the values in the first field in the index. This window was one of the most impressive additions to SQL Server 6.0 — you don't have to calculate statistical distribution values. Instead, you must know only how to interpret the significant values on this screen, which is no easy task — each statistic has far-reaching implications.

Figure 17.2 displays the distribution statistics in an easy-to-understand fashion. SQL Server distribution pages keep an *even distribution*, as opposed to a normal or standard distribution. An even distribution simply tracks every nth value in the first field of the index. To find the value of n, divide the number of rows in the table by the length, in bytes, of the first field in the index. This calculation may not be so simple when you are using a variable-length field. SQL Server tracks as many values as it can with variable-length fields, using the maximum length of the field to calculate an initial number of steps. The number of steps is shown in list of statistics at the top, and the value in each step is shown in the scrollable window at the bottom.

Figure 17.2
*Index Distribution
Statistics*

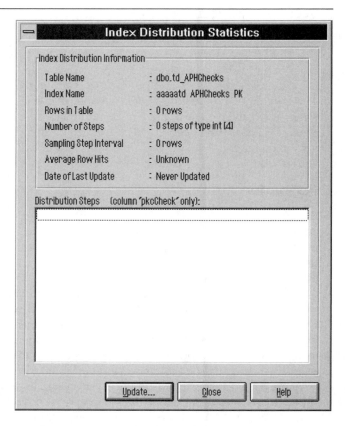

The value for the Sampling Step Interval indicates how many rows are represented by each recorded step. In the bottom window of the screen, the last value on the right is a pseudo record number representing the rows sorted by this field. Subtracting one value from the prior one in the list gives you the Sampling Step Interval.

The value of Average Row Hits is the most significant statistic on this page. The optimizer uses this statistic to determine which index has the best *selectivity.* Selectivity is an estimate of the number of rows that will be returned by a query that uses the equal sign in the Where clause for the first field in the index. (The best selectivity is the lowest number.) Selectivity is calculated by dividing the number of rows by the number of unique values in the first field in the index. You can find the number of unique values in a field with the following query:

```
SELECT COUNT(DISTINCT field) FROM table
```

The lower the density of the values, the higher the selectivity. The fewer number of duplicate entries you have in the table, the lower the density and the faster the retrieval. As the selectivity decreases, the usefulness of the index decreases.

What is a good selectivity percentage? Finding out is simpler than you might think. Figure 17.2 tells you if the percentage is excellent, good, fair, or poor. Use Table 17.2 to help you understand the meaning of the selectivity on your distribution page.

TABLE 17.2 INTERPRETING SELECTIVITY RATING

Rating	Rows Returned	Best Index Type	Comments
Optimal	1 row	Unique nonclustered	Good candidate for primary key
Very good	Between 1 row and 0.5 percent of rows	Nonclustered	
Good	Between 0.5 percent and 1 percent of rows	Nonclustered or clustered	Try both index types and use SHOWPLAN to determine which one you should use
Fair	Between 1 percent and 2.5 percent of rows	Nonclustered or clustered	Try both index types and use SHOWPLAN to determine which one you should use
Poor	Between 2.5 percent and 5 percent of rows	Clustered	Usually not indexed unless a covering query can be used frequently
Very poor	> 5 percent of rows	N/A	Don't bother indexing for performance; queries will use a table scan. Index for uniqueness if necessary, instead of indexing for performance.

To rebuild the distribution page, you must either run the Update Statistics command (discussed below) or rebuild the indexes. Distribution pages are not kept up-to-date online whenever tables are modified, for two reasons. First, it is very expensive to keep data up-to-date in real time. Second, the selectivity ratio may not change enough on each modification to make a difference to the optimizer.

The Update Statistics Command

This command updates the distribution page for an index. You can run this command for each index or for all indexes on a table. You cannot use one command for all indexes in the database. The syntax for the command is

```
UPDATE STATISTICS [[database].owner].table.[indexname]
```

where "table" is the only required parameter. Using indexname updates the statistics for one index in the table. Removing the indexname parameter causes all indexes for that table to be updated.

In SQL 6.5, use the Database Maintenance Wizard to set up a job that periodically updates the statistics for all indexes in your database. If this job takes too long to run, split it so that the most active tables are updated more often. Run the job at least once per week, except when the database is first installed and the users are adding a statistically significant amount of records; at that point, run it every night.

Distribution Notes

- A Truncate Table command clears the distribution page.
- The first record in the table is always recorded. If the index is nonclustered, the first record is used to satisfy the MIN( ) aggregate function on the first field in the index.
- The last value in the table is not always recorded, so the MAX( ) aggregate function must perform a serial scan of a nonclustered index, if one exists that contains the field referenced in the MAX( ) function. If multiple indexes that satisfy this criterion exist, the one with the fewest pages is used.
- The Average Row Hits field is used by the optimizer only if the table has more than 200 rows. Otherwise, the optimizer performs a table scan. Only in rare join queries does a table with 200 or fewer rows use an index.

Table Size

This small box on the left side of the Manage Indexes dialog box in Figure 17.1 shows the number of rows in the table and its size in K. This statistic is not always accurate, but it is usually very close. These numbers come from the sysindexes table and are not kept up-to-date in real time. To get an accurate number, you must use one of the following DBCC commands: CHECKTABLE (tablename), UPDATEUSAGE, or CHECKDB. Unless you are in dire need of an exact count, don't run the DBCC commands while others are using these tables, because they lock the tables and slow down the system.

Index Size

The bottom of the Manage Indexes dialog box shows some useful statistics about the index. These numbers, as well as those in the Table Size box described above, come from the sysindexes table and are not kept up-to-date in real time.

The first value in this part of the dialog box, Actual Size, shows the size of the index in K. Sample values for the last three fields are shown below.

Estimated Min./Avg./Max. Potential Size (K)	1000	1000	1000
Estimated Min./Avg./Max. Rows per Index Page	100	100	100
Estimated Min./Avg./Max. Index B-Tree Levels	3	3	3

The minimum, average, and maximum numbers can be different if the indexed column is a variable-length field. Each one can be a meaningful number for performance analysis. The bottom line is the B-Tree Levels; each level indicates one I/O. We go into more depth about index levels in the discussion below.

Advanced Topics

Now that you know the basics of indexing and managing your indexes, we'll consider some advanced topics, including the relationship between index levels and I/O, covering indexes, and data modifications.

Index Levels and I/O

Each index level (shown in the Index Size box of the Manage Indexes dialog box; see Figure 17.1) results in one I/O operation. Nonclustered indexes require one extra I/O beyond the leaf level, so a nonclustered index with four index levels takes five I/Os to read one record. Most indexes on transaction data contain three or four levels. Moving to a fifth level can be very expensive, and it would be wise to consider a horizontal split of the data. (See Chapter 16, "Performance Tuning," for more information about horizontal splits.) Sometimes very wide indexes have five levels, so consider narrowing your key if you have this many levels.

Update statements are the most expensive in terms of I/O; they can cause considerable performance problems for tables with four- and five-level indexes. Consider re-coding your application to use direct in-place updates (explained on page 363) if you have multi-level indexes. Chapter 18, "Optimizing Queries," gives an example of how to use cursors to force a direct in-place update.

Covering Index

A *covering index* is a nonclustered index that can solve a query by accessing only leaf-level index pages, not data pages. Covering indexes should save you I/O. Sometimes adding one or two fields that are used frequently in a Select list, Where clause, Order By clause, or Group By clause to an index can create a covering index. A clustered index can never be a covering index because the leaf-level pages are the data pages.

Data Modifications

While you read this section, keep in mind that you should strive for direct Updates in-place. They are absolutely the fastest data modifications, but they are the most difficult to achieve because of SQL Server's restrictions.

Deferred Data Modifications

Deferred data modifications are Updates, Inserts, or Deletes that SQL Server defers; SQL Server splits the modification into several behind-the-scenes batch processes. Don't get confused — if a modification is deferred, an Update trigger, if one exists, is still the only trigger executed by the Update statement. If the Update is deferred, SQL performs the Delete and Insert commands behind the scenes, so it does not execute the Delete and Insert triggers.

Let's take a look at the steps in each kind of deferred data modification.

Deferred Updates

1. All affected records are first copied to the transaction log. Two copies are made — a copy of the original records and a copy of the new records with updated values.

2. As the copy is made, an update lock is placed on each page.

3. SQL Server reads the log and, for each data page involved, obtains an exclusive lock on the page, then deletes the rows from the data page.

4. As the rows are deleted from the data pages, each index on the table is also deleted.

5. As the indexes are deleted, entries are added to the transaction log.

6. Lock entries are added to the syslocks table for the affected index pages.

7. If an Update trigger exists on the table, a special Deleted table is created, and this table is filled with all the deleted records.

8. The transaction log is read again and the new records are inserted in the table.

9. If an Update trigger exists on the table, a special Inserted table is created, and this table is filled with all the new records.

10. As the Inserts are done, each index on the table gets its corresponding Inserts. These index Inserts are logged in the transaction log. Additional lock entries are added to the syslock tables only if the new records get inserted on a new index page.

11. The Update trigger, if any, is executed.

12. The Commit statement is added to the log.

13. The locks are released and SQL Server breathes a sigh of relief because another successful transaction has finally completed.

In terms of performance, deferred Updates are the most expensive operations SQL Server can do, and we didn't even take into consideration the possibility of split pages. This operation creates more than the normal number of log records. Let's look at the above steps from a different point of view. This operation creates the following items:

- four log records for each modified data row (the two original copies, the deleted records, and the inserted records)
- three data page accesses for each row (the original copy, the Delete, the Insert)
- two log records for each corresponding index entry (the Delete and the Insert)
- two traversals of each index from root level to leaf level (to find the Delete, then to find where the Insert goes)
- two scans of the log records (one for the Delete, one for the Insert)

Deferred Inserts

A deferred Insert is one in which SQL Server uses completely separate processes, as well as temporary work tables, to complete an Insert statement. As an example, consider the following query:

```
INSERT authors SELECT * FROM authors
```

If SQL Server inserts one row at a time, then reads the next record, how does it know when to stop? Unless it could see a better strategy, it would go into an infinite loop. The better strategy is called a *deferred insert*.

To solve the above problem without going into an infinite loop, SQL Server performs the following steps:

1. The records are copied to the transaction log.
2. As the copy is made, an update lock is placed on each page.
3. The transaction log is read and the new records are inserted in the table.
4. If an Insert trigger exists on the table, a special Inserted table is created, and this table is filled with all the new records.
5. As the Inserts are completed, each index on the table gets its corresponding Inserts. These index Inserts get logged in the transaction log. Lock entries are added to the syslock tables for the new index records.
6. The Insert trigger, if any, is executed.
7. The Commit statement is added to the log.
8. The locks are released and SQL Server breathes a sigh of relief because another successful transaction has finally completed.

Deferred Deletes

When SQL Server determines that a deferred delete is needed, it follows this sequence of tasks:

1. The records are copied to the transaction log.
2. As the copy is made, an update lock is placed on each page.
3. The transaction log is read and the new records are deleted from the table.
4. If a delete trigger exists on the table, a special Deleted table is created, and this table is filled with all the removed records.
5. As the Deletes are completed, each index on the table gets its corresponding Deletes. These index Deletes are added to the transaction

log. Lock entries are added to the syslock tables before the Deletes occur on the index pages.

6. The Delete trigger, if any, is executed.

7. The Commit statement is added to the log.

8. The locks are released and SQL Server breathes a sigh of relief because another successful transaction has finally completed.

Now that we have read about these types of modifications, let's see them in action. The following Update statement updates a key value, which causes the worst kind of performance on the system; you can see the evidence in the syslogs table. To understand the output from syslogs, see Appendix A. Contrast this Update statement with the cursor example in the next chapter, which updates a non-key value in the Authors table and does a direct update-in-place.

The example below was performed with five rows in the Authors table and two indexes on the table. One was a unique, clustered index on the au_id field, and the other was a nonunique, nonclustered index on au_lname and au_fname.

```
UPDATE authors set au_id= au_id
SELECT * FROM syslogs

xactid                  op
────────────────        ──
0x140300002300          0
0x140300002300          12
0x140300002300          11
0x140300002300          12
0x140300002300          11
0x140300002300          12
0x140300002300          11
0x140300002300          12
0x140300002300          11
0x140300002300          12
0x140300002300          11
0x140300002300          8
0x140300002300          5
0x140300002300          8
0x140300002300          5
0x140300002300          8
0x140300002300          5
0x140300002300          8
```

```
0x140300002300          5
0x140300002300          8
0x140300002300          5
0x140300002300          6
0x140300002300          7
0x140300002300          6
0x140300002300          7
0x140300002300          6
0x140300002300          7
0x140300002300          6
0x140300002300          7
0x140300002300          6
0x140300002300          7
0x140300002300         30
```

Direct Updates

Direct Updates come in two kinds: in-place and not-in-place. In-place Updates are significantly faster than any other type of Update, but setting up in-place Updates is complex. Like deferred Updates, not-in-place Updates are basically a Delete operation followed by an Insert operation, but they are performed with less work than a deferred Update.

Direct Updates Not-In-Place

SQL Server uses several rules to decide whether it needs to do a deferred Update or a direct Update not-in-place. The following rules determine whether a direct Update is possible:

1. No join clauses are allowed.
2. The index used by the optimizer cannot be updated.
3. Only one row is updated by an Update statement. The optimizer must be able to determine the number of rows to be updated at the time the query is compiled. For the optimizer to determine the number of rows, you must have a unique index on the table and the Where clause must use this index with a search argument (SARG) that the optimizer can recognize as a unique value.

The row is added to the log file, deleted, updated, then added back to the table. Where is the new row placed? As in a normal Insert, it depends upon whether the table has a clustered index. With no clustered index, the row is inserted at the end of the table, which causes extra overhead because the index entries must be adjusted to point to the new place. If the table has a clustered index and the index value has changed, SQL Server moves the row so that the value is in the correct sorted order. If the clustered index value has not changed, the new record must still fit on the original page. If values in variable-length fields have increased the size of the record so much that it can no longer fits on the page, a new page is added to the table to hold the new record. If the index is a unique clustered index, a page split occurs. If the clustered index allows duplicate entries, an overflow page is created. Any movement of rows, either with a page split or with an overflow page, also causes the corresponding index entries to be updated and logged.

Direct Updates In-Place

Direct Updates in-place are absolutely the fastest Updates in SQL Server. If you can get your application to do Updates in-place, you have achieved something that is difficult to accomplish. And it is difficult to recognize when you have achieved this goal. The only way to tell whether your application does Updates in-place is to decipher the transaction log. See Appendix A for more details than you ever wanted to know about interpreting the transaction log.

Why is it so difficult to do an Update in-place? Well, here are the general rules:

- You must not change any value in the unique index chosen by the optimizer.
- You must not change a value in a clustered index that requires the record to be moved to a different location.
- The table cannot have an Update trigger. Because an Update in-place does not follow the normal Delete and Insert routine for an Update, it does not create the Deleted and Inserted tables.
- The table cannot be marked for replication.
- You cannot change the values of an image or text field in the Update statement.

Wait — we have more rules to consider. Single-row and multiple-row updates have their own separate rules. For single-row updates, the following rules also apply:

- If the updated columns are variable length, the new row must fit on the same page as the original row. This rule has relaxed from the prior versions of SQL Server where the row could not get any longer.
- The updated columns can be part of a nonunique nonclustered index, but they must be of fixed length. Remember that a column with a fixed-length

data type, such as a character column, that allows Null values is treated as a variable-length column.

Finally, to be updated, single-row updates must conform to the following two weird rules:

- The updated columns can be part of a unique nonclustered index if the key is fixed-width and the Where clause has an exact match with one and only one row.
- More than 50 percent of the number of bytes in the row cannot change, and fewer than 24 discontiguous bytes cannot change. Let's see the hotshot programmers in the SQL Server lab explain this one!

Here are the rules for multiple-row Updates in-place (a new feature added in SQL 6.0). Remember that the general rules for Updates in-place still apply.

- The columns being updated must be fixed-length columns.
- The columns being updated must not be part of a unique nonclustered index.
- The table cannot contain a column with the timestamp datatype.
- The updated columns can be part of a unique nonclustered index if the key is fixed-width and if the index is not the index used by the optimizer to satisfy the query.

Indexing Strategies

This section contains a few recommendations about what to index, what not to index, and other indexing strategies. It even includes a small test of your indexing savvy.

What to Index

- Columns used frequently in Where clauses
- Columns used in joins, usually primary and foreign keys
- Columns used in Group by clauses
- Columns used in Order by clauses
- Columns used in aggregate functions

What Not to Index

- Tables with a small number of rows
- Tables with heavy transaction-based I/O
- Columns not used in Where clause
- Columns with greater than 5 percent selectivity
- Wide columns (greater than 25 bytes in width)

Other Strategies

- Narrow indexes are sometimes better than multiple-column composite indexes unless they are used as covering queries. Wider indexes cause more index pages.
- Do not have more than one index with the same first column.
- Do you index every field in every table? Of course not; too much overhead is required to keep indexes updated. What is a good number of indexes to have? Four or five is usually the most you should have on a table. You can have more indexes on a table in a data warehouse and fewer indexes in an online transaction processing table.
- In general, integer fields make more efficient indexes than character fields and fixed-length data types are more efficient than variable types.
- Tables with a small number of rows should have a unique index only to prevent duplicates. The SQL Server optimizer does not consider an index when the table has fewer than 200 rows. It almost always uses a table scan for this table. The only time the optimizer may choose to use an index on a small table is in a join operation.
- Adding columns to a nonclustered index may be expensive in terms of increased I/O but may be a good choice if the index is a covering query so that the query only reads the index pages and does not go to the data pages.
- When you're importing data in batches, it may be faster to drop the indexes, insert all the data, then rebuild the indexes.

Trick Question

If you see a Select statement with the following Where clause and the field has a unique index, is a clustered or nonclustered index better?

```
WHERE field = value
```

Because this query uses an equal sign and the field has a unique index, it is going to return at most one row. Remember that in a clustered index, the leaf level of the index is the data, so a clustered index has one fewer I/O operation to perform. Therefore, you might pick a clustered index. But don't be so hasty. You should also remember that Table 17.2 says if one row is returned, you should use a nonclustered index. Why is that, because nonclustered indexes are more expensive and the optimizer is trying to minimize I/O?

This question illustrates this rule of thumb: Performance tuning is about saving many I/Os, not just one. You can put only one clustered index on a table, so you should use it wisely to save many I/Os. In our earlier discussions of clustered and nonclustered indexes, we learned that it is better to use clustered indexes to solve queries asking for ranges of data, not one row.

Summary

A good foundation in SQL Server indexes is necessary before you can continue performance tuning. It is a good idea to learn as much as you can now, while SQL Server only offers b-tree indexing. We will likely see other indexing strategies in future versions of SQL Server; hashing, inverted lists, or other strategies may be added someday. Although these indexing strategies will give you even more opportunity for creating efficient indexes, they will also dramatically increase your learning curve.

Chapter 18

Optimizing Queries

In this chapter, we discuss techniques and strategies for optimizing queries. In Chapter 16, we learned to tune the server, the network, and your SQL Server configuration. Chapter 17 looked at indexing strategies from different angles and introduced you to the optimizer. This chapter explains the issues that application developers need to be familiar with to tune programs.

First, we show you how to analyze queries so that the optimizer's decisions won't surprise you. After a quick discussion of the optimizer, we learn the steps the optimizer goes through before your query returns data.

We then consider a variety of strategies for optimizing queries. A discussion of cursors as they relate to performance shows you where cursors can be both better and worse than a regular query. Understanding SQL Server locking, especially the pros and cons of the new row-level locking options, is a good step in learning how to avoid locking and associated problems. Finally, we look at hot spots, page splits, and other issues. These topics are a good wrap-up, because they tie together a lot of the underlying features of SQL Server.

To understand the last part of this chapter, you need to read Chapter 17, "Indexing," and the first part of this chapter to get a solid foundation in the defining characteristics of the SQL Server optimizer.

Analyzing Queries

An understanding of the optimizer is necessary before you can address performance problems your queries might cause. We also consider ways to analyze queries so you can see what the optimizer does, both from Set statement options and from DBCC commands. DBCC is a collection of commands that check for internal database errors, set trace flags, and analyze performance. We consider the following three ways to analyze queries:

- Set options
- DBCC TRACE options
- DBCC SHOWCONTIG options

SQL Server Optimizer

The SQL Server optimizer, which is called into action only when your query contains a Where clause, is considered one of the best optimizers in the database industry. It is a cost-based optimizer, backed by a simple collection of statistics you can find in the distribution page (see Chapter 17, "Indexing," for a complete discussion of the distribution page). The optimizer is smart enough to know when it is taking too long to search for an optimal index and either performs a table scan, which performs your requested transaction row by row, or takes the best index it has found to that point.

The optimizer has a difficult task, because it must make decisions about indexing, join orders, the use of Tempdb for work tables, and sorts. It must make these decisions in a remarkably short time so as to not affect the performance of the query. Efficient algorithms and simple statistics make it possible for the optimizer to work quickly. Setting some of the trace flags lets you look at the choices and decisions the optimizer is making. DBCC TRACEON (310) displays the join analysis, and DBCC TRACEON (304) shows the optimizer's index analysis.

Using Set Options

The options available with the Set command tell you the steps the optimizer takes to satisfy a query, the steps it takes to search for the optimal join order, and how the optimizer finds its choice for the best index.

First, we need to discuss the three Set command options. You can turn on these options either by typing them at the beginning of a TRANSACT-SQL script or, if you are using a GUI tool, by turning them on in the query options. We use the SQL Enterprise Manager because it comes with SQL Server; however, other GUI tools from third-party vendors have these and other options.

The three commands are

- Set statistics I/O on
- Set statistics time on
- Set Showplan on

You can use the two buttons at the bottom left of the SQL Enterprise Manager screen, shown in Figure 18.1, to turn on the No Execute option, which parses the SQL command without executing it, or the statistics I/O option. You can also set these (and more) options with the yellow wrench icon at the top of the query window (Figure 18.2).

Figure 18.1
The No Execute and Statistics I/O Buttons

Figure 18.2
Wrench Button

We use the following query of the Pubs database (the sample publisher's database that comes with SQL Server) to demonstrate the query analysis tools. The query links the Authors, Titleauthor, and Titles tables in a three-table join. You can open a query window and test these queries yourself.

```
SELECT a.au_id ID,
       a.au_lname 'Last Name',
             title Title
FROM authors a,
       titleauthor ta,
             titles t
WHERE a.au_id = ta.au_id
AND t.title_id= ta.title_id
```

The Statistics I/O Option

Overall, this option is the best to use to gather information because it gives the bottom-line results of the I/O performed by the SQL Select command. The command returns scan count, logical I/O, physical I/O, and the order of table/view access. You can view these statistics in two ways. A graph (Figure 18.3) depicts the scan count, logical I/O, and physical I/O. You can also see the statistics after the results of the query are displayed in the Results window. Figure 18.4 shows the end of the results of the sample query with the statistics listed.

Figure 18.3

Statistics I/O Graph

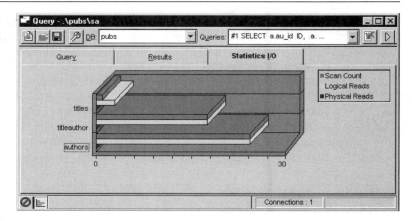

Figure 18.4

Statistics Shown with Results

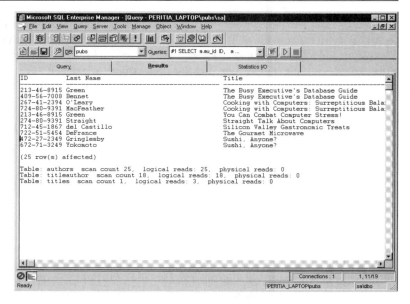

The scan count is the number of times the focus was switched to a particular table. Switching focus is expensive, but in a join, one table must be the foundation table, and SQL Server switches back and forth among all the other tables. Physical I/O indicates the number of pages that must be read from disk physically. Logical I/O is total I/O, both from cache and disk.

The order of the tables in the list in Figure 18.4 is significant because the first table is the foundation table. The query optimizer uses the foundation table as the base table and joins the other tables to it. The scan count is almost always 1 on this table. Work tables can also have a scan count of 1. This list not only shows the order of the tables but also gives you a quick glance at the number of tables and work tables involved in solving the query.

If you run a query one time and the physical I/O is high, run it again immediately. The physical I/O will drop and the logical I/O will rise because SQL Server keeps the pages in memory after the first read.

The Statistics Time Option

This option gives the time, in milliseconds, that each step of the query takes to run. It is not always accurate and should only be used as a comparison between different runs of the same query. This statistic can be misleading if the system is busy on one run of a query and not busy on another run. This option is not used very often, but if you are curious, turn it on.

The Showplan Option

This tool is another good one to get to know well. It outlines the steps the optimizer takes to get to a final decision about the query. From turning on Showplan, you can find out the order in which the tables are worked on, the indexes (if any) that are chosen, and the work tables used.

If you are running ISQL/w or the SQL Enterprise Manager, the graphical view of Showplan is a good place to start. The two buttons on the bottom left of a query screen correspond to Set noexec on and Set statistics I/O on. The optimizer's first step is shown below.

```
STEP 1
The type of query is SELECT
FROM TABLE
titles t
Nested iteration
Table Scan
FROM TABLE
titleauthor ta
Nested iteration
```

```
Table Scan
FROM TABLE
authors a
Nested iteration
Table Scan
```

It can take a while to use Showplan effectively because the results use many key words and phrases. Several good articles have been written that go into the details of Showplan's output. In particular, see the Microsoft TechNet CD and the Microsoft Knowledge Base for SQL Server.

DBCC Trace Options 302, 310, 325, 326, 3604

DBCC is a SQL Server utility whose main task is to check the internal consistency of the database. However, it has other functions, one of which is to trace options within a database. To thoroughly analyze the performance of a query, you need to use DBCC's trace options.

- DBCC TRACEON (302) indicates whether the distribution page is used in the decision-making process. It gives the selectivity percentage of the index used (if any) and the optimizer's estimate of the I/O for each index considered.

- DBCC TRACEON (310) displays the join order of the tables. The detail of this option includes the steps the optimizer went through to narrow the selection to the final index selection and the join order. Use options 302 and 310 together to show the actual join order.

- DBCC TRACEON (325) compares the cost of using a sort and using a non-clustered index to process an Order by clause.

- DBCC TRACEON (326) lists the estimated and the actual costs of a sort.

- DBCC TRACEON (3604) option forces the trace results to appear in the online results window. Without it, the results appear only in the SQL error log.

The information in the query window is shown below.

```
DBCC TRACEON (3604, 302)
GO
SELECT a.au_id ID,
       a.au_lname 'Last Name',
       title Title
FROM authors a,
```

```
        titleauthor ta,
        titles t
WHERE a.au_id = ta.au_id
AND t.title_id = ta.title_id
GO
DBCC TRACEOFF (3604, 302)
GO
```

The results of this query are shown in Figures 18.5 and 18.6. As you can see, the optimizer considers all indexes on all the tables involved in the query, and it considers them very rapidly. Index 0 (table scan) is chosen for the tables because the tables don't contain enough data to make it worthwhile to consider an index.

The output in Figure 18.5 is the result of the query optimizer's three basic jobs. The first section identifies the tables and indexes and shows the best index for each table in the query. The optimizer has already searched each index in each table, assigning a score to each index based on the statistics stored in the distribution page.

```
DBCC execution completed. If DBCC printed error messages, see
your System Administrator.
*******************************
Leaving q_init_sclause() for table 'authors' (varno 0).
The table has 23 rows and 1 pages.
Cheapest index is index 0, costing 1 pages per scan.
*******************************
Leaving q_init_sclause() for table 'titleauthor' (varno 1).
The table has 25 rows and 1 pages.
Cheapest index is index 0, costing 1 pages per scan.
*******************************
Leaving q_init_sclause() for table 'titles' (varno 2).
The table has 18 rows and 3 pages.
Cheapest index is index 0, costing 3 pages per scan.
```

Figure 18.5
DBCC TRACEON (302) Output, Index Analysis

Here are a few notes on how to decipher this cryptic output. Each table in the From clause of the query is given a number, starting at zero. The output identifies the tables as <varno *n*>. The estimate of the number of rows and pages is based on the sysindexes table. The cheapest index to use is identified by a number, which the optimizer gets from the INDID column in the sysindexes table. When the optimizer specifies index 0, it performs a table scan of the data pages instead of using an index. If the cheapest index is index 1, the optimizer has found a clustered index on the table and has chosen to use it. Values greater than 1 mean that the optimizer has chosen a non-clustered index whose INDID matches the number reported as the cheapest index.

The rest of the output, shown in Figure 18.6, analyzes the search arguments (SARGS) in the query. This output is basically a step-by-step analysis of the Where clause. The optimizer must get the fields involved and the field attributes such as datatype and length. The datatypes are important because SQL Server does not allow joins between two disparate data types, and even datatypes that can be implicitly converted cause a conversion on every record involved in the join.

Figure 18.6
DBCC
TRACEON
(302)
Output,
Where
Clause and
Join Analysis

```
*******************************
Entering q_score_join() for table 'authors' (varno 0).
The table has 23 rows and 1 pages.
Scoring the join clause:
AND (!:0x18dd004)  (andstat:0x2)
  EQ (L:0x18dcf20)  ( rsltype(0x2f):CHAR rsllen:255 rslprec:11
  rslscale:0 opstat:0x0)
    VAR (L:0x18dcb4e)  (varname:au_id varno:0 colid:1
    coltype(0x27):VARCHAR colen:11 coloff:-1 colprec:11
colscale:0
    vartypeid:101 varusecnt:2 varstat:0x1 varlevel:0 varsubq:0)
    VAR (R:0x18dced6)  (varname:au_id varno:1 colid:1
    coltype(0x27):VARCHAR colen:11 coloff:-1 colprec:11
colscale:0
    vartypeid:101 varusecnt:1 varlevel:0 varsubq:0)

Unique clustered index found—return rows 1 pages 2
Cheapest index is index 0, costing 1 pages and generating 1 rows
per scan.
Join selectivity is 23.
*******************************


*******************************
Entering q_score_join() for table 'titleauthor' (varno 1).
The table has 25 rows and 1 pages.
Scoring the join clause:
AND (!:0x18dd010)  (andstat:0x2)
  EQ (L:0x18dcfe4)  ( rsltype(0x2f):CHAR rsllen:255 rslprec:6
```

Figure 18.6
continued

```
 rslscale:0 opstat:0x0)
   VAR (L:0x18dcf98)  (varname:title_id varno:1 colid:2
   coltype(0x27):VARCHAR colen:6 coloff:-2 colprec:6 colscale:0
   vartypeid:102 varnext:18dced6 varusecnt:1 varlevel:0
   varsubq:0)
   VAR (R:0x18dcf40)  (varname:title_id varno:2 colid:1
   coltype(0x27):VARCHAR colen:6 coloff:-1 colprec:6 colscale:0
   vartypeid:102 varnext:18dcc62 varusecnt:1 varlevel:0
   varsubq:0)

Scoring clause for index 3
Relop bits are: 0x80,0x4
Estimate: indid 3, selectivity 7.142857e-002, rows 1 pages 3
Cheapest index is index 0, costing 1 pages and generating 25 rows
per scan.
Cost join selectivity is 1.
Best join selectivity is 14.
******************************

******************************
Entering q_score_join() for table 'titleauthor' (varno 1).
The table has 25 rows and 1 pages.
Scoring the join clause:
AND (!:0x18dd004)  (andstat:0x2)
  EQ (L:0x18dcf20)  ( rsltype(0x2f):CHAR rsllen:255 rslprec:11
  rslscale:0 opstat:0x0)
    VAR (L:0x18dced6)  (varname:au_id varno:1 colid:1
    coltype(0x27):VARCHAR colen:11 coloff:-1 colprec:11
    colscale:0
    vartypeid:101 varusecnt:1 varlevel:0 varsubq:0)
    VAR (R:0x18dcb4e)  (varname:au_id right:18dced6 varno:0
    colid:1
    coltype(0x27):VARCHAR colen:11 coloff:-1 colprec:11
    colscale:0
    vartypeid:101 varusecnt:2 varstat:0x885 varlevel:0 varsubq:0)

Unique clustered index found—return rows 1 pages 2
Scoring clause for index 1
Relop bits are: 0x1000,0x800,0x80,0x4
Estimate: indid 1, selectivity 6.250000e-002, rows 1 pages 2
Scoring clause for index 2
Relop bits are: 0x1000,0x800,0x80,0x4
Estimate: indid 2, selectivity 6.250000e-002, rows 1 pages 3
Cheapest index is index 0, costing 1 pages and generating 25 rows
per scan.
Cost join selectivity is 1.
Best join selectivity is 16.
******************************
```

Figure 18.6
continued

```
********************************
Entering q_score_join() for table 'titles' (varno 2).
The table has 18 rows and 3 pages.
Scoring the join clause:
AND (!:0x18dd010) (andstat:0x2)
   EQ (L:0x18dcfe4) ( rsltype(0x2f):CHAR rsllen:255 rslprec:6
   rslscale:0 opstat:0x0)
      VAR (L:0x18dcf40) (varname:title_id varno:2 colid:1
      coltype(0x27):VARCHAR colen:6 coloff:-1 colprec:6 colscale:0
      vartypeid:102 varnext:18dcc62 varusecnt:1 varlevel:0
varsubq:0)
      VAR (R:0x18dcf98) (varname:title_id right:18dcf40 varno:1
      colid:2 coltype(0x27):VARCHAR colen:6 coloff:-2 colprec:6
      colscale:0 vartypeid:102 varnext:18dced6 varusecnt:1
varstat:0x4
      varlevel:0 varsubq:0)

Unique clustered index found—return rows 1 pages 2
Cheapest index is index 1, costing 2 pages and generating 1 rows
per scan.
Join selectivity is 18.
********************************
```

ID	Last Name	Title
213-46-8915	Green	The Busy Executive's Database Guide
672-71-3249	Yokomoto	Sushi, Anyone?

```
(25 row(s) affected)
**

DBCC execution completed. If DBCC printed error messages, see
your System Administrator.
```

The optimizer must also decipher whether the SARG can be used by the optimizer to improve performance. One example of an invalid search argument is an entry in the Where clause that has complex expressions. The following Where clause

```
WHERE table.column + 1 = 3
```

is not considered by the optimizer, even if table.column has the best available index, because the column reference has a mathematical calculation. A better SARG, showing a valid search argument, is

```
WHERE table.column = 2
```

The output also shows an analysis of the joins between each table in the query. The optimizer scores each index in the tables involved in the join according to the calculated selectivity from the distribution page. It chooses the best index and displays its associated cost (in terms of selectivity).

The DBCC Join Analyzer

Now let's look at the same query with trace flag 310. This flag analyzes the joins in the query to find the base table and the most efficient indexes for joining the tables.

```
DBCC TRACEON (3604, 310)
GO
SELECT a.au_id       ID,
            a.au_lname    'Last Name',
            title  Title
FROM    authors a,
            titleauthor ta,
            titles t
WHERE   a.au_id      = ta.au_id
AND     t.title_id   = ta.title_id
GO
DBCC TRACEOFF (3604, 310)
GO
```

The results of this query are shown in Figure 18.7. One of the most important pieces of information is on the first line: QUERY IS CONNECTED. This message tells you whether you have enough entries in your Where clause to join all the tables. If you get a QUERY IS NOT CONNECTED message, you need to add more joins to your Where clause. A query that is not connected performs a Cartesian product, which causes a lot of I/O. The number of rows returned from a Cartesian product is the number of rows in one table multiplied by the number of rows in the other table.

The next line of the output (J_OPTMIZE) indicates the start of the join analysis. The "vars=[n,n,n]" information is the same as the variables in the DBCC 302 output above; that is, each table involved in the query is assigned a number in the order it appears in the From clause.

Figure 18.7
*DBCC
TRACEON
(310) Output*

```
QUERY IS CONNECTED

J_OPTIMIZE: Remaining vars=[0,1,2]

permutation: 0 - 1 - 2

NEW PLAN #1 (total cost = 268):
JPLAN (0x374f4a0) varno=0 indexid=0 totcost=16 pathtype=sclause
class=join optype=? method=NESTED ITERATION outerrows=1 rows=23
joinsel=1 lp=1 pp=1 cpages=1 ctotpages=1 corder=1 cstat=0x20
maxpages=1 matcost=10144 matpages=1 crows=23 cjoinsel=1

JPLAN (0x374f504) varno=1 indexid=0 totcost=60 pathtype=sclause
class=join optype=? method=NESTED ITERATION outerrows=23
rows=25
joinsel=16 lp=23 pp=1 cpages=1 ctotpages=1 corder=1 cstat=0x20
maxpages=1 matcost=10168 matpages=2 crows=25 cjoinsel=1
joinmap=[0]

JPLAN (0x374f568) varno=2 indexid=0 totcost=192
pathtype=sclause
class=join optype=? method=NESTED ITERATION outerrows=25
rows=25
joinsel=14 lp=75 pp=3 cpages=3 ctotpages=3 corder=1 cstat=0x20
maxpages=3 crows=18 cjoinsel=1 joinmap=[1]


NEW PLAN #2 (total cost = 218):
JPLAN (0x374f4a0) varno=0 indexid=0 totcost=16 pathtype=sclause
class=join optype=? method=NESTED ITERATION outerrows=1 rows=23
joinsel=1 lp=1 pp=1 cpages=1 ctotpages=1 corder=1 cstat=0x20
maxpages=1 matcost=10144 matpages=1 crows=23 cjoinsel=1

JPLAN (0x374f504) varno=1 indexid=0 totcost=60 pathtype=sclause
class=join optype=? method=NESTED ITERATION outerrows=23
rows=25
joinsel=16 lp=23 pp=1 cpages=1 ctotpages=1 corder=1 cstat=0x20
maxpages=1 matcost=10168 matpages=2 crows=25 cjoinsel=1
joinmap=[0]

JPLAN (0x374f568) varno=2 indexid=1 totcost=142 pathtype=join
class=join optype=? method=NESTED ITERATION outerrows=25
rows=25
joinsel=14 lp=50 pp=3 cpages=2 ctotpages=3 corder=1 cstat=0x4
maxpages=3 crows=1 cjoinsel=18 joinmap=[1] jnvar=1 refindid=0
```

```
refcost=0 refpages=0 reftotpages=0 ordercol[0]=1 ordercol[1]=2

WORK PLAN #3 (total cost = 10418):


permutation: 0 - 2 - 1
IGNORING THIS PERMUTATION


permutation: 1 - 0 - 2
WORK PLAN #4 (total cost = 272):
WORK PLAN #5 (total cost = 222):
WORK PLAN #6 (total cost = 10392):


permutation: 2 - 0 - 1
IGNORING THIS PERMUTATION


permutation: 1 - 2 - 0
WORK PLAN #7 (total cost = 272):
WORK PLAN #8 (total cost = 222):
WORK PLAN #9 (total cost = 10392):


permutation: 2 - 1 - 0

NEW PLAN #10 (total cost = 162):
JPLAN (0x374f4a0) varno=2 indexid=0 totcost=48
pathtype=sclause
class=join optype=? method=NESTED ITERATION outerrows=1
rows=18
joinsel=1 lp=3 pp=3 cpages=3 ctotpages=3 corder=1 cstat=0x20
maxpages=3 matcost=10119 matpages=1 crows=18 cjoinsel=1

JPLAN (0x374f504) varno=1 indexid=0 totcost=50
pathtype=sclause
class=join optype=? method=NESTED ITERATION outerrows=18
rows=25
joinsel=14 lp=18 pp=1 cpages=1 ctotpages=1 corder=1 cstat=0x20
maxpages=1 matcost=10168 matpages=2 crows=25 cjoinsel=1
joinmap=[2]

JPLAN (0x374f568) varno=0 indexid=0 totcost=64
pathtype=sclause
class=join optype=? method=NESTED ITERATION outerrows=25
rows=25
joinsel=16 lp=25 pp=1 cpages=1 ctotpages=1 corder=1 cstat=0x20
maxpages=1 crows=23 cjoinsel=1 joinmap=[1]
```

Figure 18.7,
continued

Figure 18.7
continued

```
BEST PERMUTATION (total cost = 162):
JPLAN (0x374e800) varno=2 indexid=0 totcost=48 pathtype=sclause
class=join optype=? method=NESTED ITERATION outerrows=1 rows=18
joinsel=1 lp=3 pp=3 cpages=3 ctotpages=3 corder=1 cstat=0x20
maxpages=3 matcost=10119 matpages=1 crows=18 cjoinsel=1

JPLAN (0x374e864) varno=1 indexid=0 totcost=50 pathtype=sclause
class=join optype=? method=NESTED ITERATION outerrows=18
rows=25
joinsel=14 lp=18 pp=1 cpages=1 ctotpages=1 corder=1 cstat=0x20
maxpages=1 matcost=10168 matpages=2 crows=25 cjoinsel=1
joinmap=[2]

JPLAN (0x374e8c8) varno=0 indexid=0 totcost=64 pathtype=sclause
class=join optype=? method=NESTED ITERATION outerrows=25
rows=25
joinsel=16 lp=25 pp=1 cpages=1 ctotpages=1 corder=1 cstat=0x20
maxpages=1 crows=23 cjoinsel=1 joinmap=[1]


TOTAL # COMBINATIONS: 1
TOTAL # PERMUTATIONS: 6
TOTAL # PLANS CONSIDERED: 10

FINAL PLAN (total cost = 162, maxpages = 5):
JPLAN (0x374e800) varno=2 indexid=0 totcost=48 pathtype=sclause
class=join optype=SUBSTITUTE method=NESTED ITERATION outer-
rows=1
rows=18 joinsel=1 lp=3 pp=3 cpages=3 ctotpages=3 corder=1
cstat=0x20
maxpages=3 matcost=10119 matpages=1 crows=18 cjoinsel=1

JPLAN (0x374e864) varno=1 indexid=0 totcost=50 pathtype=sclause
class=join optype=SUBSTITUTE method=NESTED ITERATION outer-
rows=18
rows=25 joinsel=14 lp=18 pp=1 cpages=1 ctotpages=1 corder=1
cstat=0x20 maxpages=1 matcost=10168 matpages=2 crows=25
cjoinsel=1
joinmap=[2]

JPLAN (0x374e8c8) varno=0 indexid=0 totcost=64 pathtype=sclause
class=join optype=SUBSTITUTE method=NESTED ITERATION outer-
rows=25
rows=25 joinsel=16 lp=25 pp=1 cpages=1 ctotpages=1 corder=1
```

```
cstat=0x20 maxpages=1 crows=23 cjoinsel=1 joinmap=[1]
```

Figure 18.7
continued

```
*******************************
ID            Last Name    Title
_____  _____  _____
213-46-8915   Green        The Busy Executive's Database Guide
672-71-3249   Yokomoto     Sushi, Anyone?
(25 row(s) affected)
**

DBCC execution completed. If DBCC printed error messages, see
your System Administrator.
```

The "permutation: 0-1-2" line of the output shows how the optimizer steps through all possibilities to complete the analysis. It analyzes each permutation of the tables in the From clause, with each table considered in turn as the base table.

The significant part of the "NEW PLAN #1 (total cost = 268)" line is total cost. This value estimates the I/O cost, in milliseconds, of the entire query. The total cost is the sum of the cost of each JPLAN (listed below the NEW PLAN line). A JPLAN is an analysis of each table in the query; each table gets its own JPLAN. JPLAN analyses are run in order of the current permutation. Table 18.1 defines the pieces of a JPLAN. The last four items in the table appear only if the reformatting strategy is used in your query.

TABLE 18.1 DEFINITION OF JPLAN TERMS	
Item	**Definition**
Varno	The number of the table. Tables are assigned a number, starting with 0, based on their order in the From clause.
Indexid	The value in the INDID column in sysindexes for the index being analyzed. A value of 0 indicates a table without a clustered index; a 1 indicates a table with a clustered index; a value between 1 and 250 is a nonclustered index.
Totcost	Total I/O in milliseconds for this table. This value is shown when DBCC TRACEON (330) is used in conjunction with Set Showplan on.

continued

TABLE 18.1 DEFINITION OF JPLAN TERMS, CONTINUED

Item	Definition
Pathtype	Describes how this table is accessed as the query is processed. If the path type is sclause, the table is accessed by a search clause index or table scan; "join" means a join clause is used in the Where clause; and orstruct means a dynamic index using the OR strategy.
Method	The search method. NESTED ITERATION means that one or more passes will be made at the table; REFORMATTING means that it will use temporary work tables and build a clustered index on the columns it determines would be best; OR OPTIMIZATION means it uses temporary work tables and the OR strategy to track duplicate rows from different subsets (and builds a dynamic index on the work table).
Outerrows	The number of times this table will be accessed. This value corresponds to the scan count in the Set statistics I/O on results.
Rows	The estimated number of rows to read from this table. This value comes from the selectivity of the distribution page. Use Update Statistics to keep this number optimized.
Joinsel	The join selectivity. Look at the DBCC TRACEON (302) output earlier in this chapter to see the best cost join selectivity.
Lp	The number of logical page reads the optimizer estimates it must perform. The formula for this is (cpages × outerrows).
Pp	The number of physical page reads the optimizer estimates it must perform.
Cpages	The estimated number of index and data pages per table access. The number of table accesses is the outerrows item above.
Ctotpages	The estimated total number of pages to be read by this query. In tables with fewer total pages than the configured data cache, this value is the same as physical page reads. In tables larger than the configured data cache, this value is logical page reads.

continued

TABLE 18.1 DEFINITION OF JPLAN TERMS, CONTINUED

Item	Definition
Corder	The value of colid in syscolumns for the first column in the index.
Cstat	The status field in syscolumns to describe the column properties; i.e., Identity, Null/Not Null, Output, Ansipadding, or a fixed-length column treated as variable-length column.
Maxpages	The maximum number of pages in the table.
Crows	The estimated number of rows looked at per table access.
Cjoinsel	Look at the DBCC TRACEON (302) output earlier in this chapter to see the join selectivity for this index on this table.
Joinmap	The relative position of the table in the join for this permutation.
Jnvar	The varno assigned to the tables in the joinmap.
Ordercol[n]	The columns in an assumed or specified Order By clause.
Refindid	The ID for the clustered index built in the temporary table.
Refcost	Total I/O cost, in milliseconds, of the reformatting strategy.
Refpages	Number of pages per access of the temporary clustered index.
Reftotpages	Total cost, in pages, accessed during the reformatting strategy.

Each permutation can generate many NEW PLANS, depending upon the number of indexes in each table. How many NEW PLANS does a permutation get? The answer depends on the results we saw above in the DBCC 302 output, which estimates the efficiency of each index in each table in the join. DBCC 310 plan uses the best indexes from each table. If several indexes are close in efficiency, it considers each in this analysis. You can see in the first permutation (page 378) that New Plan #1 and New Plan #2 are relatively close in the total cost (268 and 218, respectively). However, New Plan #3 is so much higher that the detail is not even printed.

After the first two New Plans, you see the entry IGNORING THIS PERMU-TATION. This message means that the optimizer determines that the permutation is not worth considering. In rare cases, it is wrong and the permutation should not be ignored. Although the optimizer does not print any information about why it is being ignored, you can change the query to see for yourself. If you change the order of the tables in the From clause to match the order in the permutation, the output prints the detail, because DBCC always does permutation 0-1-2. We suspect that those of you who have read this far in the book will try changing the order to satisfy your curiosity about why this permutation is being ignored.

Near the end of the listing, three summary lines show the number of combinations, the number of permutations, and the total number of plans considered. Last, but certainly not least, is the FINAL PLAN, the one with the lowest cost. The output shows the detail for this plan.

The formula DBCC uses for total cost is

```
(Total logical page reads [lp] x 2 ms) + (Total physical page
reads [pp] x 14 ms)
```

In this formula, the values of 2 and 14 milliseconds are hardcoded in SQL Server. It doesn't matter that your disk drives may be faster than 14 milliseconds, because the total cost of each NEW PLAN is rated relative to the total of the other plans and doesn't estimate the actual time.

In its analysis and calculation of the total cost, SQL Server makes the following assumptions:

- the first time, SQL Server always reads the pages from disk, which means a physical I/O
- in subsequent reads from the same table, the pages are already in memory

Each permutation and NEW PLAN analysis stands alone — each analysis assumes it starts by retrieving the pages from disk.

The DBCC SHOWCONTIG Option

This new option shows how packed the pages are. When you run reports, you want the pages to be as packed as possible to minimize I/O. However, when you are inserting and updating data, you do not want the table packed if you have a clustered index on a key and rows are inserted throughout the table, because you want to keep page splits on full pages to a minimum. If a clustered index is on a monotonic (ever-increasing) key that always inserts at the end of the table, then it is OK to have a packed table.

The entire syntax of the option is DBCC SHOWCONTIG (123456789, 2), where the first parameter is the table ID number and the second is the index ID number. You can find these ID numbers easily with this query:

```
SELECT id, indid, name FROM sysindexes
WHERE OBJECT_NAME(id) = 'authors'.
```

This query returns the table ID (id in the query above), the index number ID (indid), and the index name (name) of all the indexes on the authors table. The OBJECT_NAME(id) is a system function that returns the name of the object from the sysobjects table. You could also use the following select and join statements to find the ID numbers.

```
SELECT o.id, i.indid, i.name FROM sysobjects o, sysindexes I WHERE
o.name = 'authors' AND o.id = i.id.
```

You may be tempted to take a shortcut, but it doesn't work. The following example gives a syntax error:

```
DBCC SHOWCONTIG (OBJECT_ID('authors'), 2)
```

Although it seems as if this example should work, remember that not all SQL Server commands are as flexible as the Select statement.

The DBCC SHOWCONTIG statement returns the information shown in Table 18.2. As indicated in the second line of the output, it scans the leaf-level pages in the specified index to avoid scanning the data pages.

TABLE 18.2 RESULTS FROM DBCC SHOWCONTIG	
DBCC SHOWCONTIG scanning 'authors' table...	**[SHOW_CONTIG – SCAN ANALYSIS]**
Table: 'authors' (16003088) Indid: 2 dbid:4	
LEAF level scan performed.	
- Pages Scanned	1
- Extent Switches	0
- Avg. Pages per Extent	2.0
- Scan Density [Best Count:Actual Count]	100.00% [0:1]
- Avg. Bytes free per page	1404.0
- Avg. Page density (full)	30.29%
- Overflow Pages	0
- Disconnected Overflow Pages	0

The value of Extent Switches is the number of times the next page in the scan is on a different extent. When this value is almost as high as the number of pages, the table needs to be repacked. When the table is packed optimally, this value is the number of pages divided by eight (because an extent is eight pages). The "Avg. Pages per Extent" value indicates how well-packed the data is. A low value indicates that a lot of delete action has occurred on the table, or, as in our example, that the table doesn't contain much data.

The Scan Density figure is the quickest way to see how well the table is packed. The best value you can achieve is 100 percent. Best Count is the ideal number of extent switches if the table is optimally packed; Actual Count is the actual number of extents in the table.

Let's switch from looking at pages per extent and look inside the pages. "Avg. Bytes free per page" shows the average of the free space in each page. The number of usable bytes per page is 2,016. Note that the largest single row size is 1,962 bytes. A related statistic, "Avg. Page density (full)," shows the percent full each page is.

Another way to look at the index is the Overflow Pages count. This line has a value only when a nonunique clustered index inserts duplicate values at the end of the index pages and an overflow page is created. This situation is the only time a normal page split does not occur. The Disconnected Overflow Page indicator is for SQL Server's internal use only.

How do you repack the data? The easiest way is to drop the clustered index and re-create it. Choosing the Rebuild button or the Sorted Data button on the Manage Indexes dialog box does not always repack the data. You must perform a sort to repack the data, so the best option is to drop the index and re-create it. Of course, this method has ramifications, because all the nonclustered indexes are rebuilt when the clustered index is created. If the clustered index is on the primary key and foreign keys that relate to this table exist, you cannot drop the index — you can only rebuild it, either with the Rebuild button or with the DBCC REINDEX command.

What can you do if you don't want a clustered index on the table? You can always create the clustered index and then drop it. Waiting for all the nonclustered indexes to be rebuilt is usually faster than unloading the data with BCP, truncating the table, and loading the data with BCP again.

Strategies for Optimizing Queries

You have many choices for ways to improve the efficiency of your queries. They range from the complex, such as forcing the optimizer to do what you want, to the relatively simple, such as tweaking your queries and scheduling them to run at night. We cover these and other strategies in the rest of this chapter.

Forcing the Optimizer to Do What You Want

Even though the optimizer is very good about choosing the right index, sometimes it just won't pick the right one. At these times, you must take over and
bypass the optimizer. The optimizer hints, which you add to the From clause
of the Select statement, are among the newest improvements in controlling the
optimizer. If you want to force a query to always use a specific index on the
table, add the hint to the command, as shown in three examples below.

```
SELECT * FROM TableName T (INDEX = Ø)
SELECT * FROM TableName T (INDEX = idx1) WHERE Field1 = 'A'
SELECT * FROM TableName T (HOLDLOCK)
```

The items in parentheses are the optimizer hints, which can specify one of
three things:

no index (Example #1)

the index (Example #2)

the locking method (Example #3)

You can also combine hints, separated by a space, although some are not
compatible. For example, you can use PAGLOCK and TABLOCK together
without creating a syntax error, even though they are mutually exclusive. The
most restrictive option is the one used.

In the examples above, the first example comes from the Department of
Redundancy Department. The INDEX = 0 hint forces a table scan, but because
no Where clause is used in the Select statement, the optimizer does not even
kick in, so it never gets the hint.

The second example uses the index name, but we have no idea whether
it is the most efficient one for this query. It would be the best index to use
only if Field1 is the first field in the index definition.

The third example forces a table scan (also called a serial read) and holds
the page locks instead of releasing them as the pages are completed. This
example would benefit by using the TABLOCK option so that the entire table
would be locked throughout the transaction and SQL wouldn't have to waste
resources managing page locks.

The valid options, listed in Table 18.3, can be used in any combination.

TABLE 18.3 OPTIMIZER HINTS FOR FROM CLAUSES

Optimizer Hint	Notes
INDEX = index name or INDEX = index ID	This hint forces the optimizer to use the named index. An Index ID of 0 forces a table scan. If the Index ID is 1, the clustered index is used (if one exists). If a clustered index does not exist, the hint is ignored. Any other number forces the optimizer to use the nonclustered index associated with that number, if one exists. A Select * From sysindexes statement shows all the indexes in the database; look for the indid field to find a number to use. However, dropping and re-creating an index changes the index ID to the next highest number available for that table, so it is better to use the name.
HOLDLOCK	Normally, locks on a page are released as soon as the table or page is no longer needed. A HOLDLOCK retains the locks until the end of a transaction. An aborted transaction releases the locks, even though the transaction has not completed. HOLDLOCK can be used with a view. HOLDLOCK cannot be used with the FOR BROWSE option when using DBLIB programming routines.
NOLOCK	This option is potentially dangerous, because it lets you read through exclusive locks while a table is being updated. If you have read pages that get rolled back by another transaction, it can generate errors 605, 606, 625, and 626. When you get errors, retry the Read. This option can get around the problems that occur when long-running reports get in the way of data modification statements. So even though you can achieve higher concurrency, it is at the sacrifice of consistency.
PAGLOCK	This hint forces the lock manager to keep doing page locks, even when it determines that it would be more efficient to escalate to a table lock. This option is particularly useful when you're using long-running data

continued

TABLE 18.3 OPTIMIZER HINTS FOR FROM CLAUSES, CONTINUED

Optimizer Hint	Notes
	modifications to update pages that aren't being requested by other users. When this option is turned on, the page locks won't escalate to a table lock, which would force other users to wait until the operation is finished with the entire table. When used with a Select statement, this option does not override the Lock Escalation configuration settings.
TABLOCK	This lock starts as a table lock instead of a page lock. It is held until the command is completed. If HOLDLOCK is used in conjunction with TABLOCK, the table lock is held until the end of the transaction. If the command is a Select statement, read locks are generated on the whole table, which lets other readers share the table. If the command is an Update, Insert, or Delete, this command has the same effect as the TABLOCKX.
TABLOCKX	The command (a Read or Modify) starts with an exclusive table lock until the end of the command. If HOLDLOCK is used in conjunction with the TABLOCK, the table lock is held until the end of the transaction.
UPDLOCK	This lock forces a command reading a table to use update locks instead of shared locks until the end of the command. If HOLDLOCK is used in conjunction with the TABLOCK, the update lock is held until the end of the transaction.
FASTFIRSTROW	This option tells the optimizer to use a nonclustered index (if one matches the Order by clause) to avoid the sort and return the first row as soon as possible. The total query time is probably longer than letting the optimizer do the sort. Sorts can be faster because of the improvements to the asynchronous read-aheads. This option is useful when a large result set is displayed in a Windows program. You see the first row without waiting until the entire query completed.

With the improvements in the optimizer hints, the optimizer should pick the correct index. However, sometimes it won't. When the optimizer does not pick the correct index no matter what you do, you can rewrite the query and force the optimizer to become a code-based optimizer. The order of the tables in the From clause determines the join order and indexing selections. First, set Forceplan on. If the Forceplan option is used in a stored procedure or trigger, remember to set it off after the query statement so other queries can use the optimizer properly. Forceplan and other options from the Set statement are automatically turned off after the stored procedure or trigger completes. You should rarely need to use Forceplan.

General Tuning Tips

In this section, we cover general strategies for tuning queries and some specific tips for making queries run better. When you have a performance problem, the first decision you need to make is whether performance is poor generally or if poor performance is specific to certain queries. If the poor performance is general, read Chapter 16, "Performance Tuning." If it's specific to certain queries, use the techniques in this section.

In optimizing a query, the first step is to isolate the offending query. Copy it from the front-end application, trigger, or stored procedure into a query window in ISQL/w or the Enterprise Manager. Here, you have the appropriate tools to analyze the query.

If you have an application that generates dynamic queries on the front end, you have several ways to capture the query when it gets to SQL Server. The new SQLTrace program is the easiest way to see the commands. You can also see the commands by running DBCC TRACEON (4032) or DBCC INPUT-BUFFER (spid) or clicking Current Activity on the toolbar of the Enterprise Manager to see all the sessions. Double-click on the session to show the last command from that user.

After you isolate the query, the second step is to inspect the Where clause to determine whether all the Join clauses are covered. Make sure that you have enough links between the foreign and primary keys in the tables by running a quick test. Add lines to the Where clause to return a small amount of data. If the answers are correct, you have probably done the joins correctly. If the query is doing aggregate functions, like SUM or AVG, and the sums seem too big or if the results appear to be repeating primary key values, then the joins are not correct.

Next, match the Where clause with the indexes on each table. If an index is not selective enough or if the fields in the Where clause are not the first fields in the indexes, it is time to experiment with different indexes. Try different combinations — let different fields take turns being the first field in a composite index. Try different clustered indexes. Turn on the Set Statistics I/O

option before you start experimenting with indexing to give you the best indication of whether the index changes are effective.

Look for danger signs, such as a table with no unique index. This situation could cause duplicate rows to be returned when you don't expect it.

If you haven't improved your query by now, run the query with Showplan on. Look for bad signs, such as "Worktable created for reformatting" messages or table scans when you expect the optimizer to use an index. Try to
eliminate the number of steps or the use of worktables.

If Showplan indicates that the query is using the wrong index or no index,
use the optimizer hints or, in the worst case, set Forceplan on.

If the query is using a view in the From clause, you may have some
hidden problems. A view on a view can bury performance problems. Test the
views separately from the query by running the views separately with Showplan on. Solve any performance problems caused by the views, like table
scans, then test the main query again.

Data modification statements may have the same problems as Select statements. They also bring additional opportunities to increase your knowledge of
SQL Server (a fancy way of saying they are more difficult to diagnose). First,
look for triggers; they may be the cause of the problem. Test and improve the
trigger code, then go back and test your data modification statement again.

Is the data modification performance problem caused by a clustered
index? Are too many pages being split? Are the updates all deferred? Are the
updates being blocked by a long report? See the following sections to find
more strategies for identifying and fixing these types of problems.

Recompiling Stored Procedures, Triggers, and Views

A regular job to add to your operations schedule is one that recompiles stored
procedures, triggers, and views. They need to be recompiled because as each
object is run multiple times, the execution plan is added to the memory block
in the procedure cache. When too many plans are in the procedure cache,
SQL Server seems to get confused and different problems start appearing.
Among the most serious are

- procedures that normally run quickly seem to take forever to run

- procedures abort unexpectedly

- sessions cannot quit

When these symptoms occur, it is time to drop the procedures and
recompile them. For best control, you should have already saved the code in
external files, preferably using a version control system like Microsoft Visual
Source Safe.

The new Database Maintenance Wizard, documented in Chapter 7, "Scheduling and Performing Administrative Tasks," can set up a job to recompile all the code objects in the database. However, it uses the current copy of the source code in the syscomments table. If something goes wrong after it drops the procedure and tries to recompile it, the procedure is lost. So, to be safe, you must have a backup copy.

Evaluating the Performance of Cursors

Cursors have a Jekyll-and-Hyde personality. Using cursors violates relational theory because all relational concepts are based on manipulating a set of records at a time and cursors allow row-at-a-time processing.

Set-oriented commands, such as select, insert, update, and delete, are generally considered faster than the fetch commands of a cursor. When you use a While loop and a Fetch statement, the statements start at the beginning of a table and read each record until the end of the table, which takes much longer than a corresponding set-oriented command.

When are cursors faster? The best time to use cursors is to try to force a direct Update in place. In Chapter 17, we detailed the far-reaching restrictions that you must overcome to achieve an Update in place. The one restriction that was most difficult to overcome was updating just one row, which is the specialty of cursors.

Another time to use cursors is when more than one action needs to be taken on each record. It is especially efficient when the source of each action is in a different table. In conditions like these, set-at-a-time processing requires multiple steps, with temporary tables used in the intermediate step — a more complicated and slower process.

Figures 18.8 through 18.11 show examples of a cursor and how to improve it. Figure 18.8 shows a cursor for a row-at-a-time update; Figure 18.9 gives the associated syslogs contents. For these examples, we used five rows in the authors table. At the time the examples were taken, the table had two indexes — a unique, clustered index on the au_id field and a nonunique, nonclustered index on au_lname and au_fname. In Figure 18.9, notice the Begin Transaction (op=0), the Modify-in-Place (op=9), and the End Transaction (op=30) for every record. See Appendix A for a more detailed explanation of the syslogs op coder.

Figure 18.10 shows a cursor for a direct Update in place, and Figure 18.11 has its associated syslogs contents. In Figure 18.11, the syslogs contents for the improved query, the Begin Transaction (op=0), the Modify-in-Place (op=9) and the End Transaction (op=30) occur only once, for the entire transaction.

```
DECLARE @phone varchar(30)
DECLARE TestCursor CURSOR FOR SELECT phone from authors

OPEN TestCursor
FETCH NEXT FROM TestCursor INTO @phone
WHILE (@@FETCH_STATUS <> -1)
BEGIN
        IF (@@FETCH_STATUS <> -2)
        BEGIN
        Update authors set phone = 'A' where current of TestCursor
        END
        FETCH NEXT FROM TestCursor INTO @phone
END
CLOSE TestCursor
DEALLOCATE TestCursor
go
select * from syslogs
go
```

Figure 18.8
Cursor for Row-at-a-Time Update

xactid	op
0x170300000900	17
0x0c0300000b00	0
0x0c0300000b00	9
0x0c0300000b00	30
0x0c0300000e00	0
0x0c0300000e00	9
0x0c0300000e00	30
0x0c0300001100	0
0x0c0300001100	9
0x0c0300001100	30
0x0c0300001400	0
0x0c0300001400	9
0x0c0300001400	30
0x0c0300001700	0
0x0c0300001700	9
0x0c0300001700	30

Figure 18.9
Syslogs Contents

Figure 18.10

Cursor for a Direct Update in Place

```
DECLARE @phone varchar(30)
DECLARE TestCursor CURSOR FOR SELECT phone from authors

OPEN TestCursor
FETCH NEXT FROM TestCursor INTO @phone

BEGIN TRANSACTION TEST      -- added line to improve effi-
ciency
WHILE (@@FETCH_STATUS <> -1)
BEGIN
        IF (@@FETCH_STATUS <> -2)
        BEGIN
        Update authors set phone = 'B' where current of TestCursor
        END
        FETCH NEXT FROM TestCursor INTO @phone
END
COMMIT TRANSACTION TEST      -- added line to improve effi-
ciency
CLOSE TestCursor
DEALLOCATE TestCursor
go
select * from syslogs
go
```

Figure 18.11

Syslogs Contents after Improvements

```
0x170300000200 0
0x170300000200 9
0x170300000200 9
0x170300000200 9
0x170300000200 9
0x170300000200 9
0x170300000200 30
```

Preventing Locking

In most database systems, locks control the consistency of a database. SQL Server uses locks to ensure that only one data modification occurs at one time on a page. We don't cover the basics of SQL Server locking; the SQL Server

Books Online cover the types and purposes of different locks in great detail. Here, we look at locks in relation to their performance implications.

Types of Locks

Extent Lock — Exclusive

Extent Lock — Shared

Intent Lock — Exclusive

Intent Lock — Shared

Page Lock — Exclusive

Page Lock — Shared

Page Lock — Update

Page Lock — Insert_Page (New in 6.5 for row-level locking)

Page Lock — Link_Page (New in 6.5 for row-level locking)

Table Lock — Exclusive

Table Lock — Shared

New Insert Row-Level Locking

The new row-level locking feature, which works only for Insert statements, can be both a blessing and a curse. It can assist in reducing the effect of hot spots (a page that many users or operations try to access at the same time) by letting multiple transactions update the same page at the same time. However, the negative effects can outweigh the good side of this feature. The lock manager must handle an increased number of entries in the syslocks table, which takes extra effort. Additional information must be tracked in the log file to handle rollback recovery. It's easier to cause deadlocks because an Update statement still does a page lock. The system stored procedure sp_tableoption enables row-level locking.

A row lock escalates to a page lock when the Insert statement grabs an Insert_Page lock to signify that it intends to add a row to that page. If that page is full, a Link_Page lock is generated, which prevents other Insert_Page locks from occurring and forces them into the lock-wait queue. The new page is then allocated, the row inserted, and the Link_Page lock reverts back to the Insert_Page lock. Only then can other Insert_Page locks be obtained simultaneously on the same page.

Deadlocks

It is possible for the row-level locking feature to cause deadlocks. Deadlocks occur when an application has a transaction that does a row-level insert, then updates the row it just inserted (or another row on the same page). By itself, this situation does not cause a deadlock, because you cannot deadlock yourself in the same session. However, when more than one person is running same transaction at the same time, a deadlock can occur because multiple row-level locks exist on the same page when a transaction requests a page-level lock from one of the Update statements.

However, the situation we just described is probably hypothetical, because a lot of things have to happen for a row-level lock to cause a deadlock. First, anyone silly enough to insert a record and update the same record in the same transaction deserves a deadlock. If you know the values you will be updating, it is usually simpler to move the logic from the Update statement to the original Insert statement. Second, chances are good that another record you want to update is not on the same page as the row you just inserted. Third, multiple transactions must have row-level locking set on the same page at the same time that one of them requests a page-level lock. So even though it is possible for row-level locking to cause deadlocks, it is highly unlikely unless the application is improperly written.

In general, one way to prevent deadlocks is to do the data modification statements in the same order within different transactions in the same database. For example, if different transactions need to update Table A and Table B, each transaction should update Table A and Table B in the same order. If the first transaction updates Table B first and locks it and another transaction updates the tables in the reverse order and locks Table A first, then each transaction requests a lock on the other table and isn't able to get it.

Another way to avoid deadlocks is to reduce the result set size in a transaction and do multiple transactions. For example, if you need to update 10,000 rows, consider doing two transactions of 5,000 rows each, or even ten transactions of 1,000 rows each.

A third way to prevent deadlocks is to do data validation on both client and server. It does duplicate effort, but if you are having trouble with deadlocks, it can be a lifesaver. Business rules enforced in triggers and stored procedures can be duplicated or moved to the front-end programs.

Blocked!

If your screens are taking a long time to save records, you may be experiencing a block. A block occurs when you need to modify a record but must wait because someone else has a lock on that page. A long-running report can have a read lock that prevents exclusive locks from modifying the page. Or vice versa — a modification statement can prevent a report from completing or other data modifications from finishing.

What do you do when you see a blocked process? First, you should go to the Current Activity window in the Enterprise Manager and double-click on the blocked session to find out the command that is running for that session. Knowing the command that's running gives you a good idea of how long you might wait until the block is cleared. The Current Activity window is static, so keep refreshing the display to see whether the block has cleared. You can see almost the same information by typing **sp_who** in a query window.

Your options at this point are to wait until the block has cleared or to kill the session. One way to kill a session is to go to the Current Activity screen, double-click on the blocking session to see the current command, then click the Kill Session button. You can also open a query window and type **kill *nnn***, where *nnn* is the session ID of the blocking session.

Taking Advantage of Night Jobs

Standalone jobs that run at night, particularly if only one job is running, offer opportunities for unique performance tuning. Take full advantage of optimizer hints such as TABLOCK to minimize the work of the lock manager. Increase the Logwrite sleep configuration parameter to let more log records fill the buffer before a physical write is done.

Avoiding Hot Spots and Page Splits

Now for the long-awaited discussion of hot spots. A hot spot happens when everyone wants to get to the same page at the same time. When a hot spot occurs, everyone has to wait for locks to be freed before they can get their locks processed. In a typical scenario, all records are added to the bottom of the table while other portions of the applications are trying to read the same pages. The bottom of the table is the most likely place to see a hot spot.

One way to fix this particular scenario is to place a clustered index on a different field to spread the inserts around throughout the file. Creating a clustered index repacks the data and index pages, thereby creating a lot of page splits for a while. These splits can be solved by creating the clustered index with a lower fill factor. A fill factor in the range of 65–75 percent is a good estimate unless you know you will be adding a significant amount of data.

Another way to prevent hot spots is to try row-level locking on Inserts. Using this option may be enough to solve the problem, but be aware of the extra overhead that may be involved with the lock manager and the extra logging overhead.

A more drastic solution, but perhaps a better long-term one, is to create another database for reporting purposes. That way, the long-running reports do not get in the way of the short-burst transactions. A duplicate database is more work initially, but it can be worth it for larger databases. With the improvements in performance and stability in replication, this option is worth considering.

Uncovering the Effects of Alter Table Commands

If you have tried all the tricks to fix a performance problem without luck, you may have one hidden problem that is difficult to find but easy to solve. If you have altered a table to add a new column, you may have caused a problem. The command to alter a table is carried out very quickly, so it is easy to figure out that SQL Server has not gone through every record on every page to add the new column. The actual adjustment is done the next time any record on a page is updated. When a data modification statement affects a page, all the records on the page are modified — a holding spot for the new field is added and a null value is inserted in the field. This modification may be enough to cause the page to overflow, causing a page split. A massive update on a packed table could cause every page to split!

Another side effect of altering a table to add a column occurs when you create a nonclustered index on that new column. Because the records in the data pages do not have a spot reserved for this new column, SQL Server cannot use the index. You get no error message or warning, and subsequent attempts to analyze or tune a query to use this index can be very frustrating.

Fixing this problem is quite easy. Do a dummy Update on the table by setting a column to itself. For example, use the following Update statement.

```
UPDATE myTable SET column1 = column1
```

This statement might take a while to run because it causes every row in the table to be updated, forcing all the full pages to be split.

The exception to this Alter Table problem is when you add an Identity column. The Alter Table statement updates every row in the table and puts a value in the new Identity column. The order in which the identity values are assigned is the current order of the rows in the table. If you have a clustered index, the numbers are assigned in the order of the index. If you don't have a clustered index on the table, the highest number assigned in the identity field is the last row updated or inserted. Most Update statements in SQL Server are processed as deferred updates, which moves the updated row(s) to the end of the table.

Special Note

Murphy's Law for DBAs: Just when you have a good feel for performance tuning, the next version of the software is announced.

Increasing Actual Page Size

It is well documented that 1,962 bytes are reserved for data space. However, you can actually get 2,016 bytes of data on a page if you don't have a page footer. The page footer normally carries the record description. However, under certain conditions, the page footer is not added. Our guess is that the page footer isn't added on a fixed row size, which occurs when the record contains no variable-length fields. So a normal page size of 2K (2,048 bytes) less 32 bytes for the header leaves 2,016 bytes for the data space.

To get a closer look at a page, run the unsupported command

```
DBCC PAGE (database_id, page number, [option])
```

To get the database_id for the above command, execute the query Select * From master..sysdatabases. You can pick any page number greater than zero. A better way to get a starting page number is to find the first page associated with a table; to get the first page, execute the query Select * From sysindexes and look for the firstpage column. Using a 1 in the option parameter of the DBCC PAGE command shows hex and ASCII representations of the data on the page; leaving off the 1 gives a brief overview of the page.

Summary

This chapter covers a lot of detail. Read this chapter and Chapter 17, "Indexing," very carefully, perhaps even more than once. A sentence hidden in the middle of a paragraph may be the one clue you have been searching for to solve a particularly difficult problem.

Performance tuning is simply clearing a series of bottlenecks. Patience is your best tool, especially in the trial-and-error phase of tuning. Test your theories, dig into different books and sources of knowledge, and know when you have just too much data to get sub-second response time.

Chapter 19

Diagnosing and Troubleshooting Problems

In many circumstances, you need to gather and review detailed information about SQL Server's operational state. In general, you will face two categories of problems: those that occur while SQL Server is running and those that occur at server start up. You diagnose and fix these problems with two overlapping sets of tools: those that analyze the internal workings of the database and those that present information about the interaction of SQL Server and its environment. We cover both of these tool sets in this chapter.

The Basics

You can determine the health of your server from information you gather from a variety of sources. These sources range from errors that were generated and logged before the SQL server terminated to the messages generated during automatic recovery at startup. This information is especially important if your server shuts down unexpectedly, because internal errors that cause the shutdown can often corrupt data at the same time, and this sort of problem commonly requires special workarounds to overcome. Other problems are evident in other sources of information, such as entries in the event log that relate to user connection and usage. If users are having problems logging on or maintaining their connections, the Event Viewer and the SQL Server Error log can both hold error messages that tell you why those connections are failing.

Sometimes problems are internal to SQL Server or specific processes that are running. If the server is performing poorly or users are getting deadlocked and losing connections, the DBA needs to be able to tell what people are doing and how they are affecting the system. You can create a detailed view of how processes are behaving by monitoring activity from within SQL Server and through Performance Monitor.

The Event Viewer

A very useful tool for troubleshooting most problems in a Windows NT environment is Windows NT's built-in error message handler, the Event Viewer. The Event Viewer is a system tool you use to look at error messages and to configure the logging options.

The Event Viewer provides an interface for three separate error logs: the Security log, the Application log, and the System log. For most problems related to SQL Server, the System and Application logs are most relevant. The System log contains error messages generated by system processes, including the installation and functioning of network drivers, disk controllers, and system services. Any application-generated system errors — those errors that are created when the application interacts with the operating system — are written into the Application log.

The main window of the Event Viewer, shown in Figure 19.1, contains the date, time, and source of the error. A category, error number, the user who owns the process that generated the error, and the computer from which the error came are also displayed.

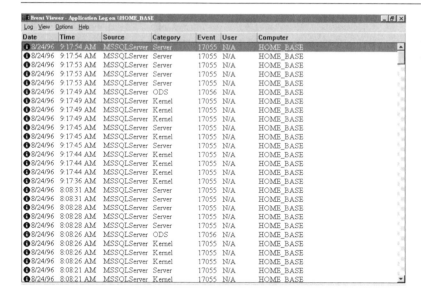

Figure 19.1
Event Viewer
Application Log

You can see details about any event shown in the Event Viewer by double-clicking an event or by selecting an event and choosing Detail from the View menu. The Event Detail dialog box is shown in Figure 19.2. The text of the message is displayed as well as the data that the error generated. Although not all errors generate data, the data logged can be very important to understanding the cause of the problem in some applications.

You can switch between the Application, Security, and System logs in the Event Viewer (Figure 19.1) by going to the Log menu and selecting a different log. With this menu item, you can also set logging options, save or clear the log, or view a log on a remote machine.

The log settings determine how big the log will get and how the log wraps when it is full. You can set the log to overwrite events as it needs to or to overwrite events only if they are older than a specified number of days. You can also set up the log so that events can be cleared only manually.

When you clear a log, you can save it as an archive and see it in the Event Viewer by selecting Open from the Log menu. The Event Viewer displays the most recent events at the top of the list by default, but you can reverse the order of the events using the View menu. You can also filter the events based on any of the fields in the display. This feature can be useful when you're troubleshooting a specific problem or, for example, if you want to display only the SQL Server messages. You can perform searches for specific errors on any fields that are not time-related. If you're viewing a log in

Figure 19.2

Event Detail Window

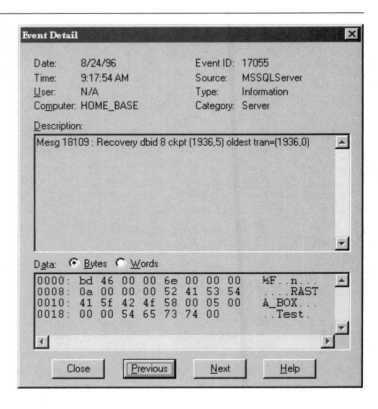

the Event Viewer in real time to see if a problem will occur, remember to refresh the log by choosing Refresh from the View menu if you leave the log open for a long time.

Most programs currently do not log internal errors to the Application log; however, SQL Server is set up to do so by default. Because the alert engine that runs under SQL Executive uses the Application log as its driving element, the errors must be logged to the Windows NT Event log for it to function.

The alert engine constantly monitors the Application log and uses its database to recognize the events that have been assigned alerts. If SQL Server fails to start for some reason, the errors that it generates as it fails are written to the Application log and to SQL Server's own Error log. Startup problems are sometimes caused by other service failures. For example, if a network service fails to start and SQL Server depends on the service, SQL Server does not run. In this case, the System log, which contains error messages for services, is the only place to find the information you need to troubleshoot SQL Server's failure.

User connectivity problems often generate messages in the Application log. As part of its client management function, SQL Server polls the client connections, asking them to verify that they are still in use. If the client fails to respond, SQL Server terminates the connection. Sometimes clients are still connected but fail to respond when polled because of network problems or speed issues. When SQL Server loses or kills a client connection, it writes an error message to its own Error log and to the Windows NT Event log (if you keep the default configuration). These error messages display the cause and can be useful in determining who is responsible for terminating the connection.

User connectivity problems can also be caused by the failure of other services, so you should examine the System log as well. If you have set up SQL Server with integrated or mixed security (see Chapter 10, "Administering Users and Security"), user connection issues are sometimes rooted in the Windows NT security system. These problems are usually easily recognized when the application reports that access to a specific resource has been denied. When you examine issues that are related to resources of any kind within the system, remember that some applications may not send the proper error messages, and the Security log can be useful in determining the cause. You must enable security auditing for the log to be useful, but in general, tracking security events is usually a good idea. (Security auditing is managed through the User Manager for Domains administrator tool.)

Adding Error Messages to the Application Log

SQL Server gives you the flexibility to add error messages to the system that are specific to your SQL Server implementation. This feature lets your database application log its specific errors or informative messages to the Windows NT Application log. SQL Server's error messages have three parts: an error number (unique identifier), a severity ranging from 1 to 25 (with 25 being most severe), and the message text. Error messages can be added to the Master database through the Enterprise Manager's Manage Alerts and Operators dialog box (see Chapter 7, "Scheduling and Performing Administrative Tasks"). You can use the following system stored procedure to add user-defined messages to the sysmessages table in the Master database:

```
sp_addmessage msg_id, severity, 'text of message' [, language
[, {true | false} [, REPLACE]]]
```

This message can then be called by the Raiserror command or xp_logevent. If the fifth argument to the sp_addmessage procedure is set to true, the error message is written to the Windows NT event log. The message can be stored with format indicators (as in the C language printf) that let it be customized at runtime. For example, the message "This error message was generated by %d" allows the message to be generated with a number for identification replacing the "%d." Only the Raiserror call can utilize the formatting in the error messages, so logging the error with a formatted message using xp_logevent results in a literal recording of the message, string format identifiers and all.

Whoever creates a user-defined error message assigns its number. This number must be unique, and it is a good idea to plan the numbering system in the design phase. The lower limit on user-defined error numbers is suggested to be 50,000, though basing your error messages at a higher value may avert future collisions with system-defined messages.

Error messages are assigned a severity on a scale of 1 to 25. An error of severity 10 or less is an informative message rather than an error message. Only the SA can add a message with a severity 19 to 25. The Replace option in the stored procedure above causes the new entry to overwrite a previously existing entry. If this argument is not given and the error number specified in the sp_addmessage duplicates an existing error message, the procedure fails.

If logging on to the NT event log is enabled on installation, the Raiserror command and xp_logevent procedure can write error messages to the event log.

```
RAISERROR ({msg_id | msg_str}, severity, state
[, argument1 [, argument2]] )
[WITH LOG]

xp_logevent error_number, message, [severity]
```

The Raiserror call has two basic forms. The first form uses messages stored in the sysmessages table in the Master database and the message ID in the Raiserror call. If the error was added to the error table in SQL Server using the sp_addmessage system stored procedure with the "Always write to NT Event Log" flag set to true, the error is logged in the event log and SQL Server's Error log. The second basic form of the Raiserror call is made with the message string in place of the message ID. Using the With Log option with the message string gives the same result as an error message called by number that has the Event Log flag set to true. Messages with format strings can be used with either of the basic Raiserror calls. It is not necessary to use the With Log option if the messages are added with the Event Log flag set to true, but the With Log option can be used in conjunction with a call using the error message ID if that message was added without the "Always write to NT Event Log" flag.

The xp_logevent extended procedure writes messages only to the SQL Server's Error log and the NT Event Log and does not send information to the client or set the @@ERROR global variable value. This feature can be useful if a message that the client is not to see is to be logged. For example, access to specific data could be monitored through error logging without informing the client that the actions are being recorded. Although this information can be useful for debugging applications, it is not normally useful in troubleshooting system-type problems, because this information exists only if the application is designed to accommodate appropriate error logging.

The SQL Server Error Log

SQL Server maintains its own Error log in addition to writing messages to the event log. The errors in the Error log duplicate those in the event log, and the Event Viewer logs have the advantage of being addressable from remote machines, which allows for centralized error handling in enterprise systems. Messages about SQL Server startup conditions and any automatic recovery strategies attempted are written into the SQL Server Error log. The log also contains information about errors in user connections.

The SQL Server Error log is written out as a plain ASCII file stored in the mssql\log directory on the server and can be viewed through a text editor. One current log and six archived logs are stored at any given time. A new log is created each time you stop and start SQL Server, so in one day you could conceivably generate all seven files. On the other hand, if you never shut down SQL Server or re-boot your server, one file could contain several months of information.

You can also see any of the last six logs through the Enterprise Manager by selecting Error Log under the Server menu (Figure 19.3). For each of the archived logs, the drop-down list displays the date the last log entry was created, not the date the log was created. The log itself is displayed in time order, with the earliest events at the top. The date and time and the source of the error are displayed, along with descriptive text. Double-clicking an entry displays a message box with the error message. This information is pretty useless, except that it does give the line number of the error message in the caption of the message box.

If you're looking at the log in real time to observe a problem as it is happening, you need to remember to refresh it by clicking the refresh button or closing and reopening it.

Figure 19.3
Error Log Viewer

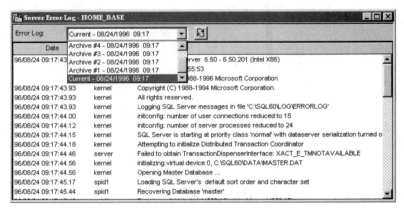

Monitoring Users and Locks

You can see the processes within SQL Server in use at any given time by looking at the Current Activity window in the Enterprise Manager. You get to the window by clicking the Current Activity toolbar button or selecting Current Activity from the Server menu. The window has three tabs: the first displays current activity grouped by user, the second details all the processes, and the third breaks down by object the use of system resources. Figure 19.4 shows the User Activity Tab of the Current Activity window.

Each tab includes many ways to kill a process, send a message to the owner of a process, or view the detail of the activity. Right-clicking any of the entries in the lists displays a menu with entries that correspond to the first three toolbar buttons on the Current Activity window. The buttons shown in Figure 19.4, from left to right, correspond to the View Detail, Send Message, Kill Process, Refresh Screen, and Display Legend commands.

To see details of a particular process, you can double-click the list entry, select More Info from the Enterprise Manager's File menu, or click the View Detail button on the toolbar. Any of these actions brings up the Process Details dialog box shown in Figure 19.5. The process, and the user and server the process is connected to, are displayed in the caption of this box. The last SQL buffer executed and the accumulated CPU and Disk I/O for the process are also displayed.

From the window shown in Figure 19.4, you can kill a process by clicking the Kill Process button; you can send a message to the owner of the process by clicking the Send Message button.

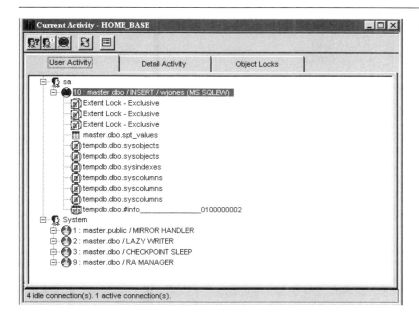

Figure 19.4
User Activity Tab

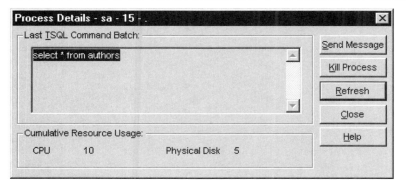

Figure 19.5
Process Detail Box

The User Activity tab groups processes by user. The list is presented in a tree structure showing users, the processes the user owns, and the locks the processes have in the database. Activity is shown for all the databases on the current server. From this tab, you can get an overview of what resources are used by certain actions on the database. If you know what the user is doing, you can determine the impact that certain processes will have on other users by looking at the tables that are touched and how many pages are locked. If you want the information you're looking at to stay current, remember to refresh the window regularly by clicking the fourth (Refresh Display) button.

The Detail Activity tab (Figure 19.6) displays a wide variety of information about all the processes on the current server. This list is not a hierarchy, as the other two tabs are; instead, it presents a detailed view of all the activity broken down to the lowest possible level. The locks and blocks are displayed, letting you analyze blocking problems by user and table. All of the locks on every process are displayed, down to the page level, if applicable. The name of the object and the type of lock that the process has on it are listed, and the total CPU usage and cumulative I/O time are displayed. The information on the Detail Activity tab can be sorted on any of the displayed fields by clicking the column heading. This tab is useful in determining what specific action is causing a problem and how the blocks or locks escalate.

Figure 19.6

Detail Activity Tab

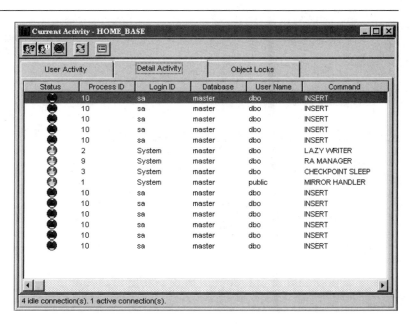

You can see the last command buffer executed in the user process by double-clicking the listing or selecting More Detail from the File menu in the Enterprise Manager. This detail dialog box shows the last SQL statement and presents buttons for sending messages and killing the listed process. A process is *blocked* if it cannot continue execution because a database object is unavailable. Blocking occurs when data-altering queries are executed and is to be expected. Blocking becomes a problem only during long-running queries, transactions, or poorly written stored procedures or triggers. If a locking contention problem arises, the Process Details dialog box provides information that can be used to optimize the table layout or index.

The Object Locks tab, shown in Figure 19.7, displays all the objects that have locks on them and details the type of locks and what process owns the lock. This display can help reveal tables with hot spots and let you reconfigure indexes or device layout based on usage. Remember to refresh the window regularly to have the latest information added.

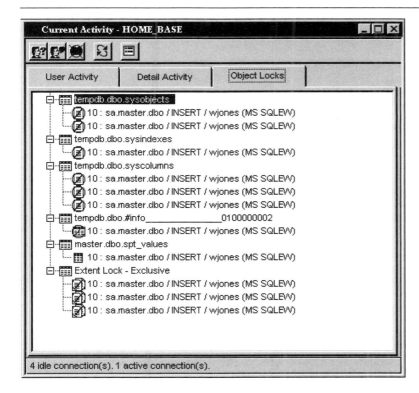

Figure 19.7
Object Locks Tab

Most of the time, you can kill processes from any of the tabs on the Current Activity window; however, sometimes processes do not respond to Kill commands. In these cases, you must restart SQL Server to terminate them. If the process is consuming a lot of resources, restarting may be the only solution.

The tabs of the Current Activity window give you a nice graphical way to get the information that comes from executing the sp_who and sp_lock stored procedures, followed by the DBCC utility with the inputbuffer(spid) option. Sometimes you may want to type the commands in a query window for faster results. You can also execute the Kill statement from the query window, using the SPID of the process you want to stop.

The DBCC Utility and Trace Flags

The database consistency checking (DBCC) utility has many uses. It can provide a wide variety of data, including file-level consistency information and the runtime behavior of database processes. You can use DBCC to report detailed information about deadlocks and about database performance and integrity. In addition, when you use DBCC, you can set trace flags that produce detailed information about runtime execution. You can also set trace flags to appear on the command line of the executable to bypass startup problems. We look at several DBCC commands in this section.

DBCC MEMUSAGE

The DBCC MEMUSAGE command displays relevant information concerning the use of objects and execution of stored procedures. The first part of the output, shown in Table 19.1, is a breakdown of the memory utilization of the server given in megabytes, 2K pages, and bytes.

TABLE 19.1 INITIAL OUTPUT FROM MEMUSAGE			
	MB	**2K Pages**	**Bytes**
Configured Memory	8.0000	4096	8,388,608
Code Size	1.7166	879	1,800,000
Static Structures	0.2385	123	250,064
Locks	0.2861	147	300,000
Open Objects	0.1144	59	120,000
Open Databases	0.0031	2	3,220
User Context Areas	0.7505	385	787,002
Page Cache	3.3269	1704	3,488,480
Proc Headers	0.0800	41	83,936
Proc Cache Bufs	1.3457	689	1,411,072

The configured memory is obviously the amount of memory that SQL server is configured to use. The code size is the size of the SQL Server application. The static structures are permanently allocated memory that SQL Server uses to perform its tasks. The locks, open objects, and open databases all reflect the amount of memory that is being used to keep track of the database state. The user context area is memory used by user processes, and the page cache is the buffer SQL Server uses to work on queries; it provides a queue as well as a work space. The procedures headers (proc headers) memory is used to reference the stored procedures in the stored procedure cache, and the procedure cache (proc cache bufs) holds the execution plans for the twenty most-used procedures.

The second segment of the output from the DBCC MEMUSAGE command is a list of the top 20 objects in the buffer cache, listed in descending order by the amount of memory they consume. The database ID, the object ID, and the index ID are displayed. This information can be useful for optimization, because it presents the most-used objects on the server, and these objects are good candidates for initial examination.

The last section of the output from the DBCC MEMUSAGE command lists the 20 most-used procedures in the procedure cache, displaying the most-used procedure first. This list includes stored procedures, triggers, and views and displays information regarding the type, size, and number of execution plans or trees that have been generated. The number of trees or plans that exist indicates the relative frequency with which the object has been accessed while currently in use by another process. These objects represent additional hotspots in the database and are therefore likely candidates for optimization or locking issues.

DBCC NEWALLOC and CHECKDB

The DBCC NEWALLOC and CHECKDB commands provide information regarding the internal consistency of a database. This information can help diagnose severe runtime failures as long as the server is not shut down. If you encounter runtime errors, think twice about stopping the server without performing consistency checks — restarting SQL Server triggers automatic recovery, which can cause the database to be marked suspect if internal consistency is a problem.

In cases in which the database is marked suspect during recovery, you must reset the status flag in the sysdatabases system table before the DBCC commands can be executed. SQL Server can also be restarted with the trace flag 3607 set on (flag 3608 if the Master database is suspect) to bypass the automatic recovery. (The trace flag is given as –T<*number*> on the command line of Sqlservr.exe.)

As discussed in Chapter 8, you cannot delete a device that contains allocations for a database without first dropping those databases. If you wish to consolidate the device structure so that SQL Server will reduce the number of devices being used, first back up the databases that have allocations on the devices you wish to remove. After they are backed up, drop the databases and delete the devices that you are removing, and create the new device(s) and re-create the databases on the new device(s). Then restore the databases from the dumps.

The restoration will produce error warnings about the segment mappings of the restored databases, but the DBCC NEWALLOC command occasionally removes these errors when it is run. Allocation pages mapped to segments that do not exist because the segment mapping has changed are most easily fixed by dropping and rebuilding the clustered index on the table that has the error. If no clustered index exists, one of the nonclustered indexes can be created as a clustered index and then re-created as a nonclustered index. If DBCC reports that a system table has allocation pages on segments that no longer exist, the best course of action is to drop and re-create the user-defined objects on the database. For example, if the sysprocedures table has allocation pages that are not contained on a valid segment, the triggers, procedures, and views can be dropped and re-created.

DBCC SQLPERF

The DBCC SQLPERF command displays performance statistics relating to network, I/O, read ahead, thread generation, and log space. It can be run with any one of the values listed below. The values correspond directly to values displayed by SQL Performance Monitor (see Chapter 15, "Performance Monitoring Guidelines").

```
DBCC SQLPERF ({IOSTATS | LRUSTATS | NETSTATS | RASTATS [, CLEAR]}
        {THREADS} | {LOGSPACE})
```

DBCC TRACEON Flags

The DBCC TRACEON flags let you analyze a lot of very detailed information about query execution, including the creation of temporary objects. The flags can be used to display information about deadlocks and the command that caused the deadlock. A complete list of TRACEON flags is provided in the Transact-SQL manual. Some of the flags can also be used on the command line to control various startup processes.

External Sources of Help

If you have a severe problem, Microsoft support can be absolutely irreplace-able. The experts on the support lines deal with hundreds of different types of problems, and your problem is probably not unique. Be sure to save copies of SQL Server Error logs and/or Windows NT event logs in case you need to send them to the support person. The logs can provide the technical support person with additional information that you may not recognize as valuable. Technical support can often provide a quick and direct solution to your problem.

Before contacting Microsoft support, it is often worth the time and effort to examine the TechNet CD. TechNet is a valuable source of information about errors and bugs in a number of Microsoft products. Normally, you can find a great deal of information about specific errors, and it often gives workarounds. TechNet is delivered by subscription and is well worth the investment, especially in development environments.

Of course, the World Wide Web and the Internet can be invaluable when you're facing complex issues, because they make it possible to contact a wide variety of vendors and experts. You can often gather free advice in Usenet groups or other newsgroups that can help you solve difficult problems. Naturally, you have no guarantee that the advice is correct, but it can provide you with clues as to how to begin.

Finally, where a significant number of users are clustered in one geographic area, you can usually find a user group. These groups can be great sources of information and provide an excellent method for contacting more advanced users or experts who have very specific knowledge about the kinds of problems you may face. Local consulting firms often have information about user groups; if none exist in your area, you may want to consider starting one yourself.

Summary

You can gather and analyze server information in a number of ways.

- The event log in Windows NT is a common repository for system and application errors; SQL Server can also use the event log, so it is the best place to start investigating errors after they occur.

- SQL Server's own Error log contains a lot of the same information that is written into the event log. Startup problems and user connection errors are also displayed in the SQL Server Error log.

- SQL Server's internal error handling can record application-specific error messages along with system messages. This feature can help trap errors as they occur.

- User activity also can be monitored from the Enterprise Manager. Activity monitoring lets you analyze table locks and the connection between the locks and user deadlocking.

- Finally, DBCC provides very detailed information about runtime behavior of database processes. It can be used to bypass startup problems and to report detailed information about deadlocks and about database performance.

- A variety of external sources can help solve SQL Server problems. Microsoft's support line and the TechNet CDs are invaluable and community experts can often be solicited for advice. A user group provides a venue to distribute and gather information about a variety of topics related to database administration.

Analyzing failures within SQL Server requires a firm scientific approach to problem solving. The first step should always be laying out all the detected problems and all the information that you can gather about the problem. You should then pursue a solution by trying to fix the most likely causes first, followed by an examination of more obscure possibilities. There is no cornucopia of answers for solving any problems, but the information that you can gather with the tools and methods in this chapter give you a good foundation.

Chapter 20

Extended Stored Procedures

Extended stored procedures can ease the implementation and maintenance of a database because they extend the functions available in the SQL Server environment. In this chapter, we examine in detail basic information about extended stored procedures, including

- what extended stored procedures are
- what they do
- how to use them
- the role of Open Data Services (ODS) in relationship to extended stored procedures
- how to add and drop them

SQL Server includes a number of predefined extended stored procedures, and we also look at some of the most commonly used procedures, including extended stored procedures that aren't mentioned in SQL Server documentation. Finally, we mention a few issues related to user-written extended stored procedures. Although writing these procedures may be out of the scope of most database administrator positions, you will find an understanding of how they work to be indispensable in solving complicated data processing problems.

The Basics of Extended Stored Procedures

What is an Extended Stored Procedure?

An extended stored procedure is simply a procedure that is implemented in a dynamic link library (DLL) — a library that is called by an application at runtime. Extended stored procedures can be used in much the same way as database stored procedures, except that extended stored procedures normally perform tasks related to the interaction of SQL Server with its operating environment. Tasks that are either too complicated or just not possible using Transact-SQL can often be performed with extended stored procedures.

Extended stored procedures are written using the Open Data Services (ODS) API. ODS is written and supported by Microsoft and is available on the Workstation version of SQL Server and as a separate product (and in the BackOffice Development Kit). The ODS development package includes both a static-link library (Opends60.lib) and C header files that let you create fully functional database services. ODS applications are dynamically linked with Opends60.dll.

Special Note

Extended stored procedures that have been created with the previous version of ODS for SQL Server 4.2x or 6.0 will not run under SQL Server 6.5. They must be recompiled and linked with the 6.5 libraries and headers.

What Do They Do?

An extended stored procedure is used within the database in the same way that a database stored procedure is. An extended stored procedure is called and takes parameters in the same way that a database stored procedure does, and the data that an extended stored procedure returns can be formatted just as a database stored procedure's can.

Extended procedures can return result sets, output parameters, or send error messages in the same way that Raiserror does. They can be called anywhere a database procedure can be called. Because extended procedures are based in the C/C++ programming languages, any of the capabilities of C/C++ can be used in the execution of the procedure, including using routines in other languages linked to C, such as Assembly or Fortran.

The ODS API library allows full communication with the database for processing requests, sending sets of data, and maintaining and addressing user connections. Extended procedures can have all the functionality of SQL Server. Combining the ODBC API or DBLIB with the capability of both C and SQL gives you the power to accomplish almost any task with extended stored procedures.

How Can I Use Them?

Implementing a process in an extended stored procedure increases the process's performance and reduces its overhead. Extended stored procedures are best for performing tasks that fall outside the capabilities of Transact-SQL. One good example of a task suited for an extended stored procedure is performing an advanced statistical analysis of database information where strong C libraries exist and can be used with very little code-writing. Another example is generating images from data stored on the server when more than just a simple graph is required. You can also use extended procedures to load information into or extract data from the database in non-standard formats that may require translations; for example, character sets or monetary units.

Extended procedures can access the database through ODBC connections or DBLIB calls, which let the procedure query the database and process those results. In a distributed computing environment, extended stored procedures can perform remote procedure calls, thereby allowing remote processing of data and the distribution of work loads. SQL Server itself uses extended procedures for such tasks as registry manipulation, security integration with Windows NT, and replication.

The ODS revision that was released with SQL Server 6.5 lets extended procedures share the lock space of the process that initiates them. Therefore, if an extended stored procedure makes a connection to the database that creates another process in SQL Server (for example, reading a set of data to perform some complicated analysis), the procedure can read through locks that the calling process may have generated. In other words, if a complicated process that requires strict concurrency across tables locks the tables before calling an extended procedure, the extended procedure can get to the locked tables even if it creates a secondary process to access the database.

The list of possible applications for extended stored procedures is endless, making it possible to use them to solve nearly every data processing problem.

The Concept Behind ODS

Open Data Services, or ODS, provides more functionality than merely the creation of extended stored procedures. It lets programmers create fully enabled servers that mimic the behavior of SQL Server. With ODS, you can create an executable that can respond to requests in exactly the same way SQL Server would respond. An ODS application can communicate directly with a calling process in the same way SQL Server does, using the same methods to form result sets and process requests.

When the ODS API is used to create an extended procedure, the execution of the extended procedure creates another worker thread within SQL Server. The extended procedure running on this thread is treated the same as any other thread executing within SQL Server's process space. The extended procedure can allocate memory for use within the memory space of SQL Server and can create result rows consisting of any valid server data types. These result sets are identical to the sets SQL Server creates, and any application that is capable of processing results from SQL Server can process the result set of an ODS process. This mimicking of SQL Server is what allows the creation of extended stored procedures. It lets SQL Server call the procedure in exactly the same way that it calls a database procedure, passing parameters and processing results the same way.

Adding and Removing Extended Stored Procedures

The Enterprise Manager provides a graphical interface for adding and removing extended stored procedures to the server. Adding extended procedures creates entries in the Master database's sysobjects system table. To add an extended procedure to a SQL server, highlight the Master database in the Server Manager window, then select Extended Procedure from the Manage menu. It is possible to edit the entry of a stored procedure by double-clicking its name in the Extended Stored Procedures collection under the Objects of the Master database. The Manage Extended Procedure dialog box, which lets you drop procedures, will appear (see Figure 20.1).

To add or drop an extended stored procedure, you can also use the sp_addextendedproc and sp_dropextendedproc system stored procedures, as shown below.

```
sp_addextendedproc function_name, dll_name
sp_dropextendedproc function_name
```

These system procedures exist only in the Master database. Executing the sp_addextendedproc procedure adds a row to both the sysobjects table and to

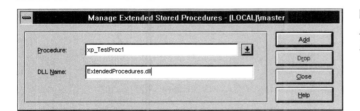

Figure 20.1
*Manage Extended
Procedures Dialog Box*

the sysprocedures table in the Master database. The record in sysobjects associates an ID with the procedure and has a type of 'X.' The sp_addextended-proc system procedure makes the Master database DBO the owner of all of the extended procedures by default. You can change this setup only by directly updating the sysobjects table and replacing the user ID. (The record in sysprocedures identifies the DLL name that the stored procedure is implemented in.)

Only the system administrator can add extended stored procedures, and no one can grant the right to execute the system procedures to other users. The right to execute an extended stored procedure can be granted and revoked in the same way as a database procedure. However, if the extended procedure will be executed in a database other than the Master database, managing security can be difficult, because all the logins that need access to the procedure will need to be added to the Master database. If you put the call of the extended procedure within a database procedure in the database from which it will be called, you can manage security for it in the usual fashion.

Built-In Extended Stored Procedures

SQL Server has several built-in extended stored procedures. These procedures provide basic operating system functions, core functionality for replication and integrated security, and other system tasks. Most of these system extended stored procedures are prefixed with xp_. In this section, we discuss some of the most commonly used built-in extended stored procedures.

The extended stored procedures below allow communication with the Windows NT system for Integrated Security.

- xp_enumgroups
- xp_logininfo
- xp_grantlogin

- xp_revokelogin
- xp_loginconfig

SQLMail extended stored procedures are listed below.

- xp_deletemail
- xp_sendmail
- xp_findnextmsg
- xp_startmail
- xp_readmail
- xp_stopmail

Here are a few general extended stored procedures.

- xp_cmdshell
- xp_sprintf
- xp_logevent
- xp_sscanf
- xp_msver

All the stored procedures listed above are well documented in the Transact-SQL reference. The arguments for each procedure are given, as are usage examples.

The following procedures are not documented in SQL Server *Books Online*. They are defined in the Master database.

- xp_availablemedia: lists all available storage devices that you can write to.
- xp_dirtree <DirPath>: shows subdirectory under <DirPath>.
- xp_enumerrorlogs: shows the complete list of error logs, their archive numbers, and their date of creation.
- xp_enumqueuedtasks: shows the tasks waiting to be processed by SQL Executive.
- xp_fixeddrives: shows the permanent drives attached to the computer.
- xp_readerrorlog <ArchiveNumber>: reads the <ArchiveNumber> error log. If no archive number is specified, the most recent archive (numbered 0) is used.
- xp_regenumvalues @hive(char), @keyname(char): returns the value names and the value contents of the specified key as a two-column result set.

- xp_regread @hive, @keyname, @valuename, @param OUT: returns the named value in the output parameter. The type of the output parameter is dependent on the type of registry value to be read.

- xp_regwrite @hive, @keyname, @valuename, @valuetype, @value: writes the specified value into the registry. If the value exists, the current data is overwritten. If the value does not exist, it is created and the specified data is inserted.

- xp_regdeletevalue @hive, @keyname, @valuename: removes the named value from the registry.

- xp_regaddmultistring @hive, @keyname, @valuename: adds the specified multistring to the registry.

- xp_regremovemultistring @hive, @keyname, @valuename: removes the specified multistring from the registry.

Although SQL Server includes more undocumented extended stored procedures, the ones listed above are probably the most useful. Just remember that these procedures are not documented and therefore may not be supported or carried into future releases.

User-Written Extended Stored Procedures

A full explanation of designing and implementing an original extended stored procedure is a complex undertaking that falls outside the scope of this book, because it is more properly the role of a programmer, not a DBA. A lot of time and effort is required to properly construct extended stored procedures, but when implemented correctly, they can significantly enhance the capability of a database application. In this section, we discuss some issues of user-defined extended stored procedures that DBAs should be aware of.

When you name your own stored procedures, we strongly recommend that you use a naming convention, but don't use the xp_ or sp_ (system stored procedure) prefix that SQL Server uses. A naming convention that indicates when a procedure is an extended procedure can be very useful when debugging code. User-written procedures won't show up in the stored procedure lists for the database, which can cause confusion during code analysis.

In our experience, user-defined DLLs seem to work only when they are located in the <Sqlroot>\Binn directory, along with the Sqlservr.exe executable. This setup eliminates some problems associated with incorrect paths.

When an extended stored procedure is executed, the DLL that contains it is loaded into memory and stays there until SQL Server is shut down or the DLL is freed from memory by the DBCC Free command, as shown below:

```
DBCC <DLL Name>(free)
```

This statement must be run before a DLL will be replaced and the operating system will let the file be overwritten.

Almost everything an extended procedure does through its implementation as a DLL could also be accomplished using the xp_cmdshell and a standalone executable. The result set could be formulated in the same way as SQL Server's result sets and returned to the server using the ODS library. This method creates a whole new process space, which requires security verification and creates the overhead of its own virtual memory table. However, in some cases, using xp_cmdshell is more desirable than running within the process space of SQL Server, especially if the process needs to continue to run after SQL Server shuts down.

The extended stored procedure call is executed within the context of SQL Server so that it behaves just like any other process on the database, sharing memory space and the security context of the SQL Server executable. This setup gives the extended procedure the benefit of acting as an agent of SQL Server, with all of its permissions. However, an adverse effect of this setup is that it makes SQL Server susceptible to errors in the procedure code. Memory violations performed by errant extended procedures can crash the SQL Server executable, forcing a shutdown. Memory errors that may go unnoticed in standalone testing can make DLL code exceptionally dangerous to production environments. You should create rigid guidelines for programs that are intended to be used as DLL procedures, and you should test these programs thoroughly for all cases before you release them into production environments.

Summary

You can use extended stored procedures in innumerable ways to ease the implementation and maintenance of a database. The ease with which system functions can be performed from an extended procedure allow rapid development of expansions and add-on systems to SQL Server. The practice of using external components to provide flexibility to the database environment will continue to grow as three-tiered architectures become utilized more frequently. Extended stored procedures are excellent tools for enabling the creation of business rule components external to the database and allow tremendous opportunities to build cross-platform data services.

Appendix A

Understanding the Transaction Log

SQL Server's transaction log plays a critical role in replication and in the automatic roll-forward and rollback recovery process. In this appendix, we explain how to use the operation codes (*op codes*) to decipher a log. We then show you how to get detailed information about transactions in a log using DBCC and give you an example DBCC listing to analyze.

Insert and Delete Statements

When an Insert statement is sent to the server, it is identified with an op code of 4 in the transaction log. It is also the only statement that causes insert triggers to execute. Similarly, when a Delete statement is sent to the server, it gets an operation code of 5 in the transaction log and is the only statement that causes delete triggers to execute.

Update Statements

Update statements are more difficult to analyze because of the different ways SQL Server interprets and handles them. The two primary types of Updates, direct and deferred, are explained in detail Chapter 16, "Performance Tuning." We focus here on the log entries related to direct and deferred Updates.

When you analyze the performance of Update statements in your application, reviewing entries in transaction log is the only way to know whether you have succeeded in setting up a direct update-in-place. A direct update-in-place, the fastest type of update, gets an op code of 9. The first entry is op code 0, which is a Begin Transaction command. All data modifications get this code, regardless of whether you have actually specified the Begin Transaction statement yourself. The op code of 9 comes next, followed by a 30, which is an End Transaction. You always get an End Transaction, even if you specify a Commit Transaction or Rollback Transaction. Commit and Rollback do not have separate op codes.

A direct, same-page Update occurs when a record is deleted from a page and inserted onto that same page, usually because of increasing row length. Because the record does not move to a new page, none of the indexes needs to be updated, unless, of course, an indexed field is updated. This type of Update gets two records, an op code of 5 (Delete), followed by an op code of 6 (Indirect Insert).

A deferred update is the most expensive. A deferred Update is actually a Delete operation followed by an Insert, but everything is done twice. The operation is first performed as a no-op Delete and Insert (op codes 11 and 12), then as the actual Delete and Insert (op codes 5 and 6). The record is usually placed on another page, which means that the index entries are also deleted and inserted (op codes 7 and 8).

Table A.1 lists the op codes in the transaction logs.

TABLE A.1 TRANSACTION LOG OPERATION CODES

Op Code	Description
0	BEGINXACT: Begin Transaction
4	Insert
5	Delete
6	Indirect Insert
7	Index Insert
8	Index Delete
9	MODIFY: Modify the record on the page
11	Deferred Insert (NO-OP)
12	Deferred Delete (NO-OP)
13	Page Allocation
15	Extent Allocation
16	Page Split
17	Checkpoint
20	DEXTENT
30	End Transaction (Either a commit or rollback)
38	CHGSYSINDSTAT — A change to the statistics page in sysindexes
39	CHGSYSINDPG — Change to a page in the sysindexes table

DBCC LOG Command

Run DBCC TRACEON (3604) then DBCC LOG to get a printout containing more information on each record in the log file. The following pages show an example of the output from the DBCC LOG command. Use the table above to help you decipher it.

```
LOG RECORDS:
    BEGINXACT      (791 , 2)
    attcnt=1 rno=2 op=0 padlen=3 xactid=(791 , 2) len=64
status=0x0000
xendstat=XBEG_ENDXACT
    masterid=(0 , 0)     lastrec=(0 , 0)      spid=3 suid=1
uid=1 masterdbid=0
mastersite=0 endstat=3
    name=dmpxact  time=Apr 21 1997 11:59PM

    MODIFY         (791 , 4)
    attcnt=1 rno=4 op=9 padlen=2 xactid=(791 , 2) len=64
status=0x0000
    tabid=2 pageno=24 offset=1163 status=0x0000
    old ts=0x0001 0x00001ae2  new ts=0x0001 0x00001afd

    ENDXACT        (791 , 8)
    attcnt=1 rno=8 op=30 padlen=0 xactid=(791 , 2) len=36
status=0x0000
xendstat=
    endstat=COMMIT time=Apr 21 1997 11:59PM

    BEGINXACT      (791 , 9)
    attcnt=1 rno=9 op=0 padlen=3 xactid=(791 , 9) len=64
status=0x0000
xendstat=XBEG_ENDXACT
    masterid=(0 , 0)     lastrec=(0 , 0)      spid=3 suid=1
uid=1 masterdbid=0
mastersite=0 endstat=3
    name=dmpxact  time=Apr 22 1997 12:00AM

    DEXTENT        (791 , 11)
    attcnt=1 rno=11 op=20 padlen=0 xactid=(791 , 9) len=60
status=0x0000
```

```
   DEXTENT       Extentid=776 endextid=0 count=1 bitmap=
0x0 0x0 0x0 0x0
   EXTENT  next=0, prev=0, objid=8, alloc=0xff,
dealloc=0x0,
indexid=0, status=0x0

   CHGSYSINDPG   (791 , 13)
   attcnt=1 rno=13 op=39 padlen=0 xactid=(791 , 9) len=36
status=0x0000
   FIRSTPAGE
   tabid=8 indexid=0 oldvalue=776 newvalue=791

   MODIFY        (791 , 14)
   attcnt=1 rno=14 op=9 padlen=2 xactid=(791 , 9) len=56
status=0x0000
   tabid=8 pageno=791 offset=8 status=0x0000
   old ts=0x0001 0x00001afb  new ts=0x0001 0x00001afb

   ENDXACT       (791 , 19)
   attcnt=1 rno=19 op=30 padlen=0 xactid=(791 , 9) len=36
status=0x0000
 xendstat=
   endstat=COMMIT time=Apr 22 1997 12:00AM

   BEGINXACT     (791 , 22)
   attcnt=1 rno=22 op=0 padlen=3 xactid=(791 , 22) len=60
status=0x0000
 xendstat=XBEG_ENDXACT
   masterid=(0 , 0)    lastrec=(0 , 0)       spid=12 suid=1
uid=1 masterdbid=0
mastersite=0 endstat=3
   name=ins  time=Apr 25 1997 3:46PM

   INSERT        (791 , 23)
   attcnt=1 rno=23 op=4 padlen=3 xactid=(791 , 22) len=84
status=0x0000
   tabid=16003088 pageno=360 offset=927 status=0x0000
   old ts=0x0001 0x00001afa  new ts=0x0001 0x00001b08

   IINSERT       (791 , 24)
   attcnt=1 rno=24 op=7 padlen=3 xactid=(791 , 22) len=64
status=0x0000
   tabid=16003088 pageno=544 offset=327 status=0x0000
   old ts=0x0001 0x00001a55  new ts=0x0001 0x00001b09
```

```
    CHGSYSINDSTAT (791 , 25)
    attcnt=1 rno=25 op=38 padlen=0 xactid=(791 , 22) len=52
status=0x0000
    tabid=16003088 rows=1 used=0 dpages=0 reserved=0
    uts_chg=0x0000000100000019 uts_undo=0xffffffffffffffff

    ENDXACT        (791 , 26)
    attcnt=1 rno=26 op=30 padlen=0 xactid=(791 , 22) len=36
status=0x0000
xendstat=
    endstat=COMMIT time=Apr 25 1997 3:46PM

    BEGINXACT      (791 , 30)
    attcnt=1 rno=30 op=0 padlen=3 xactid=(791 , 30) len=60
status=0x0000
xendstat=XBEG_ENDXACT
    masterid=(0 , 0)     lastrec=(0 , 0)        spid=12 suid=1
uid=1 masterdbid=0
mastersite=0 endstat=3
    name=upd  time=Apr 25 1997 3:52PM

    DNOOP         (791 , 31)
    attcnt=1 rno=31 op=12 padlen=0 xactid=(791 , 30) len=24
status=0x0000
    noopdel=(360 , 23)

    INOOP         (791 , 32)
    attcnt=1 rno=32 op=11 padlen=3 xactid=(791 , 30) len=56
status=0x0000

    IDELETE       (791 , 33)
    attcnt=1 rno=33 op=8 padlen=3 xactid=(791 , 30) len=64
status=0x0000
    tabid=16003088 pageno=544 offset=327 status=0x0000
    old ts=0x0001 0x00001b09  new ts=0x0001 0x00001b0d

    DELETE        (791 , 34)
    attcnt=1 rno=34 op=5 padlen=3 xactid=(791 , 30) len=84
status=0x0000
    tabid=16003088 pageno=360 offset=927 status=0x0000
    old ts=0x0001 0x00001b0b  new ts=0x0001 0x00001b0e
```

```
   INSIND        (790 , 0)
   attcnt=1 rno=0 op=6 padlen=0 xactid=(791 , 30) len=52
status=0x0000
   tabid=16003088 pageno=360 offset=927 status=0x0000
   old ts=0x0001 0x00001b0e  new ts=0x0001 0x00001b0f
   ptr=(791 , 32)

   IINSERT       (790 , 1)
   attcnt=1 rno=1 op=7 padlen=3 xactid=(791 , 30) len=64
status=0x0000
   tabid=16003088 pageno=544 offset=327 status=0x0000
   old ts=0x0001 0x00001b0d  new ts=0x0001 0x00001b11

   ENDXACT       (790 , 2)
   attcnt=1 rno=2 op=30 padlen=0 xactid=(791 , 30) len=36
status=0x0000 xendstat=        endstat=COMMIT time=Apr 25
1997 3:52PM

   CHECKPOINT    (791 , 3)
   attcnt=1 rno=3 op=17 padlen=0 xactid=(0 , 0) len=60
status=0x0000
   rows=-44, pages=0 extents=8
   timestamp=0x0001 0x00001afc active xacts:(776 , 15)


DBCC execution completed. If DBCC printed error messages,
see your System Administrator.
```

Appendix B

Knowledge Sources

Web Sites

- http://www.microsoft.com/sql/whitepapers.htm
- http://www.sqlink.com
- http://www.compaq.com — One of the best white papers on SQL configurations and performance tuning, even if it is specific to Compaq machines.
- http://www.winpub.com

Other Electronic Resources

- SQL Server *Books Online* — One of the best sources for the basics of SQL Server. It is one of the best implementations of an online reference manual for any product.
- SQL Server Resource Kit — Sample programs, white papers, utilities and more, available at http://www.microsoft.com/sql.
- TechNet, Developers Network, MSN — Good articles, white papers, workarounds to problems, and sample programs.

Books and Magazines

- *Windows NT Magazine* (http://www.winntmag.com)
- *SQL Server Professional* (http://www.pinpub.com)
- *Database Programming and Design* (http://www.dbpd.com)

Certification

Certification — It is advisable to obtain any of the Microsoft certifications. You learn a lot of details about each product or technology just by studying for the tests.

- Microsoft Product Specialist (MCP) — Take one of the certification tests to become a product specialist.
- Microsoft Certified Systems Engineer (MCSE) — One of four required tests is "SQL Server Administration."
- Microsoft Certified Solutions Developer (MCSD) — One of the required tests is "Design and Implementation of SQL Server."

Other Resources

- Microsoft Support — Very knowledgeable people to assist with problems, find workarounds, and explain solutions.

Microsoft Classes

- SQL Server Administration
- Design and Implementation of SQL Server Applications
- Performance, Tuning, and Optimizations

Appendix C

SQL 7.0 Features

Code-named Sphinx, SQL Server 7.0 is reportedly due out sometime in late 1997 or early 1998. It represents another step for Microsoft toward support for larger enterprises. Even though the features targeting large databases and distributed systems will be getting all the press, the best features may be the ones that assist the common DBA.

Performance improvements are the emphasis of SQL 7.0. Microsoft has publicly demonstrated a server configuration capable of handling one billion transactions per day.

As you may have noticed with releases of other software packages, it is almost impossible to predict the features that will make it into the final version. This appendix gives you all the information available at the time of publication about the new and improved features of SQL Server 7.0. The information was gathered from various conferences and discussions with anyone having detailed knowledge.

Features of SQL Server 7.0

- 8K page size — More data per page means less physical I/O and improved memory management.

- New optimizer — An unsubstantiated rumor is circulating that the query optimizer was entirely rewritten.

- Shared-nothing clustering — This feature brings the server clustering concept to Windows NT and SQL Server.

- Dynamic database expansion — No more running out of database and log space.

- Easier installation — It can't get much easier than it already is, although it would be nice to have a one-button-take-all-the-defaults installation option.

- Easier maintenance and administration — New wizards, administration commands, and utilities.

- Versatile locking functions — Row-level locking and de-escalation.

- Heterogeneous replication to and from SQL Server — Any ODBC data-source can replicate to SQL Server.

- Replication.

  - Multi-master — Two remote servers can own and modify the same table at the same time

  - Peer-to-peer replication — Better support for "insert/update anywhere" (mobile clients) with conflict detection and resolution

  - Improve scalability — larger batches, faster

  - Improved monitoring and administration

  - Interface for heterogeneous publishers (to SQL Server)

- Self managing resources — Dynamic reconfiguration and tuning of memory, connections, and other configuration parameters.

- Distributed SQL Server joins — Will we be able to join tables on two different servers?

- User-defined functions — Instead of having only the system functions.

- Internet optimizations — Connection pooling and other improvements in handling a high volume of database hits.

- New configuration options — For example, the procedure cache configuration parameter will be a floating point number so that you can give the procedure cache less than 1 percent of your SQL Server memory. On super servers with gigabytes of memory, even 1 percent is too large for procedure cache.

- Improved utilities — Improved tracing, additional performance monitor counters, improved transfer manager.
- Proactive DBCC — A database utility that monitors and fixes potential problems?
- Support of 8 CPU machines — Only 8? Some companies are ready to demonstrate Windows NT on machines with more than 8 processors.
- Desktop version of SQL Server — Develop on a desktop and install on a superserver.
- Transact-SQL debugger — Available now in C++ 4.2 and 5.0 and Visual Basic 5.0 development kits. Improvements to SQL debugger. Rumor has it that this feature may come with SQL Server instead of with the development products.
- Improved NT security integration — Elimination of dual Windows NT/SQL Server user names.
- Group/User follow Windows NT model — Perhaps roles will also be supported; i.e., Operator role, Administrator role.

NT and SQL Integration Products

It appears that Microsoft's strategy is to roll out products that are used with SQL Server 7.0 before the database program itself is ready. Microsoft Transaction Server (code named Viper) and OLE DB have already been released. These and other products aimed at the improvements in the integration of the Windows NT operating system and SQL Server are listed below.

Transaction Server (Code Name: Viper)

- Multifaceted integration and middle-tier software
- DTC must be on same node as SQL Server
- DTC will run in-process with SQL Server
- Improved communications transport
- Reduced messages for two-phase commit
- Connection pooling
- Support for *n*-tier transactions
- Heterogeneous transactions — relational databases, non-relational databases, spreadsheets, files, isam, etc.

Wolfpack Fail-Over Recovery

- Servers can share the same disk drives, so that if one server goes down, the other can take over.

OLE DB, Multifaceted Integration and Middle-Tier Software

An OLE COM interface that

- Provides access to all types of data
- Extends functionality via "service providers"
- Supports disconnected data access
  - Supports rowset as a self-contained object
  - Supports buffered update mode
  - Keeps current values, original values, changes
- Designed as component technology
  - Objects/data can be shared by multiple components
  - Each component operates directly on the data
- Avoids duplication of data at different levels
  - Components invoked only when needed
  - Notifications allow synchronization

Active Server Pages (Code Name: Denali)

- Language independent
- Server-based scripting (useful beyond databases)
- Extensible using components
- .asp files
- Separation of logic and layout
- ADO (instead of RDO, DAO) — Active Data Objects

Beyond 7.0

- Shared-nothing clustering (if it doesn't make it into SQL Server 7.0)
- Self-healing database

- Very large memory support
- Language-independent APIs
- Abstract data types
- Beyond 8 CPU SMP support

Index

M

New Books in the Duke Press Library

DEVELOPING YOUR AS/400 INTERNET STRATEGY

By Alan Arnold

Addresses the issues unique to deploying your AS/400 on the Internet. Includes procedures for configuring AS/400 TCP/IP and information about which client and server technologies the AS/400 supports natively. Don't put precious corporate data and systems in harm's way. Arnold shows you how to reconcile the AS/400 security-conscious mindset with the less secure philosophy of the Internet community. This enterprise-class tutorial evaluates the AS/400 as an Internet server and teaches you how to design, program, and manage your Web home page. 225 pages.

INSIDE THE AS/400, SECOND EDITION
An in-depth look at the AS/400's design, architecture, and history

By Frank G. Soltis

The inside story every AS/400 developer has been waiting for, told by Dr. Frank G. Soltis, IBM's AS/400 chief architect. Never before has IBM provided an in-depth look at the AS/400's design, architecture, and history. This authoritative book does just that — and also looks at some of the people behind the scenes who created this revolutionary system for you. Whether you are an executive looking for a high-level overview or a "bit-twiddling techie" who wants all the details, *Inside the AS/400* demystifies this system, shedding light on how it came to be, how it can do the things it does, and what its future may hold — especially in light of its new PowerPC RISC processors. 475 pages.

THE MICROSOFT EXCHANGE SERVER INTERNET MAIL CONNECTOR

By Spyros Sakellariadis

Presents everything you need to know about how to plan, install, and configure the servers in your Exchange environment to achieve the Internet connectivity users demand. 234 pages.

THE MICROSOFT EXCHANGE USER'S HANDBOOK

By Sue Mosher

A must-have, complete guide for users who need to know how to set up and use all the features of the Microsoft Exchange client product. Includes chapters about Microsoft Exchange Server 5.0 and Microsoft Outlook. 692 pages. CD included.

MIGRATING TO WINDOWS NT 4.0

By Sean Daily

A comprehensive yet concise guide to the significant changes users will encounter as they make the move to Windows NT 4.0. Includes a wealth of tips and techniques. 475 pages.

POWERING YOUR WEB SITE WITH WINDOWS NT SERVER

By Nik Simpson

Explores the tools necessary to establish a presence on the Internet or on an internal corporate intranet using Web technology and Windows NT Server. 661 pages. CD included.

THE TECHNOLOGY GUIDE TO ACCOUNTING SOFTWARE
A Handbook for Evaluating Vendor Applications

By Stewart McKie

Are you involved in recommending or selecting financial software for your department or company? Whether you are a CFO, an IS professional, or a practicing accountant, if the answer is Yes, then this book is must reading! It is designed to help managers evaluate accounting software, with an emphasis on the issues in a client/server environment. McKie cuts the marketing hype and provides a range of useful checklists for shortlisting products to evaluate in more detail. More than 50 vendors are profiled, and a resource guide and a glossary are included. 256 pages.

Also Published by Duke Press

THE A TO Z OF EDI

By Nahid M. Jilovec

Electronic Data Interchange (EDI) can help reduce administrative costs, accelerate information processing, ensure data accuracy, and streamline business procedures. Here's a comprehensive guide to EDI to help in planning, startup, and implementation. The author reveals all the benefits, challenges, standards, and implementation secrets gained through extensive experience. She shows how to evaluate your business procedures, select special hardware and software, establish communications requirements and standards, address audit issues, and employ the legal support necessary for EDI activities. 263 pages.

APPLICATION DEVELOPER'S HANDBOOK FOR THE AS/400

Edited by Mike Otey, a **NEWS/400** *technical editor*

Explains how to effectively use the AS/400 to build reliable, flexible, and efficient business applications. Contains RPG/400 and CL coding examples and tips, and provides both step-by-step instructions and handy reference material. Includes diskette. 768 pages.

AS/400 DISK SAVING TIPS & TECHNIQUES

By James R. Plunkett

Want specific help for cleaning up and maintaining your disks? Here are more than 50 tips, plus design techniques for minimizing your disk usage. Each tip is completely explained with the "symptom," the problem, and the technique or code you need to correct it. 72 pages.

AS/400 SUBFILES IN RPG

Edited by Catherine T. Rivera

On the AS/400, subfiles are powerful and easy to use, and with this book you can start working with subfiles in just a few hours — no need to wade through page after page of technical jargon. You'll start with the concept behind subfiles, then discover how easy they are to program. The book contains all of the DDS subfile keywords announced in V2R3 of OS/400. Five complete RPG subfile programs are included, and the book comes complete with a 3.5" PC diskette containing all those programs plus DDS. The book is an updated version of the popular *Programming Subfiles in RPG/400*. 200 pages.

C FOR RPG PROGRAMMERS

By Jennifer Hamilton, a **NEWS/400** *author*

Written from the perspective of an RPG programmer, this book includes side-by-side coding examples written in both C and RPG clear identification of unique C constructs, and a comparison of RPG op-codes to equivalent C concepts. Includes many tips and examples covering the use of C/400. 292 pages.

CL BY EXAMPLE

By Virgil Green

CL by Example gives programmers and operators more than 850 pages of practical information you can use in your day-to-day job. It's full of application examples, tips, and techniques, along with a sprinkling of humor. The examples will speed you through the learning curve to help you become a more proficient, more productive CL programmer. 864 pages.

CLIENT ACCESS TOKEN-RING CONNECTIVITY

By Chris Patterson

Attaching PCs to AS/400s via a Token-Ring can become a complicated subject — when things go wrong, an understanding of PCs, the Token-Ring, and OS/400 is often required. *Client Access Token-Ring Connectivity* details all that is required in these areas to successfully maintain and troubleshoot a Token-Ring network. The first half of the book introduces the Token-Ring and describes the Client Access communications architecture, the Token-Ring connection from both the PC side and the AS/400 side, and the Client Access applications. The second half provides a useful guide to Token-Ring management, strategies for Token-Ring error identification and recovery, and tactics for resolving Client Access error messages. 125 pages.

COMMON-SENSE C

Advice and Warnings for C and C++ Programmers

By Paul Conte, a **NEWS/400** technical editor

C programming language has its risks; this book shows how C programmers get themselves into trouble, includes tips to help you avoid C's pitfalls, and suggests how to manage C and C++ application development. 100 pages.

CONTROL LANGUAGE PROGRAMMING FOR THE AS/400

By Bryan Meyers and Dan Riehl, **NEWS/400** *technical editors*

This comprehensive CL programming textbook offers students up-to-the-minute knowledge of the skills they will need in today's MIS environment. Progresses methodically from CL basics to more complex processes and concepts, guiding readers toward a professional grasp of CL programming techniques and style. 512 pages.

DDS PROGRAMMING FOR DISPLAY & PRINTER FILES

By James Coolbaugh

Offers a thorough, straightforward explanation of how to use Data Description Specifications (DDS) to program display files and printer files. Covers basic to complex tasks using DDS functions. The author uses DDS programming examples for CL and RPG extensively throughout the book, and you can put these examples to use immediately. Focuses on topics such as general screen presentations, the A specification, defining data on the screen, record-format and field definitions, defining data fields, using indicators, data and text attributes, cursor and keyboard control, editing data, validity checking, response keywords, and function keys. A complimentary diskette includes all the source code presented in the book. 446 pages.

DATABASE DESIGN AND PROGRAMMING FOR DB2/400

By Paul Conte

This textbook is the comprehensive guide for creating flexible and efficient application databases in DB2/400. The author shows you everything you need to know about physical and logical file DDS, SQL/400, and RPG IV and COBOL/400 database programming. Clear explanations illustrated by a wealth of examples, including complete RPG IV and COBOL/400 programs, demonstrate efficient database programming and error handling with both DDS and SQL/400. Each programming chapter includes a specific list of "Coding Suggestions" that will help you write faster and more maintainable code. In addition, the author provides an extensive section on practical database design for DB2/400. This is the most complete guide to DB2/400 design and programming available anywhere. 772 pages.

DESKTOP GUIDE TO THE S/36

By Mel Beckman, Gary Kratzer, and Roger Pence, **NEWS/400** *technical editors*

This definitive S/36 survival manual includes practical techniques to supercharge your S/36, including ready-to-use information for maximum system performance tuning, effective application development, and smart Disk Data Management. Includes a review of two popular Unix-based S/36 work-alike migration alternatives. Diskette contains ready-to-run utilities to help you save machine time and implement power programming techniques such as External Program Calls. 387 pages.

THE ESSENTIAL GUIDE TO CLIENT ACCESS FOR DOS EXTENDED

By John Enck, Robert E. Anderson, and Michael Otey

The Essential Guide to Client Access for DOS Extended contains key insights and need-to-know technical information about Client Access for DOS Extended, IBM's strategic AS/400 product for DOS and Windows client/server connectivity. This book provides background information about the history and architecture of Client Access for DOS Extended; fundamental information about how to install and configure Client Access; and advanced information about integrating Client Access with other types of networks, managing how Client Access for DOS Extended operates under Windows, and developing client/server applications with Client Access. Written by industry experts based on their personal and professional experiences with Client Access, this book can help you avoid time-consuming pitfalls that litter the path of AS/400 client/ server computing. 430 pages.

ILE: A FIRST LOOK

By George Farr and Shailan Topiwala

This book begins by showing the differences between ILE and its predecessors, then goes on to explain the essentials of an ILE program — using concepts such as modules, binding, service programs, and binding directories. You'll discover how ILE program activation works and how ILE works with its predecessor environments. The book covers the new APIs and new debugging facilities and explains the benefits of ILE's new exception-handling model. You also get answers to the most commonly asked questions about ILE. 183 pages.

IMPLEMENTING AS/400 SECURITY, SECOND EDITION

A practical guide to implementing, evaluating, and auditing your AS/400 security strategy

By Wayne Madden, a **NEWS/400** *technical editor*

Concise and practical, this second edition brings together in one place the fundamental AS/400 security tools and experience-based recommendations that you need and also includes specifics on the latest security enhancements available in OS/400 Version 3 Release 1. Completely updated from the first edition, this is the only source for the latest information about how to protect your system against attack from its increasing exposure to hackers. 389 pages.

INTRODUCTION TO AS/400 SYSTEM OPERATIONS

By Patrice Gapen and Heidi Rothenbuehler

Here's the textbook that covers what you need to know to become a successful AS/400 system operator. System operators typically help users resolve problems, manage printed reports, and perform regularly scheduled procedures. *Introduction to AS/400 System Operations* introduces a broad range of topics, including system architecture; DB2/400 and Query; user interface and Operational Assistant; managing jobs and printed reports; backup and restore; system configuration and networks; performance; security; and Client Access (PC Support).

The information presented here covers typical daily, weekly, and monthly AS/400 operations using V3R1M0 of the OS/400 operating system. You can benefit from this book even if you have only a very basic knowledge of the AS/400. If you know how to sign on to the AS/400, and how to use the function keys, you're ready for the material in this book. 234 pages.

AN INTRODUCTION TO COMMUNICATIONS FOR THE AS/400, SECOND EDITION

By John Enck and Ruggero Adinolfi

This second edition has been revised to address the sweeping communications changes introduced with V3R1 of OS/400. As a result, this book now covers the broad range of AS/400 communications technology topics, ranging from Ethernet to X.25, and from APPN to AnyNet. The book presents an introduction to data communications and then covers communications fundamentals, types of networks, OSI, SNA, APPN, networking roles, the AS/400 as host and server, TCP/IP, and the AS/400-DEC connection. 210 pages.

JIM SLOAN'S CL TIPS & TECHNIQUES

By Jim Sloan, developer of QUSRTOOL's TAA Tools

Written for those who understand CL, this book draws from Jim Sloan's knowledge and experience as a developer for the S/38 and the AS/400, and his creation of QUSRTOOL's TAA tools, to give you tips that can help you write better CL programs and become more productive. Includes more than 200 field-tested techniques, plus exercises to help you understand and apply many of the techniques presented. 564 pages.

MASTERING AS/400 PERFORMANCE

By Alan Arnold, Charly Jones, Jim Stewart, and Rick Turner

If you want more from your AS/400 — faster interactive response time, more batch jobs completed on time, and maximum use of your expensive resources — this book is for you. In *Mastering AS/400 Performance*, the experts tell you how to measure, evaluate, and tune your AS/400's performance. From the authors' experience in the field, they give you techniques for improving performance beyond simply buying additional hardware. Learn the techniques, gain the insight, and help your company profit from the experience of the top AS/400 performance professionals in the country. 259 pages.

MASTERING THE AS/400
A Practical, Hands-On Guide
By Jerry Fottral
This introductory textbook to AS/400 concepts and facilities has a utilitarian approach that stresses student participation. A natural prerequisite to programming and database management courses, it emphasizes mastery of system/user interface, member-object-library relationship, utilization of CL commands, and basic database and program development utilities. Also includes labs focusing on essential topics such as printer spooling; library lists; creating and maintaining physical files; using logical files; using CL and DDS; working in the PDM environment; and using SEU, DFU, Query, and SDA. 484 pages.

OBJECT-ORIENTED PROGRAMMING FOR AS/400 PROGRAMMERS
By Jennifer Hamilton, a **NEWS/400** *author*
Explains basic OOP concepts such as classes and inheritance in simple, easy-to-understand terminology. The OS/400 object-oriented architecture serves as the basis for the discussion throughout, and concepts presented are reinforced through an introduction to the C++ object-oriented programming language, using examples based on the OS/400 object model. 114 pages.

PERFORMANCE PROGRAMMING — MAKING RPG SIZZLE
By Mike Dawson, CDP
Mike Dawson spent more than two years preparing this book — evaluating programming options, comparing techniques, and establishing benchmarks on thousands of programs. "Using the techniques in this book," he says, "I have made program after program run 30%, 40%, even 50% faster." To help you do the same, Mike gives you code and benchmark results for initializing and clearing arrays, performing string manipulation, using validation arrays with look-up techniques, using arrays in arithmetic routines, and a lot more. 257 pages.

POWER TOOLS FOR THE AS/400, VOLUMES I AND II
Edited by Frederick L. Dick and Dan Riehl
NEWS 3X/400's Power Tools for the AS/400 is a two-volume reference series for people who work with the AS/400. *Volume I* (originally titled *AS/400 Power Tools*) is a collection of the best tools, tips, and techniques published in *NEWS/34-38* (pre-August 1988) and *NEWS 3X/400* (August 1988 through October 1991) that are applicable to the AS/400. *Volume II* extends this original collection by including material that appeared through 1994. Each book includes a diskette that provides load-and-go code for easy-to-use solutions to many everyday problems. *Volume I:* 709 pages; *Volume II:* 702 pages.

PROGRAMMING IN RPG IV
By Judy Yaeger, Ph.D., a **NEWS/400** *technical editor*
This textbook provides a strong foundation in the essentials of business programming, featuring the newest version of the RPG language: RPG IV. Focusing on real-world problems and down-to-earth solutions using the latest techniques and features of RPG, this book provides everything you need to know to write a well-designed RPG IV program. Each chapter includes informative, easy-to-read explanations and examples as well as a section of thought-provoking questions, exercises,

and programming assignments. Four appendices and a handy, comprehensive glossary support the topics presented throughout the book. An instructor's kit is available. 450 pages.

PROGRAMMING IN RPG/400, SECOND EDITION

By Judy Yaeger, Ph.D., a **NEWS/400** *technical editor*

This second edition refines and extends the comprehensive instructional material contained in the original textbook and features a new section that introduces externally described printer files, a new chapter that highlights the fundamentals of RPG IV, and a new appendix that correlates the key concepts from each chapter with their RPG IV counterparts. Includes everything you need to learn how to write a well-designed RPG program, from the most basic to the more complex, and each chapter includes a section of questions, exercises, and programming assignments that reinforce the knowledge you have gained from the chapter and strengthen the groundwork for succeeding chapters. An instructor's kit is available. 464 pages.

PROGRAMMING SUBFILES IN COBOL/400

By Jerry Goldson

Learn how to program subfiles in COBOL/400 in a matter of hours! This powerful and flexible programming technique no longer needs to elude you. You can begin programming with subfiles the same day you get the book. You don't have to wade through page after page, chapter after chapter of rules and parameters and keywords. Instead, you get solid, helpful information and working examples that you can apply to your application programs right away. 204 pages.

THE QUINTESSENTIAL GUIDE TO PC SUPPORT

By John Enck, Robert E. Anderson, Michael Otey, and Michael Ryan

This comprehensive book about IBM's AS/400 PC Support connectivity product defines the architecture of PC Support and its role in midrange networks, describes PC Support's installation and configuration procedures, and shows you how you can configure and use PC Support to solve real-life problems. 345 pages.

RPG ERROR HANDLING TECHNIQUE
Bulletproofing Your Applications

By Russell Popeil

RPG Error Handling Technique teaches you the skills you need to use the powerful tools provided by OS/400 and RPG to handle almost any error from within your programs. The book explains the INFSR, INFDS, PSSR, and SDS in programming terms, with examples that show you how all these tools work together and which tools are most appropriate for which kind of error or exception situation. It continues by presenting a robust suite of error/exception handling techniques within RPG programs. Each technique is explained in an application setting, using both RPG III and RPG IV code. 164 pages.

RPG IV BY EXAMPLE

By George Farr and Shailan Topiwala

RPG IV by Example addresses the needs and concerns of RPG programmers at any level of experience. The focus is on RPG IV in a practical context that lets AS/400 professionals quickly grasp what's new without dwelling on the old. Beginning with an overview of RPG IV specifications, the authors prepare the way for examining all the features of the new version of the language. The chapters that follow explore RPG IV further with practical, easy-to-use applications. 500 pages.

RPG IV JUMP START, SECOND EDITION
Moving Ahead With the New RPG

By Bryan Meyers, a **NEWS/400** *technical editor*

In this second edition of *RPG IV Jump Start*, Bryan Meyers has added coverage for new releases of the RPG IV compiler (V3R2, V3R6, and V3R7) and amplified the coverage of RPG IV's participation in the integrated language environment (ILE). As in the first edition, he covers RPG IV's changed and new specifications and data types. He presents the new RPG from the perspective of a programmer who already knows the old RPG, pointing out the differences between the two and demonstrating how to take advantage of the new syntax and function. 204 pages.

RPG/400 INTERACTIVE TEMPLATE TECHNIQUE

By Carson Soule, CDP, CCP, CSP

Here's an updated version of Carson Soule's *Interactive RPG/400 Programming*. The book shows you time-saving, program-sharpening concepts behind the template approach, and includes all the code you need to build one perfect program after another. These templates include code for cursor-sensitive prompting in DDS, for handling messages in resident RPG programs, for using the CLEAR opcode to eliminate hard-coded field initialization, and much more. There's even a new select template with a pop-up window. 258 pages.

S/36 POWER TOOLS

Edited by Chuck Lundgren, a **NEWS/400** *technical editor*

Winner of an STC Award of Achievement in 1992, this book contains five years' worth of articles, tips, and programs published in *NEWS 3X/400* from 1986 to October 1990, including more than 280 programs and procedures. Extensively cross-referenced for fast and easy problem solving, and complete with diskette containing all the programming code. 738 pages.

STARTER KIT FOR THE AS/400, SECOND EDITION
An indispensable guide for novice to intermediate AS/400 programmers and system operators

By Wayne Madden, a **NEWS/400** *technical editor*
with contributions by Bryan Meyers, Andrew Smith, and Peter Rowley

This second edition contains updates of the material in the first edition and incorporates new material to enhance its value as a resource to help you learn important basic concepts and nuances of the AS/400 system. New material focuses on installing a new release, working with PTFs, AS/400 message handling, working with and securing printed output, using operational assistant to manage disk space, job scheduling, save and restore basics, and more basic CL programming concepts. Optional diskette available. 429 pages.

SUBFILE TECHNIQUE FOR RPG/400 PROGRAMMERS

By Jonathan Yergin, CDP, and Wayne Madden

Here's the code you need for a complete library of shell subfile programs: RPG/400 code, DDS, CL, and sample data files. There's even an example for programming windows. You even get some "whiz bang" techniques that add punch to your applications. This book explains the code in simple, straightforward style and tells you when each technique should be used for best results. 326 pages, 3.5" PC diskette included.

TECHNICAL REFERENCE SERIES: DESKTOP GUIDES

Edited by Bryan Meyers, a **NEWS/400** *technical editor*

Written by experts — such as John Enck, Bryan Meyers, Julian Monypenny, Roger Pence, Dan Riehl — these unique desktop guides put the latest AS/400 applications and techniques at your fingertips. These "just-do-it" books (featuring wire-o binding to open flat at every page) are priced so you can keep your personal set handy. Optional online Windows help diskette available for each book.

Desktop Guide to AS/400 Programmers' Tools

By Dan Riehl, a **NEWS/400** *technical editor*

This second book of the **NEWS/400** *Technical Reference Series* gives you the "how-to" behind all the tools included in *Application Development ToolSet/400* (ADTS/400), IBM's Licensed Program Product for Version 3 of OS/400; includes Source Entry Utility (SEU), Programming Development Manager (PDM), Screen Design Aid (SDA), Report Layout Utility (RLU), File Compare/Merge Utility (FCMU), and Interactive Source Debugger. Highlights topics and functions specific to Version 3 of OS/400. 266 pages.

Desktop Guide to CL Programming

By Bryan Meyers, a **NEWS/400** *technical editor*

This first book of the **NEWS/400** *Technical Reference Series* is packed with easy-to-find notes, short explanations, practical tips, answers to most of your everyday questions about CL, and CL code segments you can use in your own CL programming. Complete "short reference" lists every command and explains the most-often-used ones, along with names of the files they use and the MONMSG messages to use with them. 205 pages.

Desktop Guide to Creating CL Commands

By Lynn Nelson

In *Desktop Guide to Creating CL Commands*, author Lynn Nelson shows you how to create your own CL commands with the same functionality and power as the IBM commands you use every day, including automatic parameter editing, all the function keys, F4 prompt for values, expanding lists of values, and conditional prompting. After you have read this book, you can write macros for the operations you do over and over every day or write application commands that prompt users for essential information. Whether you're in operations or programming, don't miss this opportunity to enhance your career-building skills. 164 pages.

Desktop Guide to DDS

By James Coolbaugh

This third book of the **NEWS/400** *Technical Reference Series* provides a complete reference to all DDS keywords for physical, logical, display, printer, and ICF files. Each keyword is briefly explained, with syntax rules and examples showing how to code the keyword. All basic and pertinent information is provided for quick and easy access. While this guide explains every parameter for a keyword, it doesn't explain every possible exception that might exist. Rather, the guide includes the basics about what each keyword is designed to accomplish. The *Desktop Guide to DDS* is designed to give quick, "at your fingertips" information about every keyword — with this in hand, you won't need to refer to IBM's bulky *DDS Reference* manual. 132 pages.

Desktop Guide to OPNQRYF

By Mike Dawson and Mike Manto

The OPNQRYF command is the single most dynamic and versatile command on the AS/400. But unless you understand just what it is and what it does, it can seem mysterious. Our new Desktop Guide leads you through the details with lots of examples to bring you up to speed quickly. 150 pages.

Desktop Guide to RPG/400

By Roger Pence and Julian Monypenny, **NEWS/400** *technical editors*

This fourth book in the *Technical Reference Series* provides a variety of RPG templates, subroutines, and copy modules, sprinkled with evangelical advice that will help you write robust and effective RPG/400 programs. Highlights of the information provided include string-handling routines, numeric editing routines, date routines, error-handling modules, tips for using OS/400 APIs with RPG/400, and interactive programming techniques. For all types of RPG projects, this book's tested and ready-to-run building blocks will easily snap into your RPG. The programming solutions provided here would otherwise take you days or even weeks to write and test. 211 pages.

Desktop Guide to SQL

By James Coolbaugh

The *Desktop Guide to SQL* is an invaluable reference guide for any programmer looking to gain a better understanding of SQL syntax and rules. For the novice SQL user, the book features plenty of introductory-level explanatory text and examples. More experienced users will appreciate the in-depth treatment of key SQL concepts, including using SQL on distributive databases, accessing a database with SQL's powerful data manipulation language, and much more. 210 pages.

UNDERSTANDING BAR CODES

By James R. Plunkett

One of the most important waves of technology sweeping American industry is the use of bar coding to capture and track data. The wave is powered by two needs: the need to gather information in a more accurate and timely manner and the need to track that information once it is gathered. Bar coding meets these needs and provides creative and cost-effective solutions for many applications. With so many leading-edge technologies, it can be difficult for IS professionals to keep up with the concepts and applications they need to make solid decisions. This book gives you an overview of bar code technology including a discussion of the bar codes themselves, the hardware that supports bar coding, how and when to justify and then implement a bar code application, plus examples of many different applications and how bar coding can be used to solve problems. 70 pages.

USING QUERY/400

By Patrice Gapen and Catherine Stoughton

This textbook, designed for any AS/400 user from student to professional with or without prior programming knowledge, presents Query as an easy and fast tool for creating reports and files from AS/400 databases. Topics are ordered from simple to complex and emphasize hands-on AS/400 use; they include defining database files to Query, selecting and sequencing fields, generating new numeric and character fields, sorting within Query, joining database files, defining custom headings, creating new database files, and more. Instructor's kit available. 92 pages.

USING VISUAL BASIC WITH CLIENT ACCESS APIs

By Ron Jones

This book is for programmers who want to develop client/server solutions on the AS/400 and the personal computer. Whether you are a VB novice or a VB expert, you will gain by reading this book because it provides a thorough overview of the principles and requirements for programming in Windows using VB. Companion diskettes contain source code for all the programming projects referenced in the book, as well as for numerous other utilities and programs. All the projects are compatible with Windows 95 and VB 4.0. 680 pages.

FOR A COMPLETE CATALOG OR TO PLACE AN ORDER, CONTACT

NEWS/400 and Duke Press
Duke Communications International
221 E. 29th Street • Loveland, CO 80538-2727
(800) 621-1544 • (970) 663-4700 • Fax: (970) 669-3016
or shop our Web site: **www.dukepress.com**